RED
—LETTER—
LEADERSHIP

LEADERSHIP LESSONS FROM THE LIFE OF CHRIST

Foreword by Chad Robichaux

JORDAN AMES
BEN HUNTER
ERIC ALBRIGHT

Tremendous Leadership
PO Box 267 • Boiling Springs, PA 17007
(717) 701 - 8159 • (800) 233 - 2665
www.TremendousLeadership.com

Tremendous Leadership's titles may be bulk purchased for business or promotional use or for special sales. Please contact Tremendous Leadership for more information.

Tremendous Leadership and its logo are trademarks of Tremendous Leadership. All rights reserved.

No part of this publication may be reproduced, stored in or introduced into a retrieval system, or transmitted in any form, or by any means (electronic, mechanical, photocopying, recording, or otherwise) without prior written permission of both the copyright owner and the above publisher of this book except by a newspaper or magazine reviewer who wishes to quote brief passages in connection with a review.

Scripture references are from the New International Version (NIV). The references may show different editions of the NIV. Red Letter Leadership took the liberty to emphasize the words of Jesus in red to call out words attributed to Him. When pronouns reference any person of the Trinity, they are capitalized.

Copyright © 2025 Red Letter Leadership
All rights reserved.

Paperback ISBN: 978-1-961202-58-0
Hardcover ISBN: 978-1-961202-59-7
eBook ISBN: 978-1-961202-60-3

DESIGNED & PRINTED IN THE
UNITED STATES OF AMERICA

WHAT KEY LEADERS ARE SAYING ABOUT RED LETTER LEADERSHIP

"Jesus set the ultimate standard for leadership. *Red Letter Leadership* will help you follow in His footsteps. Practical, insightful, and deeply rooted in faith, this book is a gift to leaders at all levels."

— **Mark Cole**, CEO, Maxwell Leadership

"Leadership is the study of a lifetime. *Red Letter Leadership* highlights principles of leadership from a faith perspective that will make anyone a more effective leader. A great read for any student of leadership and certainly for leaders whose world view includes faith as a foundational element."

— **Chaplain (Major General) William "Bill" Green, Jr.**, U.S. Army

"Jesus was a true 'rebel.' *Red Letter Leadership* teaches how Jesus rebelled against the religious and cultural norms, and in doing so, redirected the course of humanity through His leadership. This book will inspire you to live and lead in the purpose for which you were created"

— **Graham Cochrane**, USA Today bestselling author of *Rebel: Find Yourself by Not Following The Crowd*

"*Red Letter Leadership* is an inspiring and transformative guide to Christ-centered leadership, offering profound lessons drawn from the ultimate leader—Jesus Christ. Having served as Jordan Ames' Commanding Officer at Marine Special Operations Command, I have witnessed firsthand his unwavering commitment to leadership under the most challenging conditions. His ability to lead and grow with humility, discipline, and proficiency—principles deeply rooted in faith—makes this book a powerful resource for anyone seeking to lead and grow with integrity and purpose. Jordan embodies the very leadership values he and his team writes about, and this book is a testament to their experience, wisdom, and dedication to serving and empowering others through the example of Christ."

— **Major Fred Galvin USMC (Ret.)**, Best-Selling Author of *A Few Bad Men: The True Story of U.S. Marines Ambushed in Afghanistan and Betrayed in America*

"This is truly a wonderful book, full of truth and sound wisdom. I highly recommend it to anyone who desires to enhance their leadership skills."

— **Richard E Simmons**, Best-selling author of *The True Measure of a Man* and founder of The Center for Executive Leadership

TABLE OF CONTENTS

Red Letter Leadership's Seven Pillars vii
Foreword ix
Preface xi

The Book of Matthew 1
The Book of Mark 149
The Book of Luke 245
The Book of John 393

Epilogue 491
Acknowledgements 495
Index 499
Notes 509
About the Authors 513

RED LETTER LEADERSHIP'S

SEVEN PILLARS

1. Jesus of Nazareth is the greatest leader of all-time and should be studied by all.

2. The Bible is the infallible word of God and hosts the words and accounts of Jesus.

3. As image bearers of God, we all have the capacity to lead (Gen 1:27).

4. The Great Commission is a command for every person to be a leader (Matt 28:19).

5. The essence of leadership is not derived from a title.

6. Leadership must be a daily effort.

7. The same three principles that will grow us in our relationship with Christ are the same three that will grow us as leaders.

Be Humble
Be Disciplined
Be Proficient

FOREWORD

When the Red Letter Leadership team asked me to write the foreword for this book, I was both humbled and honored. As a follower of Jesus and a leader shaped by my time in special operations, professional mixed martial arts, and the trenches of both war and ministry, I was excited to hear about a team of veterans and warriors stepping up to highlight the leadership of our Savior. This isn't just another leadership book—this is a bold and much-needed deep dive into the greatest leader who ever lived: Jesus Christ.

When I met Jordan, Ben, and Eric, I knew right away they were the real deal. These men are not only seasoned combat leaders with 22 overseas deployments between them, but they're also godly husbands and fathers who lead their families in a Christ-honoring way. They've led in combat and politically sensitive areas where every decision had life-or-death consequences. And now they're pointing us to the One who led perfectly in every situation: Jesus.

There are plenty of leadership books out there. Names like John Maxwell, Stephen Covey, and Craig Groeschel come to mind. And while many of them point to Christ as their example, *Red Letter Leadership* is different. It's not just a book with biblical values sprinkled throughout. It doesn't just borrow from the Bible—it builds entirely on the words and actions of Jesus Himself and events surrounding His life. There has been no single volume compiled with such an extensive study on the leadership of Jesus Christ. This book offers over 370 leadership lessons drawn directly from the four Gospels. I've never seen anything like it.

I've spent years training warriors—men broken by battle, trauma, and hardship—and one truth always holds: the only leadership that truly transforms is the kind rooted in Christ. I've seen men rise from addiction, depression, and moral failure, not because of motivational speeches, but because they encountered the red letters of Jesus and followed His example of servant leadership. That's the power behind this book.

What makes this book powerful isn't just its content—it's the conviction behind it. These men didn't just study Christ's leadership from a distance. They've lived it, tested it under fire, and applied it in war zones, boardrooms, foxholes, and even while leading their children through difficult seasons. That matters. And it gives this book a credibility that's rare.

This book is grounded in two powerful truths: Jesus is the greatest leader of all time, and the Bible is God's perfect Word. If you already believe that, this book will sharpen your leadership and deepen your faith. If you're still searching, I challenge you—read these pages with an open heart. Read the Scriptures listed with each lesson. Let Jesus speak for Himself.

Red Letter Leadership doesn't claim to be perfect, but it points to the One who is. The study isn't exhaustive—God's Word is too rich for that—but it opens a door. A door to real transformation. A door to leading with humility, courage, conviction, and grace. A door to leading like Jesus, whether you're heading into combat, leading a team, or just trying to love your family well. I invite you to walk through it. Join the conversation. Let the Holy Spirit shape you into the leader God created you to be—for your family, your community, your church, and beyond. Start with this book and become a world-changer.

Chad Robichaux
Founder, Mighty Oaks Foundation
Host, The Resilient Show

PREFACE

The vision behind the lessons in this book is in its name: "Red Letter Leadership." As I prepared to retire from the military in 2022, I developed a passion for being a leadership coach. I truly love watching people grow and succeed as leaders. But as I considered what entering the leadership development space looked like for me, I believed God was leading me to do so from a Christ-centered perspective. Christ has been my number one leadership coach, so why shouldn't I point people to Him?

Red Letter Leadership was founded on the belief that to be truly great leaders, we must first humble ourselves to Christ's lordship in our lives, and then we must commit to studying Christ's words and examples from a leadership perspective. We hold this belief for two reasons: 1) Jesus is the greatest leader of all-time and is God incarnate, and 2) He calls us to deny ourselves and submit to His will. Our definition of greatness is Biblical, not worldly. God has given each of us a certain potential and capacity to be great. He has stamped His image on each of us—you, me, and everyone that has ever lived. But if we are unwilling to deny ourselves, we stand in the way of the greatness that is His image. We block the great potential He has given us when we seek to gratify our own ambitions outside of His will. When we submit to Him and therefore align our will with His, He begins to grow our capacity to lead and advance His kingdom.

God's commands to us are universal across mankind: 1) *"Love the LORD your God with all your heart and with all your soul and with all your mind and with all your strength,"* and 2) *"Love your* neighbor as yourself" (Mark 12:30–31). His task to us is also universal: "go and make disciples" (Matt 28:19). Following His commands will allow us to accomplish His task.

Nested in His universal purpose for all of us are the individual purposes that He's placed on each of our lives. He's given each of us unique personalities, strengths, talents, and gifts which we use to fulfill the individual purposes He's given us. As we fulfill our individual purposes, we serve our role on God's team—the Body of Christ, the Church. And His team—the Church—is who will advance His kingdom.

So, the question is not 'what do we do?' but rather 'how do we do it?' How do we love? How do we make disciples? How do we use our strengths and talents?

We believe that God gave us the 'how' through the life of Jesus. The 'how' is also summed up in one word: "leadership." Through leadership, as Jesus Christ has defined it through His words and examples, we will serve the role He's given us and the greater purpose of advancing His kingdom. Information about how Jesus led is not hidden from us. Jesus' leadership was recorded by those who had firsthand knowledge of His words and actions, and who were developed directly by His leadership. Knowledge of His leadership was also recorded through committed research by some outside Jesus' inner circle who didn't possess all the firsthand knowledge of Him. Who He was and what He did and said has been corroborated by many different sources with the foremost accounts being that of Matthew, Mark, Luke, and John.

Jesus Christ's leadership is not a different kind or style of leadership from that which is best for families, for businesses, for government leaders, for local church organizations, or other local community organizations. We believe the red letters are the original source of great leadership and so these lessons on leadership, team development, and personal growth are designed to grow leaders of all types and organizations while also giving them the opportunity to grow closer to Christ.

What this book is not is a peer reviewed book on theology. It was written by three common men who love Jesus, follow Him intensely, and have decades worth of broad leadership experience. This book is not meant to enter the theological debate. It was written to pull leadership lessons from the four Gospels not to contribute to a theological discussion. It is a leader's handbook for those seeking to lead like Jesus.

The Red Letter Leadership Team has, collectively, over six decades of leadership experience within the special operations, infantry, and aviation communities; and spanning 22 overseas deployments. We love Jesus and want His leadership known from front-line workers to top decision makers, from privates to presidents. We leverage our experience to add value to you through these lessons. We wrote these lessons as committed followers of Jesus Christ, as fathers, as husbands, as leaders in the Church, and through our professional perspectives and experiences.

I began writing the Book of Matthew lessons thinking that I would write for all four Gospels myself. I praise God that He placed Ben Hunter and Eric Albright in my path and that they both saw my vision for these and saw the great value that we could add to others as we committed our time and energy to allow God to speak through us to you. Some of the passages have many leadership lessons packed into them. We don't extrapolate all of them. Our goal was to guide you to and illuminate the leadership of Jesus and those close to His life, and mistakes in leadership made by others surrounding Jesus such as the religious leaders. There is much more to be learned, and we hope you continue your study of Him long after you finish reading these lessons.

I wrote all the lessons for the Book of Matthew. Ben and Eric began co-authoring the early passages of Mark. For the Books of Mark, Luke, and John, our initials are placed next to the title of the lessons for the ones each of us wrote so you understand whose writing you are reading.

We not only wrote this for you, but we also wrote these for our own reference and leadership development. We are by no means the authority on Christ-centered leadership. These lessons are as much for us to apply in our own lives as they are for you. They continue to serve as a reference for us as we commit to being constant students of God's word and true Christ-centered leaders.

As you embark on this journey through the Gospel accounts, commit to reading no more than one lesson a day. This book is not intended to be finished in a certain amount of time. If you feel you must remain on one lesson for more than a day and work its application in your life, then do so, and allow the Holy Spirit to refine and grow you as a leader. This will allow time for reflection and growth as you engage with the Scripture readings, lessons, and suggested applications that follow each named lesson.

Growth doesn't happen passively—it requires intentionality. It also requires consistency. As John Maxwell, the recognized #1 leadership expert in the world, says, "consistency compounds." I encourage you to record your reflections in a written or digital manner so that you will be able to reference your notes for continuous study and application.

At Red Letter Leadership, we believe that developing any skill requires a commitment to three core principles, and we ask you to embrace these before moving forward to develop your leadership skills:

BE HUMBLE | BE DISCIPLINED | BE PROFICIENT

Humility is an attitude that must be consciously chosen every day and in every situation. Discipline involves forming new routines and habits based on what we learn through humility. Proficiency is the result we strive for in the form of specific and measurable goals, taking actions steps to become competent in the skill in which we seek proficiency. The application suggestions at the end of each lesson are opportunities for you to humble yourself to the Scripture and lesson, discipline yourself to applying it to your life, and commit to taking action to increase your proficiency as a leader.

Red Letter Leadership wants to inspire you to step out of your comfort zone and begin to shape your environments so that, together, we drive change and advance the kingdom of God each day. We want to help you navigate challenges. We want to see families, workplaces, and communities transform because leaders are modeling the leadership of Christ. We want to help grow the capacity of the Body of Christ to advance the kingdom of heaven. If the kingdom of heaven is going to advance, it will take strong leadership.

We pray that these lessons will enable you to grow and equip you to face the adversity within our fallen world. We all have the capacity to lead, and we all must. Leadership is not a trait that some are born with more than others; it's a skill that anyone can develop. However, only those who are humble and committed to growth and improvement should assume the responsibility of leading others.

Thank you for joining us on this journey through the Gospels. Together, we'll explore what it truly means to be a Christ-centered leader. I'll give you a sneak peek: it'll involve a lot of **love**, a lot of **sacrifice**, and a lot of **service**. Begin today if you want to grow into a Christ-centered leader.

Let's go!

Jordan

THE BOOK OF MATTHEW

STRENGTH IN DIVERSITY

"Thus there were fourteen generations in all from Abraham to David, fourteen from David to the exile to Babylon, and fourteen from the exile to the Christ."
—Matt 1:17

Read: Matthew 1:1–17 "The Genealogy of Jesus"
The genealogy of Jesus is far from a random list of ancestors; it is a powerful story of God's redemption. It reveals His plan to come to us, live among us, and show us both Himself and how to be 'more than conquerors' in the midst of a fallen world. Jesus' ancestors committed some of the worst sins—prostitution, adultery, and even murder. He was not of purely Israelite descent. By Jesus' time, the Jewish people had become a melting pot of ethnicities due to assimilation, wars, commerce, and 70 years of exile in Babylon. Like all nations, Israel was diverse.

If all humanity descended from Adam and Eve, then there is no such thing as a pure ethnicity, except the human race. Despite our unity as humans, we are wonderfully diverse, and our differences should be seen as strengths that can make our unity even more profound.

Without recognizing God's hand in Jesus' genealogy, we might only see a lineage of foolish, womanizing, arrogant, murderous, manipulative, and corrupt men. But when we view it through the lens of God's gracious and merciful plan for redemption, we see Jesus as the perfect culmination of that lineage—born at the perfect time, fully equipped and prepared to carry out God's plan to redeem mankind.

Humble yourself to the diverse strengths of those on your team.

Application: Elevate one teammate's strengths today. Consider speaking a word of praise about their strength, leveraging their strength to accomplish a task and then praise them, or acknowledge their strengths to other teammates.

STAND IN THE GAP

> "Because Joseph her husband was a righteous man and did not want to expose her to public disgrace, he had in mind to divorce her quietly."
> —Matt 1:19

Read: Matthew 1:18–25 "The Birth of Jesus Christ"
In the culture into which Jesus was born, adultery was punishable by death. Mary could have faced this severe consequence, and her best-case scenario might have been a quiet divorce from Joseph to avoid bringing shame upon herself or her family. Understandably, Joseph was deeply hurt and initially resolved not to marry her. As a righteous man, he had every right in that society to expose her to public disgrace, yet he chose a different path.

Even today, there are cultures that disgrace and shame people for similar sins, and some even still carry death penalties as a punishment for adultery. However, there are also righteous men who stand in the gap within these cultures, protecting potential victims and acting with integrity.

Like Joseph, we are called to be men and women of honor—righteous individuals who discern what is right in God's eyes, even when cultural norms and expectations might suggest otherwise. This requires a deliberate, consistent effort to immerse ourselves in God's word, seek His wisdom, and allow Him to guide our understanding. Once we have that understanding, we must be ready to act with courage and compassion.

Leaders must stand in the gap, discern God's will, and act with integrity, even when culture or emotions pull us in a different direction.

Application: Our culture is increasingly distancing itself from our Holy God. Find one environment, one social group, etc., where God is not praised and determine today to change your actions and your speech that others may see Him in you.

COMPETING vs. COLLABORATING

> "When King Herod heard this he was disturbed, and all Jerusalem with him."
>
> —Matt 2:3

Read: Matthew 2:1–12 "The Visit of the Magi"
King Herod was determined to protect his throne at all costs. If even the slightest opposition to his rule arose, he would crush it without hesitation. Like many kings of that time and dictators today, Herod dealt with any threat to his power swiftly and ruthlessly.

In contrast, the Magi from the East, who were also men of great wealth and influence, responded differently. Despite their own status, they were not threatened by the newborn King. Instead, they recognized His significance and came to worship Him, acknowledging that His power and influence surpassed their own.

As leaders, we face a similar choice. Are we disturbed, as King Herod was, when we encounter someone more powerful, influential, or proficient in our field? Do we respond with selfishness, seeking to discredit or undermine our competition? Or do we act as the Magi did—recognizing others' strengths, humbly supporting them, collaborating with them, and celebrating their success?

True leadership is not threatened by the strengths of others; it recognizes and embraces them, finding ways to collaborate and uplift rather than compete and diminish.

Application: Change your attitude with your competitors today. Learn how to collaborate with them. Find one area where you compete and seek their advice to grow yourself and your team in that area.

DRASTIC MEASURES

> "So he got up, took the child and His mother during the night and left for Egypt."
>
> —Matt 2:14

Read: Matthew 2:13–23 "The Escape to Egypt and Return to Nazareth"

Shortly after Jesus' birth, Joseph received instructions from "an angel of the Lord" to take Jesus and Mary and flee to Egypt until Herod died. He did this because in Herod's fear that there was a newborn king to come and take his throne, he ordered "all the boys in Bethlehem and its vicinity who were two years old and under" to be killed (Matt 2:16).

In our own lives, our families, or in the workplace, sometimes there comes times for leaders to take drastic measures. One of the boys my older sons played soccer with when we lived in NC suffered from asthma as a young child. At the time, his family lived in Ohio and when the doctors said that it would be best for the child if he lived in a warmer and more humid climate, they picked up and moved south. There are situations many of us could probably recall of stories we've heard or decisions that we have had to make that have drastically altered our life's path. Sometimes we just need to remove ourselves from a region and start afresh somewhere else for the betterment of those we lead.

When faced with a difficult situation that could alter your life and that of your family's, first seek God for wisdom, then consider the risks of your options.

Great leaders are willing to make difficult decisions, even drastic ones, for the well-being of those they lead.

Application: Reflect on a time when you were faced with the decision to take a drastic measure that potentially altered your life or the lives of your family. If you have none, reflect on such a decision that you've seen someone you know make or a story you heard. What was the decision? How was the risk calculated, and the cost counted?

BE SELECTIVE

> "The ax is already at the root of the trees, and every tree that does not produce good fruit will be cut down and thrown into the fire."
> —Matt 3:10

Read: Matthew 3:1–12 "John the Baptist Prepares the Way"
Jesus is selective in His judgment. He makes it clear that not everyone will receive the reward of eternal life. In this passage, John prophesies that the time is near when those who do not produce good fruit will be cut down and thrown into the fire. Similarly, in John 15, during the Last Supper, Jesus teaches His disciples that they must remain in Him to bear fruit. Those who do not will face the consequences of being thrown into the fire.

While we are not God and should never assume His role, we are called to exercise discernment and selectivity in our leadership. In the workplace, this means being selective in hiring, promoting, and retaining team members. It means distinguishing between those who work hard and those who do not, between those who are prepared for challenges and those who are not. Effective leadership requires us to build strong teams by holding others accountable for their actions.

Discriminating in this context is not about unfair bias but about making wise and just decisions that reflect the values and goals of the team or organization.

Strong leadership requires discernment—making tough choices to build and maintain teams that align with your values and goals. Accountability is key to ensuring success and fostering growth.

Application: What tough choices are you faced with today? Be selective in discerning wisely what is the best decision for accomplishing the task and upholding the welfare of the team. Do not seek to make everyone happy. Instead, seek to serve what is best for the team even if it takes some of your teammates out of their comfort zone.

BEGIN WITH HUMILITY

"Jesus replied, 'Let it be so now; it is proper for us to do this to fulfill all righteousness.' Then John consented."

—Matt 3:15

Read: Matthew 3:13–17 "The Baptism of Jesus"
Why did Jesus receive baptism from John? John himself questioned this, saying, "I need to be baptized by you." Baptism is traditionally a public proclamation of one's commitment to follow Jesus Christ. While Wikipedia defines baptism as a "rite of passage," and Merriam-Webster describes it as "an act, experience, or ordeal by which one is purified, sanctified, initiated, or named," Jesus' baptism held a much deeper meaning.

Jesus was baptized not because He needed purification but to set an example for us and to live above reproach before those who witnessed His life. His baptism fully identified Him with humanity's sin, despite His sinlessness. Those present likely heard the Father's voice from heaven affirming, "This is my Son, whom I love; with Him I am well pleased" (Matt 3:17).

Jesus' baptism marked the beginning of His earthly ministry, signifying His readiness to fulfill His divine mission. Immediately afterward, the Spirit led Him into the wilderness to be tempted by the devil and tested.

Jesus' baptism teaches us the importance of leading with humility, identifying with others, and preparing for the challenges that lie ahead in our journey of leadership.

Application: What does it look like to begin transformation with humility in your own life? Where do you need to change? Where do you need to grow? Are you prepared for the trials, the adversity that will come? Must you start with an apology and asking for forgiveness? Or maybe you need to be more empathetic in how you relate to others and seek better ways to connect? Beginning with humility will open doors for improved connections and stronger relationships.

ARE YOU PREPARED?

"Then the devil left Him, and the angels came and attended Him."

—Matt 4:11

Read: Matthew 4:1–11 "The Temptation of Jesus"
Following Jesus' baptism, the Spirit led Him into the wilderness to be tempted by the devil (Matt 4:1). Before Jesus could begin His ministry and make disciples, He had to endure the same trials and temptations that we all face. Hebrews 4:15 reminds us, "For we do not have a high priest who is unable to sympathize with our weaknesses, but we have one who has been tempted in every way, just as we are—yet was without sin."

God led Jesus out of His comfort zone to discipline Him for His ministry. From this passage, we can draw three key lessons on discipline:

1. **Know the Word of God:** Jesus responded to Satan's temptations with Scripture. To resist the enemy's tactics, we must be deeply rooted in God's Word and ready to apply it in our lives.
2. **Discern the Truth:** Satan used Scripture to try and deceive Jesus. Similarly, others may misuse the Bible to discredit its message. We must know God's Word well enough to discern truth from deception and respond with both our actions and words.
3. **Prepare for Trials:** Jesus faced temptation alone, without immediate assistance. It wasn't until after the devil left Him, that angels came and attended to Him. We must be prepared and equipped to handle challenges on our own, trusting that God's help will come in due time.

Jesus humbled Himself at His baptism, disciplined Himself in the wilderness, and became proficient to minister and make disciples.

True leadership requires preparation and discipline to be ready to face challenges with resilience and faith.

Application: Where must you discipline yourself to know and understand God's word better? Do you commit Scripture or a specific lesson you learned to memory? Do you journal your reflections so that you can go back and see where you've grown from? If you don't do one of these or something similar to grow your understanding of God's word, commit today to start.

ANSWER HIS CALL

"Come, follow Me, and I will make you fishers of men."

—Matt 4:19

Read: Matthew 4:12–22 "The Calling of the First Disciples"
After overcoming temptation in the wilderness, Jesus moved to Capernaum in Galilee and began His public ministry with the message, "Repent, for the kingdom of heaven is near" (Matt 4:17). From the outset, Jesus was presenting Himself with authority and establishing His credibility as a teacher and leader.

In this passage, Jesus calls His first four disciples—fishermen who He challenges to become "fishers of men." By this time, these young men were likely familiar with Jesus and His teachings, so the opportunity to be chosen by Him must have been both surprising and exciting.

For us today, this story prompts an important question: Are you ready to stop what you are doing and follow Christ? Sometimes, following God's will requires a drastic change that takes us out of our comfort zone.

Christ-centered leadership requires us to be willing to follow Christ's lead even when it challenges us to change direction.

Application: Take a moment to reflect: Are you aligning your life with God's purpose, or are you resisting it? Consider where your comfort zones are. Pick one comfortable area of your life and make one change today in that area to test and challenge yourself to enable and enhance your growth today.

INTEGRITY

"Large crowds from Galilee, the Decapolis, Jerusalem, Judea and the region across the Jordan followed Him."
—Matt 4:25

Read: Matthew 4:23–25 "Jesus Heals the Sick"
As Jesus went throughout Galilee, teaching, preaching, and healing, His reputation quickly spread. People were drawn to Him, not just by His words, but by His actions. His teachings were powerful, but without the accompanying miracles, His words might have seemed empty. And even those miracles would have been incomplete without His ultimate act of integrity—His resurrection from the dead.

Jesus' life demonstrated perfect integrity from the beginning to the end. His words and actions were always in alignment, even when it led Him to the cross. His integrity is what made Him credible and trustworthy, and it's what drew so many to follow Him.

How is your integrity? Do your words and actions match? Are you credible in what you say and what you do? In a world that is desperate for trustworthy leaders, the need for men and women who possess and model integrity has never been greater.

Integrity is the foundation of credible leadership. Ensure your words and actions are consistently aligned, so others can trust and follow you with confidence.

Application: Reflect today on how your words and actions match across different environments in which you live (i.e., family, social circles, church, community, etc.). If you cannot honestly say that you are the same person regardless of your environment, commit today to a life of integrity which can only be ensured by following the truest standard, which is Christ.

POOR IN SPIRIT

"Blessed are the poor in spirit, for theirs is the kingdom of heaven."

—Matt 5:3

Read: Matthew 5:1–12 "The Beatitudes"

God's heart is deeply connected to the broken spirit, the powerless, the poor, the widow, and the orphan. In Matthew 22:37, we are reminded that the greatest commandment is to love Him with all our heart, soul, and mind. But for the love to be genuine, it must be a choice, not something forced upon us. True love for God arises when we recognize our need for Him and understand the depth of what He has done for us.

When we are poor in spirit, we find ourselves in a place where we can truly see our need for Jesus. This spiritual poverty creates the ideal opportunity for us to turn to Him. However, not everyone who experiences this brokenness reaches out to God, and that is a profoundly tragic situation.

In America, we have been richly blessed by God, yet many have grown conceited and entitled, believing that we deserve His blessings. But we do not. This attitude, if unchecked, can lead to our downfall. Sometimes, God may lift His blessings to bring us to a point of spiritual poverty, helping us realize our desperate need for Him.

Spiritual poverty reveals our need for God. Even leaders will experience spiritual and emotional lows and must humble themselves to seek God.

Application: Where have you experienced spiritual poverty? Did you turn to God or someone/something else? Use your past experience to prepare for the next low. As a Christ-centered leader, prepare yourself now to help your teammates through times of spiritual poverty.

BE A COMFORTER

"Blessed are those who mourn, for they will be comforted."
                                                              –Matt 5:4

Read: Matthew 5:1–12 "The Beatitudes"
In this verse, Jesus promises to comfort those who mourn, showing His deep compassion for those who are sad, distressed, depressed, and downtrodden. When we turn to Him, He wipes away our tears and brings us the comfort only He can provide.

We live in a fallen world where many tragedies defy explanation. Yet, in the midst of our sadness, Jesus promises His comfort. Death does not mark the end—His glory does. Death does not have the final word—His resurrection does.

As the world grows darker with hate and people turning away from God, the light of Christ's followers will shine even brighter. With a darker world will come more tragedies. Are we prepared to shine brighter, no matter the cost?

Leaders who seek Christ's comfort can effectively offer it to others, shining brighter in a dark world and bringing hope where it's needed most.

Application: Do you need comfort today? Are you in a position to extend comfort to those who are mourning? Speak a word of hope, write a note of encouragement, or offer an act of kindness that will bring comfort to someone who desperately needs it.

STRENGTH UNDER CONTROL

"Blessed are the meek, for they will inherit the earth."
—Matt 5:5

Read: Matthew 5:1–12 "The Beatitudes"
Matt Chandler aptly said, "Meekness is strength under control."[1] To expand on that, true meekness is strength under God's control, and that is the essence of self-control.

Our world often mistakes meekness for weakness. But nothing could be further from the truth. How could the weak inherit anything of value? On the contrary, strength that is wild and out of control leads to constant conflict, war, and tragedy. True peace comes from strength that is under God's control.

Do you use your strength, power, and influence to create peace? Or do you wield your authority like a big stick, ensuring your dominance? Are you worried that others might take advantage of you if you exhibit meekness?

Submit to Christ all the areas of your life where you are strong and where He does not yet have full control. It's easy to seek Him in our weaknesses, but don't stop there—surrender your strengths to Him as well.

True strength lies not in dominance, but in submitting our power to God's control, creating peace and stability in every aspect of leadership.

<u>Application</u>: Commit today to giving all your strengths over to serve your King. Pick one area in your life where you are strong (talents, abilities, maybe finances) and do something to serve and sacrifice for the kingdom which you have not done with that specific strength.

SETTING PRIORITIES

"Blessed are those who hunger and thirst for righteousness, for they will be filled."

–Matt 5:6

<u>Read</u>: Matthew 5:1–12 "The Beatitudes"
When we humble ourselves to God's will and discipline ourselves to seek Him, we will be filled by Him. Jesus calls us to "hunger

and thirst for righteousness." In this fallen world, where we are born into a nature inclined to sin, righteousness doesn't come naturally—it requires desire and effort.

Many people demand that God prove Himself to them, yet they are not prepared to receive Him—they are not truly hungry for Him. But for those who are ready, who genuinely thirst for His presence, God will reveal Himself. He longs for a relationship with His children, but He will never force Himself upon us. We must actively seek Him.

Are you hungry for Him? Do you pursue Jesus as if you haven't eaten in days and He is the only sustenance available? Or is your time consumed with the busyness of life—running kids to activities, working long hours to meet deadlines, or chasing other distractions? Perhaps you haven't yet realized your need for Jesus. Regardless of your circumstances, we must cultivate a hunger for Christ. When we do, He promises to fill us, and we will be satisfied.

The great reformer, Martin Luther, once said that when he began spending the first three hours of his day with God, he found more time to accomplish everything else he needed to do.[2] If we want to increase our productivity and truly fulfill our purpose, it starts with hungering and thirsting for Christ.

Prioritize your relationship with Christ above all else, and you will find that He fills you and empowers you to accomplish more than you could on your own.

Application: Make deliberate time today to spend time with Jesus. Pursue Him. If you aren't in a habit of pursuing Him, make changes today that will help you build a habit. Wake up 15 minutes earlier and start spending 15 minutes seeking Him in prayer before your day starts. B.U.S.Y. = Burdened Under Satan's Yoke. Don't let your B.U.S.Y. lives take precedence over pursuing your Savior.

BE MERCIFUL

"Blessed are the merciful, for they will be shown mercy."
—Matt 5:7

Read: Matthew 5:1–12 "The Beatitudes"

It's natural to want others to brush off our mistakes because we rationalize that "it's not a big deal." Yet, when others wrong us, we often seek justice. This reaction is natural because it stems from our sinful nature. However, just because it's natural doesn't mean it's right. Seeking justice for wrongs done to us while expecting others to excuse our mistakes is inconsistent with Christ's teachings.

We must humble ourselves daily and recognize that none of us are deserving of mercy. Yet, Jesus promises that when we show mercy, it will be shown to us. How often do we point fingers at others—in our families, communities, or workplaces? We want to protect our reputation, so we are quick to highlight others' faults. But in doing so, we miss the opportunity to show mercy.

Mercy is an opportunity—an opportunity to empower those around us to be great, to influence others to lead. By being merciful, we create an atmosphere of growth and a culture where people can thrive. Leaders who extend mercy cultivate an environment where risks can be taken, mistakes can be learned from, and goals that once seemed impossible can be achieved.

So, be merciful, receive mercy, and become a leader who fosters greatness. Embrace mercy as a foundation for leadership that transforms both individuals and teams.

When you extend mercy you cultivate a culture of growth, empowerment, and achievement in your team.

Application: Who do you need to show mercy to today? Who on your team needs your mercy to recharge, to be empowered, and to feel redeemed? Offer mercy today without hesitation.

PURE IN HEART

"Blessed are the pure in heart, for they will see God."
—Matt 5:8

Read: Matthew 5:1–12 "The Beatitudes"
We cannot see God without Jesus, nor can we achieve a pure heart without Him. Scripture reminds us that all have sinned and fallen short of God's glory (Rom 3:23) and that no one does good on their own (Rom 3:10, 12). To have a heart that is truly pure, we must fully submit to Christ and His sovereign authority over our lives. Only then will we see God.

Have you completely surrendered your will to Christ's authority? Or are you still trying to be your own authority? Our culture often portrays submission as weakness, but those who have yielded to Christ and acknowledge His authority understand true strength. They possess a power that cannot be taken from them, regardless of their circumstances. They live without fear of what mortal men can do (Ps 56:4, 11), knowing that their account is settled, and they will see God.

True strength and purity of heart come from fully submitting to Christ's authority, which grants us peace and power beyond worldly understanding.

Application: What power are you holding on to? Reflect right now and ask God to show you where you are not fully submitting to His authority in your life.

MAKE PEACE

"Blessed are the peacemakers, for they will be called sons of God."
—Matt 5:9

Read: Matthew 5:1–12 "The Beatitudes"

My unique personality style, according to my Maxwell DISC Personality Indicator (MDPI) report, is "SC." The report uses the word "peacemaker" to describe the "SC" style. I cherish this description of me because of the key verse.

For those unfamiliar with the DISC styles, they are: Dominant, Influencer, Steady, and Compliant. So, very generally speaking, my own style is "steady/compliant."

Each of our unique personalities is a gift from the Creator. Jesus, who was fully God and fully human, perfectly embodies all personality styles. Where we have blind spots and weaknesses, He is strong. Where our unique styles may limit us from connecting with others due to our sin, He can connect with us right where we are.

For example, my own behavior style may naturally make me a peacemaker, but like anyone, my sin can get in the way. A "dominant" behavior style may take charge more easily yet may struggle to bring peace. For any style, our ability to adapt and provide the influence needed in a situation begins with humility. We must recognize what the situation requires and assess whether we are the best ones to provide it.

We are all capable of being peacemakers. Similarly, we are all capable—and commanded—to be leaders (Matt 28:19–20). By understanding our behavior style, we can see the unique pattern of how God designed us, recognizing our strengths and limitations. When we are humble, we can accept that pattern and use it for His glory, even if it means stepping aside for someone whose strengths better suit the situation.

Effective leadership and peacemaking begin with understanding our God-given personality, humbly assessing the needs of a situation, and being willing to adapt or step aside for the greater good.

Application: Do you know your own unique behavior style? If not, invest in a behavior assessment today. The results will show you the science of who you are and allow you to better apply the Word of God and the art of leadership to your life.

YOU ARE ROYALTY

> "Blessed are those who are persecuted because of righteousness, for theirs is the kingdom of heaven."
> —Matt 5:10

Read: Matthew 5:1–12 "The Beatitudes"
Why do we so often view hardship, defiance, and persecution as something negative, undeserved, or unjust? Living in arguably the greatest and freest nation the world has ever known, we enjoy comforts at our fingertips and have come to feel that we are entitled to our freedoms.

Yes, God desires us to enjoy life and live in freedom. Thankfully, our American Founders understood and believed this. However, as people born into a sinful nature, we compromise our entitlement to freedom through our own sin. Because of sin, we live in a fallen, chaotic world where people violate others' freedoms for their selfish desires. In that environment, those who live and walk in the righteousness that Christ provides will be persecuted.

If we are truly Christlike, we will face persecution. Yet, if we are truly Christlike, He promises to share His inheritance of the kingdom of heaven with us. Romans 8:17 tells us, "Now if we are children, then we are heirs—heirs of God and co-heirs with Christ, if indeed we share in His sufferings in order that we may also share in His glory."

To illustrate, think of the typical Disney princess story (because I have four daughters). In this analogy, God is the King who lives in the castle. The angels of heaven are His servants and subjects. Those of us who seek the righteousness of Christ and are willing to endure the persecution that comes with it are the princes and princesses in the castle—we are and will be royalty in God's kingdom. What an incredible thought! We are not mere servants; we are royalty!

> **Embrace persecution and suffering for Christ as a path to our royal inheritance, recognizing that enduring hardship in His name leads to sharing in His glory.**

Application: Are you prepared for persecution or are you scared? Read about real, present-day stories of Christians being persecuted all over the world from "The Voice of the Martyrs" organization.[3] Consider what enduring suffering may look like for you and your family.

BE GLAD

> "Rejoice and be glad, because great is your reward in heaven, for in the same way they persecuted the prophets who were before you."
> —Matt 5:12

Read: Matthew 5:1–12 "The Beatitudes"
Jesus continues by explaining that we are blessed when persecuted because of Him. Not only does He encourage us by telling us we are "blessed," but in verse 12, He even tells us to "rejoice and be glad." He isn't asking us to merely endure persecution with gritted teeth; He encourages us to embrace it with joy and gladness!

Being Christlike is not for the weak or faint of heart. It requires the utmost toughness, courage, and resilience—qualities we all desire in our teams. Christ-centered leadership does not promise riches, wealth, power, or worldly success, but it does promise a great reward in heaven. Is that enough for you? Are you content with your heavenly reward, or is your definition of success still tethered to the fleeting things of this world?

Be bold. Stand firm. "Rejoice and be glad" in the midst of persecution "because great is your reward in heaven" (Matt 5:12). Period. Be content with that. Nothing more is needed.

Christ-centered leadership embraces persecution with joy, focusing on eternal rewards rather than worldly success.

Application: I hope you read at least one story from "The Voice of the Martyrs."[3] Were you inspired by the joy that the persecuted believer had in the story? I always am. I constantly ask myself, 'could I find that kind of joy if I was being persecuted in the same way?' I pray that I could, and I encourage you to do the same.

REFLECT HIS LIGHT

"In the same way, let your light shine before men, that they may see your good deeds and praise your Father in heaven."

–Matt 5:16

Read: Matthew 5:13–16 "Salt and Light"
We are to let our light shine, not keep it hidden. Jesus does not tell us to do this so that people will recognize us, praise us, and exalt us. He explains that the whole point is for others to "see [our] good deeds and praise [our] Father in heaven." That takes humility

on our part and there's no greater example of that humility than Christ.

So, what is "our light?" Let's take a moment and reflect on what is light. Here are some ideas:

- The Fruits of the Spirit: love, joy, peace, patience, kindness, goodness, faithfulness, gentleness, and self-control (Gal 5:22–23).
- Live above reproach. Have integrity.
- Be humble.
- Be disciplined in all aspects of your being (physically, mentally, emotionally, and spiritually).
- "Whatever you do, work at it with all your heart, as working for the Lord and not for men" (Col 3:23).
- Be an ambassador for Christ.
- The "Platinum Rule:" Treat others as they would like to be treated.[4]
- "Act justly, love mercy, and walk humbly with your God" (Mic 6:8).
- Comfort those who mourn.
- Take care of the poor, orphaned, oppressed, distressed, and downtrodden.

These ideas on what our "light" is only scratch the surface. However, our light is only the reflection of Christ's. If our "good" deeds do not reflect Christ, then they are not "good" at all.

Christ-centered leaders reflect the character of Christ, inspiring others to follow a higher standard.

<u>Application</u>: Pick one way to reflect the character of Christ today and be intentional about seeing it through. Consider bringing others like family members, friends, or coworkers along with you.

GOD'S HOLY STANDARD

"Do not think that I have come to abolish the Law or the Prophets; I have not come to abolish them but to fulfill them."

—Matt 5:17

Read: Matthew 5:17–20 "The Fulfillment of the Law"
Some people who claim Christ as their Savior believe it gives them a license to sin, thinking they can act as they please because Christ will forgive them. While it is true that His death covers our past, present, and future sins, this mindset misinterprets the true purpose of grace. In this passage, Christ clearly states that He did not come to "abolish" or remove the Law but to "fulfill" it. This means the Law continues to stand, and we are called to follow it. Christ came to fulfill the whole purpose of the Law, which exists to make us holy before God.

The reality is that we fall short in keeping the Law. That's why Christ's fulfillment of it is so crucial. Jesus teaches us that holiness in God's eyes comes from keeping and obeying the Law. But we also recognize that only through Christ can we achieve holiness according to God's standard. If Jesus had come to abolish the Law, there would have been no need for His sacrifice.

We must hold and keep God's standard. His holy standard still stands, even today. When you encounter something that contradicts God's Word—whether you hear it, see it, or read it—you must rebuke it immediately. Allowing such contradictions to take root can give the devil a foothold in your life, leading you to question if God's Law still applies in 2025.

Christ-centered leaders uphold God's standards with vigilance, discernment, and the courage to rebuke anything that contradicts His Word, while leading with grace.

Application: How do you view God's standard of holiness? Do you take it as seriously as Jesus going to the cross for your sin and mine. Be humble and view each of your sins, no matter how large or small, as what directly put Christ on the cross.

SEEK RECONCILIATION

"First, go and be reconciled to your brother; then come and offer your gift."

—Matt 5:24

Read: Matthew 5:21–26 "Murder"
Be humble and seek reconciliation. Take action to reconcile with others, for only then can you be in a position to truly worship God.

This passage challenges the notion that simply going to church or performing good deeds can reconcile us with God. Jesus emphasizes that it is more important to reconcile with someone who has something against us than to come and worship Him. Our commitment to attending church every Sunday, serving the needy, and giving to the poor does not fool God when He knows there is a broken relationship in our life that needs healing.

To seek reconciliation, we must first humble ourselves to understand what needs to be reconciled and then discipline ourselves to pursue it. Only through this process will we become proficient in reconciliation. Who might you need to reconcile with? Are you the one who needs to be forgiven, or are you the one who needs to forgive? Make it right first and then bring your worship to God.

Leaders reconcile and restore the unity of the team.

Application: Is there disunity among your family or organization? Seek reconciliation today. Be the one with the courage to take the first step to make amends.

BE SIN CONSCIOUS

"If your right hand causes you to sin, gouge it out and throw it away. It is better for you to lose one part of your body than for your whole body to be thrown into hell."
—Matt 5:29

Read: Matthew 5:27–30 "Adultery"

Jesus raises the standard of righteousness far beyond the simple adherence to the Law. He tells us that it is not enough to merely avoid actions like murder or adultery; we must also address the deeper issues of anger and lust. By doing this, Jesus highlights the seriousness of sin and its capacity to separate us from God if we do not confront and conquer it.

Jesus' call here is about the condition of our hearts. He is helping His audience, and us today, understand how deeply ingrained sin can be and how essential it is to humble ourselves before God. It's not enough to follow the letter of the Law; we need to transform our hearts and deal with the sin at its root. This transformation only comes through Christ, who equips us to conquer sin.

As leaders, when we take this teaching as seriously as "do not murder" or "do not commit adultery," we become more conscious of our own sinful tendencies. This awareness positions us to cultivate healthier, more effective relationships. And when we foster healthy relationships, we naturally build stronger and more efficient teams, whether at work, in our homes, or in our communities.

Leadership starts with inner transformation— addressing sin at its root will allow you to foster healthier relationships and lead more effectively.

Application: Honestly examine yourself today. We can't lead others if we are incapable of leading ourselves. Identify 2–3 struggles you have. Then, seek to identify the source of those struggles. Commit today to addressing those struggles right at the source.

KEEPING OUR WORD

*"Simply let your 'Yes' be 'Yes,' and your 'No,' 'No';
anything beyond this comes from the evil one."*

—Matt 5:37

<u>Read</u>: Matthew 5:31–37 "Divorce" and "Oaths"
Remember when we used to cross our fingers to get out of a promise? While that may have seemed harmless as kids, it doesn't work in real life, especially when it comes to integrity. In this portion of the "Sermon on the Mount," Jesus emphasizes the importance of being men and women of our word. He's telling us that we shouldn't need to swear an oath to be trustworthy—our word should be enough.

In today's society, written agreements and contracts are often necessary to ensure trust and accountability. While this is understandable given the world we live in, imagine if everyone upheld the integrity that Jesus calls for. Marriages would remain strong because spouses would keep their vows. Business relationships would be built on trust, free from scandals and betrayals. Politics would be honest and transparent. Though we don't live in a sinless society, we would at least have stronger relationships, teams, partnerships, and governments built on integrity.

Commit to keeping your word. If unforeseen circumstances force you to change a commitment, address it with humility and honesty, and do what you can to help those affected. People are much more understanding when your life has been a model of integrity.

**Keep your word, and when priorities change
address it with humility and honesty.**

<u>Application</u>: Reflect on where your integrity stands today. Can people trust you to be a person of your word? If you must go back on your word, do so with clear explanations to those who are affected

and only for reasons that are unselfish and with the best interests of the team and the team's mission in mind.

TOUGHNESS

> "But I tell you, do not resist an evil person. If someone strikes you on the right cheek, turn to him the other also."
> —Matt 5:39

Read: Matthew 5:38–42 "An Eye for an Eye"
In sports, who's often the one to get the penalty after a scuffle? It's usually the second person to throw a punch—the one who retaliates. This illustrates the principle Jesus is teaching in this passage about turning the other cheek. Many misunderstand this teaching, especially those in military or law enforcement roles who see themselves as protectors. They can misinterpret it as a call to weakness or passivity.

In reality, this passage calls for a strength that goes beyond physical force. Jesus is not asking us to be weak or passive in the face of evil, but rather, He's calling us to a deeper, tougher kind of strength—one rooted in resilience and self-control. He's telling us to be so physically, mentally, and emotionally strong in Him that we can absorb hatred and persecution without letting it corrupt our hearts or drive us to retaliate.

This is about having the courage to stand firm in your faith and identity, knowing that your strength comes from Christ, and not from defending your pride or reputation. Responding with love and grace in the face of hostility demonstrates a toughness far greater than a retaliatory punch. When you walk with Christ, you don't need to defend yourself, because your identity and value are secure in Him.

**Let your toughness be grounded in
Christ, not in your defense of self.**

<u>Application</u>: Think of the last time someone attacked your pride or reputation. How did you respond? Did you fire back in defense of yourself or did you respond with your identity fully secured in Christ?

EXPERIENCING GOD

"Be perfect, therefore, as your heavenly Father is perfect."
—Matt 5:48

<u>Read</u>: Matthew 5:43–48 "Love Your Enemies"
Jesus ends a challenging lesson with the command to "be perfect" (Matt 5:48), which feels like an impossible standard. Loving family and friends can be hard enough, but He goes even further, commanding us to love our enemies. Then, as if to remind us not to falter, He adds the call to perfection—placing the ultimate challenge before us.

However, Jesus isn't trying to burden us with impossible expectations. He's inviting us to experience the fullness of God's presence in our lives. Perfection, in this context, isn't about flawless performance but about being transformed by the love, grace, and character of God.

I've had a lifetime of thrilling experiences—jumping from planes, diving deep beneath the ocean's surface, hiking through some of the world's most rugged terrains, and even standing where Jesus lived, died, and rose again. But none of these exhilarating moments compares to the experience of God working within me. When we love like Jesus loved, serve like He served, and sacrifice like He sacrificed, we don't just imitate Him—we encounter Him.

The real tragedy is when we try to assume God's position without surrendering to His authority, but when we allow Him to shape us, we begin to reflect His image. It's not about achieving perfection on our own but letting Him refine us, knowing He is faithful to complete the work He started in us (Phil 1:6).

Love how God loves not how the world does.

<u>Application</u>: Find someone who you've been at odds with and consider making a gesture of love toward them. Reconnect with an encouraging note or phone call. Commit to unconditional love.

BE A GIVER

> "So when you give to the needy, do not announce it with trumpets, as the hypocrites do in the synagogues and on the streets, to be honored by men. I tell you the truth, they have received their reward in full."
>
> —Matt 6:2

<u>Read</u>: Matthew 6:1–4 "Giving to the Needy"
Jesus calls us to give generously and sacrificially, without seeking attention or expecting praise in return (Matt 6:3–4). True giving isn't about being seen but about serving others from a place of humility and love. After you've given, give again. This is the heart of servant leadership.

As a leader, give of your time, talents, and resources generously to those around you—your family, friends, colleagues, and community. Give to those in authority over you, those under your care, and those who work alongside you. Be a consistent and selfless giver.

But take care: even when you give, don't fall into the trap of being a "taker." Giving for the purpose of recognition is still a form of taking. True generosity flows from a heart that serves, not one seeking personal gain.

True servant leadership inspires others by the purity of your actions rather than the visibility of your deeds.

Application: Find a way to be a giver today. Pick one way to give off your time, talent, or resources, no matter how small of a way you think it is. But pick something that serves someone else and adds value to them and neither them nor anyone else will know it was you that gave.

WHERE IS YOUR HEART?

"And when you pray, do not keep on babbling like pagans, for they think they will be heard because of their many words."

—Matt 6:7

Read: Matthew 6:5–18 "Prayer and Fasting"
In this passage, Jesus teaches His disciples to pray through what we call "The Lord's Prayer." Yet, more important than the specific words is the condition of the heart behind the prayer. Jesus reminds us that religious practices—whether praying, singing, attending church, fasting, or giving—are meaningless if our hearts are not truly engaged. God cannot be impressed by empty actions or rituals because He sees our true motives and will not be mocked (Gal 6:7).

When our hearts are genuinely aligned with humility and submission to God, we seek His will earnestly, and He responds. However, even when we don't see immediate answers, true obedience is revealed in trusting God's timing and His perfect plan. Prayer is not just about asking for things—it's about aligning ourselves with God's heart and will, being patient for His action, and trusting His process.

Before praying, ask yourself: Where is my heart? Start from a place of humility, and your prayer will be authentic and meaningful, whether brief or long. Remember, prayer is not for God's sake—it's for us to be aligned with Him.

> **Christ-centered leaders examine their hearts before taking action and allow God to guide their decisions through prayer.**

Application: Pray the above prayer and then take 10 minutes to consider upcoming decisions you may have. Also reflect on the recent past decisions where you did not seek God's will.

WHERE IS YOUR TREASURE?

"For where your treasure is, there your heart will be also."
—Matt 6:21

Read: Matthew 6:19–24 "Treasures in Heaven"
Do you store up your wealth to satisfy your own desires, or do you allow yourself to be a conduit of God's resources for His kingdom purposes? The way you handle your treasure reveals where your heart truly lies. Jesus teaches, "Where your treasure is, there your heart will be also" (Matt 6:21). God doesn't need your wealth—He wants your heart; and your stewardship reflects your devotion to Him.

When you accept that "The earth is the LORD's, and everything in it" (Ps 24:1), it becomes easier to see yourself as a steward, not an owner, of the resources God entrusts to you. These resources are meant to flow through you to fulfill His purposes, not to be hoarded for personal gain.

If you haven't yet, I challenge you to start by giving 10% of your gross profit to God. This is not about legalism but about positioning yourself to trust in God's provision and blessings. Malachi 3:10 says, "Test me in this... and see if I will not throw open the floodgates of heaven and pour out so much blessing that you will not have room enough for it." Trusting God with your finances demonstrates a shift in your heart and mindset, recognizing that everything you have is His, and He can multiply your obedience in ways beyond your imagination.

Let this shift in perspective guide how you manage your family finances, handle profits in your business, and steward all other resources God has given you.

True leaders understand that resources, like money, are tools for serving a greater purpose. By surrendering our finances to God, we demonstrate trust in Him and position ourselves to be used for His kingdom work.

<u>Application</u>: If you currently do not give 10% of your gross profit (i.e., your first fruits) to God, commit to doing that today. God says to test Him, so do it. Remember, all of it belongs to Him. He's letting you keep 90% of what is His.

CHRIST FIRST AND FOREMOST

> "If that is how God clothes the grass of the field, which is here today and tomorrow is thrown into the fire, will He not much more clothe you, O you of little faith?"
>
> —Matt 6:30

<u>Read</u>: Matthew 6:25–34 "Do Not Worry"

"Can any one of you by worrying add a single hour to your life?" (Matt 6:27). Worry often tricks us into believing that we have some measure of control over a situation, but in reality, it distracts us from trusting God's greater plan. We worry because we fear that what God considers "good" might not align with our own desires or expectations. We are afraid of where God might lead us, and of stepping outside our comfort zone into the unknown.

Jesus, in this passage, addresses these fears with a simple yet profound instruction: "Do not worry." Instead of allowing fear to rule our hearts, He urges us to "seek first His kingdom and His righteousness" (Matt 6:33). This is the antidote to worry—shifting our focus from the problem to God's purpose. As Jesus promised earlier in Matthew 5:6, "Blessed are those who hunger and thirst for righteousness, for they will be filled." Our lives are filled not by our own efforts to control, but by seeking God's will above all else.

When we seek God first, everything else falls into place. It doesn't mean life will always be easy, but it does mean that He will provide for our needs. Trusting Him requires us to let go of our own plans and trust that His ways are higher and better than our own.

Christ-centered leaders must relinquish the illusion of control, trusting that God's plan will always provide what is needed. Leading with faith instead of fear enables us to focus on what truly matters—seeking God's kingdom and righteousness above all.

Application: What fears or concerns are weighing on you at the moment? Reflect. Now, take those to God in prayer and give that burden to Him through faith. Allow Him to lead you through handling those concerns.

BE VULNERABLE

"For in the same way you judge others, you will be judged, and with the measure you use, it will be measured to you."
—Matt 7:2

Read: Matthew 7:1–6 "Judging Others"

Jesus warns us against judging from a position of arrogance, as if we hold all the answers and others merely need to conform to our wisdom. When we judge, He tells us to do so with the same measure that we expect to be judged (Matt 7:2). This creates a posture of humility, reminding us that we, too, are flawed and in need of grace.

In verse 6, Jesus also cautions us not to waste our judgment on those who are not ready to receive it. This is particularly relevant for new believers and non-believers who may not yet have the capacity to understand or embrace spiritual truths. Rather than being an obstacle for the Gospel in our judgments, let's be a pathway through our love and grace.

When we judge, we must do so from a place of selfless vulnerability, willing to accept judgment and correction in return. Jesus Himself judged the religious leaders, His disciples, and others He encountered, but He did so from a position of sacrificial love. Ultimately, He bore the judgment of the world through His crucifixion—though He was the only one who never deserved it. His example shows us that true judgment comes with humility, vulnerability, and love.

Effective leaders recognize the power of judgment but wield it with humility, love, and vulnerability, inviting accountability and self-reflection to foster stronger, more compassionate relationships.

Application: Reflect on who you may have passed judgment on recently before examining yourself and making yourself vulnerable to being judged in the same way. Go to that person, apologize, and seek their forgiveness. Commit to examining yourself before passing judgment.

WHAT IS YOUR RESPONSE?

"So in everything, do to others what you would have them do to you for this sums up the Law and the Prophets."

—Matt 7:12

Read: Matthew 7:7–12 "Ask, Seek, Knock"
It's easy to focus on the well-known "Golden Rule" in this passage: "Do to others what you would have them do to you" (Matt 7:12). Even non-believers recognize its value for building relationships and fostering collaboration within teams. But Jesus' teaching in these six verses holds much more than just this powerful statement. He uses the Golden Rule as the culmination of His lesson on generosity and responsiveness.

Before making His famous point about treating others as we want to be treated, Jesus emphasizes God's willingness to give us good gifts. He reminds us that even though we are flawed, we still give good gifts to those we love—how much more will our perfect Heavenly Father give us what is good when we ask Him? But before we expect God to respond to our requests, Jesus challenges us to consider how we respond to the needs of others.

Too often, we hesitate to ask, seek, or knock on God's door, fearing we might be asking for too much or seeking Him too often. Yet, when it's our turn to respond to someone else's need, we can be quick to overlook it or delay our help. Jesus is teaching us not only to trust that God will answer us when we ask, but also to reflect that same generosity and responsiveness in our own relationships.

Whether it's a teammate asking for support, a family member seeking attention, or a friend knocking on our door for help, we are called to give, seek, and knock on behalf of others with the same urgency and care we desire from God.

> **Christ-centered leaders reflect God's generosity by responding to the needs of others with the same care, attention, and willingness they hope to receive from Him.**

Application: Seek out someone today who has a need that you are capable of meeting. You may be the one who God is using to answer their prayer.

HOLINESS OVER HAPPINESS

"But small is the gate and narrow the road that leads to life, and only a few find it."

—Matt 7:14

<u>Read</u>: Matthew 7:13–14 "The Narrow and Wide Gates"

Why do we need to consistently strive to **be humble, be disciplined, and be proficient** every day? Because the path to life—true, meaningful life—is narrow and difficult. As Jesus said, *"small is the gate and narrow the road that leads to life, and only a few find it"* (Matt 7:14). This journey isn't easy, and leadership, whether at home or in any other area of life, requires more than just maintaining the status quo or making others comfortable.

Nick Saban's quote captures this well: "If you want to make everyone happy, don't be a leader; sell ice cream."[5] Leadership is not about pleasing everyone or indulging in temporary comforts. Instead, it's about guiding those you lead—whether it's your children, your team, or your community—on the path of holiness and growth, even when it's uncomfortable.

True joy comes from walking in the righteousness of Christ, which ultimately brings a deeper fulfillment than mere momentary happiness. In leading your family, workplace, or community, your responsibility is not to keep everyone content but to guide them toward lasting growth and transformation, even if that means stepping into the heat of refinement.

Precious metals are forged in fire, and the same is true for us. The refining process may be uncomfortable, but it produces lasting character, integrity, and righteousness. You can enter the heat and the pressure of the Refiner's fire with the few, or you can stand in the line for ice cream with the many to continue indulging the desires of your flesh. The choice is yours.

Effective leaders prioritize long-term growth and holiness over short-term comfort and happiness, recognizing that refining through discipline and sacrifice leads to lasting transformation.

<u>Application</u>: Change a comfortable practice today that is impeding your growth. Step out of your comfort zone and embrace the heat of your own refining process.

HOW ARE YOU RECOGNIZED?

"Thus, by their fruit you will recognize them."
—Matt 7:20

<u>Read</u>: Matthew 7:15–23 "A Tree and Its Fruit"
We've all heard the saying, "character is tested only in adversity." It's in those tough moments, when the pressure is on and comfort is stripped away, that our true nature is revealed. Jesus emphasized this principle in Matthew 5:46, when He challenged us to love not just those who love us, but also those who challenge us. The same principle applies to producing good fruit in our lives. It's easy to give, love, and serve when it's 70 degrees and sunny. But what about when the storms come, and the waters rise?

Jesus expects us to bear fruit not only when it's easy, but especially in times of adversity. Are you only generous when your finances are abundant, or are you continuing to give when things are tight? Do you only serve when it's convenient, or are you making time, even when life is busy and overwhelming?

In the movie *National Treasure* (2004), there's a line that I've always found impactful. Nicholas Cage's character is reading from The Declaration of Independence when his partner asks, "What does that even mean?" Cage responds, "It means those who have the ability to take action, have the responsibility to take action." This statement rings true in each of our lives. We are given gifts, resources, and abilities not just for our own benefit, but to serve others, especially in challenging times.

As followers of Christ, we have a responsibility to give, serve, and lead, even when it's inconvenient or uncomfortable. True character shines when we continue to produce good fruit in the midst of adversity, and true generosity flows when we give not just from our surplus but from sacrifice.

Character and generosity are most authentically demonstrated in times of adversity, when we continue to give, serve, and lead even when it's difficult or uncomfortable.

<u>Application</u>: Where are your abilities? Your talents? Your strengths and your team's strengths? God gave them to you. Bear the fruits of the Spirit through those abilities.

BUILD YOUR HOUSE ON THE ROCK

> "Therefore everyone who hears these words of Mine and puts them into practice is like a wise man who built his house on the rock."
>
> —Matt 7:24

<u>Read</u>: Matthew 7:24–29 "The Wise and Foolish Builders"
Jesus concludes His "Sermon on the Mount" with a clear analogy between the wise and foolish builders. Those who hear His teachings and put them into practice are likened to a wise builder who constructs a house on a solid foundation, a rock. In contrast, those who hear but do not apply His teachings are like a builder who erects a house on sand, easily washed away by the storms of life.

Jesus is not saying that following His teachings is easy, but it is necessary. Earlier in His sermon, He commands us to "Be perfect, therefore, as your Heavenly Father is perfect" (Matt 5:48). This perfection is not about being flawless but about striving toward complete alignment with God's will and walking in His ways.

As a former military commander of Marine infantry and special operations units, I understood my responsibility to ensure that those I led had the support they needed to accomplish their mission. Jesus, as the greatest leader to ever walk the earth, takes this even further. If He commands us to do something, He will give us the support and strength to accomplish it. "For nothing is impossible with God" (Luke 1:37).

Be wise and build your leadership, your family, and your life on the solid Rock—Jesus Christ. He is the Cornerstone upon which everything stands.

A Christ-centered leader builds on the unshakable foundation of Jesus, trusting that He will provide the support to accomplish the difficult tasks He commands.

Application: Reflect on the teachings we've explored from reading the first Beatitude until now. Which of these do you struggle to apply in your life? What areas do you need to surrender to God so that He can disciple and grow you?

WILLPOWER

> "Jesus reached out His hand and touched the man. 'I am willing,' He said. 'Be clean!' Immediately he was cured of his leprosy."
>
> —Matt 8:3

Read: Matthew 8:1–4 "The Man with Leprosy"

In this passage, we see a man with leprosy approach Jesus in faith, acknowledging Jesus' power to heal. His request was simple: "Lord, if you are willing, you can make me clean." Jesus, full of compassion, responded, "I am willing," and healed the man.

This story challenges us to reflect on our willingness to help others in need. The man with leprosy had no doubt that Jesus had the power to heal him, but what he asked was whether Jesus was willing. Jesus' willingness is a model for how we should respond to those around us who are hurting or in need.

In our lives, we encounter family members, friends, coworkers, and even strangers who may be struggling. Do we have the power, influence, or resources to make a difference? And more importantly, are we willing? Sometimes we might not be the best person to meet a specific need, but we can influence others or help coordinate the support necessary to bring comfort and aid.

Leadership is not just about having the capacity to act; it's about having the willingness to serve. When we are willing to step up, there is no need too great to meet, no hurt too profound to comfort, and no problem too difficult to solve.

> **Making a true impact is less about our abilities and more about our willpower.**

Application: Where do you have a desire to serve but you've been hesitant with excuses? Adopt a willpower to make a real impact and take a step of faith to serve the needs God has placed in your life and in your heart.

SUBJUGATING YOUR AUTHORITY

> "The centurion replied, 'Lord, I do not deserve to have You come under my roof. But just say the word, and my servant will be healed.'"
>
> —Matt 8:8

Read: Matthew 8:5–13 "The Faith of the Centurion"
After Jesus delivered His famous "Sermon on the Mount," the crowds were amazed because He taught with authority unlike anyone they had ever heard (Matt 7:28–29). One person who clearly recognized this authority was the Roman centurion in this passage. Although a military leader himself, the centurion understood that Jesus' authority was far greater than his own. When his servant was gravely ill, he didn't ask Jesus to come in person but humbly said that if Jesus only spoke the word his servant would be healed. His faith was so great that even Jesus was astonished by it (Matt 8:10).

In verse 9, the centurion makes a striking comparison between his own authority and Jesus'. As a military commander, he gave orders to his soldiers, and they were expected to obey immediately, often under penalty. Yet, he knew that Jesus' authority was limitless. If Jesus spoke, even illness and death had to obey. This Roman officer recognized his place as a leader but understood he was ultimately subjugated to Jesus' supreme authority. His faith acknowledged the true power behind leadership—knowing who holds ultimate control.

As leaders, do we recognize the limits of our own authority? Are we willing to subjugate ourselves to a higher authority to accomplish our goals? Leadership is not always about being "in charge" or "the boss." It's more often about knowing how to maneuver your own authority by humbly subjugating yourself to another in order to coordinate efforts toward a common goal. The centurion's example teaches us a lot about subjugating our authority to someone else.

Effective leaders recognize the limits of their authority and know when to humbly submit to a greater authority for the sake of the mission.

Application: Consider what the limits are in the authority you possess. Do those limits keep you from accomplishing the mission you have at home, at work, or in your community? Oftentimes they do. Connect with someone whose authority is not limited in the same way yours is and continue your mission.

HE HEALS

> "This was to fulfill what was spoken through the prophet Isaiah: 'He took up our infirmities and carried our diseases.'"
> —Matt 8:17

<u>Read</u>: Matthew 8:14–17 "Jesus Heals Many"
Jesus is a healer. When He chooses to heal, He does so completely. When He restores, He makes things brand new. The greatest act of His willingness to heal and restore was seen when He remained on the cross for our sake. Though He had the power to come down, He stayed, willingly sacrificing Himself to bring us eternal healing.

Jesus heals because He is willing, and He died for us because He is willing. Yet, how often do we hold onto our burdens, struggles, and fears, afraid to fully trust Him? He has already borne our infirmities and carried our diseases, but the question remains—are we willing to let Him take them from us? Jesus desires to bear our burdens, but we must be willing to hand them over to Him, trusting that He will make us whole.

Leadership involves recognizing when to release control, trusting others to handle what we cannot carry on our own.

<u>Application</u>: What are you holding on to because you lack trust? Are you failing to trust a teammate or leader in your life? Have you committed to fully trusting Christ or do you want to keep controlling the situation your own way? Trust Christ to place people in your life that you can trust with burdens you can't carry on your own.

BE INTENTIONAL

> "But Jesus told him, 'Follow me and let the dead bury their own dead.'"
>
> —Matt 8:22

<u>Read</u>: Matthew 8:18–22 "The Cost of Following Jesus"

There is no time to waste. The longer we make excuses for why we can't follow Jesus now, the more room we give the devil to work his schemes in our lives. Putting off that decision allows distractions, fear, and temptation to take root.

In John Maxwell's book, *The 15 Invaluable Laws of Growth*, his first principle is "The Law of Intentionality."[6] He explains that growth doesn't happen by accident; it requires intentional effort. This applies not just to personal growth, but also to our decision to follow Jesus and deepen our relationship with Him. It must be a conscious, deliberate choice.

Are you making excuses? Do you need to be more intentional in your relationships, how you communicate with your teammates, or how you lead others? Most importantly, are you being intentional in your relationship with Christ? Now is the time to humble yourself before His calling and discipline yourself to follow Him. Jesus is the greatest leader of all time, and if you let Him, He will guide you on the path of growth and purpose.

> **Growth in leadership—and in faith— requires intentionality and discipline; excuses only delay progress.**

<u>Application</u>: What area or areas in your life must you be more intentional about growing? List three areas today, pick one, and get after it. Find an accountability partner to help you through your growth and hold you accountable to your plan.

LET JESUS SPEAK

"He replied, 'You of little faith, why are you so afraid?'"
—Matt 8:26

Read: Matthew 8:23–27 "Jesus Calms the Storm"
It's easy to be hard on the disciples for doubting during the storm on the Sea of Galilee, but we should remember that they were still new to following Jesus. Many of them had only been with Him for days or weeks, and not all Twelve had been called yet (Matthew's calling is recorded in chapter 9). By this time, they had witnessed Jesus heal the sick and teach with authority, including the powerful "Sermon on the Mount." But in the midst of this sudden, violent storm their fear took over, and they thought they would drown. Even with all they'd seen, it hadn't crossed their minds, yet, that Jesus might be God.

As the storm raged, Jesus rebuked the wind and waves with a simple command, and they instantly calmed. Stunned, the disciples asked, "What kind of man is this? Even the winds and the waves obey Him!" (Matt 8:27). In that moment, they glimpsed Jesus' power over creation, something they'd never imagined was possible for any teacher or prophet.

Jesus has shown His power before—healing the blind, cleansing lepers, making the lame walk, and even raising the dead (Luke 7:22). Your storm isn't His first miracle, and it won't be His last. Invite Jesus to speak into your storm, and trust in His power to bring peace.

**Let Jesus stand between you and
your storm, and bring calm.**

Application: What storm in your life do you need Jesus to calm? Are you facing difficulties in your family, workplace, church, or community? Write down a relationship or situation that is causing a storm and ask Jesus to specifically bring peace to it. Trust that He will, submit to His authority and ability to do so, and stay out of His way, but commit all your faith to His way.

GET IN THE GAME

> "Then the whole town went out to meet Jesus. And when they saw Him, they pleaded with Him to leave their region."
> –Matt 8:34

Read: Matthew 8:28–34 "The Healing of Two Demon-possessed Men"

When Jesus crossed over to the eastern side of the Sea of Galilee, He was entering new territory. Up until then, His teaching, healing, and casting out demons had largely taken place on the western side. In the first-century world, news traveled slowly, so many people on the eastern side may not have heard much about Jesus or witnessed His miracles firsthand. This is an important context to help us understand the reaction of the townspeople in the region of the Gadarenes, who asked Jesus to leave after He performed a powerful miracle.

In this account, Jesus encounters two demon-possessed men and drives the demons into a herd of pigs, which then rushes over a cliff and drowns into the sea. This act, while freeing the men, came at a cost—the destruction of a herder's property and livelihood. From the townspeople's perspective, Jesus' actions may have seemed disruptive, frightening, or even financially harmful. And the men He healed, though now free, were likely still outcasts, carrying the stigma of their past for years to come.

There's a lesson here for us, too. Like the townspeople, we may witness Jesus' work in someone else's life, but hold back from joining in. Perhaps it seems too costly, requiring us to step outside our comfort zone, invest time, or use our resources to support those He has restored. We can be so focused on our own comfort that we hesitate to embrace the work God is doing around us.

Instead of staying on the sidelines hoping that Jesus will "play in our game," our question should be, "How can I be part of His?"

Christ-centered leaders find where God is moving and bring influence and value even when it is out of their comfort zone.

<u>Application</u>: God doesn't call us to every area He is moving. But He does call us. We are His hands and feet. Is there an area or cause where God is moving that He's urging you to join Him but it's out of your comfort zone? Take the step and embrace His work in your life.

ACTIONS SPEAK

> "'But so that you may know that the Son of Man has authority on earth to forgive sins...' **Then He said to the paralytic,** 'Get up, take your mat, and go home.'"
>
> —Matt 9:6

<u>Read</u>: Matthew 9:1–8 "Jesus Heals a Paralytic"
We've all heard the saying, "Actions speak louder than words." While words can either breathe life into someone or cut deep like a knife, actions carry a weight that words alone do not.

In this passage, Jesus performs three miracles. Two of these—only He can do: forgiving sins and knowing the hearts and thoughts of the teachers of the law present. The third miracle, however, is one that His disciples performed, and that Christians continue to do today: He heals the paralytic's physical body. The first two miracles occurred solely in the spiritual realm, while the third took place in the natural realm, showing His divine authority in both realms.

This is a powerful lesson in leadership. As leaders, do our selfless actions display our authority within the team? Do they show that accomplishing the mission and caring for our teammates come before our personal interests? Or do we rely on titles and expect obedience simply because of our position? Jesus prioritized His mission of forgiving sins, cared for the team by examining their hearts and minds, and then demonstrated His authority as the Son of Man through an undeniable act of healing.

True leadership is shown through selfless actions that prioritize mission and team over personal gain.

<u>Application</u>: Do you put the mission and the team before yourself? Reflect and write down one time from recent memory where you did not put the "mission" or team before yourself. Whether that was your family team, work team, or a community team? Write it down and be aware of the next time you have that decision to make.

CLEAR OBJECTIVES

> "When the Pharisees saw this, they asked His disciples, 'Why does your teacher eat with tax collectors and sinners?'"
>
> –Matt 9:11

<u>Read</u>: Matthew 9:9–13 "The Calling of Matthew"
Early in His ministry, Jesus' disciples were still young in their faith. Though they had witnessed much by this point, they remained in the early stages of learning from Him. In fact, Matthew had just become a follower that very day, and this event takes place in his own home.

When the Pharisees—prestigious religious leaders—question why Jesus spends time with sinners, they direct their question to the disciples rather than Jesus Himself. Jesus, however, steps in without hesitation and answers for His disciples. As a wise leader, He doesn't expect His spiritually young and potentially vulnerable disciples to respond to such an intimidating question. His direct, clear answer not only silences the Pharisees but also reassures His disciples, strengthening their confidence in Him as their leader.

This moment offers a valuable lesson in leadership. Jesus' response shows how essential it is for leaders to protect and support their teams, especially when they're inexperienced or uncertain. For leaders today, this account encourages a commitment to continual growth—spiritually, mentally, physically, and emotionally—so we can lead by example, stand above reproach, and be ready to answer questions or defend our team.

Strong leadership steps in to protect and reassure your team, especially in challenging moments.

Application: Have you empowered your team by providing clear objectives? Do your team members understand why they do what they do? When challenged, do you have the courage and wisdom to respond effectively?

COMMIT THE RESERVES

"Jesus answered, 'How can the guests of the bridegroom mourn while he is with them? The time will come when the bridegroom will be taken from them; then they will fast.'"
—Matt 9:15

Read: Matthew 9:14–17 "Jesus Questioned about Fasting"
John the Baptist's disciples were curious. If Jesus was indeed a greater teacher than John, why didn't He and His followers practice fasting? They even pointed out that the Pharisees, the religious leaders of the time, set the example for how and when to carry out these practices.

It seems likely that John's disciples didn't know Jesus had fasted for 40 days in the wilderness before beginning His ministry. That period of fasting was part of His preparation. Now that Jesus was fully prepared and bringing the good news, there was no need for additional fasting at that moment.

Fasting, as a spiritual practice, is often a way to seek God's intervention, expressing deep commitment and faith. Choosing to fast, especially when food is readily available, shows a strong resolve to draw closer to God. Using a military analogy, if prayer is fighting a battle in spiritual warfare, fasting is like sending in your reserves to achieve an overwhelming victory. When prayer alone doesn't seem enough, fasting shows a heightened commitment to seeking God's answer.

In this passage, Jesus explains that He is the "reserves." Humanity's fallen state couldn't be redeemed without God's intervention—and so—He sent Jesus. Jesus was telling them that there was no need to plead for additional help while He, the ultimate help, was already present with them.

Leaders provide what is needed at the moment bringing encouragement, resources, or reassurance when the team needs it most.

Application: What struggles are you going through, to which you need to "commit the reserves?" Fasting tests our commitment to seeing God move in a situation. If you are struggling in a battle where losing is not an option, then fast.

CONSIDER THE SPIRITUAL REALM

"He said, 'Go away. The girl is not dead but asleep.' But they laughed at Him."

—Matt 9:24

Read: Matthew 9:18–26 "A Dead Girl and a Sick Woman"

Jesus consistently observed what was happening in the spiritual realm before acting in the natural realm. Over the years, this concept has weighed heavily on me. Am I focusing on what is unfolding spiritually before responding in the natural? I've learned that when I overlook the spiritual realm, I am most vulnerable to sin. When we view situations solely through a natural lens, our flesh often takes over, leading us to act in ways that stray from God's guidance.

When Jesus told the flute players and noisy crowd to leave, saying the girl was only asleep, they laughed at Him. Yet, Jesus wasn't surprised or offended by their response; He understood that their faith was weak, and they couldn't perceive what was happening spiritually. His calm reaction shows that His actions were rooted in a firm understanding of the spiritual reality.

Do you pause to consider the spiritual aspect of a situation, or do you react impulsively to what you see in the natural? Every event in the natural world has a spiritual dimension, though not everything spiritual manifests naturally. If we want to succeed in the natural realm, we must first engage in the spiritual realm. Ignoring the spiritual aspect makes us vulnerable to failure in the natural.

True leadership discerns both spiritual and natural realities, responding from a foundation rooted in spiritual awareness.

Application: Before reacting in kind to someone who is being mean or malicious toward you, consider how your real enemy, the devil, is deceiving them to do so. Pray for that person and ask God to give you the appropriate response. We must always fight in the spiritual, "For our struggle is not against flesh and blood, but against the rulers, against the authorities, against the powers of this dark world and against the spiritual forces of evil in the heavenly realms" (Eph 6:12).

SIGNIFICANCE OVER SUCCESS

"...and their sight was restored. Jesus warned them sternly, 'See that no one knows about this.'"
—Matt 9:30

Read: Matthew 9:27–34 "Jesus Heals the Blind and the Mute"
Why did Jesus "warn them sternly" not to tell anyone? And why did they "spread the news" anyway (Matt 9:31)? It's easy to understand why they couldn't keep quiet. Imagine their excitement: "Guess what Jesus did for me! But don't tell anyone because He told me not to say a word." We all know how that story usually ends—it's hard to contain good news, especially when it's life-changing.

The bigger question is why Jesus didn't want His incredible deeds to be publicized. Throughout His early ministry, Jesus often instructed those He healed to keep it quiet. While each instance may have had a unique reason, it seems here Jesus was emphasizing that His mission was about healing, restoration, and redemption—not about gaining fame or followers. Jesus came to give life to the dead and set captives free, not to draw attention to Himself or build popularity.

This lesson really convicts me. I deeply desire to share the insights God has given me and the experiences He has used to develop me as a leader. Yet, I sometimes catch myself focusing on gathering a crowd or generating income. This is a sin, and I know it. I must refocus on serving people and developing leaders with a heart that isn't concerned with the "return on investment" (ROI), but with genuine impact. Do you ever find yourself focusing more on success than on significance? Remember, when you focus on God's purpose for your life, success becomes the byproduct.

True leaders focus on significance through service and adding value to others, letting success become the byproduct of their efforts.

Application: Write down one area at work where you may be focused on your success before adding value to others and write down another area outside of work where you also notice yourself focusing on your own success. Commit these to God today and ask Him to help you completely turn your eyes away from what you want out of it and seek to add value each day to others.

LEADERS DIRECT THE PLANNING PROCESS

"Then He said to His disciples, 'The harvest is plentiful, but the workers are few.'"

—Matt 9:37

Read: Matthew 9:35–38 "The Workers are Few"

Verse 35 describes Jesus going "through all the towns," teaching, preaching the good news, and healing various diseases and sicknesses. By this point, He was doing all the work Himself. Likely many months or even over a year into His ministry, Jesus was now preparing to give His disciples the authority to preach, heal, and drive out demons, sharing His mission with them.

In military terms, this phase resembles the "Mission Analysis" in the Military Decision-Making Process (MDMP) or "Problem Framing" in the Marine Corps Planning Process (MCPP). In fact, one could argue that Jesus had been engaged in problem framing since He began His ministry. This passage suggests He was now ready to give His disciples their mission, having fully assessed the need and trained them to address it.

The challenge Jesus identified is that His mission was never intended to be a solo effort. Jesus wanted not only a relationship with each of us but also for us to serve and build relationships with one another. So, He prepared His disciples to continue His work, empowering them to serve in the same ways He had been serving.

Do you have a solid planning process for yourself and your team? Jesus led by planning intentionally and giving clear instructions. Leaders owe their teams a thorough planning process and clear guidance to achieve their tasks. Like Jesus, involve your team in planning rather than working in isolation. Jesus included His disciples in His process from the start, teaching them directly, showing them miracles, and letting them observe how He handled individuals and crowds. Prepare your team, involve them in planning, and enable decentralized execution.

Clear, detailed planning enables team involvement and empowers them to execute the mission.

Application: For a role you have as an organizational leader, how do you do with driving the planning process? Do you provide clear objectives to the team you are planning with? Do you follow a planning process? If not, commit today to learning and adopting a sound planning process that produces a clear, detailed plan to enable your team to follow it while giving them the flexibility to execute the mission in a decentralized manner.

WORTHY OF YOUR WORK

"Freely you have received, freely give. Do not take along any gold or silver or copper in your belts; take no bag for the journey, or extra tunic, or sandals or a staff; for the worker is worth his keep."

—Matt 10:13–14

Read: Matthew 10:1–15 "Jesus Commissions His Disciples"
Jesus sends His disciples on their mission in the humblest manner possible. Unlike the business trips we're accustomed to, where

logistics are often arranged by the organization, Jesus instructs His disciples to rely on those they serve for support. This reliance was not just practical—it was a test of faith. Jesus wanted them to trust that God would care for them, especially when they faced rejection.

From this passage, we can draw three essential lessons. First, always seek to give rather than to receive. Our focus should be on serving others, trusting that provision will come as we fulfill God's purpose. Second, trust God to take care of you and your family while you remain faithful to His plan. Don't compromise His word out of fear; stand firm, knowing He is your ultimate provider. Third, be worthy of your work. As leaders, teachers, or coaches it's vital to practice what we preach. If we fail to live by the principles we promote, we lose credibility and diminish the value of our work.

Jesus' instructions remind us to prioritize humility, trust, and integrity in our work and relationships. Leading from this foundation allows us to serve others sincerely and with unwavering faith.

Serve with humility, trust God's provision, and embody the values you teach.

Application: When you review the points above, which one(s) do you feel are the hardest for you to keep? Is your trust completely placed on Christ for everything you need and the needs of your team? If not, write down how you will commit to trusting solely in Him for you and your team.

SEND ME!

"I am sending you out like sheep among wolves. Therefore, be as shrewd as snakes and as innocent as doves."

—Matt 10:16

Read: Matthew 10:16–23 "A Hard Road for the Disciples"

Jesus doesn't keep us in our comfort zones. In this passage, He sends His disciples out to face tasks they've never done before, knowing that some people may reject them. He warns them to expect mistreatment, yet instructs them to maintain their innocence. Jesus emphasizes the need for shrewdness—urging them to recognize danger and be on guard. Though the places they're sent are challenging and often unwelcoming, He sends them anyway.

It's a sad reality that many non-Christians avoid church because of hurtful things they've seen Christians do or say. Jesus called us to be "as innocent as doves," but some Christians place their methods and traditions of their form of Christianity above reaching the lost with love and grace. This misrepresents Christ's heart for others and risks pushing people further away from Him.

Jesus isn't interested in our wealth or how polished our church buildings look; He wants us to step out in faith, beyond our comfort zones, to bless and reach others. Are you willing to let Him stretch you beyond what feels safe? He's sending you out every day, so be on mission. Listen closely and be willing to adapt as He opens new mission fields around you.

Embrace each day as a mission, moving beyond comfort to reach others with Christ's love.

Application: Don't waste today. Today is a gift from God to be used for His glory. It has with it tremendous responsibilities. Write down at least one way you will use your time, talents, or resources to bless someone in Jesus' name today. Do this at least once a week for a month, and then twice a week for a month, and then three times a week, and continue until it is your habit to do it every day.

RECEPTION AND REJECTION

"He who receives you receives Me, and he who receives Me receives the One who sent Me."
—Matt 10:40

Read: Matthew 10:24–42 "The Meaning of Discipleship"
In this final part of Jesus' instructions, He offers His disciples powerful encouragement. He tells them not to fear those "who kill the body but cannot kill the soul," (Matt 10:28) and assures them, "he who receives you receives Me." Although He has warned them to be vigilant and expects them to face hatred, He also comforts them with the reminder that their true value and purpose are beyond human opinion.

As we live our daily lives committed to Christ, we can rest in the assurance that He is with us. Those who welcome us are welcoming Him, and those who reject us are ultimately rejecting Him. This understanding frees us from bearing the weight of others' decisions and actions, which are not our responsibility. Like parenting, where our children ultimately choose their paths, our task as believers is to pursue our own growth in Christ, to trust in His discipline, and to let Him work through us.

Today, hostility toward Christians is growing, especially in the West, as society moves further from biblical values. Stand firm in your faith, prioritize your relationship with Christ, and live in a way that reflects the eternal hope we hold. Remember, your life is a testimony of God's grace, even if the world does not recognize it.

Stand firm, focus on your growth in Christ, and let Him handle the responses of others.

Application: Reflect on how you are focused on your growth in Christ each day. Maybe it is a commitment to use these lessons to read through the Gospels. I pray that it is blessing you. If not, consider what actions or steps you must take to adopt habitual disciplines to grow in your walk with Christ.

FORCEFULLY SACRIFICIAL

"From the days of John the Baptist until now, the kingdom of heaven has been forcefully advancing, and forceful men lay hold of it."

—Matt 11:12

Read: Matthew 11:1–19 "Jesus and John the Baptist"
In prison, John the Baptist sends his disciples to ask Jesus if He is truly "the One who was to come." Jesus responds by affirming His actions and describing John as more than a prophet—he is the prophesied one from Malachi who prepares the way for Christ. In front of the crowd, Jesus speaks not only of John's legacy but delivers a powerful message to all willing to listen: *"The kingdom of heaven has been forcefully advancing, and forceful men lay hold of it."*

This verse highlights the boldness Christians are called to embody in our approach to the world. For me, it's a foundational truth behind Red Letter Leadership. In the face of an evil world, Christians cannot be passive or content within comfort zones, particularly in environments that challenge godly values. Instead, we are called to be resilient—to be "aggressively patient," "aggressively grace-giving," and to "stand tough," even when facing blows. Like an unwavering boxer in the ring receiving blow after blow, we are unfazed, steady, and confident in the strength of Christ.

Too often, Christians attempt to match the world's evil blow for blow. But true strength lies not in reciprocating hostility but in standing resolute and merciful, knowing evil ultimately has no power over God's kingdom. Why engage in a fight you're already promised to win? Show mercy, and let the opposition wear itself out.

Christians are commanded to lead, and leadership requires service and sacrifice, which ultimately advances the kingdom of heaven.

True leaders don't just react; they serve and sacrifice for a higher purpose.

Application: Are you "forcefully sacrificial?" Are you aggressively and intentionally going out of your way to serve and sacrifice your goals and ambitions for that of your team? That's a tall order to which we are called. Commit today to that level of sacrifice in your life.

CONCEITED OR GRATEFUL?

> "But I tell you that it will be more bearable for Sodom on the day of judgment than for you."
>
> —Matt 11:24

Read: Matthew 11:20–24 "Woe on Unrepentant Cities"
Jesus denounces several cities where He had performed miracles, including Capernaum, His primary residence at that time. Despite witnessing His miracles, these cities refused to repent. Jesus even states that if Sodom had experienced these same wonders, they would have turned from their ways. For Jesus to compare them to Sodom—a city notorious for its extreme wickedness—reveals the gravity of their unrepentance.

We could put ourselves in the position of these cities or even look at it from the perspective of our teams. What do we want, or what do we want for our teams, but we are unwilling to change? Are we seeking grace, success, or blessings while resisting the transformation needed to truly receive them? Often, we may justify our shortcomings by thinking, "we're not that bad," but whose standard are we using? If it's not God's, then we are likely off course.

True repentance comes from recognizing that we are not entitled to forgiveness, success, or any earthly blessing; everything belongs to God. With this perspective, entitlement falls away, and we are left with gratitude for all He provides, big or small. Only then can we genuinely turn away from self-centered desires and live with a heart open to God's guidance and provision.

Embrace humility and gratitude, understanding that everything is a gift from God, not a reward we are owed.

Application: Do you take anything for granted? Truly examine yourself today and reflect if you feel entitled to the blessings you have. Consider how you are using those blessings for His glory. "The LORD gave, and the LORD hath taken away; blessed be the name of the LORD" (Job 1:21, KJV).

FOLLOW HIS LEAD

"Take My yoke upon you and learn from Me, for I am gentle and humble in heart, and you will find rest for your souls."
—Matt 11:29

Read: Matthew 11:25–30 "Rest for the Weary"
This key verse is a profound reminder that leadership, true and meaningful, begins with the red letters—the teachings of Jesus. Jesus invites us to give Him our burdens, promising that He will carry them and give us rest. He describes Himself as *"gentle and humble in heart,"* which assures us that His leadership offers comfort and strength to our weary souls.

In the military, leaders carry what's often called "the burden of command." Having been a commander, I know this responsibility well. The commander is accountable for everything the command does or fails to do. When their time of command ends, there's a bittersweet relief, a lifting of the weight they've shouldered. The burden is transferred to the succeeding commander. Yet, with Jesus, the burden we place on Him is never transferred; He bears it fully and eternally. His shoulders are strong enough for whatever we carry.

As leaders, we should consider what burdens we're lifting off our teams. Are we easing their load so they can focus fully on the mission? Leadership in Christ's example means serving our team by understanding their struggles and sharing their load. By doing this, we allow them to thrive and grow without unnecessary strain, just as Christ does for us.

Lead by lightening the load for others—take on your team's burdens so they can succeed in the mission.

Application: As leaders, what burdens are we carrying for our teams? Reflect now. Are you taking strain from your team so that they can focus on the mission? Remember, they don't serve you. You serve them. Engage them. Understand their burdens and then make them yours.

RELENTLESS SERVICE

"How much more valuable is a man than a sheep?! Therefore, it is lawful to do good on the Sabbath."
—Matt 12:12

Read: Matthew 12:1–14 "Lord of the Sabbath"
It's striking that Jesus had to remind the religious leaders that doing good—even on the Sabbath—is honoring to God. They were so caught up in the letter of the Law that they overlooked its purpose: to guide us toward love and mercy. Jesus even had to remind them that human life holds more value than livestock, a truth clouded by their obsession with rule-keeping. Instead of seeing the

Law as a way to serve and bless, they used it to criticize, judge, and ultimately plot against Jesus for healing on the Sabbath.

The Law was intended to benefit humanity, to draw us closer to God, and to set us apart in holiness—not as a tool to control or condemn. When Jesus says He came to fulfill the Law, He means that His life and sacrifice bring the Law's true purpose to completion: to lead us into right standing with God. His mission was to serve, sacrifice, and redeem, knowing that some would reject His message.

Reflecting on this, we should ask ourselves: Does our leadership serve and uplift others, honoring God's call to love? Or are we sometimes guilty of prioritizing personal goals, material gain, or control over God's command to do good? True leadership aligns with God's purpose, putting others' well-being before ambition or control.

Lead with a heart focused on serving others, not controlling them.

Application: Where do you think you try to exact control over your team before serving them? Write down three ways that you have controlled your team over serving them by empowering them to carry out the mission or tasks of the team. If you do a good job not controlling and micromanaging them, then write three areas that you've witnessed other leaders control their teams. Then write how you need to rectify those situations to empower the team and serve them over controlling them.

KEEP YOUR FOCUS

> "Aware of this, Jesus withdrew from that place.
> Many followed Him, and He healed all their sick."
> —Matt 12:15

Read: Matthew 12:15–21 "God's Chosen Servant"
When Jesus learned that the Pharisees were plotting against Him, He didn't argue or plead with them to change. He knew they weren't

willing to listen, as they were only looking for reasons to condemn Him, not to understand Him. Instead, Jesus chose to withdraw. He understood that forcing influence on those who reject it is fruitless and distracts from reaching those ready to receive.

Jesus didn't quarrel, argue, or seek validation in the public square. As verse 19 emphasizes, "[He] will not quarrel or cry out; no one will hear his voice in the streets." His mission was not to win arguments or rally crowds for the sake of approval; His purpose was to set captives free. This focus allowed Him to prioritize those truly seeking Him, rather than becoming sidetracked by those determined to resist Him. Despite the opposition, "many followed Him," highlighting that even when some reject, others are still drawn to authentic leadership.

This passage challenges us to focus our leadership on those open to our influence and their growth rather than being discouraged by those who resist or reject us.

Lead with purpose and focus, prioritizing those willing to receive guidance, and avoid spending energy on those who only seek to oppose.

Application: Who would you like to have a positive influence on, but who consistently rejects or resists you? Consider disengaging them and focus your efforts on those who seek your influence and are intentional about their personal growth. Maintain your integrity and the ones who reject you now may return to you as they mature.

UNITE YOUR TEAM

"Every kingdom divided against itself will be ruined, and every city or household divided against itself will not stand."

—Matt 12:25

Read: Matthew 12:22–29 "Rebukes the Pharisees"

The Pharisees felt their authority threatened by Jesus' growing influence, leading them to accuse Him of casting out demons by Satan's power, calling Him an agent of "Beelzebub." Jesus, "knowing their thoughts," responded with grace, explaining that a divided kingdom or house cannot stand. He pointed out the illogic in their accusation: it would make no sense for Satan to empower someone to dismantle his own work.

Jesus' ministry showed His true mission—to heal, restore, and redeem, revealing God's kingdom at work. Through His actions, Jesus modeled unity and alignment with God's purpose, healing hearts and bringing people closer to God. His ministry teaches us that true influence brings life, not division, and works against evil, not alongside it.

As leaders, we should evaluate whether our actions unify our teams or create division. Are we empowering them with a shared mission and vision, or do we inadvertently create friction and conflict? Uniting a team, especially in times of disagreement, is the leader's responsibility. Conflict may delay progress, but a clear vision, empowerment, and effective communication keep the team moving forward. Leaders who align their team's goals and give clear direction inspire their people to accomplish the mission with greater success and cohesion.

Effective leadership unites the team under a shared vision and mission, fostering collaboration and strength that drives lasting success.

Application: Reflect now. Is/Are your team(s) united? If not, where is the divide? Write down where your team(s) may be divided and bring your thoughts to your team. Then, seek their input for how to become more united. What core values will everyone get behind? What vision and mission do they want to pursue (this of course, if you have a team that can design their own. In the workplace environment, this may not be possible.)?

WORDS REVEAL CHARACTER

"For by your words you will be acquitted, and by your words you will be condemned."
—Matt 12:37

Read: Matthew 12:30–37 "Words Reveal Character"
Jesus' rebuke of the Pharisees highlights how their words reveal the state of their hearts. Although actions can speak louder than words, words hold a unique power: they can either uplift and heal or undermine and destroy. The Pharisees' harsh words toward Jesus showed their hardened hearts and the hypocrisy in their actions. Jesus' response underscores the truth that our words not only reflect our character but also shape the impact we have on those around us.

Words are powerful; they were instrumental in creation itself when God spoke the world into existence. Yet, as James reminds us, the tongue is like a fire that can consume and devastate if left unchecked (James 3:5–6). In leadership, effective communication is essential for a team to accomplish its mission. Our words should be clear, concise, and aligned with our intentions. A leader who inspires and encourages his team with well-chosen words strengthens their morale and unity, while a leader who belittles or criticizes risks eroding their trust and losing their respect.

As leaders, we hold the responsibility to wield our words wisely. Choose to build up, encourage, and guide your team. Remember that the right words can empower others to achieve great things, just as the wrong ones can diminish progress and morale.

Words reveal the heart; speak with integrity, uplifting your team to foster unity and inspire growth.

Application: When was the last time your words have negatively influenced, or worse, impacted another's life? Give yourself an honest examination today of how you use words and the tone of your voice. Write down a few ways you can improve your speech to be uplifting and inspiring to those around you.

GOD'S GRACE WHEN IT FEELS LIKE HIS JUDGMENT

> "He answered, 'A wicked and adulterous generation asks for a miraculous sign! But none will be given it except the sign of the prophet Jonah.'"
>
> —Matt 12:39

Read: Matthew 12:38–45 "The Sign of Jonah"
The Pharisees ask Jesus for a "miraculous sign" to prove Himself, despite the countless miracles He has already performed out of compassion and love for people. Their request reflects a refusal to believe, not a genuine need for proof. Jesus rebukes their stubbornness, pointing to the "sign of Jonah." Jonah's journey, spent in the belly of a fish for three days, was both a correction and a grace from God, redirecting Jonah back to his mission in Nineveh. Jesus draws a parallel, foretelling His own three days in the grave as the ultimate sign of His authority and mission.

Sometimes God's intervention can feel uncomfortable or even like judgment, but it's often a sign of His grace, not condemnation. Jonah's time in the fish wasn't pleasant, but it set him back on course to fulfill his calling. Similarly, when we face challenges or correction, it may be God's way of realigning us with His will, offering a second chance to grow and obey.

When life feels like a storm, consider that God may be lovingly steering you back to His purpose. His signs aren't always peaceful and easy—they may feel like a "big fish" moment, but they're designed to bring us closer to Him.

Sometimes God's grace feels uncomfortable, but it's His way of guiding us back to His purpose. Embrace His course corrections as opportunities for growth.

Application: Has God taken you somewhere that seems like a storm of His judgment? Consider that He may have taken you out of your comfort zone to redirect you and to grow you. Have you thought that what He is really doing is giving you an opportunity to come back to His will?

OPPOSITION WITHIN OUR FAMILIES

> "For whoever does the will of My Father in heaven is My brother and sister and mother."
>
> —Matt 12:50

Read: Matthew 12:46–50 "Jesus' Mother and Brothers"
In this passage, Jesus teaches that our spiritual family—those who follow God's will—holds a unique and profound significance. While our earthly families are essential, they should not surpass our commitment to God's purposes. Jesus is not calling us to neglect our families but to prioritize God's will even when it may conflict with family expectations. This principle would have been especially challenging if His own family, as hinted in Luke 8:19, was unsure of His mission and possibly pressured by religious leaders' accusations. Despite any tension, Jesus remained resolute in His dedication to His Father's will.

For believers today, this can be a difficult reality, particularly for those from non-Christian backgrounds. New believers may find themselves ridiculed or even rejected by their families for their faith. In such moments, the support of the Body of Christ becomes essential. Ministries like "The Voice of the Martyrs" highlight stories of people coming to know Jesus from predominantly Islamic and Hindu cultures and then facing beatings and persecutions from members of their own family.[3] It is sad but also encouraging to hear how those believers keep the faith. These accounts remind us of the resilience required to stay faithful, even when it means standing alone.

If you find yourself torn between family expectations and God's call, remember to stay steadfast in your commitment to Him. When the challenges feel overwhelming, "stand" in faith, as Ephesians 6:13 urges.

When family pressures weigh heavy, lean on the support of the Body of Christ to stay faithful.

Application: Do you or have you faced opposition from your own family for choices you made that you believed were in-line with God's will? First, examine the choice and ask God to give you confirmation that you are in fact following His will. Open up Scripture and ask Him to reveal the truth. Seek support from the Body of Christ in your local church to help you endure opposition that you receive from your family and elsewhere.

WORK THE SOIL...DAILY

"But blessed are your eyes because they see and your ears because they hear."

—Matt 13:16

Read: Matthew 13:1–23 "The Parable of the Sower"
The Parable of the Sower, recorded here in Matthew, is one of Jesus' profound teachings on receptivity to God's word. When His disciples asked why He used parables, Jesus explained that while

they were given direct insight into the mysteries of heaven, the crowds were not. It wasn't that He was hiding truth from them but their "calloused" hearts (Matt 13:15) prevented them from seeking it sincerely. Parables allowed those genuinely interested in truth to pursue it, while others simply walked away. This approach highlighted the principle that those who truly desire God's word will seek it with open hearts and minds.

In Galatians 6:7, we're reminded, "Do not be deceived: God cannot be mocked. A man reaps what he sows." God is calling us to take ownership of the state of our hearts and lives. This parable is often seen as a call to avoid "bad soil" in our own hearts, but it's more than that. We are also called to be Sowers, taking responsibility to cultivate not only our own "soil," but also that of those we influence—our families, colleagues, and friends. Whether we are planting seeds or merely preparing the soil, we play a vital role in nurturing an environment that allows God's truth to grow. We may not always be the ones planting the seeds or even watering them, but we all should be preparing the soil.

Leadership cultivates the soil of our hearts and the soil of others' hearts, making way for God's truth to take root and grow.

Application: With your thoughts, words, and actions are you cultivating soil in your own life? Are you preparing to always be receptive to God's word? Write down two ways you are and two ways you can improve how you cultivate your own soil and the soil of those you influence.

INVEST IN WHAT'S GOOD

"'No,' He answered, 'because while you are pulling the weeds, you may root up the wheat with them.'"
—Matt 13:29

Read: Matthew 13:24–30, 36–43 "The Parable of the Weeds" and "The Parable of the Weeds Explained"

This passage offers a profound answer to the age-old question of why God allows evil to persist in the world. Many question, "If there is a God, why does He permit such tragedy?" The answer lies in God's dual nature of mercy and justice. He desires that everyone has a chance to turn from wrongdoing and come to Him. Despite knowing who will ultimately accept or reject Him, God allows all to coexist, knowing that tragedy touches everyone. It's a reminder that though evil persists, God's desire for redemption remains open to all.

We may not understand all of God's ways, but as believers, we trust His character. He is perfectly just and merciful, and He cannot commit evil. This means that even when we see injustice or tragedy, we recognize that God will use it for good. In the parable, Jesus suggests that we are the wheat growing among weeds. Instead of condemning the weeds, we should focus on becoming the healthiest "wheat" possible and supporting others in their growth. God may call us to protect, nurture, or even inspire others to join His kingdom, and all of this is done by living out His love and grace.

> **Christ-centered leaders don't waste their time condemning. Instead, they invest it in developing themselves and others focusing on growth instead of judgment.**

Application: How might you be too focused or being too committed to condemning the evil around you that you miss opportunities to cultivate the good around you? Write down two people who you wish to invest in developing and commit to connecting with them.

HIS KINGDOM STILL GROWS

"Though it is the smallest of all your seeds, yet when it grows, it is the largest of garden plants and becomes a tree, so that the birds of the air come and perch in its branches."
—Matt 13:32

Read: Matthew 13:31–35 "The Parable of the Mustard Seed and the Yeast"

Jesus often used familiar imagery, like the mustard seed and yeast, to illustrate the kingdom of heaven's growth, showing how it begins small and spreads into something vast and life-changing. When we view history through this lens, we see a continuous spread of God's kingdom across nations, despite opposition or misuse of His name.

I took a class titled "Foundations of Western Civilization" when I was working toward my Master's in History. We started in Ancient Greece and finished with the founding of America during the "Age of Enlightenment." It was incredible to see, amid evil government oppression over hundreds of years, how the Holy Spirit continued its work and changed hearts. There was much evil done in the name of Christianity, but do not connect that with God. Christianity does not always get it right, but Christ does. We must follow Him, not a worldly religion. This isn't a slam on Christianity. I certainly practice it. However, Christianity—the practice of worshipping God with other fallible human beings—sometimes gets it wrong. "God will not be mocked" (Gal 6:7). He will not be fooled by us taking His word out of context and using it for our worldly gain.

Leaders, do not believe everything a "Christian" tells you, even if he/she is behind a pulpit. Find the truth in God's word yourself. Grow Christ's kingdom. Do not oppose it in your ignorance.

Christ-centered leaders discern truth from error, standing firm in God's word and guiding others to do the same.

<u>Application</u>: Are you so stubborn in your religious traditions that you miss true religion? Many Christians prioritize the way their church practices Christianity over God's word. Commit today to be a critical thinker in everything you read, hear, and see regarding the Word of God. When you truly test His word and seek the truth, you will find it and the deception will be exposed.

JOY THROUGH SACRIFICE

> "The kingdom of heaven is like treasure hidden in a field. When a man found it, he hid it again, and then in his joy went and sold all he had and bought that field."
>
> —Matt 13:44

<u>Read</u>: Matthew 13:44–46 "The Parable of the Hidden Treasure and the Pearl"

Reflecting on the kingdom of heaven, we might ask ourselves: are we, like so many around the world, willing to give up comfort for the sake of Christ's calling? In America, it's easy to water down the kingdom of heaven, hoping to balance both worldly comforts and God's purpose. Yet, Jesus clearly says, "You cannot serve both God and money" (Matt 6:24). Recently, I urged you to subscribe to "The Voice of the Martyrs," where stories of believers enduring intense suffering and sacrifice for Christ illustrate their deep commitment and increasing joy.[3] Their lives reveal the real connection between the spiritual and natural realms—trading comfort for Christ brings them an ever-deepening joy, a joy rooted in knowing Jesus as their Savior.

Leadership is sacrifice. To lead effectively, one must embrace the reality that leadership often requires sacrifice for the sake of the team. This doesn't mean giving up everything in every situation, but it does mean leaders must be willing to make necessary sacrifices, demonstrating that the mission is more important than themselves. If leaders are not willing to make necessary sacrifices, then they cannot expect those they lead to sacrifice either.

True leadership demands the sacrifice of personal comfort for the sake of the mission, showing others the path to follow.

Application: What sacrifices do you make for your team? What sacrifices are you not making that you need to make? Is there a game on that you want to watch when your son or daughter want your attention? Do you need to take on more work from a teammate because they are going through a rough time in their personal life and their productivity has decreased? Be willing and joyful in making sacrifices.

LIVE HIS WORD AND GAIN HIS JOY

> "He said to them, 'therefore every teacher of the law who has been instructed about the kingdom of heaven is like the owner of a house who brings out of his storeroom new treasures as well as old.'"
>
> —Matt 13:52

Read: Matthew 13:47–52 "The Parable of the Net"
The Parable of the Net reflects a similar teaching on the kingdom of heaven as seen in the Parable of the Weeds, but Jesus emphasizes something new in verse 52, our key verse here. He reaffirms that the Law remains, yet His presence has introduced new treasures, insights "hidden since the creation of the world" (Ps 78:2). This

highlights the unity between God's timeless principles and the fresh revelation Jesus brings.

We cannot experience the new treasure while neglecting the old. We cannot have the joy of God's kingdom without submitting to His authority. Many people in the world seem to want God's riches while wanting nothing to do with His family. They say things like, 'if there was a God, then this wouldn't happen, or I would have this or that.' How foolish?! They close their eyes to seeing that the truly good things in their lives are from God and continue to turn their back on Him because they don't have 'this' or don't experience 'that.'

To truly experience the joy of God's kingdom, we must fully commit to His truth and principles. We cannot have one without the other; God's joy and our obedience are intertwined. While living by His standards can be challenging, it's through this commitment that we find lasting joy. God will not withhold His joy from those who walk in His righteousness, even when it comes through hardship.

Christ-centered leaders add great value to people living God's word and exposing His glorious truth day after day.

<u>Application</u>: Consider what living His word means to you. In what ways in your home, your community, and your workplace can you be a leader who lives God's word? Write down one new way for each of those environments where you can live God's word, and by doing so add great value to the people around you.

CREDIBILITY

"And they took offense at Him. But Jesus said to them, 'Only in his hometown and in his own house is a prophet without honor.'"

–Matt 13:57

Read: Matthew 13:53–58 "A Prophet without Honor"
Jesus' wisdom and miraculous works were met with skepticism by those who knew His humble origins. They "took offense at Him" because their familiarity with His earthly family blinded them to His true identity and potential. This dynamic can resonate deeply with many of us, especially when our pasts overshadow the greatness God wants to achieve through us.

Do you ever feel disheartened by those who remember your past mistakes while you strive to embrace God's calling for your present and future? It's important to recognize that we all have a history, and often, our hometowns know our shortcomings best. Rather than harboring resentment, focus on serving others and building your credibility outside of familiar circles.

Consider how you view others from your past. You may see them as ordinary or remember their previous failures, yet they might now be accomplishing remarkable things for God's kingdom. Celebrate their successes and seek opportunities for growth in your own life. If your hometown doesn't recognize your potential, don't dwell on it; instead, "knock the dust off your feet" and take your message or mission to new places. God can use you powerfully, regardless of where you start.

Your past does not define your future; seek to grow beyond your hometown's perceptions and let God use you for His glory.

Application: Are you weighed down by negative connotations that exist about you in your hometown? Be encouraged; we all have areas we can grow. But also, be encouraged; we all have a message—a testimony—that God has imprinted on our lives and He wants us to use it to serve Him. Be bold today and live your message.

SPEAK TRUTH TO POWER

"...for John had been saying to him: 'It is
not lawful for you to have her.'"

—Matt 14:4

Read: Matthew 14:1–12 "John the Baptist Beheaded"
Even in prison, John the Baptist boldly speaks truth to power, challenging the moral corruption of Herod. Here verse 5 reveals that Herod wanted John killed because he couldn't control him, mirroring the Pharisees' attitude toward anyone who defied their authority. John understood his life's purpose—to prepare the way for Jesus—and remained unshaken, confronting evil even though it might cost him his life.

Today, as we witness the rise of evil, the urgency to stand for truth has only grown. We cannot afford to remain silent when faced with immorality, even if society deems it "acceptable" or considers it "modern." As leaders, we must have the courage to call out wrongdoing without sugar-coating it and remain rooted in our principles regardless of societal shifts.

Ask yourself: are you the type of leader who speaks truth to power? Do you expect accountability from those around you? Whether your role calls you to address a leader's actions or uphold your team's values, start by seeking wisdom through prayer. Consult trusted advisors and carefully plan how you will approach the situation. Lead with a spirit of sacrifice and prepare yourself for any potential consequences, knowing that true leadership often demands bravery and integrity.

> **Leaders must have the courage to confront wrongdoing with humility and the strength to accept any consequences that result.**

Application: Are you approachable to your teams, inviting and encouraging them to speak truth even if it may incriminate you?

We are to trust each other and be vulnerable to the accounting from those closest to us. Call two close friends of the same gender and ask them if you are an approachable person. Regardless of their answer, ask them to give you a few ideas on how to be more approachable.

YOU FEED THEM

> "Jesus replied, 'They do not need to go away. You give them something to eat.'"
>
> —Matt 14:16

<u>Read</u>: Matthew 14:13–21 "Jesus Feeds the Five Thousand"
Jesus is God. We all need Him. Yet, when the disciples identified a problem—that the crowds were getting hungry—they advised Jesus to send them away so that they could eat.

This passage tells us that Jesus had compassion on them and began healing their sick. The crowds yearned for Christ and the disciples' response was to send them away from Jehovah Jirah, our Provider, for their needs to be met elsewhere. Clearly, the disciples were not focused in the spiritual realm, where Jesus was always operating. They were focused in the natural realm.

Jesus shows His disciples that what these people really need is their Savior, and what the disciples need to do is bring them to Jesus, not send them away. Jesus wants to include us in His miracles. He wants us to be involved in His ministry. His kingdom includes us.

What happened on that hillside over 2,000 years ago was the very kingdom of heaven. The multitudes came and ate with their Savior, a bounty that only God could provide. And the disciples would have missed it if they executed their plan to send the crowds away.

We are not here to send the crowds away from Jesus. We are here to bring them to Jesus.

Leaders, you give them something to eat. Don't wait for someone else to.

<u>Application</u>: Jesus wants to use us in His ministry. Are you available and willing for Him to use you? Reflect today on the needs that you can meet but which you originally thought to yourself, 'someone else will do that.' Consider praying and asking God if you are the one to meet that need.

FACE YOUR FEARS

> "But Jesus immediately said to them: 'Take courage! It is I. Don't be afraid.'"
>
> —Matt 14:27

<u>Read</u>: Matthew 14:22–36 "Jesus Walks on the Water"

The boat that held the disciples that night was not unlike the smaller, exposed boats used as whaleboats in the American Revolutionary War or today's lifeboats on cruise ships—meant only for short journeys. When Jesus approached them, walking on the water between 3:00 and 6:00 a.m. ("the fourth watch"), the disciples, exhausted and vulnerable, thought He was a ghost. It's an understandable reaction—most of us would have felt the same way! But Jesus quickly calmed their fears with a command: "Take courage!" and an assurance: "It is I."

"Courage is not the absence of fear, rather; it is the strength to overcome it" (MCDP-1 *Warfighting*, 15). This Marine Corps Doctrinal Publication reminds us that fear is part of the journey, not a sign of failure. True leadership doesn't ignore fear but studies it, prepares for it, and leads others through it.

As leaders, we are not called to be without fear; we are called to be courageous in the face of it. Jesus doesn't just suggest we take courage—He commands it. When we don't follow His command, it raises a deeper question: Do we trust Him enough to overcome our fear?

Leaders embrace courage as a response to fear.

<u>Application</u>: What fears do you face? What fears must you face? Write three of your most prominent fears down and take the next three days to study each one. When you finish, develop a plan to face each of those fears and trust that Jesus will be with you each step of the way.

A MATTER OF THE HEART

> "Listen and understand. What goes into a man's mouth does not make him 'unclean,' but what comes out of his mouth, that is what makes him 'unclean.'"
>
> —Matt 15:10–11

<u>Read</u>: Matthew 15:1–14 "Clean and Unclean"
This teaching may seem straightforward to us, given over 2,000 years of the Holy Spirit's guidance and freedom from a legalistic religious culture. Jesus explains to the Pharisees that traditions shouldn't supersede obedience to God. When traditions distort God's Word, it is not the Word that needs revision, but the traditions themselves.

Jesus isn't dismissing hygiene or healthy eating, rather, He focuses on honoring God through authentic practices, not empty rituals. He calls out the Pharisees as hypocrites for their surface-level obedience, while their hearts are far from God. His words, though true, offend them because they reveal the real issue—the heart.

Our words and actions, rather than food or drink, are what should reflect our devotion. However, we should also consider how food or drink influences us—immediately (such as with alcohol or drugs) or over time (like with poor dietary habits). We honor God by what comes out of our mouths, yet what we put into our bodies can affect this as well. As leaders, we are called to set an example by loving God with all that we are: body, mind, soul, and heart.

Our behaviors and how we communicate are how we will be perceived.

<u>Application</u>: Examine yourself today. Has your communication and behaviors over the past week displayed the fruits of the Spirit (Gal 5:22–23)? If they have not, first make it right with the one you may have wronged, and then ask that person, 'how could I have said that better?' or 'how could I have acted in a way that was uplifting rather than degrading?'

HUMBLE POWER

> "'Yes, Lord,' she said, 'but even the dogs eat the crumbs that fall from their masters' table.'"
> –Matt 15:27

<u>Read</u>: Matthew 15:21–28 "The Faith of the Canaanite Woman"
The Canaanite woman's faith is a powerful display of humility toward Jesus. Recognizing herself as "only a dog in comparison to God's children—the Israelites," she shows unwavering faith despite discouragement. When the disciples urge Jesus to send her away, implying that His grace is exclusive to them, Jesus tests her persistence further. First, He ignores her, then He says He was not sent for her, and finally, He compares her to a dog. Yet, she humbly

accepts this comparison, persisting in faith until Jesus ultimately honors her request and heals her daughter.

The Apostle Paul echoes this theme, sharing that Christ told him, "My grace is sufficient for you, for My power is made perfect in weakness" (2 Cor 12:9). This woman's humility opened her to Christ's power, perfecting her in her weakest moment.

For leaders, this example is a reminder that effective leadership isn't about asserting one's own strength but acknowledging limitations. Many leaders assume they must know everything because they're in charge, yet often the collective expertise of the team surpasses that of any single leader. A wise leader will, like the Canaanite woman, embrace humility and seek solutions from the team.

Humble leaders know that real strength often comes from recognizing one's limitations and seeking wisdom from others.

Application: In your roles as a leader, do you sometimes feel like you need to have all the answers, offer all the good ideas, or provide all the solutions? It is easy for leaders to feel this way because the responsibility of the mission lies on their shoulders. However, this thinking is a burden that the leader does not need to carry and will only lead to a toxic environment. Find the strength in someone on your team today and seek an idea or solution to a problem from them. Empower them.

HIS HANDS AND FEET

"Then He took the seven loaves and the fish, and when He had given thanks, He broke them and gave them to the disciples, and they in turn to the people."

—Matt 15:36

Read: Matthew 15:29–39 "Jesus Feeds the Four Thousand"
This miracle, Jesus' second feeding of thousands with only a few loaves of bread and fish, highlights both His compassion and His invitation for us to participate in His work. Jesus saw that although the crowd's spirits were nourished, they still needed food; and He responded to this physical need just as He had healed their lame, sick, mute, and blind. With thousands gathered, not everyone likely saw Jesus praying over the bread and fish or instructing His disciples. If this event happened today, it would be captured by cameras and broadcast across social media, but at that moment, the focus was on meeting people's needs, not gaining attention.

What stands out in this miracle is how Jesus involved His disciples in serving the crowd. While He performed the miracle, the disciples carried out His work by distributing food to those who were hungry. Some in the back of the crowd may not have known how little food Jesus started with, but everyone felt the impact of the miracle. This scene beautifully illustrates how God builds our credibility through His power. He calls us to bring Him to others by serving them, and through this, His power flows through us, meeting real needs.

> **Christ-centered leaders are channels of His power, serving others and building credibility through our faithful actions.**

Application: How do you involve your team in acts of service? You may be seen as credible by others, but are you bringing your team along with you and developing their credibility too? Decide how you can include your family team, work team, or a community team in an act of service and plan to do so.

BE ON GUARD

"'Be careful,' Jesus said to them. 'Be on your guard against the yeast of the Pharisees and Sadducees.'"

—Matt 16:6

Read: Matthew 16:1–4 "The Demand for a Sign"
Despite all that Jesus did, many of the religious leaders—the very people appointed to lead God's chosen people in worship—were hardened to His true identity. A few recognized His divinity, but most did not. Jesus rebuked their stubbornness and then urged His disciples to guard themselves against the influence of the Pharisees and Sadducees.

Today, just as in Jesus' time, we must protect ourselves from false teachings. The Body of Christ is led by the Holy Spirit, not popularity or numbers. Even now, some teachers claim to follow Christ, but spread unbiblical doctrines, leading people astray. As leaders, we must know how to distinguish truth from deception, which requires deep familiarity with Scripture. In an age flooded with information, discernment is essential; we need to be in the Word consistently to strengthen that discernment.

Thank you for joining me in this journey through the Gospels. But let these lessons only be a part of your time in the Bible. I encourage you to read the Scriptures linked to each lesson, inviting the Holy Spirit to guide you personally. Trust Him to speak directly through His Word, and let your prayers continue to flow from your own heart.

Leaders must guard against false teachings by anchoring themselves in Scripture and seeking the guidance of the Holy Spirit.

Application: Have you been disciplined to read each of the passages of Scripture with these lessons? If you haven't, commit to beginning to do so today. By reading all passages and not only the key verse, we become aware of the context of the writing which will reveal the truth and how we can apply it to our lives.

JESUS OF NAZARETH IS THE CHRIST

"'But what about you?' He asked. 'Who do you say I am?'"
—Matt 16:15

Read: Matthew 16:13–20 "Peter's Confession of Christ"
Jesus asks each of us the same question He asked His disciples: "Who do you say I am?" Our answer to this is foundational to our faith and our relationship with Him. Peter's response, "You are the Christ, the Son of the living God" (Matt 16:16), is the simplest and truest statement of Christianity. Without answering this question correctly, no relationship with Christ can endure.

From this confession flows the essence of Christian living: loving God and loving others. Let's not complicate it. Everything in Scripture builds upon these two truths: 1) Jesus is the Christ, the Son of the living God, and 2) He commands us to love Him and love others. This is the core of our faith, the foundation upon which we grow and act in love.

Have you answered Jesus' question? If not, consider doing so today.

Christ-centered leaders acknowledge Christ as Lord and commit to living the Great Commission.

Application: If you have not professed your faith in Christ, do so today. Do not hesitate any longer. He is the King. There will never be a dominion over Him. He wants to connect with you, be in a close relationship with you, and lead you to develop others who desire Him.

KEEP YOUR MIND ON THINGS OF GOD

"Jesus turned and said to Peter, 'Get behind Me, Satan! You are a stumbling block to Me; you do not have in mind the things of God, but the things of men.'"

–Matt 16:23

Read: Matthew 16:21–23 "Jesus Predicts His Death"
Not long after Jesus blessed Peter with the words, "on this rock I will build my church," He delivered a strong rebuke to him.

Though the exact time between these events is unclear, Matthew records Jesus' rebuke as the next significant interaction. The quick shift highlights how Peter's understanding was rooted in a natural, earthly view of the Messiah. Like many Jews, Peter likely envisioned a Messiah who would deliver Israel through political or military strength.

Jesus blessed Peter for recognizing His true spiritual identity. But when Jesus spoke of His coming suffering and death, Peter's perspective shifted to his own ideas about what the Messiah's path should be. His newfound role clouded his view, and his response, "Never, Lord!" was rooted in human thinking rather than spiritual wisdom. Jesus rebuked Peter's arrogance, not as a withdrawal of His blessing, but as a correction and reminder of God's greater purpose.

We too can fall into the same trap when we react with "Never, Lord!" to situations that seem uncomfortable or conflicting. Before assuming a difficulty isn't God's will, we should examine our own biases and ask if God might be leading us through it for a greater purpose. Often, He calls us to walk through challenges, both to grow us and to reveal His presence alongside us.

> **Christ-centered leaders surrender their ideas of comfort and control, embracing even difficult paths as opportunities for spiritual growth.**

Application: Reflect on the last time you experienced an uncomfortable time in your life—even time "in the valley." Did you see that time as an opportunity for your growth? John Maxwell's Law of Pain states, "Good management of bad situations leads to great growth."[7] Ask God to grow you through bad situations you experience. Do not try to retreat from them, but rather embrace them as an opportunity to grow as a leader.

A DAILY EFFORT

> "Then Jesus said to His disciples, 'If anyone would come after Me, he must deny himself and take up his cross and follow Me.'"
>
> —Matt 16:24

Read: Matthew 16:24–28 "Discipleship is Costly"
Following His rebuke of Peter, Jesus taught His disciples the true cost of following Him. Denying oneself to follow Christ isn't a one-time decision but a continual choice, one that requires us to surrender our worldly inclinations and ambitions each day. In Red Letter Leadership's Seven Pillars, I emphasize, "Leadership must be a daily effort," mirroring Jesus' call to take up our cross daily.

Jesus highlighted that true discipleship means giving up our own desires and surrendering everything to God, the rightful owner of our lives. Our society often encourages us to prioritize personal comfort and success, but Jesus flips that script, calling us to seek holiness even when it places us at odds with the world. In verse 25, He reminds us that true life is found not by clinging to it, but by releasing it to God's control. God owns it all, but He invites us to be His stewards. We cannot be His stewards without giving up the ownership to the rightful owner—Him.

Jesus asks a profound question in verse 26: "What good will it be for someone to gain the whole world, yet forfeit their soul?" This question challenges our tendency toward materialism and self-centered ambition. Our lives are fleeting, and in the end, worldly gain has no eternal value. True stewardship is about releasing control to God and aligning our pursuits with His kingdom.

Effective leadership demands a commitment to daily self-denial, grounding ourselves in the things of God rather than the fleeting desires of this world.

Application: Thankfully, leadership is a daily effort. Which means, when we fail as leaders—and you will—we can immediately humble ourselves, pick ourselves up, correct our deficiencies, and be better the next day. Part of that is adopting an attitude to deny 'self' every day. Choose one area of your life today that only gratifies you and choose to deny yourself that gratification and replace it with an effort to serve those you lead in a new way.

"LISTEN TO HIM!"

> "While He was still speaking, a bright cloud enveloped them, and a voice from the cloud said, 'This is My Son, whom I love; with Him I am well pleased. Listen to Him!'"
> —Matt 17:5

Read: Matthew 17:1–13 "The Transfiguration"
Peter witnesses Jesus' face become bright like the sun, His clothes become as white as the light (Matt 17:2). Then he sees Moses and Elijah talking with Jesus (Matt 17:3). What is Peter's response? He wants to memorialize the occasion with a sort of monument—"shelters" (Matt 17:4).

In the previous chapter, Jesus told Peter that he will build Christ's Church (Matt 16:18). Peter has yet to understand that he is Christ's monument. Those of us who testify to Christ's deity, His death, and His resurrection—we are His monuments. He needs no "shelter" on the side of a mountain to where people can pilgrimage.

God, the Father, interrupts Peter's arrogant speech about memorializing the occasion with some earthly rubble and emphatically states, "This is My Son...Listen to Him!" It's like God is telling Peter, 'shut your mouth and listen to Jesus.' Wow! Who else beside me needs to hear that, and even more, is comforted by it?

As *I* think about how I want Red Letter Leadership to add value to individual people and teams through our mission statement, I forget to listen to how **God** wants to use Red Letter Leadership to add value to individual people and teams. Like Peter, I want to make a suggestion so I can say that it was my idea, when what I really need to be doing is falling face down and "Listen to Him!"

Christ-centered leaders listen to God's guidance over their own ambition.

<u>Application</u>: What situation in your life do you seem to be trying to direct, but, like Peter, God the Father is simply telling you to just listen to Jesus? Sometimes we need to be go-getters, but sometimes we need to stop, be still, and listen to Jesus. Consider what situation or decision you are dealing with, where you just need to stop and listen to Jesus.

MOVING MOUNTAINS

> "He replied, 'Because you have so little faith. I tell you the truth, if you have faith as small as a mustard seed, you can say to this mountain, 'Move from here to there' and it will move. Nothing will be impossible for you.'"
>
> —Matt 17:20

<u>Read</u>: Matthew 17:14–23 "The Healing of a Boy with a Demon"
When Jesus rebukes the disciples' lack of faith, He emphasizes that even "faith as small as a mustard seed" can accomplish the seemingly impossible. The disciples had already witnessed Jesus' power over sickness, death, blindness, and demonic forces—and had been empowered to do the same. Yet, something about this particular case must have unsettled or intimidated them, causing their faith to falter. Instead of focusing on Christ's authority, they may have let fear overtake their confidence in His power.

If we think of "mountains" as obstacles, Jesus' words challenge us to approach our struggles with unwavering faith. God puts mountains in our lives so that we can watch Him move them. Don't be discouraged by the size of the mountain in front of you. Have faith that He will move it. He will either give you stronger legs to endure the climb so that it doesn't feel like a mountain, or He will pick the whole mountain up and throw it into the heart of the sea. Either way, He expects you to face the mountain and have faith that He will act.

> **Christ-centered leaders approach each obstacle with faith that God will deliver them and provide the solution.**

<u>Application</u>: Sometimes we feel like our mountains are too big and so we try to avoid them and go a different direction. God wants us to put our faith in Him to deal with or navigate the mountain. What mountain do you need God to help you address? Write down and clearly identify the mountain in your life that you need to overcome and commit it to the One who throws them into the sea.

WE OWN NOTHING

> "But so that we may not offend them, go to the lake and throw out your line. Take the first fish you catch; open its mouth and you will find a four-drachma coin. Take it and give it to them for my tax and yours."
>
> —Matt 17:27

<u>Read</u>: Matthew 17:24–27 "The Temple Tax"
By now in Jesus' ministry, many people throughout the towns surrounding the region of Galilee knew that Jesus was at odds with the religious leaders. Some, like the collectors of the temple tax in this passage, assumed that Jesus wouldn't pay the tax since He openly opposed their teaching. Yet, in this miracle, not only did He live

above their reproach of Him, but He showed Peter, and likely the other disciples, that all creation and all wealth serves Him.

This miracle displays that earthly currency does not put limitations on God. My first full year of service in the Marine Corps was 2002 (I entered active duty in June 2001). I remember tithing around $1500 that year. I also remember receiving a refund of around $1500 when I filed my tax return in the early spring of 2003. Not that I expected to get back in a tax return what I tithed that year, or I ever thought that would happen again, but I do remember that God was impressing on me, 'If you can continue to obey My command to tithe, you will never be in need.' I can testify to you today: I've never been in need. I encourage you all to tithe. It's freeing to know that you don't own anything. It is God who gives and who takes away….and who can provide what you need in the mouth of a fish.

Christ-centered leaders trust God with their resources and are assured that He will meet every need.

Application: Do you think you own your company, or your house, or your health? If so, choose to change your attitude with that belief. God owns it all. Have the attitude that you are one of His many stewards and trust Him with your resources. Write down one thing which you have been treating and making decisions about as if you own it, and commit today to beginning to make the decisions as the chief steward.

CHILD-LIKE FAITH

"Therefore, whoever humbles himself like this child is the greatest in the kingdom of heaven."

–Matt 18:4

Read: Matthew 18:1–9 "The Greatest in the Kingdom of Heaven"
Children are the greatest in the kingdom of heaven. Why? As a father, I've learned this to be true by watching my youngest grow from birth. She trusts me and has faith in me as her father with no hesitation. That's the kind of faith God wants us to have in Him and that's what will elevate us to greatness. Sometimes as leaders, we think we need to display our 'power.' On the contrary, we are to humble ourselves and retain our child-like faith no matter how high we climb up the organizational ladder.

We are to protect children from evil while mimicking their faith. I have consulted with a nonprofit organization whose mission is to combat human trafficking by focusing on rescues and high-risk interventions, while also pursuing justice through arrests and the judicial system of the host nation. Slavery is one of the greatest evils and human trafficking is indeed slavery. "Anyone who kidnaps another and either sells him or still has him when he is caught must be put to death" (Exo 21:16). For a grown man or woman to take advantage of the trust and faith a child has in them and then use them and abuse them for their own advantage is something that God commands us to adamantly oppose. "They trample on the heads of the poor as on the dust of the ground and deny justice to the oppressed. Father and son use the same girl and so profane my holy name" (Amos 2:7). Consider how you may be able to support the fight against this wretched evil.

The true greatness God values in His kingdom lies in child-like faith, humility, and a commitment to protect and honor those who are vulnerable.

Application: Do you trust God like a young child who needs their father to meet all their needs including to protect them? Trust in your Heavenly Father today for all your needs. Consider also how you can serve, support, and protect children who are misused and abused all over the world. You may very well be how God is providing them their needs and protection.

NOT ONE IS FORGOTTEN

> "In the same way your Father in heaven is not willing that any of these little ones should be lost."
>
> —Matt 18:14

Read: Matthew 18:10–14 "The Parable of the Lost Sheep"
Jesus is explaining to His disciples that the Father cares as much for any of His children that have gone astray as He cares for those who haven't. He even states that He is happier about finding the one than about 99 who did not go astray.

There is no person in any race, religion, or country on the globe, who has gone astray which God has forgotten. And some are just weeds that He knows will never humble themselves to Him and will eventually be picked and thrown into the fire (Matt 13:24–30). But we don't know that. Therefore, we are to "be as shrewd as snakes and as innocent as doves" (Matt 10:16).

This passage spoke to my wife and I as we decided to adopt. Hundreds of thousands of children are waiting in the foster care system to be adopted. We knew God had given us an ability to adopt and so we believed He was also placing that responsibility on us. We didn't know how tough the road would be, but we took a step of faith.

You and I are placed on this earth for a reason—for kingdom purpose. Find your purpose within His will. I had a lot of help as I was transitioning out of the military to craft my "why" statement. My personal why is: To empower the greatness in others, so that they become 'more than conquerors.' This statement drove me to be a father, to seek challenging assignments in the military, to step out of my comfort zone and start Red Letter Leadership, and to serve in the fight against human trafficking.

Christ-centered leaders use their influence and resources to seek and support those who need God's saving grace.

Application: Though we are all commanded to "go and make disciples," God has given each of us different "why's" to guide us in fulfilling His Great Commission. Do you know your "why?" Consider having a life coach help you formulate your "why." If you are walking in God's will, you are likely already living your "why." Being able to write it out in a statement helps us refer to it and stay focused and encouraged by it.

TEAMWORK

> "For where two or three come together in My name, there am I with them."
>
> —Matt 18:20

Read: Matthew 18:15–20 "A Brother Who Sins against You"
Jesus outlines a clear process for resolving conflicts among believers, with the ultimate aim of fostering unity. First, He advises addressing the issue privately with the person involved. If that approach is met with humility and understanding, the matter is resolved. Should the individual not listen, Jesus instructs us to bring one or two others to reinforce the testimony. If the individual remains unresponsive, the matter should be presented to the larger church community. Finally, if the person continues to resist correction, they should temporarily step back from serving until they repent, as their unwillingness to acknowledge their fault hinders the unity of the church.

At the heart of this teaching is Christ's desire for unity within His Body. He calls us to handle conflicts not through division, but by fostering reconciliation and understanding. Ecclesiastes 4:12 states, "Though one may be overpowered, two can defend themselves. A cord of three strands is not quickly broken." Hours before His death, He prayed earnestly for the unity of all believers

(John 17), emphasizing how critical it is to our faith and witness. This process is not simply about conflict resolution. it's about cultivating healthy relationships and teamwork within the Church, strengthening our collective service to Him and to others.

Christ-centered leaders foster a culture of healthy relationships and of conflict resolution, resulting in unmatched teamwork.

<u>Application</u>: What was the last conflict you were involved in? Was it with fellow believers? Did you follow the guidelines from this passage to resolve the conflict? Recount how you handled the conflict and then write down what you would do differently the next time. How will following Jesus' instruction in this passage resolve the conflict, reconcile parties, and grow the team?

FORGIVE...EVERY TIME

"Jesus answered, 'I tell you, not seven times, but seventy-seven times.'"

—Matt 18:22

<u>Read</u>: Matthew 18:21–35 "The Parable of the Unmerciful Servant"
We are called to forgive because God, in His boundless mercy, forgives us. Even if those who wrong us repeatedly seem undeserving of forgiveness, withholding it would imply that God should likewise withhold His forgiveness from us—a notion none of us would want. Our forgiveness of others is a reflection of God's grace to us through Christ's sacrifice. It's not about what others deserve but about mirroring the mercy God has extended to each of us.

Forgiveness, whether given or sought, requires deep humility. When we forgive those who have wronged us, we show humility by releasing resentment and restoring peace. When we seek forgiveness, we humbly acknowledge our shortcomings. This mutual humility strengthens relationships and builds resilient teams, prepared to face any challenge. Forgiveness isn't always easy, but it is essential for unity and strength. Jesus bore our guilt without any of His own, setting a high standard of mercy. "Freely you have received; freely give" (Matt 10:8) is our guide to extending the same forgiveness we've received.

Forgiveness, grounded in humility, restores relationships and builds strong, united, and unstoppable teams.

Application: When was the last time someone needed your forgiveness? Did you give it? Write down three of the top ways in which someone has wronged you throughout your life. Ask God to give you the strength and courage to forgive. Ask Him to give you the humility to feel the freedom that He has given you through His forgiveness. You can offer that same freedom to yourself and someone else today.

LEADERSHIP IN MARRIAGE

"So they are no longer two, but one. Therefore, what God has joined together, let man not separate."
—Matt 19:6

Read: Matthew 19:1–12 "Divorce"
The Pharisees approach Jesus to test Him, hoping to catch Him contradicting Mosaic Law by addressing divorce. But instead of dwelling on the subject of divorce, Jesus turns their attention to God's design for marriage. Our key verse emphasizes that it is God who joins man and woman together, and no person should separate that bond. Marriage, as Jesus explains, creates a unique "one flesh" relationship—a closeness that mirrors the spiritual union between Christ and His followers.

Jesus uses marriage to illustrate His relationship with the Church, positioning Himself as the groom and the Church as His bride. The Apostle Paul extends this analogy, urging wives to submit to their husbands as to the Lord and husbands to love their wives as Christ loved the Church (Eph 5:22–25). True leadership in marriage, then, is not about who holds a position, but about each spouse fulfilling their God-given roles in a way that reflects God's influence and love.

When husband and wife honor these roles, they both lead in their unique ways—living examples of God's design for influence within the family. A wife, in her submission, wields powerful influence for God's kingdom, just as a husband, in his sacrificial love, leads by Christ's example. Together, their marriage becomes a testimony to others and to the next generation, showing that leadership is about faithfully reflecting God's commands, regardless of position.

True leadership in marriage flows from both spouses fulfilling God-given roles, enabling them to influence others for God's kingdom through love, respect, and obedience to His commands.

Application: If you are married, consider how you fulfill your role. Are you a wife? God's command to you to respect and be submissive to your husband does not remove you from leadership responsibilities. In fact, it enables your ability to lead your family. Are you a husband? God's command to serve, sanctify, and sacrifice for your wife is the greatest form of leadership there is. Take time now to reflect how you lead in your marriage.

PRIORITIES OF HEAVEN

"Jesus said, 'Let the little children come to Me, and do not hinder them, for the kingdom of heaven belongs to such as these.'"

–Matt 19:14

Read: Matthew 19:13–15 "Jesus Blesses Little Children"
In this passage, we see the disciples rebuking people for bringing their children to Jesus, likely influenced by their cultural beliefs that prioritized power and status. They may have thought that Jesus, now a figure of great influence and authority, was too important to spend time with children. Yet, Jesus challenges this notion by demonstrating His care for children and affirming their significance in the kingdom of heaven.

There are three key takeaways from this moment:

1. **Concern for Children:** Jesus actively shows that children hold a special place in His heart and in the kingdom of God.
2. **Prioritization of Time:** Jesus pauses His important ministry to bless the children, illustrating that true leadership is not about being busy with significant tasks, but rather making space for what truly matters—relationships.
3. **Rebellion Against Cultural Norms:** By welcoming the children, Jesus subverts the prevailing cultural attitudes that dismissed their importance, revealing a revolutionary and relational approach to leadership that prioritizes love over status.

I had the privilege of speaking with the former Bloomsburg University football head coach, Danny Hale, over the phone. As a recent inductee into the College Football Hall of Fame, he could easily use his fame for personal gain. However, he chooses to invest his time in babysitting his grandchildren, embodying the same spirit of prioritizing relationships that Jesus demonstrates. Coach Hale's commitment to his family reflects a deep understanding of what is truly valuable, showing that impactful leadership transcends accolades and fame. No wonder he had such a great impact on the players he coached.

Leaders prioritize relationships over status.

Application: Reflect now. Do you prioritize your relationships over your status, wealth, or other self-gratifying things? Commit today to focusing on your relationships and prioritizing them over all else.

PERFECTION IS COMPLETE SUBMISSION

> "Jesus answered, 'If you want to be perfect, go, sell your possessions, and give to the poor, and you will have treasure in heaven. Then come, follow Me.'"
>
> —Matt 19:21

Read: Matthew 19:16–30 "The Rich Young Man"

The rich young man approaches Jesus with eagerness, seeking the key to eternal life. His initial interaction with Jesus seems straightforward; he is told to follow the commandments that govern relationships with others, culminating in the well-known principle to "love your neighbor as yourself" (Matt 19:18). On the surface, the rich young man appears to be a model citizen: young, successful, generous, and admired by the society. He embodies the characteristics many strive for, the proverbial "Joneses" that people often wish to emulate.

However, when he inquires, "What do I still lack?" (Matt 19:20), it becomes clear that despite his outward adherence to the commandments, there is a deeper spiritual deficiency within him. Jesus then challenges him directly, pointing to his attachment to material wealth by instructing him, "If you want to be perfect, go, sell your possessions and give to the poor" (Matt 19:21). This moment reveals a critical truth: while the young man is good by societal standards, he is not aligned with the radical call of discipleship that Jesus offers. His inability to relinquish his possessions highlights a heart that, despite its goodness, is still bound by earthly treasures.

This narrative prompts us to reflect on our own lives. Could we truly give it all away if Jesus asked us to? And is He, in fact, demanding such a sacrifice? Perhaps God has blessed us not just for our own benefit, but so that we might become vessels of His love and power in the world. The rich young man walked away saddened because he could not part with his wealth, potentially missing the transformative journey of faith that awaited him.

Our personal leadership development requires our willingness to release our earthly attachments and follow Jesus wholeheartedly, trusting that His plans for us are greater than our own desires for wealth and status.

Application: What are you holding on to that is impeding your development? While attending the International Maxwell Conference in Orlando, FL in August 2024, I heard Dan Martell, a CEO business coach and 9-figure entrepreneur, state, "poor people spend time to save money, while rich people spend money to save time." Are you trying to hoard your money? Release and trust God. It all belongs to Him anyways.

UNCONDITIONALLY UNFAIR

"Don't I have the right to do what I want with my own money? Or are you envious because I am generous?"

—Matt 20:15

Read: Matthew 20:1–16 "The Parable of the Workers in the Vineyard"

Doesn't God have the right to do what He wants with His own resources? Remember, He owns it all. "The LORD gave and the

LORD has taken away; may the name of the LORD be praised" (Job 1:21). We are not to covet His resources; we are to be good stewards of them. We are to covet Him.

In this parable, the workers who agreed to work for one denarius and who worked all day, complained that the owner paid the same amount to the workers who only worked the last hour. Wouldn't you complain about that? That's not fair at all.

But the kingdom of God is not about fairness. It's about complete humility and submission to the King and accepting that what He decides is always true, always just, and always fair according to His endless mercies.

Love isn't fair; it's unconditionally unfair to the one distributing it. That is what makes it love—true, Godly love. And to the one receiving love, it will heal any wound, mend any heart, and save the soul.

Love and unselfishness should be a leader's attitude toward others—their team and others with whom they collaborate. That attitude will help foster an environment where team members hold each other accountable, the leader is approachable, innovative ideas are considered and encouraged, change occurs, and conflict is appropriately dealt with.

Love is not fair. But it is strengthening, freeing, enabling, encouraging, and inspiring. 'Love' is arguably the only single word that can accurately define the kingdom of God.

> **True leadership is rooted in love and selflessness, fostering an environment of grace where team members are empowered and inspired to contribute their best.**

<u>Application</u>: Have you ever felt that offering your love to someone was unfair to you? Like, they don't deserve that because of what they've done to you or others? That's ok. As a matter of fact, that is expected. However, we are still commanded to love. Today, choose love over fairness.

SPEAKING WITH AUTHORITY

"They will condemn Him to death and will turn Him over to the Gentiles to be mocked and flogged and crucified. On the third day He will be raised to life!"
—Matt 20:18-19

Read: Matthew 20:17-19 "Jesus Predicts His Death a Third Time"
In this passage, Jesus predicts His death for the third time, and this time, He gives a detailed description of the suffering He will endure. He tells His disciples that He will be handed over to the Gentiles, mocked, flogged, and ultimately crucified. His earlier predictions had only mentioned His being handed over and killed, followed by His resurrection on the third day. Here, Jesus goes deeper, preparing His followers for the reality of His impending sacrifice.

By speaking with authority, Jesus demonstrates His responsibility toward His disciples, guiding them into truth, even when it's painful. He doesn't soften the message to make it more palatable, instead, He presents them with the truth to prepare them for the challenges ahead. His authority here is not domineering but protective and honest.

For leaders, speaking with authority carries an inherent responsibility. Just as Jesus spoke to equip and prepare His disciples, leaders must also ask themselves if they are genuinely shouldering responsibility when they exercise authority. Are they supporting their teams to meet expectations? Are they guiding and providing necessary resources and training to help their teams grow? Authority divorced from responsibility is empty; it's the willingness to bear responsibility that gives authority its rightful strength and integrity.

Effective leadership asserts authority with owning responsibility, offering both direction and the support needed for others to thrive.

Application: When you give tasks to your team, are you also owning the responsibility to ensure they are properly supported to accomplish the task you gave them? Are you giving them adequate time and the resources needed for the task? Consider a recent task you gave. Write down what you provided your team to accomplish that task and what you didn't provide that they needed or would have helped. In the military, we categorize the need for equipment as it relates to accomplishing a mission as "mission critical," "mission essential," or "mission enhancing."

THE ESSENCES OF GREATNESS

> "Not so with you. Instead, whoever wants to become great among you must be your servant."
> —Matt 20:26

Read: Matthew 20:20–28 "A Mother's Request"
In verse 25, Jesus states how the world sees power and authority—leadership. He states, "that the rulers of the Gentiles lord it over them, and their high officials exercise authority over them." Jesus is pointing out that those who are ruled are the servants and those who do the ruling are to be served. No matter how much the term "servant leadership" is tossed around, it seems that when people get a touch of power, they begin to think others should be serving them. This notion could not be further from the truth.

As Eric Albright recently pointed out to me, "servant leadership is just leadership." That is so true. I've grown to dislike the "servant leadership" phrase because it gives the impression like it's a kind of leadership. No. It is leadership. Without the "servant" aspect to it, it's not leadership.

A servant bears burdens.
A servant puts others before themselves.

A servant serves another's needs.
A servant endures beatings.
A servant does not respond in kind to a harsh word.
A servant finds joy in their suffering.

Leadership is inseparable from service. To lead well is to serve fully, embodying humility, sacrifice, and resilience.

<u>Application</u>: How well do you serve? The answer to that question is a good indication of how well you lead. Consider one act of service that you can do in each of the environments where you lead (family, work, church, community, etc.) to have a positive influence on your team in those environments.

BUT GOD...

"Jesus stopped and called them.
'What do you want Me to do for you?'"
—Matt 20:32

<u>Read</u>: Matthew 20:29–34 "Two Blind Men Receive Sight"
Here is another passage where Jesus ignored an inconsiderate, dispassionate crowd, and sought out the marginalized. The crowd thought that Jesus was too important to deal with these outcasts. The physically and mentally disabled in Jesus' culture were thought to be bearing the judgment of God in their disabilities. So, for those who had no disabilities, these two blind men were social outcasts and rightfully so. But God...

But God stopped, and He called to them. No one else called to them, but God. There is comfort in this passage but also conviction. The comfort is that God stops and calls us when everyone else has abandoned us. The conviction is that we are guilty of abandoning those in whom God is looking to work a miracle.

Keep your eyes open for when God stops, turns to the marginalized, and calls them. You may be positioned to witness or even be a part of a mighty miracle of God.

Christ-centered leaders are called to see people as He sees them, to stop, and to reach out, participating in the redemptive work He is already doing.

Application: Where might God be calling you to be a part of a miracle He wants to work through you? Be open to being used by Him and He will place you where He wants to use you. Write down three strengths you have to serve the marginalized in the society.

ENTHRONED FOREVER ON TRUTH

"If anyone says anything to you, tell him that the Lord needs them, and he will send them right away."
—Matt 21:3

Read: Matthew 21:1–11 "The Triumphal Entry"
According to my Bible's footnotes, the donkey was "an animal symbolic of humility, peace, and Davidic royalty." Jesus is entering Jerusalem as Messiah, from the Mount of Olives, and displaying His identity to royalty through the throne of David while offering humility and peace. And the people praised Him for it and shouted, "Hosanna to the Son of David! Blessed is He who comes in the name of the Lord! Hosanna in the highest!" (Matt 21:9).

"Of the greatness of His government and peace there will be no end. He will reign on David's throne and over His kingdom, establishing and upholding it with justice and righteousness from that time on and forever. The zeal of the Lord Almighty will accomplish this" (Isa 9:7). This is a common passage read and observed at Christmas time. Jesus' triumphal entry is His claim to David's throne while also symbolizing the most humble and peaceful way for a king to assume a throne.

In Matthew 11, Jesus states that He is "humble and gentle at heart." He entered this world in the most humble way to a lowly family, and now enters Jerusalem as king in the most humble way.

So how could a crowd crucify such a man within a week from this worship of Him? Because He brought the truth which they were too afraid to accept.

Speak truth when it hurts. Speak truth even to those who will reject it. Speak truth with your actions. Speak truth, but do so in love, humility, and peace. Your first piece of the armor of God to put on is your belt—the belt of truth—which will hold your garments in place and secure weapons to your side.

> **Christ-centered leaders speak and live truth even when others will reject it and even when it may incriminate themselves.**

<u>Application</u>: Consider a time when you did not speak the truth fully because it was uncomfortable, and you thought it would produce an outcome that you didn't agree with. What happened? How would speaking the truth have improved the situation for all involved? How can you commit today to always live and speak truth?

UPHOLDING STANDARDS

"'It is written,' He said to them, 'My house will be called a house of prayer, but you are making it a 'den of robbers.'"

—Matt 21:13

Read: Matthew 21:12–17 "Jesus at the Temple"

Jesus' actions in the Temple remind us of His passion for upholding the sanctity and purpose of God's house. After entering Jerusalem humbly on a colt, He walked straight into the Temple—the most sacred place on earth for the Jewish people—and confronted the corruption and exploitation that had seeped into its practices. Today, if someone attempted to act as Jesus did on the Temple Mount, they would likely face severe consequences from the Israeli security forces due to the tensions around the Temple Mount. This context helps us understand the weight of Jesus' actions in His time, as well as the courage and righteous anger that motivated Him.

However, we are not called to mimic His outward display of rage. Jesus' unique role as the Son of God justified His actions, but His example still teaches us valuable principles. Jesus demonstrated that accountability is essential for maintaining integrity, whether in our personal lives, our faith, or our teams. He stood against hypocrisy and upheld the holiness of a place meant for prayer and worship.

In leadership, we too are responsible for holding our people accountable. Just as Jesus insisted on reverence in His Father's house, we must ensure that our teams uphold the values and standards we set together. Having clear, measurable standards of behavior and a shared ethos can help cultivate a culture of integrity and respect within our organizations.

Leaders hold their team to a standard that aligns with the team's values, ensuring accountability and honoring the purpose behind their work.

Application: Recall a time you held the standards of your team even when it was uncomfortable to do so and even when your team appeared in disagreement with your actions. How did it maintain standards and uphold the integrity of your team?

NESTED IN KINGDOM OBJECTIVES

> "If you believe, you will receive whatever you ask for in prayer."
> —Matt 21:22

Read: Matthew 21:18-22 "The Fig Tree Withers"
When the disciples asked Jesus how the fig tree withered so quickly, He did not explain how in the scientific, natural sense of how it happened. Rather, He remained focused in the spiritual realm and taught how faith caused the fig tree to wither.

Our key verse is one that has been very hard for me, and I'm assuming for many others, to believe. There are many times that I have asked in prayer, with unselfish, Godly motives, and I feel God did not answer my prayer. But I will say, it is hard to believe, because we tend to see those unanswered requests as truly unanswered. However, in my experience, when I try to focus my mind on the grander picture of God's plan, I can start to see how He may be moving in a situation. In those times, I am encouraged to continue to pray.

Now, I am not saying I never lack faith. I wish I could say that, but the truth is that the times when I've lacked faith in prayer are too numerous. But what is very encouraging is that there are many times when my prayers were answered and I didn't realize it until days, even months, or years later.

The most important aspect of our prayer is also the most important aspect of our leadership. We must remove self.

We exist to serve kingdom purposes. We cannot do that if we seek to serve self. With kingdom purposes, we need kingdom objectives. What are some kingdom objectives? Everything else about our lives—our families, our businesses, our communities—should nest themselves within kingdom objectives.

We can only seek kingdom purposes after we have intentionally removed 'self' from the equation.

Application: List three kingdom purposes that your efforts as a leader could be nested under to advance the kingdom of heaven.

WISDOM IN THE QUESTION

"John's baptism—where did it come from? Was it from heaven, or from men."
—Matt 21:25

Read: Matthew 21:23–27 "The Authority of Jesus Questioned"
When the religious leaders questioned Jesus' authority, rather than debating them, He asked a simple question in return, which would have naturally led them to the truth. But the chief priests and elders, secure in their own authority, refused to answer. Their pride prevented them from seeing Jesus' wisdom, and they assumed that He owed them explanations, not the other way around. Jesus recognized their arrogance and chose not to engage in a pointless argument.

This is a powerful example for us in handling conflicts. Jesus didn't engage in a heated debate, nor did He defend His position. Instead, He demonstrated a humble, insightful approach by posing a clarifying question that invited understanding without escalating the situation. Often, we find ourselves in arguments where both sides are so focused on "winning" that the true understanding is lost. Jesus' approach teaches us to pause and consider if there's a better way to reach clarity.

Next time you find yourself in a heated conversation, consider following Jesus' example: ask a clarifying question to understand the other person's perspective. Even if you already know the answer, this approach shows humility and may defuse tension. Like a skilled lawyer, ask questions that reveal the core issues, helping all parties gain clarity and focus on the truth instead of ego.

Christ-centered leaders resolve conflict through seeking understanding by asking clarifying questions, prioritizing truth over winning.

Application: How often do we feed into someone else's arrogance which then leads to a heated argument? Remember Jesus' approach from this passage and consider asking a clarifying question rather than seeking to defend yourself or "win" the argument. Truth is already the victor. It does not need your defense.

ACCEPT REBUKE

> "'Which of the two did what his father wanted?' 'The first,' they answered. Jesus said to them, 'I tell you the truth, the tax collectors and the prostitutes are entering the kingdom of God ahead of you.'"
>
> —Matt 21:31

Read: Matthew 21:28–32 "The Parable of the Two Sons"
When the chief priests and elders refused to answer Jesus' question about John's authority, Jesus responded by sharing a parable that revealed their own hypocrisy. In this story, the father asks two sons to work in his vineyard. The first son initially refuses but later obeys, while the second son agrees to go but fails to act. When the religious leaders correctly identify the first son as the obedient one, Jesus uses their own admission to convict them. He explains that notorious sinners like tax collectors and prostitutes would enter the kingdom of God before them—not because of their reputation but because of their genuine repentance and obedience.

The religious leaders, focused on preserving their authority, were blind to the truth Jesus offered. Their pride and self-righteousness hindered them from acknowledging their need for God's mercy. Jesus' response was not one of condemnation but of correction, urging them to open their eyes to the true condition of their hearts.

This story challenges us to examine our own openness to rebuke. Do we approach Scripture and correction with humility, ready to be shaped by God's truth? When we're corrected, especially in matters rooted in Scripture, we should receive it with humility. As Proverbs reminds us, loving discipline and correction leads to growth and honor, while resisting it leads to shame and foolishness. But when we face correction that lacks scriptural foundation, Jesus' advice in Matthew 10:14 to "dust off our feet" can guide us to disengage gracefully.

Growth comes through a teachable heart.

<u>Application</u>: Do you consider yourself teachable? Do you accept rebukes when they come, and not immediately jump to defend yourself? Are you vulnerable and approachable to new ideas, to considering that your ideas may be in the wrong direction, and are you open to hearing from others? Write three ways or areas that you could be more teachable and approachable.

HIS WORKERS ARE FEW

"Therefore I tell you that the kingdom of God will be taken away from you and given to a people who will produce its fruit."

—Matt 21:43

Read: Matthew 21:33–46 "The Parable of the Tenants"

In this parable, Jesus highlights the resistance of the religious leaders by illustrating their rejection of God's messengers. The landowner, symbolizing God the Father, entrusts his vineyard (the world) to tenants (those with authority), sending servants (the prophets) to collect its fruit. But these servants are mistreated, and finally, the landowner sends his son (Jesus), whom the tenants ultimately kill. Through this story, Jesus confronts the religious leaders about their rejection of God's call and their hostility toward those who bring His message.

Jesus makes it clear that producing fruit for God's kingdom is a sign of true stewardship. The parable's warning that "the kingdom of God will be taken away... and given to a people who will produce its fruit" (Matt 21:43) underscores that it's not about titles or positions, but about the heart's response and the fruit of a life lived for God. For the religious leaders, the truth was too convicting to accept, prompting them to seek a way to silence Jesus rather than listen.

This message challenges us to examine our own "vineyards." Are we nurturing God's purposes, bearing fruit that honors Him, or are we focused on building our own success? True stewardship means dedicating our day-to-day efforts to the growth of God's kingdom, allowing His work to shine through us.

Christ-centered leaders are stewards who seek to produce the fruit of God's vineyard, not their own.

Application: This passage has convicted me how I have focused too much on leadership development as a business rather than a platform to produce the fruit of God's kingdom. I know God will take care of my needs and I must stay focused on producing the fruit for which He has given me the talents and resources to do. Write down an area in your life or a time where you sought to produce your own "fruit" in place of the fruit of God's kingdom.

DISCRIMATE WITH LOVE

"But when the king came in to see the guests, he noticed a man there who was not wearing wedding clothes."
—Matt 22:11

Read: Matthew 22:1–14 "The Parable of the Wedding Banquet"
In this parable, Jesus uses a wedding feast to illustrate how God extends His invitation to all people. Originally, the invitation was given to Israel, but when they rejected it, God opened the invitation to the rest of the world. Yet, even as God welcomes everyone, there is a standard: we must enter "clothed" appropriately, symbolizing the need to accept Christ's sacrifice. Jesus makes clear that, though God loves all and welcomes all, entrance into the "wedding feast" requires wearing the righteousness provided through Christ.

God's kingdom has high standards, as does any position that carries great responsibility. I have served in several units that required a very discriminative screening and selection process. I served as a Presidential Security Guard at Camp David, a Force Recon Marine, a Marine Infantry Officer, and a Marine Special Operations Officer. There was a rigorous screening and selection process for each of those positions. The communities had to maintain the elite standards of their organizations in order to carry out the mission that the nation expected. With all that said, each day was always a test. Upholding standards meant accountability, yet, I learned that taking ownership of mistakes and showing humility could restore trust, even after a failure.

For leaders, the challenge is to balance inclusivity with accountability. Upholding standards doesn't mean being harsh but ensuring everyone has a clear understanding of expectations and responsibilities. Lead with humility, set an example of grace and integrity, and make it clear that standards exist not to exclude but to honor the value and purpose of each role.

Upholding standards with humility and compassion allows for accountability without diminishing respect, helping to foster trust and growth.

<u>Application</u>: Do you get frustrated when someone isn't upholding the standards of their role or the team? I know I do. But as a leader, are you able to show humility and vulnerability when you fail to uphold a standard? Reflect and write down some ideas for how to gracefully approach a teammate who is not meeting the standard.

LIVING UNDER OPPRESSION

> "'Caesar's,' they replied. Then He said to them, 'Give to Caesar what is Caesar's, and to God what is God's.'"
>
> —Matt 22:21

<u>Read</u>: Matthew 22:15–22 "Paying Taxes to Caesar"
The Pharisees send their disciples to trap Jesus by questioning His allegiance. They hope He'll renounce Caesar's authority, which would place Him in conflict with the Roman government. But Jesus sees beyond their scheme, recognizing that their hearts are hardened, focused on earthly power rather than God's truth. In His response, "Give back to Caesar what is Caesar's, and to God what is God's" (Matt 22:21), Jesus makes a profound distinction. He acknowledges the authority of earthly governments but also establishes that divine authority is separate, ultimate, and unwavering.

Jesus' response is a powerful lesson in navigating difficult authorities. He doesn't advise rebellion, but instead calls for faithful integrity within the world's systems, all while keeping one's highest allegiance to God. This teaches us that our spiritual integrity should transcend earthly authority, not be defined by it.

In our own lives, it's challenging to submit to earthly authorities, especially when they seem to contradict our values or feel oppressive. As leaders, this passage urges us to examine whether we are creating environments where people find it easy to follow, and it challenges us to lead by first being good followers ourselves. If we approach authority with humility and integrity, we set a foundation for others to follow us willingly.

Leaders create environments that make it easy for teammates to follow even when the authority above them is oppressive.

<u>Application</u>: What authority do you have a hard time submitting to? Consider how you may be a leader your team has a hard time submitting to. Write three ways that you can properly submit to the authorities above you, while maintaining the integrity of your values and three ways that you can create an environment where your team is eager to follow you.

ONE BIG FAMILY

> "But about the resurrection of the dead—have you not read what God said to you, 'I am the God of Abraham, the God of Isaac, and the God of Jacob?' He is not the God of the dead but of the living."
> —Matt 22:31–32

<u>Read</u>: Matthew 22:23–33 "Marriage at the Resurrection"
The Sadducees, who deny the resurrection, approach Jesus with questions that reveal a limited, earthly view of eternity. They assume that life after the resurrection will simply restore the current world, complete with marriage and other earthly relationships

as they are now. Jesus corrects them, teaching that resurrection life transcends earthly institutions. The resurrection brings us into the fullness of God's plan: a family united in relationship with Him.

This message challenges us to examine our focus. Are we caught up in earthly matters, hoping for things to be restored just as they are? Or do we live with our eyes fixed on Jesus, who is "the Author and Perfector of our faith" (Heb 12:2)? Every part of our lives—our marriages, parenting, work, and daily interactions—serves the purpose of glorifying God and inviting others into His family. Our earthly relationships, even marriage, are ultimately about helping one another grow closer to God and preparing us for eternity with Him.

God desires family, and everything He ordains serves to draw us and others into that relationship with Him. Each moment, each relationship, and every responsibility is an opportunity to point others to Him and reflect His love. Let us align our priorities with God's ultimate purpose, recognizing that our lives are part of a much greater family plan.

Use every opportunity to draw others closer to Him and fulfill His desire for a united family.

Application: Reflect today on how your life's roles and the tasks you do from day-to-day support God's desire to grow His family.

LOVE GOD

"Jesus replied, 'Love the Lord your God with all your heart and with all your soul and with all your mind.'"
—Matt 22:37

Read: Matthew 22:34–40 "The Greatest Commandment"

When an expert in the law asks Jesus what the greatest commandment is, Jesus' response is simple yet profound: love God with "all of your heart, and with all your soul, and with all your mind" (Mark 12:30 adds "strength"). This is the foundation of everything in Scripture. Jesus explains that loving God and loving others is not only the core of our faith, but also a call to engage fully—all of who we are—as image-bearers of God (Gen 1:27).

Jesus' command to love God with our heart, soul, mind, and strength invites us to reflect on how we engage each aspect of ourselves in worship. Loving God with our heart means surrendering our emotions so they lead us toward love and not away from it. If your emotions hinder your ability to love others, consider bringing them to God and asking Him to reshape them for His purposes. Loving God with your soul means having a spirit that earnestly desires the salvation and well-being of others, reflecting a heart burdened for their spiritual lives.

Loving God with your mind challenges you to renew your thoughts with God's truth (Rom 12:2). Are your thoughts helping you to serve others, grounded in Scripture, or are they distracting from God's will? If you find your thinking misaligned, ask God to help you reframe it with His truth. Lastly, loving God with your strength involves caring for your physical body. Discipline in areas like exercise, diet, and rest prepares you to serve God and others fully.

A life of loving God deeply in these ways transforms not only your walk with Him but also your leadership. When we love God wholly, we lead with a purpose that aligns with Him, making our leadership a true reflection of His heart.

> **Leaders must love before they can lead,
> and their love must start with God.**

Application: Ask God to expose areas of your life today where you are not showing Him the fully committed, sacrificial love that He has shown you.

REFOCUS

> "No one could say a word in reply, and from that day on no one dared to ask Him any more questions."
> —Matt 22:46

Read: Matthew 22:41–46 "Whose Son is the Christ"
This lesson comes not from Jesus' words but from the Pharisees' response to His teaching. When Jesus questioned them about the Christ being the son of David, they answered according to their beliefs and traditions, grounded in genealogy. But Jesus, referencing Scripture, clarified that this view was incomplete. Though they had answered in part, they missed a greater truth, and Jesus corrected them. When He did, "no one could say a word in reply" (Matt 22:46). Yet, instead of humbling themselves and seeking to learn, the Pharisees only grew more resistant, focused on defending their status rather than embracing the truth.

This scene offers us a cautionary insight. The Pharisees' refusal to be corrected wasn't due to lack of knowledge; it was due to pride. This isn't a lesson solely for the obviously arrogant—it's for all of us, even those who appear humble. Pride can quietly settle in, even in the lives of those who desire humility. I've been told I'm a humble person, yet I've seen my own pride emerge, sometimes even while correcting others for theirs.

When someone rebukes us with Scripture, especially when done thoughtfully, are we quick to respond in anger, feeling judged? Or do we choose to listen, allowing God's Word to speak to us? It's easy to focus on how someone else may have delivered correction imperfectly, but if we dwell on that, are we missing the opportunity to grow in Christ? God's truth should always be our focus, even if we don't like how it's delivered.

Embrace truth even when it's uncomfortable or inconvenient—pride will only prevent growth.

Application: Does your pride stand in the way of hearing the truth of God's word? Ask Him to expose the pride you have in your life that is standing in His way of blessing you so much. Then, write down what pride you need to release to Him. What control do you need to relinquish to Him?

ACTIONS CARRY INFLUENCE

> "So you must obey them and do everything they tell you. But do not do what they do, for they do not practice what they preach."
>
> —Matt 23:3

Read: Matthew 23:1–39 "Seven Woes"

"Do as I say, not as I do." It's a phrase that, hopefully, we only hear in jest. But this mentality is exactly the opposite of what Christ teaches. Jesus points out that the religious leaders "sit in Moses' seat" (Matt 23:2), giving them the authority to teach God's law, yet they misuse this authority. They impose heavy burdens on others without lifting a finger to help, using the law to oppress rather than to uplift. This is the mark of a "do as I say, not as I do" leader.

James 1:22 instructs us, "Do not merely listen to the word and so deceive yourselves; do what it says." Listening, memorizing Scripture, and being inspired are all valuable, but if we don't live out the Word—especially in love—we fall into the same trap as the Pharisees, who missed the heart of God's message. I hope this journey through the Book of Matthew has encouraged you to live Jesus' teachings with compassion and sincerity.

As leaders, setting the example is crucial. Words alone don't carry influence, actions do. We can't ask others to do something we're unwilling to do ourselves. Leading by example doesn't just validate our words; it builds trust and inspires others to follow.

The best way to lead is to live the standard we expect, embodying integrity, and a willingness to serve.

Your actions will carry your influence further than your words.

Application: Are you a leader who walks your talk? Reflect on a time when you may have spoken truth and instructed others to do the right actions, but you did not follow your words with your own actions. Write a single statement that will inspire you to allow your actions to carry your influence. Then hang it where you will see it and be inspired.

ENDURE WHAT IS TO COME

> "Because of the increase of wickedness, the love of most will grow cold, but he who stands firm to the end will be saved."
>
> —Matt 24:12

Read: Matthew 24:1–35 "Signs of the End of the Age"
Jesus shares signs to be aware of before His return, offering us guidance on how to prepare. Here are six key points we should reflect on:

1. **Avoid Deception** (Matt 24:4): Jesus warns that many will try to mislead His followers. Staying grounded in God's Word is essential, as even well-meaning people and entire church bodies may stray into worldly deception if they're not firmly rooted in Scripture.
2. **Wars and Rumors of Wars** (Matt 24:6): Conflicts will arise, but these events don't signal the end. As tragic as they are, they're not the final indicator of Christ's return.
3. **Natural Disasters** (Matt 24:7–8): These are "birth pains"—intense, but not yet the end. Prophecy reminds us that Christ

will reign for a thousand years on earth. If we interpret this accurately, we shouldn't see global warming as a threat to our immediate survival, though we should still be good stewards of God's creation.
4. **Persecution of Believers** (Matt 24:9): Jesus warns that His followers will face tribulation, persecution, and hatred. Sadly, some who profess faith will fall away, turning against one another.
5. **Increased Lawlessness and Cold Love** (Matt 24:12): As lawlessness increases, genuine love will diminish, leading many hearts to grow cold.
6. **Global Proclamation of the Gospel** (Matt 24:14): The good news will reach every corner of the world, signaling that the end is near.

Given these prophecies, our response should be one of endurance, rooted in the truth of God's Word. As leaders, it's our responsibility to convey this truth to those we influence, preparing ourselves and others to stand firm. Knowledge of God's Word must move from our minds to our hearts, so we can remain steadfast and united as one Body, even amid trials.

Leaders anticipate opposition not out of fear, but to prepare for trials to come.

Application: Re-read this passage of Scripture and study it. Fear only God and consider how you are preparing your team for what is to come.

KEEP WATCH

"Who then is the faithful and wise servant, whom the master has put in charge of the servants in his household to give them their food at the proper time?"

—Matt 24:45

Read: Matthew 24:36–51 "The Day and the Hour Unknown"
Jesus illustrates the suddenness of His return, likening it to an unexpected event where "two men will be in the field; one will be taken and the other left" (Matt 24:40). Since the timing is unknown, Jesus commands us to "keep watch."

But how do we keep watch and demonstrate that we are "the faithful and wise servant" (Matt 24:45)? It begins with cultivating a humble, sacrificial attitude toward those God has placed around us. In Jesus' parable, one servant is devoted to serving others, while the other indulges in selfish desires. This distinction underscores the heart of true watchfulness—not just waiting passively but actively serving with love and integrity.

To stay prepared for Christ's return, we must set aside pride and choose to give continually—giving from our hearts, our souls, our minds, and our strength. This is the investment Christ calls us to, and the return on that investment will be beyond anything we could imagine.

Christ-centered leaders invest in tomorrow by humbly giving today.

Application: Consider where you stand. Are you focused on what you can give or on what you can take? Reflect on where your unselfishness shines and where selfishness might have crept in.

EQUIP YOUR TEAM

"The wise, however, took oil in jars along with their lamps."
—Matt 25:4

Read: Matthew 25:1–13 "The Parable of the Ten Virgins"
In the Parable of the Ten Virgins, Jesus emphasizes the importance of being prepared, underscoring our responsibility to equip ourselves with the right tools. For leaders, this means not

only preparing ourselves but also ensuring those we lead are well-equipped. While we aren't the sole resource for our team, we are accountable for their readiness, for guiding them toward the tools and support they need.

The foolish virgins acted on assumptions and failed to plan for potential delays, whereas the wise virgins anticipated the possibility of a late arrival and prepared for it. This foresight and readiness allowed them to be present and ready when the bridegroom arrived. Leaders must mirror this wisdom by assessing situations, understanding risks, and equipping their teams accordingly, covering every aspect of readiness—spiritual, emotional, mental, and physical.

As a military commander, I learned that equipping my team went beyond physical armament. Ensuring their personal and family affairs were in order was as vital to mission success as their combat readiness. A challenging home life or marital issue will not improve with a deployment. A Marines' personal welfare is just as important for mission accomplishment as his weapon and ability to communicate.

Prepare your team for the opposition, conflict, or risk in front of them and then lead them through it.

Application: How well have you prepared your team for the trials ahead? Have you assessed the opposition, conflict, or risk that they may face? If so, have you directly supplied them with or guided them to the tools and support they will need? Today, consider the trials ahead and take a moment to consider what your team needs to prepare.

ADD VALUE TO MULTIPLY IT

> "His master replied, 'Well done, good and faithful servant! You have been faithful with a few things; I will put you in charge of many things. Come and share your master's happiness!'"
>
> —Matt 25:21, 23

Read: Matthew 25:14–30 "The Parable of the Talents"
In the Parable of the Talents, Jesus reveals that each servant is given talents according to their abilities, and when the master returns, he rewards those who multiplied their talents and punishes the one who didn't. This teaches us that God expects us to faithfully use and multiply the abilities and resources He's entrusted to us. Complaining about what we haven't been given keeps us from seeing the opportunities within what we already have. Instead, we should focus on stewarding our gifts well and adding value to others. And as leaders, we must recognize the good and faithful stewardship efforts of those we lead and ensure we reinforce that good behavior.

Several years ago, I read the book, *Getting to Yes*, as part of a negotiation class I attended taught by a former FBI negotiator. I want to share a short story with you from the book about the burnout of our teammates when we neglect to recognize the good and faithful stewardship efforts of those we lead.[8]

"Everyone knows how hard it is to deal with a problem without people misunderstanding each other, getting angry or upset, and taking things personally.

A union leader says to his crew, 'All right, who called the walkout?'

Jones steps forward. 'I did. It was that bum foreman Campbell again. That was the fifth time in two weeks he sent me out of our group as a replacement. He's got it in for me, and I'm tired of it. Why should I get all the dirty work?'

Later the union leader confronts Campbell. 'Why do you keep picking on Jones? He says you've put him on replacement detail five times in two weeks. What's going on?'

Campbell replies, 'I pick Jones because he's the best. I know I can trust him to keep things from fouling up in a group without its point person. I send him on replacement only when it's a key person missing, otherwise I send Smith or someone else. It's just that with the flu going around there've been a lot of point people out. I never knew Jones objected. I thought he liked the responsibility.'"

This story highlights how a lack of clear communication and acknowledgment can lead to burnout and frustration. In this example, the union leader discovered that Jones, who felt undervalued and unfairly tasked, was actually trusted by his foreman due to his reliability. Yet, without proper recognition, Jones interpreted his extra work as mistreatment. This miscommunication shows that even well-intentioned leadership can miss the mark if it doesn't involve encouragement and clear communication about why a person's strengths are valued.

When we use our abilities to add value to others, we create a multiplying effect, as those we've encouraged are inspired to do the same within their own circles. By stewarding our talents well and fostering an environment of recognition and appreciation, we create a cycle of value that extends beyond ourselves.

The greatest leaders use their abilities to multiply value in others and ensure those they lead feel recognized and valued in their contributions.

<u>Application</u>: How have you added value to those in your sphere of influence this week? Write three ways that you added value. Then, write three ways that they can take the value you added to them and add value to someone else, thereby multiplying the value you gave them.

LEADERSHIP ROOTS

"The King will reply, 'I tell you the truth, whatever you did for one of the least of these brothers of mine, you did for me.'"

–Matt 25:40

Read: Matthew 25:31–46 "The Sheep and the Goats"
Jesus shows us that the true test of love is action: feeding the hungry, offering a drink to the thirsty, welcoming the stranger, clothing the needy, caring for the sick, and visiting the imprisoned. Jesus' words here underscore that love isn't merely a feeling or a sentiment expressed in "thoughts and prayers." While thinking and praying for others is vital, especially in difficult times, Jesus calls us to go further. True love requires action, especially when the need around us is so great.

This emphasis on active love aligns with the third point of my leadership philosophy which I wrote in 2013: "Leadership is rooted in love and unselfishness. If a leader does not love those he leads or seek their needs before his own, he cannot truly serve them. Leaders are servants. Any deviation from this is not leadership but tyranny." Leadership rooted in love means putting the well-being of those we lead at the forefront of our priorities. They must see that our actions stem from genuine care and commitment to their needs, not from self-interest or empty gestures.

For our leadership to be truly impactful, we must ensure that our thoughts, words, and actions align with a selfless, servant minded approach. When those we lead believe in our genuine concern for them, it builds trust, inspires loyalty, and cultivates an environment where people thrive.

> **Leaders drive change when they prioritize the needs and well-being of others above all else.**

Application: Do you actively love before trying to lead? What actions show that you do? Reflect on the acts of love that you do for those you influence. How could you love more actively and drive the change that you want to see?

THE EVIDENCE IS EVERYWHERE

"As you know, the Passover is two days away—and the Son of Man will be handed over to be crucified."
—Matt 26:2

Read: Matthew 26:1–5 "The Plot Against Jesus"

Jesus tells His disciples the exact timing of His crucifixion, and events unfold precisely as He said. This fulfillment gives us a firm foundation for trusting His word, not only in His prophecies, but also in His teachings on how we should live and lead. Jesus' foreknowledge and His fulfillment of prophecy reinforce His authority and reliability, providing a solid basis for following Him wholeheartedly.

For anyone questioning the truth of God's word or the life, death, and resurrection of Jesus, there is historical and archaeological evidence that goes beyond the Bible itself. This evidence attests to Jesus' impact, the early Christian movement, and even accounts of His resurrection that spread widely through ancient Judea and beyond. In understanding why this matters, it's helpful to consider external sources, like *The Case for Christ* by Lee Strobel.[9] Strobel, once an atheist, documents his journey to belief through examining evidence outside of Scripture. His research underscores the historical validity of Jesus' life and mission, providing a reasoned foundation for faith in Christ.

As leaders, we are called to follow the example Jesus set—in our thoughts, words, and actions—because His reliability was proven not only in His words but in His life, death, and resurrection. Jesus' truth invites us to trust deeply, live purposefully, and lead faithfully.

Leaders are critical thinkers who find truth in the evidence not in the emotions.

Application: Have you sought past the Bible for evidence to its truth? If you have any doubts to the Bible's truth, look for the evidence; it's all around us.

IT'S ALL ABOUT JESUS

"Aware of this, Jesus said to them, 'Why are you bothering this woman? She has done a beautiful thing to Me.'"

—Matt 26:10

Read: Matthew 26:6–13 "Jesus Anointed at Bethany"
Many of Jesus' teachings command us to give to the poor, to place their needs above our own, and to comfort the oppressed and powerless. Remember the "rich young man" in Matthew 19? He had kept all the commandments, but had not given Jesus his whole heart. That was the one thing he lacked. In his case, the act of selling all he had, giving it to the poor, and then following Jesus would have shown Jesus that his whole heart belonged to Him.

This passage is about a woman who poured a very expensive amount of perfume on Jesus, days before His execution. John's Gospel states that the amount of perfume she poured on Jesus was equivalent to a year's wages. Wow! So much wealth could really help the poor.

Once again, the disciples were focused on the natural realm and not the spiritual. Though Jesus just told them that He would be killed in two days, they were not focused on worshipping Him, but rather on rebuking a woman who "wasted" much wealth.

This woman's actions were foolish from a financial responsibility standpoint, but we must remember that our finances and our material is not ours. It all belongs to Him. If He wants you to give more to the poor and needy, then do it. If He wants you to worship

Him with the resources He's given you in other ways, then do that. Give Him your heart and follow Him with how He wants you to steward the many things He's given you to advance His kingdom.

> **Serving is not about the service; it's about the heart of the one serving.**

<u>Application</u>: When you serve, do you serve because you feel it is the right thing to do or because your heart drives you to? When our hearts are fixed on Jesus, the purpose behind our service is fulfilled in the most complete way. Consider how your acts of service fulfill the purpose God has placed on your heart.

OPPORTUNITIES MISSED

> "'What are you willing to give me if I hand Him over to you?' So they counted out for him thirty silver coins."
> —Matt 26:15

<u>Read</u>: Matthew 26:14–16 "Judas Agrees to Betray Jesus"
Likely, within the same day as Judas watched Jesus rebuke the disciples for stating that the perfume the woman poured on Jesus could have been sold and given to the poor, he goes to the chief priests and offers to betray Jesus to them for...money.

I've heard it said that Biblical scholars believe that Judas was the treasurer for Jesus and His disciples. He managed the group's money as they traveled around and ministered to people. He also had a front row seat to many of Jesus' teachings and so heard Jesus speak many times about the importance of giving to the poor. Jesus' rebuke to the disciples regarding the expensive perfume poured on Him probably seemed contradictory to Judas. If the perfume was worth a year's wages, Judas must have felt indignant toward Jesus to be willing to turn and betray Him.

Judas's decision was based solely on money. He must not have been present, or he forgot very quickly, that Jesus told Peter to go to the water of the Sea of Galilee and pull out a coin from a fish's mouth (Matt 17:27). Anyone that can command that is not a magician, He's God. Judas missed his many opportunities to know Jesus' heart and it cost him his soul. His priorities were not aligned with Christ.

Misaligned priorities can lead to devastating misjudgments.

<u>Application</u>: What opportunities are you missing to know Jesus' heart? What opportunities may you be missing to express Jesus' heart to someone who doesn't know Him? Do you want to know His heart unconditionally? Or do you want to know His heart only where it aligns with yours? Be careful and ensure that your priorities are in line with God's so that you can accurately and wisely judge.

JESUS HAD A JUDAS

"The Son of Man will go just as it is written about Him. But woe to that man who betrays the Son of Man! It would be better for him if he had not been born."

—Matt 26:24

<u>Read</u>: Matthew 26:17–30 "The Lord's Supper"
We live in a fallen world. So fallen that even a man can experience the incarnation of the Creator God, watch Him perform miracles, hear His teachings, and yet betray Him for money.

We all have a Judas in our lives. Sometimes our pride has caused us to be Judas to someone else. We have loved someone unconditionally and yet they betrayed us. What did Jesus do in those times? He loved anyways.

Jesus called Judas and Judas followed. Jesus ministered to Judas for three years in a small group. Judas was one of Jesus' closest friends. Yet, the love of money and the fear of the world drove Judas to betray the truth.

Hold tightly to the truth. The world loves lies. Leaders must love and follow the truth and lead with the truth, despite what "Judases" may arise in their own lives.

Don't be discouraged when someone you love, someone you are close to, someone you lead and are trying to develop, betrays you. Even Jesus had a Judas.

True leadership persists in love and integrity, even when faced with betrayal.

Application: Who has been a Judas to you? Someone you love deeply and care about. Someone who you would give your life for. Yet, they have betrayed you. Write their name down. If you have more than one come to mind, write all the names down. Now pray for their hearts to be softened and yours to be filled with love and forgiveness. Then prepare and commit to reaching out to them with forgiveness.

GO AHEAD OF YOUR TEAM

"But after I have risen, I will go ahead of you into Galilee."
—Matt 26:32

Read: Matthew 26:31–35 "Jesus Predicts Peter's Denial"
In His final hours, Jesus displayed deep, unwavering love for His disciples, even as He foretold their coming betrayal. Jesus knew Peter and the others would deny Him when He was arrested, yet He

didn't withdraw His love or service. Instead, He washed their feet, broke bread with them, and assured them of His return. His assurance that He would "go ahead of [them] into Galilee" reminded the disciples that His mission wasn't ending in shame, but would rise in victory, restoring their hope and credibility.

Leaders often face moments when their team members falter or lose faith. Jesus exemplified that leading through such moments requires patience, forgiveness, and the resolve to press forward in truth. When a leader is aligned with God's purpose, it's essential to communicate that vision clearly and embody consistency, even if doubts arise among the team. By moving forward with integrity and transparency, a leader reassures others that setbacks are not the end. They model resilience, demonstrating that the mission remains intact, and that loyalty and confidence can be rebuilt.

True leadership goes beyond assurance; it's a commitment to restoring credibility and courage when failure has sown doubt. Like Jesus going ahead of His disciples to Galilee, leaders must show that no betrayal or failure is final if one's heart remains grounded in His truth.

As a leader, if you are doing the right thing according to God's word and your team "scatters" or "disowns" you, how do you reassure them that the choices you are making and the direction you are going is right? How do you "go ahead of them" into a "region" that would consider them frauds for following you?

Strong leaders offer grace and steadfast direction, guiding their teams back to trust and purpose—even after setbacks or betrayal.

Application: Have you faced betrayal by members of your team for doing the right thing? How do you reconnect with them and assure them that your direction is the right path? We must do so with extraordinary grace if we are going to unite the team.

TAKING STRAIN

"Watch and pray so that you will not fall into temptation. The spirit is willing, but the body is weak."
—Matt 26:41

Read: Matthew 26:36–46 "Gethsemane"
In this passage, we witness the very humanism of Christ. His *"soul is overwhelmed with sorrow to the point of death"* (Matt 26:38). His *"spirit is willing, but [His] body is weak"* (Matt 26:41).

In the Garden of Gethsemane, Jesus knows that He is moments from being betrayed, His closest friends scattering, His body suffering immensely, and His soul bearing the weight of the whole world's sin. I've experienced times of despair, physical pain, grief, a sorrowful spirit, but I've never experienced the wrath of God. I may have missed God's blessings in my sin because that is not His character, but He has never poured His wrath on me, or I would be dead. But with Jesus, the full wrath of God was poured on Him on our behalf.

Do we enter/accept challengers as Christ does? Or do we make comfort-based decisions? Who are we willing to take strain for? Who are we willing to sacrifice our time, talents, and resources for, so that they see and understand the true character and love of God?

You may be the only Jesus your team, your leaders, your peers, your followers, your family, and your community, ever see.

Leaders take strain for their teams when the team faces great challenges.

Application: Recall a time when you "took strain" for your team. How can a leader lead if they are not out in front taking the initial brunt of the challenges that the team faces? Consider how you must step out of your comfort zone and take some strain on behalf of your team. Lead them through their challenges, don't cheer them through.

IT MUST BE THIS WAY

"But how then would the Scriptures be fulfilled that say it must happen in this way?"

—Matt 26:54

<u>Read</u>: Matthew 26:47–56 "Jesus Arrested"

Jesus knew His mission: to endure suffering and sacrifice for the reconciliation of all humanity to God. He foretold His betrayal, arrest, and crucifixion, knowing the exact time and place it would unfold. Despite this clear purpose, Peter, still envisioning an earthly kingdom, reacted as any king's defender might—with force. But Jesus rebuked this response, reminding Peter that His kingdom was not of this world and that reconciliation could only come through the cross. If Jesus had chosen power over sacrifice, humanity's redemption would have been lost.

Jesus' commitment invites us to examine our own convictions. Do we truly believe and stand on the truth of Scripture, or do we cling only to the comfortable parts? Leading with integrity requires courage, especially when facing opposition or discomfort. The truth is often divisive and following it may mean losing status or popularity. However, the impact of authentic, sacrificial leadership—modeled after Christ—is worth any discomfort we might face.

Leaders are committed to the truth even when it is uncomfortable and requires their extreme sacrifice.

<u>Application</u>: Reflect on a time when you stepped out of your comfort zone and committed yourself to serving and sacrificing for others, not out of what you might gain but out of love. Was the joy you felt knowing that you willingly sacrificed and denied your own comforts out of love for someone else a large enough return?

WILL YOU ENDURE?

> "'Yes, it is as you say,' Jesus replied. 'But I say to all of you: In the future you will see the Son of Man sitting at the right hand of the Might One and coming on the clouds of heaven.'"
>
> —Matt 26:64

Read: Matthew 26:57–68 "Before the Sanhedrin"

The Sanhedrin, seated in a façade of power, finally seizes the opportunity to try Jesus, doing so secretly under the cover of night—a clear sign of their intent to manipulate justice. For three years, these leaders had been powerless to entrap Jesus in His teachings and miracles, but now they act with desperation. As I often remind my children, "Nothing good happens after midnight." In this case, the late hour foreshadows the wrongful conviction that is about to unfold.

In the face of hate, Jesus stands resolute. When the Sanhedrin demands His identity, He boldly declares Himself the Christ, the Son of God. Even as they prepare to strike and mock Him, He assures them that one day He will be "seated at the right hand of the Mighty One and coming on the clouds of heaven." His composure and willingness to "turn the other cheek" demonstrate true courage, showing us how to face trials with integrity, resolve, and endurance.

Jesus' words are never empty; He has walked every road He calls us to walk. Are we willing to lay down our fears and allow Him to walk with us as we confront them? Whatever challenges—whether physical, emotional, or spiritual—await us, will we endure them for His sake?

Leaders face challenges with integrity and personify endurance for the sake of the team they serve.

Application: What beatings, whether physically or verbally, have you endured for your team? Reflect on a time you endured such abuse. If you haven't, be thankful, but write down a commitment now, while the "seas are smooth," to how you will endure for the sake of your team.

TEAM BREAKDOWN

> "Immediately a rooster crowed. Then Peter remembered the word Jesus had spoken: 'Before the rooster crows, you will disown Me three times.' And he went outside and wept bitterly."
>
> —Matt 26:75

Read: Matthew 26:69–75 "Peter Disowns Jesus"

Many factors can undermine a team: dishonesty shatters trust, arrogance divides, and rejection denies the very existence of the team. In this passage, Peter exemplifies this breakdown when he denies knowing Jesus. Scattered and frightened, the disciples felt all hope was lost; from their perspective, Jesus' arrest and crucifixion marked an end. But to Jesus, these events were the fulfillment of His purpose, with the resurrection bringing new life to those who would believe.

As Peter's leader, Jesus prepared him for his moment of denial, foretelling that he would disown Him before the rooster crowed. This warning served a critical purpose. The combination of Jesus' words and the rooster crowing brought Peter to a moment of deep conviction, forcing him to confront his actions. At that point, Peter faced a choice: seek forgiveness and return to Jesus or reject the opportunity for restoration.

Where Peter's actions threatened the team's unity, Jesus' words, example, and preparation for the disciples paved the way for reconciliation?

Leaders build strong teams by uniting them following failure and guiding them toward restoration.

Application: Consider your own influence: Do your words and actions encourage team unity and restoration, or do they lead to its disintegration? Honestly examine yourself and write down two previous situations when your words and actions unified your team and two situations when you divided them?

POWER CORRUPTS

> "'I have sinned,' he said, 'for I have betrayed innocent blood.' 'What is that to us?' they replied. 'That's your responsibility.'"
>
> —Matt 27:4

Read: Matthew 27:1–10 "Judas Hangs Himself"
When the Sanhedrin deemed Jesus deserving of death, they transferred Him to the Roman governor, Pontius Pilate, as only Rome held the authority to enforce capital punishment. Judas, upon realizing that Jesus was headed toward execution, felt convicted of his actions. He may have thought the Sanhedrin would rough Jesus up and then release Him, failing to believe Jesus' own predictions of His death.

In stark contrast, the Sanhedrin's motivation was their fierce desire to maintain power. Jesus threatened the status quo, unsettling their authority, and challenging their control over the Jewish people. Their lust for power eclipsed any concern for justice or integrity; they didn't hesitate to bend the rules and push for His swift execution without a fair trial.

Sadly, the desire for power often erodes integrity, leading to corruption that harms those under that leadership. All we must do is observe a poverty-stricken nation and we will see that it likely stems from the corruption of those in power. The solution to poverty is not more wealth, it's leadership. I first traveled to Uganda in April 2024, and learned that the eastern part of the country is in worse poverty than the western part. Why? Because western Ugandans are united by one language whereas the eastern Ugandans speak several different languages. The current president, who has been in office since 1986, is a western Ugandan. Most of the positions of power in the military are held by western Ugandans. The problem is much deeper and more complex than I could ever learn or provide in a paragraph. However, one thing is certain, the problem is a lack of leadership which exists from a lust for power.

Leadership is not a position or privilege; it's service and sacrifice.

Humility and integrity are the antidotes to a corrupt leader.

Application: When have you been susceptible to power corrupting you? Did it corrupt you? If not, how did you prevent it from corrupting you? What accountability systems and processes to remain transparent and vulnerable to constructive criticism did you put in place?

NO DEFENSE

"Meanwhile Jesus stood before the governor, and the governor asked him, 'Are You the king of the Jews?' 'Yes, it is as you say,' Jesus replied."

—Matt 27:11

Read: Matthew 27:11–26 "Jesus before Pilate"

Notice Jesus' answer to Pilate was the same as when the Sanhedrin asked Him if He was the Christ. Following His confession to Pilate when the chief priests hurled their accusations, He gave no further answer.

For three years, His life, words, and actions testified to who He was. The religious leaders never had an interest in the truth and always sought to oppose Him to ensure their own power and influence remained intact. Jesus never called for a rebellion, and He even instructed the people to submit to the governing authorities. What He called for was the kingdom of heaven, where He is the king. His life ushered in the kingdom of heaven for all of us to experience and it testified to His position as King. "Yes, it—(the truth about My power, authority, and kingdom)—is as you say" (Matt 27:11).

Jesus' life was a testimony to His position as the true King. His actions spoke for themselves, and He didn't need to defend His truth. When we align our lives with the truth of God's Word, we can stand firm in the face of any challenge or opposition.

"The safest place to be is not in the absence of danger but in the will of God." –Anonymous

True leadership needs no defense but may require a graceful explanation to the fool.

Application: Do your actions require defense? Do you live in such a way that your words and deeds invite reproach, or do you live the truth boldly, regardless of the opposition? Reflect on how you respond when you feel you must defend your actions or your reputation.

IN THE MIDST OF MOCKING

"Then the governor's soldiers took Jesus into the Praetorium and gathered the whole company of soldiers around Him."
—Matt 27:27

Read: Matthew 27:27–31 "The Soldiers Mock Jesus"
As we will soon read, the centurion, the commander of this "company of soldiers," exclaimed in Matthew 27:54, "Surely He was the

Son of God." This centurion's day began with the task to flog and then crucify Jesus along with two other criminals. By the end of the day, His witness of how Jesus carried Himself in the midst of unmatchable spiritual, emotional, and physical pain, caused him to testify that Jesus surely "was the Son of God." Why?

We so often want to fire back and defend our reputation if someone is mocking us. But really? Will that improve the situation? We need to take a lesson from Christ and stand firm in the midst of the mocking while still speaking His truth through our words and actions.

Despite what pain and turmoil our spirit, our emotions, and our body is experiencing, we must be in the appropriate mental state to serve Christ and testify to His truth in our words and deeds. To be certain that we will be able to do this in the worst of times, we must prepare now and do so daily. Jesus didn't prepare to face this mocking and humiliation the night before. He prepared before He left heaven to come to earth.

Leaders prepare their teams to face trials and opposition in the environments in which they operate.

<u>Application</u>: How are you preparing your team to face trials and opposition? Do you provide a Godly example of how to face trials and opposition? Do you clearly communicate with your team to prepare them? Do you discuss potential areas and situations where you and your team may face challenges and discuss how you will navigate those challenges?

ENDURE THE OPPOSITION

> "'He saved others,' they said, 'but He can't save Himself! He's the King of Israel! Let Him come down now from the cross, and we will believe in Him.'"
> –Matt 27:42

Read: Matthew 27:32–44 "The Crucifixion"
As Jesus hung on the cross, exposed and suffering, He faced humiliation and mockery from onlookers, including religious leaders who jeered, challenging Him to save Himself if He truly was the Son of God. Yet, Jesus did not come to serve Himself but to serve us, enduring the ultimate sacrifice to glorify His Father, who desires our reconciliation with Him. Jesus' mission was never about self-glorification; it was about fulfilling the Father's plan to restore us, even at the cost of His own dignity and life.

Corrupt leaders do not grasp this selfless love. In their view, power and honor are to be safeguarded, never surrendered. The concept of a king who would willingly sacrifice for His people is beyond their understanding, as such humility and servanthood defy their worldly perspective. But Jesus exemplified a different way—a way that calls us as leaders to deny ourselves, bear opposition, and courageously hold to the truth of God's Word, no matter the cost.

Leaders endure opposition with their team and lead the team through it.

Application: What opposition are you currently facing? Write down a few things, people, or factors that oppose your progress with family relationships, business progress, your social life, or any other hindrance to you moving in the right direction. Whether large or small, identify your opposition. Now, build a strategy with support from your team and even people external to your team to overcome your opposition.

WE ALL BEAR WITNESS

"When the centurion and those with him who were guarding Jesus saw the earthquake and all that had happened, they were terrified, and exclaimed, 'Surely He was the Son of God.'"

–Matt 27:54

Read: Matthew 27:45–56 "The Death of Jesus"

Jesus' crucifixion was a city-wide spectacle. Even those who didn't personally see Him knew of the execution and witnessed the strange events that followed—darkened skies and a tremor that shook Jerusalem. For the Roman centurion and his soldiers, these unnatural signs and Jesus' demeanor, words, and silence amid suffering made a profound impact. Though unfamiliar with Jewish Scriptures, they saw something in Jesus that no other criminal had demonstrated, leading them to recognize Him as the Son of God.

Meanwhile, the religious leaders, well-versed in Scripture, mocked Jesus because He did not fit their expectations of the Messiah. Their pride in their knowledge and traditions blinded them to the truth. Instead of recognizing Jesus' divine authority and self-sacrificial love, they dismissed Him, unwilling to let go of their preconceived notions.

As leaders, we must guard against the trap of pride, which can prevent us from seeing truth in unexpected places. A humble heart remains open to new perspectives and encourages a culture where each voice is valued. By doing so, we allow our teams to reach new heights, as we remain receptive to ideas that might lead to greater impact.

> **A prideful heart closes itself off from other perspectives; a humble heart creates a culture where there are new perspectives, innovation, and teamwork.**

Application: Where is your pride keeping you from seeing fresh perspectives and enabling teamwork? Reflect and write down an area where you can adopt a more humble attitude to engage with other perspectives and enable a healthy culture where collaboration is encouraged and comfortable.

NOTHING FROM THIS WORLD

"Joseph took the body, wrapped it in a clean linen cloth, and placed it in his own new tomb that he had cut out of the rock."
—Matt 27:59–60

<u>Read</u>: Matthew 27:57–61 "The Burial of Jesus"

When Jesus was born, He was given no place for a proper birth. When He died, there was no proper place for His body. Matthew records that Joseph was "a rich man from Arimathea," a town about 20 miles northwest of Jerusalem, "who had himself become a disciple of Jesus" (Matt 27:57). Now Joseph was not considered one of the twelve disciples, but he was committed to following Christ and for using his own resources, such as his own tomb, to worship Jesus.

Jesus did not come for anything this world could offer. He did not covet anything from this world and did not seek to gain anything from it. He did not seek its wealth, its power, or its status. He came to bring us the kingdom of heaven and allow us to share it with Him. In doing so, He showed us that the kingdom of heaven is not **of** this world, although it very much can be **in** this world. He showed us that the kingdom of heaven is a matter of the heart. He showed us that the resources of this world are meant to be used to advance the kingdom of heaven not for us to covet and keep for ourselves.

Jesus lived outside of the comforts of this world, and He invites us to do the same. I've learned that the greatest satisfaction in life comes from life's greatest challenges. My wife and I sometimes joke about the wealth we could have if we never adopted six children. But then we would have never adopted six children. The experience we've gained in the process of parenting all seven of our children, including our youngest who is not adopted, has brought us much closer to God through how we've been able to experience Him than any amount of wealth we could have accumulated by not adopting. Adoption is a great thing as it intends to bring children from an otherwise worse situation and give them a better opportunity at life. But I must confess, adopting my children was as much as God's grace and favor toward me as it ever was toward them.

Embrace discomfort and challenges while living in God's will and He will give you a joy and satisfaction that this world could never offer.

Application: Write down three challenges that you do not want to face because they are out of your comfort zone. Now pray and ask God to reveal to you if He is leading you to face them. Whatever is your decision, take a step of faith out of your comfort zone. If you don't, you'll never grow.

CAN'T STOP TRUTH

"'Take a guard,' Pilate answered. 'Go, make
the tomb as secure as you know how.'"
—Matt 27:65

Read: Matthew 27:62–66 "The Guard at the Tomb"
No one can stop the truth from accomplishing what it has set out to accomplish. That is why when we act on God's word, our actions need no defense.

2 Timothy 4:3–4 states that people will fall away from "sound doctrine" and listen to what their "itching ears want to hear." We see this all over our society today. But it was also true in Jesus' day.

The chief priests were determined to oppose Jesus and smother His influence. So, they went to Pilate and asked for guards at the tomb. Pilate granted their request, and they posted a guard and put a seal on the tomb (Matt 27:66).

We will not and cannot stand in the way of God's word accomplishing what it set out to do. Isaiah 55:11 states, "My word that goes out from My mouth: It will not return to Me empty but will accomplish what I desire and achieve the purpose for which I sent it."

When we oppose Jesus and His word, we are essentially saying, we don't want to be on the winning team. If someone were to ask us, would you rather lose or win, every single one of us would say, 'win.' When it comes to life and leadership, we win when we align ourselves with God's truth—Jesus' words and example.

Christ-centered leaders are already the victors because they align themselves with God's truth.

Application: Reflect on a time when you felt like you were maintaining your faith and values but you felt like you were on a losing team. Be encouraged today that in our fallen world, sometimes, we may feel like we are in a sealed grave with guards, but Sunday is coming. Hold true to your faith because you are already a victor.

"JUST AS HE SAID"

"Then Jesus said to them, 'Do not be afraid. Go and tell my brothers to go to Galilee; there they will see Me.'"

—Matt 28:10

Read: Matthew 28:1–10 "The Resurrection"
Less than 72 hours earlier, His "brothers" deserted and disowned Him at the time of His greatest need. Yet, the first words Matthew accounts Jesus saying after His resurrection are to call His disciples "brothers." What great love, grace, and mercy!

Nothing in Scripture has any validity if the Resurrection is not true. You can believe that Jesus was a wise teacher, even a great prophet. You can gain valuable leadership lessons from His words and examples. But if you do not believe that the Resurrection happened and that Jesus reigns forever, then He is not your God and He is not your savior.

As I wrote a few lessons back, the evidence for the death and resurrection of Christ is overwhelming. Beyond historical and archaeological evidence, the proof of cataclysmic change in a person's life after they have turned from a life of sin to follow Christ is the greatest evidence of all.

In a world that grows darker by the day, the light increases in brightness. Be the light that people will see and the leader that leads them out of their darkness.

Christ-centered leaders shine brightest in the darkest areas.

Application: We need to surround ourselves with the Body of Christ to encourage us and lift us up. But to lead others to Christ, we must get out in the darkness. Commit to two ways that you can "get out in the darkness," where people are lost and lead them to Christ directly or indirectly.

BEWARE OF THE DECEIVER

"When the chief priests had met with the elders and devised a plan, they gave the soldiers a large sum of money, telling them, 'You are to say, "His disciples came during the night and stole Him away while we were asleep."'"

—Matt 28:12–13

Read: Matthew 28:11–15 "The Guard's Report"
After Christ's resurrection, the chief priests and teachers of the law still refused to believe in Him as the Son of God. They were determined to keep their power, even if it meant deceiving the people they were meant to guide. Although they had seen the miracles and the fulfillment of prophecy, their hearts remained hardened, and they continued to lead others astray for their own control and status.

This spirit of deception persists today. Just as the religious leaders of Jesus' time misled the crowds, there are forces at work trying to turn people away from the truth of God's Word. We must remember that the ultimate deceiver is Satan, who influences people, even believers, to quarrel and divide. Our battle, therefore, is not with each other but with the forces of evil in the spiritual realm. Jesus showed us how to confront opposition: He prayed, fasted, and fought in the spiritual realm. We are called to do the same.

As St. Francis of Assisi is credited with saying, "Preach the Gospel at all times, and if necessary, use words." Let our actions, kindness, and integrity demonstrate Christ's love to others. When we choose love and prayer over confrontation, we reflect the Gospel more powerfully than words alone.

> **Christ-centered leaders must fight their battles in the spiritual realm first, trusting that love and faithfulness to God's truth are their greatest weapons.**

Application: It is easy to lose faith as we pray for God's intervention and start to think He is not listening. Do not be discouraged. He has not left you. Continue praying and interceding and living the Gospel through your love, actions, and words. Do not be deceived. God is at work in your life. As Philippians 1:6 says, "Being confident of this, that He who began a good work in you will carry it on to completion until the day of Christ Jesus."

LEADING IS A COMMANDMENT

"Therefore go and make disciples of all nations, baptizing them in the name of the Father and of the Son and of the Holy Spirit."

—Matt 28:19

Read: Matthew 28:16–20 "The Great Commission"
In Matthew's account, Jesus' final instructions after His resurrection were clear: "Go and make disciples." I recall from a sermon I heard years ago that the original Greek emphasizes "as you are going." This suggests Jesus wasn't saying we needed to stop pursuing family, career, or community involvement, but rather to integrate leading other people to him into all aspects of life. Wherever life takes us, our purpose remains to reflect Christ and lead others to Him.

This is a powerful reminder that disciple-making is not confined to specific events or times, it's a continuous mission. In every interaction, whether with family, at work, or in the community, we have an opportunity to lead others to Christ by example.

Take a moment to consider your role in each sphere of life. Are you leading your children to follow Christ? Are you influencing coworkers toward Him? In your community, are you showing others the love and truth of Jesus? Making disciples is an ongoing, everyday calling that every leader is charged to fulfill.

The Great Commission is a command for every person to be a leader.

Application: Do your purpose and priorities nest into Jesus' Great Commission for His Body? If not, how can you nest your day-to-day actions into serving the Great Commission? Write at least one way you can do so at home, at work, and at church/in your community.

THE BOOK OF MARK

A NEW WAY *JA*

"And whoever wants to be first must be slave of all. For even the Son of Man did not come to be served, but to serve, and to give His life as a ransom for many."
—Mark 10:44–45

Read: Book of Mark Introduction

John Mark, the author of the Gospel of Mark, is believed to have been a close associate of Peter. He may have been a scribe to Peter. So, the Gospel of Mark is a secondhand account of Jesus as told by Peter's firsthand account. Mark is also mentioned in the Book of Acts, written by the same Luke that wrote the Gospel of Luke, as a companion to the Apostle Paul and Barnabas.

Scholars believe that Mark's Gospel account was written around A. D. 65, around the time Peter was martyred during the persecution under the Roman Emperor Nero. In the midst of this persecution, scholars believe that it was written to Gentile (everyone except Jews) believers who are facing persecution. Mark's message encourages them: "There is One mightier who is coming, His name is Jesus."

"Jesus has come to introduce a radical new way of life that will undercut existing power relationships."[10]

Jesus' way of leadership is what is desperately needed in this world.

Christ-centered leaders must embrace and promote His example to transform their teams and organizations.

Application: As you reflect on the Gospel of Mark and its message of hope amid persecution, consider how you can introduce Jesus' radical way of leadership in your own sphere of influence. This week, identify one way to model servant leadership and challenge yourself to lead with humility, courage, and a focus on empowering others—just as Jesus did.

HE HAS ME RIGHT HERE *JA*

> "John wore clothing made of camel's hair, with a leather belt around his waist, and he ate locusts and wild honey."
> —Mark 1:6

Read: Mark 1:1–8 "John the Baptist Prepares the Way"
John the Baptist embraced his kingdom purpose, even though it led him to a life of simplicity and sacrifice. Living in the wilderness, clothed in camel's hair, and sustained by locusts and wild honey, John remained steadfast in his mission to prepare the way for the Lord. His life was not defined by worldly comforts, but by his alignment with God's will. This alignment brought him deep contentment, despite the grungy and humble nature of his circumstances.

How often do we hesitate to follow God's call because it disrupts our comfort or challenges our ambitions? The fear of the unknown or the discomfort of sacrifice often holds us back. Yet, John's life reminds us that true fulfillment comes not from pursuing our own desires, but from walking in God's purpose for us.

Each of us has been uniquely placed in this world—in a specific time, location, and set of circumstances—for God's divine plan. While our surroundings may differ vastly from John's, the choice remains the same: will we submit to God's will, even if it means stepping out of our comfort zone? Whether we are called to wear camel's hair or fine garments, the heart of the matter is obedience and trust.

True contentment and purpose come from aligning your will with God's, even when it leads to discomfort or sacrifice. Trust that His plan is greater than your own.

Application: Are you trusting God's will in your life over worldly success, wealth, and accomplishment? If you are, don't be discouraged. It is easy to do. That is why we need to be around the community of believers to encourage us when God urges us to step out of our comfort zone and even suffer. Reflect how God's will may cause you to step out of your comfort zone and ask yourself today if you are willing to do so.

THE CORNERSTONE OF CULTURE *JA*

> "And a voice came from heaven: 'You are My Son, whom I love; with You I am well pleased.'"
> —Mark 1:11

Read: Mark 1:9–13 "The Baptism and Temptation of Jesus"
At Jesus' baptism, we witness His first recorded act of humility. Jesus' baptism, like ours when we choose to follow Christ, was a public display of His submission to His Father and commitment to obey His will. Jesus' humility brought His Father great pleasure.

C. S. Lewis once said, "A man is never so proud as when striking an attitude of humility." The Father was "well pleased" with the Son's genuine humility. Think of a time when your own obedience and humility made your father proud. How did that make you feel?

Lewis is also credited with one of the simplest and most accurate definitions of humility: "Humility is not thinking less of yourself; it's thinking of yourself less." When Jesus humbled Himself in baptism, He demonstrated to all that He was prioritizing His Father's will above His own. What was the Father's will for Christ? That He would bring the kingdom of heaven to earth and ultimately sacrifice His life as a ransom for humanity—those doomed to eternal separation from God because of sin. Jesus served, and Jesus sacrificed.

Humility in a leader is the cornerstone of a healthy culture. Once this cornerstone is properly laid, the foundation of humility across a team can establish a strong and vibrant organization capable of withstanding even the most challenging circumstances. Just ask Jesus' disciples.

The leader's humility is the cornerstone of a healthy culture.

<u>Application</u>: How do you view humility? Do you think it means you must think less of yourself? True humility empowers the soul. Self-pity is thinking less of yourself. Humility is being fully self-aware and recognizing who you are compared to Christ. Only when we submit to Christ's lordship can we reach our fullest potential. What area of your life do you need to stop thinking less of yourself and maybe just think of yourself less?

THERE'S SOMETHING ABOUT JESUS *JA*

> "'The time has come,' He said. 'The kingdom of God is near. Repent and believe the good news!'"
> —Mark 1:15

<u>Read</u>: Mark 1:14–20 "The Calling of the First Disciples"
The last prophet God sent to the Jewish people spoke some 400 years before Jesus. Since the time of Malachi, God had been silent. Then Jesus arrived, declaring, "The time has come...the kingdom of God is near."

A few weeks ago, I wrote about how the kingdom of God is a matter of the heart. The Sunday School class I attend is currently studying The Lord's Prayer—not simply as a prayer to recite but as a pattern to guide how we pray. The prayer begins by acknowledging the holiness of God and submitting to His will before presenting any requests: "Your kingdom come, Your will be done, on earth as it is in heaven" (Matt 6:10). We shouldn't wait for eternity to begin when our earthly bodies perish. If we have accepted Christ as our Savior and claim victory over death through His resurrection, then our eternity has already begun. Each day, we must seek to live in the kingdom of God.

Jesus came preaching and teaching that the kingdom of God is near. His words, actions, and demeanor drew multitudes. When He called specific men to be His disciples, they responded without hesitation (Mark 1:18, 20).

What is it about us that draws people to us? God has given each of us unique strengths to serve Him and bring Him glory through discipling others to desire and know Him.

Christ-centered leadership draws others through authenticity and purpose, using God-given strengths to inspire and guide others toward His kingdom.

Application: Consider your strengths: What comes easily to you? What do you feel passionate about? What resources has God entrusted to you that could enhance your ability to influence others? Ask Him to reveal these things to you.

A GREAT RESPONSIBILITY JA

"The people were all so amazed that they asked each other, 'What is this? A new teaching—and with authority! He even gives orders to evil spirits, and they obey Him.'"
—Mark 1:27

Read: Mark 1:21–28 "Jesus Drives Out an Evil Spirit"
What was so unique about Jesus' teaching that amazed people and caused them to say He spoke "with authority?" This suggests the teachers of the law did not speak with the same authority (see, Mark 1:22). Jesus not only spoke with authority but demonstrated it through His actions. When He commanded evil spirits to

leave, they obeyed—an authority the teachers of the law could not replicate.

The teachers of the law likely relied on regurgitating the Mosaic law, using it to wield religious and political power over the people. Jesus, however, operated outside their control. He possessed an authority they did not understand and could not overpower.

And so do we. When we accept Jesus, we inherit His authority. In the Great Commission, Jesus tells His disciples, "All authority in heaven and on earth has been given to Me... And surely I am with you always, to the very end of the age" (Matt 28:18, 20). In Acts 1:8, right before His ascension, Jesus declares, "But you will receive power when the Holy Spirit comes on you; and you will be My witnesses in Jerusalem, and in all Judea and Samaria, and to the ends of the earth."

If we desire His authority, we must first deny our own. That is the first step to becoming a Christ-centered leader. Authority from Jesus carries immense responsibility, and to wield it well, we must submit to Him fully.

Christ-centered leaders must deny their own authority, fully submit to Jesus, and responsibly wield the authority He entrusts to them.

Application: What authority might you be trying to retain? Submit all your authority to Jesus and He will give you much greater authority and with it, responsibility.

YOUR ACTIONS DEFINE YOU JA

"And Jesus healed many who had various diseases. He also drove out many demons, but He would not let the demons speak because they knew who He was."

–Mark 1:34

Read: Mark 1:29–34 "Jesus Heals Many"

After teaching in the synagogue in Capernaum, Jesus went to the home of Simon (Peter) and Andrew, where He healed Simon's mother-in-law of a fever. That day marked the beginning of Jesus publicly displaying His miraculous power to heal and drive out demons.

Mark 1:34 notes that Jesus silenced the demons because they knew who He was. While He had begun to reveal Himself as a wise teacher and even as a prophet of God by proclaiming, "The kingdom of God is near," and casting out evil spirits, it was not yet time for His full identity as the Messiah to be widely known. Such a revelation early in His ministry would have hindered His mission and influence.

Jesus demonstrated humility in this restraint. He did not flaunt His position as the Christ; instead, He served. When He saw a need, He met it. In contrast, we often cling to our titles, positions, and credentials, believing they validate our worth. However, positions don't define a leader, actions do. Great leaders earn respect through service and the impact they have, not the titles they hold.

A leader's influence comes from their actions and service, not their position or title.

Application: What actions have defined you recently? Do you rely on your current actions or past reputations to speak to who you are? Write down three actions that define you or you believe would define you as a Christ-centered leader. Now, write down three actions that you are currently doing or have done in the past that may define your title or position more than your leadership.

LET'S GO TO THE TOP *JA*

"Jesus replied, 'Let us go somewhere else—to the nearby villages—so I can preach there also. That is why I have come.'"

–Mark 1:38

Read: Mark 1:35–39 "Jesus Prays in a Solitary Place"
This passage captures the day after the Sabbath from the previous two accounts. Jesus, staying at the house of Simon and Andrew, rose early in the morning and went to a solitary place to pray (Mark 1:35). This time prayer with His Father was a priority for Him before continuing His ministry.

Following this prayer time, Jesus traveled throughout Galilee, teaching, preaching, and healing—and most notably—He brought His disciples with Him. While this may seem obvious since they were His disciples, it's significant for leadership development. At this point, the disciples were still new to following Him. Jesus didn't leave them behind with instructions to study Scripture until they were "ready." Instead, He actively involved them in His ministry, modeling leadership and allowing them to learn by observing and participating.

In one of our leadership mastermind groups, we study John Maxwell's *Leadership Gold*. One key takeaway from the lesson "If It's Lonely at the Top, You're Doing Something Wrong" is that true leadership success isn't achieved in isolation. Maxwell encourages leaders to bring others with them to the top. By investing in and sharing success with their teams, leaders move from being successful to being significant.[11]

> **Great leaders invest in their teams, bringing others along on the journey to achieve not just success but significance.**

Application: Who are you bringing with you as you grow in wisdom, influence, and status? Consider how you may be able to grow your own sphere of influence by graciously bringing others up to where you are. Who are you developing? Write down at least one person to mentor and develop and invite them to start today.

PREPARE TO BE INCONVENIENCED JA

"See that you don't tell this to anyone. But go, show yourself to the priest and offer the sacrifices that Moses commanded for your cleansing, as a testimony to them."
—Mark 1:44

Read: Mark 1:40-45 "A Man with Leprosy"
The man with leprosy had great faith to be healed, and Jesus had great compassion to heal him. The man did not question Jesus' power and authority to do so but only questioned if healing him was Jesus' will.

Jesus felt compassion and healed the man but gave him clear instructions. It was the beginning of Jesus' ministry, and by following Jesus' instructions, the man would have adhered to the Mosaic law. In doing so, he would have testified that he was truly and miraculously healed. However, this man did not follow the Mosaic Law and instead boasted of his healing and cleanliness all over town. Jewish religious leaders began to despise Jesus, and His popularity with the townspeople grew so rapidly that He had to move out to the rural areas surrounding Galilee for the time.

This man's disobedience inconvenienced Jesus. Yet, knowing the man would disobey His clear instructions to follow the Mosaic law, Jesus still felt compassion and still healed him.

Are we so compassionate to those we lead and influence that we are prepared to be inconvenienced by them? Jesus was prepared to be inconvenienced. He adjusted His plans and continued His mission. Are we so concerned with maintaining our plans and schedules that we miss opportunities to give and show compassion because we have a task to complete? Leaders are responsible for completing the mission. Christ-centered leaders understand that the mission is often in the process as well.

Be prepared to be inconvenienced and make leading people as much a part of your mission as completing the task you are assigned.

Christ-centered leaders graciously serve those who inconvenience them because they value others as much as themselves.

Application: Do you welcome inconvenience by those who you influence? Do you view their time as more valuable than your own? Reflect and write down ways you can prepare yourself to be inconvenienced by those you lead.

OUR OPERATING ENVIRONMENT *JA*

"Immediately Jesus knew in His spirit that this was what they were thinking in their hearts, and He said to them, 'Why are you thinking these things?'"
—Mark 2:8

Read: Mark 2:1–12 "Jesus Heals a Paralytic"
I often like to consider what is happening in the spiritual realm and what is happening in the natural realm as separate environments. I believe that the spiritual realm is the Christ-centered leader's "operating environment." "Operating environment" is a phrase we used often in the military to encompass the area where we conducted our operations. We had to know the environment—the political, military, economic, social, informational, infrastructural, geographical, and other aspects of the environment in which we operated and conducted our missions.

I believe that the spiritual realm is the Christ follower's operating environment because he must operate, battle, and function there if he is going to be successful in the natural realm. When we only concern ourselves with the natural realm, we are often defeated in the spiritual realm.

Jesus displays this concept in this passage of Mark. The friends of this paralytic man go through great trouble to lower him so that Jesus could see the man and heal him. But when Jesus saw the man and their faith, He did not first heal him. Instead, He forgave their sins. To Jesus, as it should be to us, the man's spiritual healing was much more important than his earthly healing. If he's only healed in the natural, he may go on to break his leg or, worse, die the next day in an accident. Jesus prioritized His efforts. He operated in the spiritual and then displayed in the natural what had already occurred in the spiritual—miraculous healing.

Christ-centered leaders operate in the spiritual realm so that they achieve victories in the natural realm.

<u>Application</u>: Do you know your operating environment? Are you prioritizing your efforts to lead and serve your team for an eternal purpose? Before reacting or responding to a situation that you are experiencing in the natural realm, consider what may be occurring in the spiritual realm. As you stop, think, and reflect, how will you adjust your response to the situation so that good prevails and evil is thwarted? This will take our deliberate efforts of discerning situations and praying through our actions.

THE RIGHT INDIVIDUAL JA

"On hearing this, Jesus said to them, 'It is not the healthy who need a doctor, but the sick. I have not come to call the righteous, but sinners.'"

—Mark 2:13–17

<u>Read</u>: Mark 2:13–17 "The Calling of Levi"
In reply to the Pharisees' question directed toward Jesus' disciples, "Why does He eat with tax collectors and 'sinners?'" Jesus claims

that "sinners" are the ones He calls. Why would He not also call the righteous? Because no one is righteous except God. Eternal life is a gift, and it is not earned by anyone.

"Righteous" people don't need Jesus. He knows their hearts are hardened toward Him because they consider themselves righteous enough. So, He came to call the "sinners"—the ones who recognize that they fall short of the righteousness of a Holy God.

Who would you rather have on your team? Someone who thinks they need no improvement, or someone who recognizes their weaknesses and desires to improve those areas while also seeking to make their strengths even stronger. The latter option, of course.

It's not always about finding the person who can do the job the best. Oftentimes, it's about finding the one who is trainable, who has the right attitude to work with the team, and can add value to those around them because of their own desire to grow and improve themselves. In the selection process for the various United States special operations units from different branches of the armed forces, this is exactly the person they spend millions of dollars every year seeking to select for their units. They are not looking for the best individuals; they are looking for the right individuals.

The best teammates are the ones who are humble, teachable, and committed to learning.

Application: Are you teachable? Do you know someone who always has a response to why they did what they did as if to defend their words or actions? We are better teammates when we are coachable and committed to learning from our peers and those below us, as much as we are from those above us. Next time someone teaches you something, show gratitude in your response.

A CHANGE AGENT *BH*

"How is it that John's disciples and the disciples of the Pharisees are fasting, but Yours are not? Jesus answered, 'How can the guests of the bridegroom fast while he is with them? They cannot, so long as they have him with them. But the time will come when the bridegroom will be taken from them, and on that day they will fast.'"
—Mark 2:18–20

<u>Read</u>: Mark 2:18–22 "Jesus Questioned about Fasting"
During Jesus' time on earth, many struggled to comprehend His divinity as God incarnate. Followers of the Pharisees and John the Baptist observed fasting as a means to draw closer to God. They found it perplexing that Jesus and His disciples did not adhere to the same practice. In His characteristic fashion, Jesus told parables to elucidate why fasting was unnecessary for His followers; God was already present among them, embodied in Jesus Himself. Being with Jesus was a cause for celebration, rather than mourning or sadness as was customary during fasting traditions.

In the parables of guests celebrating with a bridegroom, a new cloth patching an old garment, and new wine being poured into old wine skins, Jesus vividly illustrates how the path to salvation—a new unshrunk patch—cannot be confined by rigid adherence to old traditions, and how the old traditions—an old wine skin—cannot contain the transformative power of the new way (Mark 2:21–22).

As a leader, you must be prepared to face questions and scrutiny. Leadership often invites challenges, and there will be moments when your methods and decisions are questioned. It's also important to recognize resistance to change, as people can be fearful of or resistant to new ideas, often clinging to the familiar refrain of "That's not the way we've always done it." However, embracing your role as an agent of change is essential. Like Jesus, leaders sometimes must introduce new ways of doing things to propel the organization forward, even if it means stepping outside of traditional practices.

Change occurs when the leader acts with humility and confidence paving the way for the team to trust the process of change.

Application: When have you lacked the confidence to affect change that was needed to grow your team? When the change that needs to be made follows God's word, you can be confident that it is the right change. Regardless of how uncomfortable they may be, consider changes that need to be made to help progress your team toward accomplishing its mission.

ALWAYS BEING WATCHED BH

> "Another time Jesus went into the synagogue, and a man with a shriveled hand was there. Some of them were looking for a reason to accuse Jesus, so they watched Him closely to see if He would heal on the Sabbath. Then Jesus asked them, 'Which is lawful on the Sabbath: to do good or to do evil, to save life or to kill?' But they remained silent."
> —Mark 3:1–4

Read: Mark 2:23—3:6 "Lord of the Sabbath"
During His time on earth, all eyes were on Jesus—some in amazement, others in eager pursuit of learning, and yet some with a critical gaze, seeking to find fault according to their traditions. As a leader, Jesus was under constant observation and scrutiny.

At the culmination of one such incident, when Jesus healed a man with a shriveled hand, the Pharisees reacted by conspiring with the Herodians to plot His demise (Mark 3:6).

Like Jesus, leaders must acknowledge that they are constantly under observation and evaluation. Just as Jesus remained steadfast in His actions because He knew His heart was aligned with God's will, we too, as leaders, can find assurance in following His example. We should be confident in our decisions when they are rooted in goodness and guided by Scripture, even in the face of scrutiny.

As a leader, it is crucial to acknowledge that you are always being watched, as your actions and decisions set the tone for others. By emulating Jesus' example, you can ensure that your intentions remain pure, demonstrating integrity and humility in your leadership. Even when faced with scrutiny, stand confidently in your decisions to do what is right, trusting that principled leadership will inspire and guide those you lead.

Leaders inspire trust and resilience by demonstrating integrity and standing firm in principled decisions, even under scrutiny.

Application: How can you maintain your integrity and remain steadfast under scrutiny? Do you live above reproach? We all make mistakes. The question is, are we humble to admit them, take ownership of them, and have the integrity to fix them? Reflect on how your integrity builds your resilience or how your lack of integrity breaks it.

REPUTATION, REST, AND HUMILITY *BH*

"Jesus withdrew with His disciples to the lake, and a large crowd from Galilee followed. When they heard about all He was doing, many people came to Him

> from Judea, Jerusalem, Idumea, and the regions across the Jordan and around Tyre and Sidon."
>
> –Mark 3:7–8

Read: Mark 3:7–12 "Crowds Follow Jesus"
Jesus frequently sought moments of solitude away from the throngs of people who constantly trailed Him. Despite His desire for solitude, His compassion led Him to continue healing the sick and casting out impure spirits (Mark 1:10–11). As His popularity surged and crowds swelled around Him, Jesus, with humility, often instructed those He helped to keep his miracles quiet.

The word of Jesus' compassion and miraculous deeds spread far and wide, drawing people from distant places to witness His acts of kindness. His loving reputation fostered a large and devoted following. Reflecting on this, it's essential for us as leaders to consider our own reputations and the reasons behind our followership. Do people follow us because of our character and actions?

Even Jesus recognized the need for periodic withdrawal from the demands of leadership to recharge, often retreating with His closest companions. Do we acknowledge our need for rest and replenishment amidst our leadership responsibilities? Just as Jesus found strength in companionship during these times, we too should seek support from those closest to us.

Furthermore, Jesus' humility shines through in His reluctance to draw attention to His remarkable deeds. His humility led Him to understanding the value of rest and replenishment. Because He didn't seek recognition or praise, He wasn't going to burn Himself out to get it. He stayed focused on doing His Father's will and adding value to others.

Compassionate leadership inspires followership through character and actions, while humility and intentional rest ensure sustained effectiveness.

Application: Do you exercise humility in your accomplishments, or do you seek recognition and praise from others? Practicing humility will lead you to the rest and refit you need. Seeking praise will only burn you out.

BUILDING THE TEAM BH

> "Jesus went up on a mountainside and called to Him those He wanted, and they came to Him. He appointed twelve that they might be with Him and that He might send them out to preach and to have authority to drive out demons."
> —Mark 3:13–15

Read: Mark 3:13–19 "The Appointing of the Twelve"
Recognizing the importance of teamwork, Jesus assembled a group of disciples whom He would teach, coach, mentor, and empower to carry out His mission. Even as the perfect leader, Jesus understood the necessity of a dedicated team to achieve His goals. Each member was carefully chosen, their unique qualities serving a purpose in fulfilling His ultimate mission.

Jesus handpicked twelve individuals to form His inner circle, knowing that their diverse talents and abilities would contribute to the success of His mission. Similarly, as leaders, we must prioritize talent management, ensuring that we have the right people with the right skillsets to advance the mission of our organization.

In a demonstration of effective leadership, Jesus delegated authority to His team members, acknowledging that He needed their assistance to fulfill His vision. This teaches us the importance of entrusting responsibilities to others. While it may seem tempting to handle everything ourselves, effective delegation allows us to focus on tasks that only we can accomplish, leading to lasting impacts on our organizations.

Just as Jesus relied on His team to accomplish His mission, so must we recognize the value of collaboration and shared responsibility in achieving our goals.

Effective leaders build diverse teams, delegate authority, and embrace collaboration to achieve lasting success.

<u>Application</u>: Assess your team composition. Do you have the right people with the necessary skills? Delegate authority to your team, allowing you to focus on tasks that require your unique expertise. Remember that even the most capable leaders need the support of others to accomplish their mission.

LEADERSHIP CAN BE LONELY BH

> "Then Jesus entered a house, and again a crowd gathered, so that He and His disciples were not even able to eat. When His family heard about this, they went to take charge of Him, for they said, 'He is out of His mind.' And the teachers of the law who came down from Jerusalem said, 'He is possessed by Beelzebul. By the prince of demons, He is driving out demons.'"
> —Mark 3:20–22

<u>Read</u>: Mark 3:20–30 "Jesus Accused by His Family and by Teachers of the Law"

In this story, Jesus faces opposition from both the teachers of the law, representing the Old Testament tradition, and His own family. The teachers accuse Him of being possessed by demons, while His family expresses concern, even suggesting He is "out of his mind." Yet, in His characteristic manner, Jesus responds not with confrontation, but with colorful parables, turning their accusations into opportunities for teaching.

As leaders, we may encounter lack of support or even opposition from those around us, including family members, despite our successes. Jesus faced a similar situation, achieving remarkable success with large crowds following Him, yet experiencing rejection from His own family. Such moments can indeed be isolating for leaders. How do you handle ridicule as a leader? It's vital to observe how Jesus navigated this scenario, transforming criticism into teachable moments. Had the teachers of the law and Jesus' family truly understood Him, they would have celebrated His success instead of criticizing Him.

Often, when leaders thrive, envy can surface among those around them, leading to rumors and attempts to undermine their achievements, mirroring the actions of the teachers of the law. How do we respond when others succeed or receive promotions? Do we support them or succumb to jealousy? It's crucial to recognize the potential for jealousy and strive to support others in their successes.

Great leaders turn criticism into teachable moments, responding with grace and using challenges to inspire understanding and growth.

Application: Consider a time when you felt like no one was following you, but you believed you were leading in a Christ-centered manner. Reflect on how lonely you felt. Now consider how you could connect with those who ridiculed you so that they could understand the truth of your leadership. Approach them from their perspective.

MAINTAIN FOCUS BH

"A crowd was sitting around Him, and they told Him, 'Your mother and brothers are outside looking for You.'

> **'Who are My mother and My brothers?'** He asked. Then He looked at those seated in a circle around Him and said, **'Here are My mother and brothers! Whoever does God's will is My brother and sister and mother.'"**
>
> —Mark 3:32–34

<u>Read</u>: Mark 3:31–35 "Jesus' Mother and Brothers"

In the previous lesson, we discovered that even Jesus' own family doubted Him, declaring Him "out of His mind." Now, we witness Jesus distancing Himself from His family. In this narrative, Jesus is surrounded by crowds eager to learn about salvation. He had a divine mission on earth: to reveal Himself as the living God and to establish the kingdom of heaven. Recall from the previous story that Jesus' family sought to intervene, but He recognized their intentions and remained steadfast in pursuing God's will for His life.

While it may appear abrupt for Jesus to rebuff His own family, He understood the greater purpose He was called to fulfill as a leader. He was dedicated to spreading the gospel, and His family's interference threatened to derail His mission. Similarly, as leaders, we encounter distractions that seek to divert our focus from our roles. Recognizing these distractions is crucial to staying on course and achieving our objectives.

In our roles as leaders within our families, we may also face distractions that we fail to recognize. God entrusts us with leadership responsibilities within our families, yet the devil works tirelessly to steer us away from this mission. It's imperative that we identify and overcome these distractions, safeguarding our commitment to lead our families with purpose and devotion.

Focused leaders recognize and overcome distractions to fulfill their mission while staying devoted to their purpose and responsibilities.

Application: List three distractions that keep you from maintaining your focus on a goal you have. How can you overcome these distractions? What support do you need to ask for from family and friends? Oftentimes we stand in our own way, and it takes those around us who love us to help.

UNDERSTAND THOSE YOU LEAD BH

> "Some people are like seed along the path, where the word is sown. As soon as they hear it, Satan comes and takes away the word that was sown in them. Others, like seed sown on rocky places, hear the word and at once receive it with joy. But since they have no root, they last only a short time. Still others, like seed sown among thorns, hear the word; but the worries of this life, the deceitfulness of wealth and the desires for other things come in and choke the word. Others, like seed sown on good soil, hear the word, accept it, and produce a crop—thirty, sixty, or even a hundred times what was sown."
>
> —Mark 4:15–20

Read: Mark 4:1–20 "The Parable of the Sower"
Jesus imparts crucial leadership insight into understanding the people we lead. The Sower represents a person of influence—a leader or anyone proclaiming the Gospel. While the Sower embodies leadership, the seeds symbolize the words imparted to the listeners. Each individual hearing the words represents various types of soil where the seeds land. Although all hear the word, not all truly internalize and act upon it. Jesus reminds us to persist in leadership, recognizing that not everyone will heed

our words. "He who has ears to hear, let them hear" (Mark 4:9). Despite knowing that not everyone will listen, we must persevere in our leadership efforts. As leaders, we will eventually reap what we sow, especially when our followers possess "good soil" and yield a bountiful harvest—thirty, sixty, or even a hundredfold.

Jesus teaches us that as leaders we must comprehend the diverse responses of those we lead. Some may resemble the seed sown "along the path," showing no inclination to heed our guidance. Others may be like the "rocky ground," initially receptive, but faltering when challenges arise. There are also those akin to "thorns," allowing the distractions of life to hinder their progress. Yet, among those we lead, there are those with "good soil," who not only embrace our leadership but also multiply our efforts by nurturing new leaders under them.

Perseverance, faith, and intentional investment in those with the greatest potential amplify a leader's impact and legacy.

Application: Do you truly understand those you lead? Do you know what makes them tick? Do you know their behavior and communication styles? Consider purchasing DISC assessments, personality assessments, strength finders, and leadership assessments.

SHINE *JA*

"Whoever has will be given more; whoever does not have, even what he has will be taken from him."

—Mark 4:25

Read: Mark 4:21–25 "A Lamp on a Stand"
In the darkness, a light serves as a beacon, revealing the path forward. Jesus, as the Light of the World, illuminates the way to the Father. John 14:6 reminds us of His declaration: "I am the way and

the truth and the life. No one comes to the Father except through me." Jesus came not only to reveal Himself but also to unveil the truth for us to receive and embody.

At first glance, this key verse may seem at odds with Jesus' teachings on generosity and caring for those in need. However, this passage transcends material possessions; it delves into the essence of God's truth. Those who embrace His truth will receive abundantly, while those who disregard it will forfeit even what they have.

God desires to bless every aspect of our lives—our families, businesses, and communities. Yet, His blessings flow exclusively through the conduit of His truth. We are called to diligently seek Him, for it is in our pursuit that we encounter Him. As the passage suggests, He has already revealed Himself; our task is simply to turn toward Him and embrace His truth.

Leaders must seek and embody the truth.

<u>Application</u>: Are you allowing God's truth to illuminate your path? Do you integrate His wisdom into your family dynamics and professional endeavors? Are you holding onto the things of this world and missing the truth about what is to come? Reflect on these questions and provide honest answers in your notes.

JUST DO IT JA

"Night and day, whether he sleeps or gets up, the seed sprouts and grows, though he does not know how."

—Mark 4:27

<u>Read</u>: Mark 4:26–29 "The Parable of the Growing Seed"
Jesus teaches us that the growth of God's kingdom isn't solely dependent on our efforts but on His divine orchestration. While we

play a crucial role as stewards of His kingdom, the timing and manner of growth are under His control—not ours.

This message resonated deeply with me as I contemplated the trajectory of Red Letter Leadership. In 2023, when I transitioned from my previous job, I didn't anticipate immediately diving into building a leadership development business. Yet, since then, God has orchestrated encounters and connections that align perfectly with the mission of Red Letter Leadership. While I may have planted the initial seed, it's God who nurtures and directs the growth of this venture according to His divine will. Though I'm still discerning His specific plans, I see immense potential for Red Letter Leadership to infuse the leadership development landscape with its Christ-centered approach.

God continually presents opportunities before us, just as He did when He brought Ben and Eric to Red Letter Leadership. In the fall of 2023, when asked about the future scale of Red Letter Leadership, I responded, "I don't really know. I want to take it wherever God wants to take it." That certainly was the right answer, but it is the one I must commit to everyday. I encourage you to do the same.

When God prompts you in a particular direction, step out in faith. He desires for us to trust Him wholeheartedly. Though I stumble at times, the moments when I align my will with His are undeniably fulfilling.

Embrace God's guidance and trust that His plan will lead to greater outcomes than your personal agenda.

Application: Are you fully trusting God's providence in your life? If we are honest, we likely fail at this more days than we don't. Proverbs 16:9 states, "In his heart a man plans his course, but the LORD determines his steps." I often want to be the one determining my steps. How can you commit to trusting God to determine your steps today and start stepping?

INVEST IN THOSE CLOSEST *JA*

"He did not say anything to them without using a parable. But when He was alone with His own disciples, He explained everything."
—Mark 4:34

Read: Mark 4:30–34 "The Parable of the Mustard Seed"

Jesus, the master storyteller, understood the profound impact stories have on shaping, understanding, and inspiring action. Most of us would agree that we enjoy hearing stories from others, too. I know I do. Just as Jesus used stories to convey abstract concepts, we too can leverage storytelling to illuminate the multifaceted realm of leadership.

In verse 34, we glimpse Jesus' teaching style with His disciples—patiently explaining everything in intimate settings. Similarly, 1:1 or small group settings foster deeper interaction, allowing individuals to ask questions, share insights, and build tighter bonds. These environments cultivate a sense of safety and vulnerability, crucial for meaningful discussions and personal growth.

Jesus invested in the development of His closest disciples, recognizing their pivotal role in advancing His mission. Likewise, we're called to nurture those closest to us, starting with our children and extending to the inner circles of our workplaces and communities. Whether in a formal coaching role or not, our own personal growth must be consistent if we are going to develop and empower others.

Effective leaders invest in their own personal growth and that of their teammates using intimate settings to inspire, develop, and empower those closest to them.

Application: Reflect on the time you take each day or each week to invest in those closest to you: your spouse, your children, your teammates. How can you improve the quality and/or quantity of that time? We only have 24 hours in our days. Time is our most precious commodity. Don't waste your time.

CALM BREEDS CALM *JA*

> "Jesus was in the stern, sleeping on a cushion.
> The disciples woke Him and said to Him,
> 'Teacher, don't You care if we drown?'"
> —Mark 4:38

Read: Mark 4:35–41 "Jesus Calms the Storm"

While the passage suggests Jesus was asleep during the storm, it's unlikely He was unaware of the chaos unfolding around Him. The disciples' question implies they perceived His calmness as indifference to their plight. Yet, Jesus' tranquil demeanor amid the storm serves as a powerful example of calm leadership in the face of chaos.

Calm breeds calm. Chaos breeds chaos. That is a common saying and understanding among military leaders and other leaders in roles that take them into stressful and austere environments. I know I've done well at this and have also failed at this many times. Whether on the job as a ground force commander in a direct-action raid or at home with my children, I've lost my cool and it did not help the situation. The wins I've had in stressful situations are when I've spoken calmly into the chaos. The calm voice of the leader brings comfort and confidence to the led.

This lesson reminds me of the actions of LT Michael Murphy, who was the US Navy SEAL leading the team of three other SEALs into the Hindu Kush mountains in June 2005 to provide overwatch and observation for a ground operation in the valley. The team's heroic actions are accounted in the book, *Lone Survivor*.[12] The team was compromised and subsequently attacked by a Taliban force that far outnumbered the four of them. Amid the storm the team was facing, as machine gun fire and RPGs came crashing toward their position, an already wounded LT Murphy left cover to attain a signal with his satellite phone so that he could inform his higher headquarters of the situation and ask for a quick reaction force to rescue them. The account states that he was calm over the phone and at the end of the conversation, said, 'thank you.' Those are said to be his last words before being mortally wounded.

Calm breeds calm. When confronted with chaos, leaders must resist the urge to react impulsively and instead respond with deliberate, measured actions. By embodying calmness and clarity amidst turmoil, leaders can guide their teams through the storm with confidence and resolve.

Calm and deliberate actions in the face of chaos inspire confidence and clarity, enabling leaders to guide their teams through challenging situations.

Application: How do you remain calm in chaotic situations? Do you recall a time when you added to the chaos and how your response may have destabilized the situation further and caused those around you to lose trust and confidence in you? Consider chaos that you may be facing at work or at home. Write down three ways you can speak calm into the chaos verbally or nonverbally.

TELL YOUR STORY *JA*

"Jesus did not let him, but said, 'Go home to your family and tell them how much the Lord has done for you, and how He has had mercy on you.'"
—Mark 5:19

Read: Mark 5:1–20 "The Healing of a Demon-Possessed Man"

In Mark, this appears to be the first time that Jesus instructs someone who He had healed to go tell their family. Following previous healings, Jesus instructs the people who were healed to not tell anyone. We also see that Jesus instructs the man to "tell them how much the Lord has done for you" (Mark 5:19). Jesus is pointing people to the Lord. Of course, we know He is the Lord, but these people did not. Jesus is not directly making claims yet that He is God. He is performing miracles and speaking with authority, while pointing others to God.

We are to tell of the good things the Lord has done for us. Our lives are our testimony, and we must share the Good News. Every one of us has a story.

Leadership involves guiding others toward higher principles and values, as exemplified by Jesus directing the healed man to share how much the Lord had done for him. Our lives serve as powerful testimonies, showcasing the transformative impact of God's grace and inspiring us to share our experiences with others. Effective leadership is not about seeking personal glory, but about recognizing and sharing the greater power and wisdom of God in our lives and leadership journeys, pointing others to Him through our actions and words.

Red Letter Leadership was founded not out of self-exaltation in leadership prowess, but out of a passion to develop leaders by sharing personal successes and failures, recognizing that Jesus holds the ultimate answers, and our stories reflect His transformative work in our lives. Tell your story.

Christ-centered leaders guide others toward higher principles inspiring them to recognize God's greater wisdom and grace.

Application: How can you be more vulnerable today in sharing your story? Sharing stories of your failures may have a greater impact on those you influence than your successes. Write down two lessons you've learned from your failures that you can share with those who you influence and who look up to you.

CASTING VISION *JA*

"Ignoring what they said, Jesus told the synagogue ruler, 'Don't be afraid; just believe.'"
–Mark 5:36

Read: Mark 5:21–43 "A Dead Girl and a Sick Woman"

Jesus healed many and drove out evil spirits, but at this point in His ministry, it is likely that only the disciples were aware of Him calming the storm on the Sea of Galilee. He healed and spoke with authority and people wanted more of Him. Even so, no one at this point, even His disciples, probably anticipated Him to be the Messiah. Raising the dead? No way!

When some men came to Jarius to tell him not to bother Jesus anymore because his daughter has died, Jesus encourages Jarius to "just believe" (Mark 5:36). Jesus casts vision where there is no hope. He then took only Peter, James, and John with Him to the house. When they arrive, He says to all of those mourning and wailing, "The child is not dead but asleep" (Mark 5:39). Jesus is providing the vision of what is in the realm of the possible, while those around Him see it as impossible.

Leaders cast vision for their teams when everyone else around can't see what is possible. Leaders see the strengths of all the individuals on the team, as Jesus saw the faith of Jarius, and cast vision for the team to see and understand what is possible. Leaders then drive the team to organize, plan, and execute that vision.

Effective leaders inspire hope and confidence by casting a clear vision of what is possible, even when others see only impossibility, driving their teams to believe, plan, and achieve extraordinary outcomes.

Application: Most of us are realists and if we don't understand a vision within the confines of our reality, then we don't have confidence in it. Christ wants us to allow Him to define reality and trust Him with achieving greater things through us. What is your vision for your team? Does it push the bounds of your reality, or can you clearly see all the steps to achieve your vision? I challenge you to have a vision that is just beyond the scope of your own reality and allow God to stretch and grow you and your team to how He will achieve that vision through you.

CREATE YOUR OPPORTUNITIES JA

> "He could not do any miracles there, except lay hands on a few sick people and heal them. And He was amazed at their lack of faith."
> —Mark 6:5–6

Read: Mark 6:1–6 "A Prophet without Honor"
As Jesus returned to Nazareth, the familiarity of His background overshadowed the profound impact of His teachings, leading many to dismiss His authority and potential based on His humble origins.

Similarly, whether due to past mistakes or the reputation of one's family, individuals may face skepticism and lack of credibility, hindering their opportunities for growth and leadership development. However, Jesus' experience serves as a reminder that even the most remarkable abilities can be overlooked by those who lack understanding and foresight.

In moments of discouragement, remember that God has endowed each of us with great potential for leadership and impact. Like Jesus, we must be willing to step beyond the confines of our comfort zones and hometowns, embracing opportunities for growth and service wherever He leads us.

Leadership requires perseverance, even when faced with skepticism or rejection, trusting in God's plan and stepping beyond familiar boundaries to fulfill your purpose.

Application: Do you let your past mistakes hinder your future potential? Be willing to step out of your comfort zone, and even, literally speaking, your hometown in pursuit of opportunities for growth and service. Write down three ways you can step out of your comfort zone to bring transformative change in your own life and in the lives you influence. Now write down one or two literal ways you can go beyond your hometown to expand your opportunities for growth and adding value to others.

TEAM DESIGN *JA*

> "Calling the Twelve to Him, He sent them out two by two and gave them authority over evil spirits."
> —Mark 6:7

Read: Mark 6:6–13 "Jesus Sends out the Twelve"
Matthew's account of how Jesus sends out His twelve disciples in Matthew 10 is much more detailed than Mark's. However, Mark records that Jesus sent them out "two by two."

In the military, the concept of having a "battle buddy" is ingrained from the moment we enter basic training. When conducting missions behind enemy lines, we must always be alert and on guard for potential enemy contact. Security is paramount, and while one person cannot achieve 360-degree security alone, two can manage it effectively. Ecclesiastes 4:12, reminds us: "Though one may be overpowered, two can defend themselves. A cord of three strands is not quickly broken."

A team becomes more formidable with the inclusion of strong and capable individuals who contribute to its success. However, the number of team members must align with the mission's requirements. In operations behind enemy lines, the team's mobility and risk of compromise must be carefully balanced against its size.

Jesus demonstrated the importance of this principle by sending His disciples out in pairs. He knew that pairs were the right size for the mission of preaching the kingdom of heaven, healing the sick, and driving out demons. Larger groups could be more difficult for the local townspeople to accommodate and would limit the number of towns they could cover in the given time.

As leaders, we must carefully consider the size, composition, and disposition of our teams to best achieve our objectives without unnecessary risk or logistical strain.

Strategic team formation and partnerships are essential for maximizing efficiency, minimizing risk, and achieving mission success.

Application: Reflect on the composition of your team. Are you employing all your teammates' strengths to the best of their abilities? Do your teammates feel they are working in their strength zones? Does everyone on the team believe that they need each other to accomplish the mission? Take a few minutes today to consider how each person is employed and ensure you communicate your reflections one-on-one with your teammates.

ALLOW FOR CONVICTION *JA*

"But she was not able to, because Herod feared John and protected him, knowing him to be a righteous

> and holy man. When Herod heard John, he was greatly puzzled; yet he liked to listen to him."
>
> —Mark 6:19–20

Read: Mark 6:14–29 "John the Baptist Beheaded"
Despite Herodias's intense hatred for John the Baptist, King Herod protected John because he feared him as a "righteous and holy man." Herod was "puzzled" by John's preaching but still "liked to listen to him," indicating a possible brewing conviction about his evil ways that he ultimately chose to ignore.

How often do we ignore conviction spoken to us by others, or directly by the Holy Spirit? Our pride, clinging to our ways and deflecting blame onto others, often causes us to disregard these convictions. When we accept God's word, we recognize that "there is no one who does good; not even one" (Ps 14:3 and Rom 3:12). This understanding should lead us to humble ourselves and seek the necessary changes in our lives.

For leaders, this is especially critical. Leaders set the greatest example for their teams. If a leader cannot or will not seek personal conviction, the team is unlikely to do so either. King Herod's failure to heed his convictions and instead listen to the evil wishes of his wife serves as a stark reminder of the importance of humble self-reflection in leadership.

Leaders must embrace personal conviction with humility, as their example profoundly influences the attitudes and actions of their teams.

Application: Does your team observe your personal convictions? Do you share your personal convictions with your team? Are you vulnerable to your team's feedback and constructive criticism? Our convictions lead to crafting our beliefs and values and our beliefs and values structure our character. Commit today to humbly living out your personal convictions as aligned with God's word.

TEAM WELFARE *JA*

> "Then, because so many people were coming and going that they did not even have a chance to eat, He said to them, 'Come with Me by yourselves to a quiet place and get some rest.'"
>
> —Mark 6:31

Read: Mark 6:30–44 "Jesus Feeds the Five Thousand"

Jesus' disciples returned after going out "two by two" to towns to preach, heal the sick, and drive out demons (Mark 6:6–13). They reported to Jesus all they had done and taught, and Jesus responded by attempting to move them to a solitary place so that they could eat and get some rest. Jesus recognized that the disciples needed to recharge—they needed to rest and refit so that they could continue their ministry.

How often do we seek rest only to be met with new demands—whether from a child, a coworker, or our church? The disciples wanted to send the crowds away, but Jesus, moved by compassion, recognized that there was still work to be done. Despite their need for rest, the mission had priority.

As a leader, Jesus knew the importance of both accomplishing the mission and caring for His team. He prioritized the mission to preach that the kingdom of heaven is near and guide people to the Father. Yet, He also ensured His disciples' needs were met. This balance is essential in leadership.

In the military, a leader's responsibility is to accomplish the mission and take care of their people. While the mission's priority is clear, the welfare of the team is equally crucial. A leader and a team exist to accomplish a mission, to reach objectives. Jesus demonstrated this balance perfectly. I'm sure the disciples ate well and rested after Jesus prayed over the five loaves and two fish.

**Effective leaders balance mission accomplishment
with caring for their team's well-being,
ensuring both objectives are met.**

<u>Application</u>: Do you effectively balance prioritizing mission accomplishment and the welfare of your team? There is no use for the team if they don't accomplish the mission, but there is also no chance of mission accomplishment without a healthy team. Sometimes we must make taking care of our team the mission that needs accomplished. Write down three tangible ways you can improve the welfare of your team.

BE STEADFAST *JA*

> "He saw the disciples straining at the oars, because
> the wind was against them. About the fourth
> watch of the night, He went out to them, walking
> on the lake. He was about to pass by them."
> —Mark 6:48

<u>Read</u>: Mark 6:45–56 "Jesus Walks on the Water"
After a long day of ministering and feeding over 5,000 men plus women and children, Jesus sends His disciples across the Sea of Galilee ahead of Him. He does this for two reasons: 1) He needs time alone to rest and pray, and 2) He is about to demonstrate His deity by walking on the water to meet them.

Despite witnessing the miracle of feeding the crowd with five loaves and two fish, the disciples do not understand its significance. Mark 6:52 tells us, "their hearts were hardened." Sensing their lack of faith and understanding, Jesus turns His compassion toward His own team. Amidst strong winds and rough waters, He walks across a large lake to reach them. When He climbs into the boat, the wind ceases.

At this moment, Jesus reminds His weary disciples of His divine strength. He reaffirms His power and capabilities, showing that He is more than a teacher—He is God, commanding His own creation.

When the team is weary and struggles to understand, leaders must remain strong. Leaders instill confidence through their actions, behavior, and conduct, providing reassurance and encouragement to their teams.

Leaders inspire confidence and perseverance by demonstrating strength and reassurance during their team's moments of doubt and weariness.

Application: How can you inspire your team when they are doubting and weary? We must ensure we have a good routine to take care of ourselves—physically, mentally, spiritually, and emotionally. Reflect on your routine. Do you even have one? Commit to your own rest and rejuvenation so that you may be steadfast in inspiring your team when they are weary.

DEFINING LEADERSHIP *JA*

"Nothing outside a man can make him 'unclean' by going into him. Rather, it is what comes out of a man that makes him 'unclean.'"

—Mark 7:15

Read: Mark 7:1–23 "Clean and Unclean"
Jesus performed numerous miracles—healing the sick, raising the dead, feeding over 5,000 people with five loaves and two fish, walking on water, and calming storms. Despite these astonishing acts, the Pharisees confronted Him with, "Hey teacher, Your disciples don't wash their hands before they eat." Jesus responded by

calling them "hypocrites" (Mark 7:6), highlighting their misguided priorities.

Jesus explained how their thinking was upside down concerning Old Testament laws and practices. He criticized them for nullifying God's word with their traditions. In verses 15 and 20, He emphasized that it is not what enters a person that makes them 'unclean,' but what comes out of them.

We must guard our hearts from evil influences and protect ourselves from harm. However, it is not the exposure to unclean things that defiles us, rather, it is how those influences manifest in our actions and conduct.

Similarly, it is not our resumes, leadership training, or preparation that make us effective leaders. These elements contribute to our capability but do not define our leadership. Our words and actions shape us as leaders. Leadership is an abstract concept until we apply it in real situations.

Our leadership is defined not by external qualifications or appearances, but by the integrity of our actions and words in real situations.

<u>Application</u>: Consider how you have leveraged your resume or reputation to promote yourself as a good leader. I know I have. Red Letter Leadership believes that leadership is a daily effort. Regardless of what our "qualifications" are, we can fail or succeed at leading each day. Commit today to being held accountable to your words and deeds in how you handle current leadership challenges more than relying on your resume or reputation.

TESTING YOUR TEAM *JA*

"Then He told her, 'For such a reply, you may go; the demon has left your daughter.'"

–Mark 7:29

Read: Mark 7:24–30 "The Faith of a Syrophoenician Woman"
Jesus travels to the town of Tyre, present-day Lebanon, and encounters a Greek woman born in Syrian Phoenicia. Despite being a foreigner to God's chosen people, she bravely seeks out Jesus and begs Him to drive a demon out of her daughter. Jesus challenges her request by comparing her ethnicity to dogs eating bread from the table of the Jews.

Even after this seemingly insulting remark, she responds by calling Him "Lord" and acknowledging that even the "crumbs" from His table would suffice. Jesus sees her faith and immense humility and immediately speaks hope to her and healing to her daughter.

James 1:3 tells us that "the testing of your faith develops perseverance." Jesus tested this woman's faith, and she persevered for her daughter's healing. Instead of reacting with anger, she showed resilience, believing that Jesus could heal her daughter. Her perseverance was met with Jesus' miraculous healing power.

Testing produces perseverance, resilience, and growth. As leaders, we should invite tests and challenges and even distribute them to our teams. This helps identify who is reliable, dependable, and trustworthy. Just as Jesus rewarded the woman's perseverance with healing, leaders should be prepared to reward their team's resilience to foster growth and strength.

> **Leaders should embrace challenges and tests, using them to build resilience and identify dependable team members, rewarding perseverance to foster growth and strength.**

Application: How do you test your team? Jesus often assesses behavior, which includes verbal communication. Write down three specific ways you can test your team—not for the purpose of passing judgment but for growing them through their perseverance. We don't always want to induce friction but when we have the opportunity and the environment is a safe place to do so, inducing friction on our team can test how they respond and persevere.

BE PERSONAL *JA*

> "After He took him aside, away from the crowd,
> Jesus put His fingers into the man's ears. Then
> He spit and touched the man's tongue."
> –Mark 7:33

Read: Mark 7:31–37 "The Healing of a Deaf and Mute Man"
Jesus travels from Tyre to the region of the Decapolis near the Sea of Galilee, where people bring Him a deaf and mute man. Prior to this, Mark had not recorded any healings of the deaf or mute. After this healing, the people's amazement grows, seeing that there seems to be no limit to Jesus' miraculous power.

In the previous passages, Jesus heals and then commands those who witnessed the healing to tell no one. Most of His healings were done away from the crowd, with only a few witnesses present.

This contrasts with modern-day healers who perform in front of large crowds and on national television. Jesus often moved away from the crowds to perform miracles. Why? Because He was real and personal, and His actions were never about Himself; they were about the person receiving His healing.

The crowd brought this deaf and mute man to Jesus, who then immediately removes him from the crowd. Jesus is personal. He seeks an intimate relationship with each of us. He doesn't bring healing before establishing a personal connection. John C. Maxwell, the renowned #1 authority on leadership in the world, stated, "We must love before we can lead."[13] Leading requires relationships, and relationships require a personal connection.

Effective leadership is rooted in love through genuine relationships, as leaders must connect personally and authentically to inspire and guide others.

Application: Reflect on how personal you are with those you lead. Do you meet with those you lead on a regular one-on-one basis? Consider today what steps you can take to improve personal connections with those on your team.

COMPASSIONATE LEADERSHIP *BH*

> "Since they had nothing to eat, Jesus called His disciples to Him and said, 'I have compassion for these people, they have already been with Me three days and have nothing to eat. If I send them home hungry, they will collapse on the way, because some of them have come a long distance.'"
>
> —Mark 8:1–3

Read: Mark 8:1–13 "Jesus Feeds the Four Thousand"
Jesus had been traveling and teaching, with crowds of thousands of people following Him to listen to His every word. While Jesus was hyper-focused on His vision and mission, He was always able to show love and compassion. In this story, Jesus had a clear understanding that His followers had sacrificed food and days of travel to follow Him. As a leader, Jesus knew He had to ensure His followers were loved and taken care of. Jesus understood their needs and made sure He provided for them.

Like Jesus, as leaders, we must understand the importance of loving and taking care of our team. If you understand your people, you will know their needs. If you understand their needs, you can take care of your people. If you take care of your people, they will take care of you.

Jesus is the perfect example of a compassionate leader. Being a compassionate leader helps you understand the needs of your team. Your team will perform at their best when they feel understood and know that their interests are being seen and cared for.

**Loving those who work for us is essential; it
builds trust, fosters a supportive environment,
and encourages mutual respect.**

Application: Are you someone that feels compassion toward your team is a sign of weakness? Consider changing that thinking. Your team wants to know that you care more about them than you do about their effectiveness. Show compassion toward them and your will grow their effectiveness.

BE VIGILANT BH

*"'Be careful,' Jesus warned them. 'Watch out for
the yeast of the Pharisees and that of Herod.'"*

—Mark 8:15

Read: Mark 8:14–21 "The Yeast of the Pharisees and Herod"
We see the metaphor for yeast used throughout the Bible. Jesus specifically uses the example of yeast to describe both good and bad influences. Jesus describes yeast as a symbol for building and growing the kingdom of heaven. However, in this instance, Jesus uses the metaphor of yeast in a negative way. Jesus tells us, "Be careful" (a clear warning) to be vigilant of the negative characteristics (yeast) "of the Pharisees and that of Herod" that have developed in them, creating character flaws.

As a young leader, some of the best lessons I learned were from observing the negative characteristics of leaders I had the opportunity to observe. Jesus provides this same situation to His disciples. Jesus tells them to observe the negative traits of some of the other leaders of those times and to avoid falling into those bad characteristics as leaders.

The Pharisees were religious leaders who exhibited self-righteousness and hypocrisy. Herod was a political leader who allowed the corruption of power and lack of empathy to grow in him. Like yeast, good or evil can grow inside leaders. As Jesus says, we must be vigilant and observe the negative character of other leaders to ensure we don't become like them.

Be vigilant and observe other leaders to learn from both the good and the bad characteristics.

Application: It is wise to learn from our failures as leaders. It is wiser to learn from the failures of other leaders and commit to not making the same mistake. Remain in God's word and surround yourself with great leaders so that you will be able to discern poor leadership.

UNDERSTAND THE ENVIRONMENT BH

> "He took the blind man by the hand and led him outside the village. When He had spit on the man's eyes and put His hands on him, Jesus asked, 'Do you see anything?' He looked up and said, 'I see people; they look like trees walking around.' Once more Jesus put His hands on the man's eyes. Then his eyes were opened, his sight was restored, and he saw everything clearly. Jesus sent him home, saying, 'Don't even go into the village.'"
> —Mark 8:23–26

Read: Mark 8:22–26 "The Healing of a Blind Man at Bethsaida"
In this story, Jesus performs a remarkable miracle by healing a blind man. While Jesus performs many different miracles throughout His time on earth, what makes this specific miracle unique is the fact that He takes the man outside of the village first. Jesus takes the blind man by the hand and leads him out of his current environment. Once Jesus has him out of the village, then He heals him.

In the previous miracles, Jesus heals people in front of others, but here He takes the person away from others. As Lord, we trust Jesus knew everything. Jesus knew that the village was not the right environment to perform His work (the miracle). Maybe there were people in the village that He didn't want to witness the miracle, or maybe He simply didn't seek recognition for His work. Jesus was often very personal with the people He healed. Jesus knew the village was not the right environment for the blind man, and so pulled Him out of it and directed Him to not return. Often when Jesus heals people, He tells them they are healed because of their faith. I believe Jesus knew the village was not the right environment for the blind man to believe and thrive. Jesus knew He needed to place the blind man in the right environment to not only be healed but also to continue on a path of faith and belief. As leaders, when a positive change happens in the life of a member of our team, we must consider that they may need help and led to a new environment from which to thrive.

Understand the environment and ensure your people are positioned in an environment where they can use their own unique design and strengths to serve the mission of the team.

<u>Application</u>: Our greatest limitation is ourselves, not our environment. However, when we remove ourselves from one environment to another, we can gain a fresh perspective and stimulate innovation and productivity. This may empower us to serve the mission better in the original environment. Reflect and journal how you can understand and help your team to understand your environment.

COMMUNICATION IS KEY *BH*

"On the way He asked them, 'Who do people say I am?' They replied, 'Some say John the Baptist; others

> say Elijah; and still others, one of the prophets.'
> **'But what about you?'** He asked. **'Who do you say I am?'** Peter answered, 'You are the Messiah.'"
>
> —Mark 8:27–29

<u>Read</u>: Mark 8:27–30 "Peter's Confession of Christ"

While we know Jesus is all-knowing and already knew what people were saying about who He was, the fact that Jesus confronts His disciples and communicates with them in this way provides a valuable leadership lesson. Even though Jesus knew the answer, He understood the importance of communicating with His disciples. Jesus sets an example of clear and concise communication. He also demonstrates the importance of not shying away from confronting our team to ask them the hard questions.

As leaders, we must have the courage to communicate openly with our team, even when it involves uncomfortable conversations. What if Peter had told Jesus, "I don't know who you are," or "I don't know what to believe?" Would you, as a leader, be able to handle rejection when asking the hard questions? Does your team feel comfortable enough to provide honest feedback?

Effective communication first requires a relational connection. Connection requires the humility of the leader. Jesus connected with His team long before He asked the tough questions.

As the perfect leader, Jesus understood the significance of good communication, being approachable, and asking the tough questions to gauge the commitment of His team.

First, evaluate the connection you have with your teammates. Then, reflect if you are approachable and if your team feels comfortable being honest with you.

<u>Application</u>: How do you handle rejection when asking hard questions? Does your team feel comfortable enough to provide honest feedback? Evaluate your connection with your team today

and commit to clearer communication so that you and your team do not operate on misplaced assumptions.

THE BIGGER PICTURE *BH*

> "He spoke plainly about this, and Peter took Him aside and began to rebuke Him. But when Jesus turned and looked at His disciples, He rebuked Peter. 'Get behind Me, Satan!' He said. 'You do not have in mind the concerns of God, but merely human concerns.'"
>
> —Mark 8:32–33

Read: Mark 8:31—9:1 "Jesus Predicts His Death"

In this story, Jesus is explaining to His disciples the vision and plan of action. He is revealing to them that He will need to suffer, be rejected, be killed, and three days later rise again. This is not what the disciples wanted to hear, nor was it the plan His team wanted to follow through with. While this revelation is spiritually significant for Jesus to predict His death and resurrection, there are also crucial leadership lessons Jesus imparts to us.

Jesus' followers didn't fully believe in His vision and even went as far as to "rebuke" Him. His disciples didn't grasp the bigger picture or understand Jesus' purpose on earth. As leaders, we can find ourselves in similar circumstances. Often, our team members don't have the opportunity to see the things that we see or understand the bigger picture. It is our responsibility as leaders to share the vision of the organization, but we must be prepared for the possibility that the team may not fully understand the "why." Remember that your team doesn't have the same perspective as you, and they may reject your plan or vision because of this. Jesus had the long game in mind, but His disciples didn't share the same perspective as their leader.

Your team will not always believe in your vision, but it is your responsibility as the leader to teach, coach, and inspire your team to see the bigger picture and understand your vision.

Application: Do you clearly convey the bigger picture with your team? Consider the environment you work in and the circumstances surrounding your team's mission today. Is everyone on the same page as to what the bigger picture is? If not, make a committed plan to ensure everyone understands the 'why' and where it exists in the big picture.

LEGITIMIZE YOUR LEADERSHIP WITH ACTION *BH*

"After six days Jesus took Peter, James and John with Him and led them up a high mountain, where they were all alone. There He was transfigured before them. His clothes became dazzling white, whiter than anyone in the world could bleach them. And there appeared before them Elijah and Moses, who were talking with Jesus."
—Mark 9:2–4

Read: Mark 9:2–13 "The Transfiguration"
As we have learned in previous lessons, Jesus faced challenges with His disciples fully embracing the vision of His mission on earth. In the previous lesson, we discussed how His disciples rejected His plan of being killed and rising again in three days. It's evident that His disciples lacked understanding of the bigger picture. In this lesson, we learn that Jesus took a select few of His disciples up on a mountain where He was transformed into a heavenly vision alongside Elijah and Moses. At one point during the transfiguration, God

even spoke out loud to the disciples, saying, "This is my Son, whom I love. Listen to Him!"

Jesus knew His disciples were struggling to see the bigger picture and His true authority, so He brought particular ones (likely the ones He knew could influence the others) up to the mountain to witness the transfiguration alongside the prophets Elijah and Moses. His followers even heard God speak to them. I believe Jesus did this to help them understand His true authority and to believe in His vision and the plan He had shared with them.

As leaders, we have to provide our team with the opportunity to see us in action, so that they trust our vision and plan for the organization. When our followers see our legitimacy and understand our authority, they are more likely to embrace what we are trying to accomplish.

> **When your team struggles to accept your vision, legitimize your leadership with the most influential people on your team.**

Application: How do you use the influence of others to help influence your team to understand the bigger picture and accept your vision? Be humble and acknowledge where your influence may be limited. Write down a few people in your life who you'd like to influence and help see the bigger picture but who seem to be unaccepting of your influence. Consider how you can work your influence through others.

LEAD FROM THE FRONT *BH*

> *"'If You can'? said Jesus. 'Everything is possible for one who believes.'"*
>
> —Mark 9:23

Read: Mark 9:14–32 "The Healing of a Boy with an Evil Spirit"

In this story, Jesus clearly grows frustrated with His disciples and even the boy's father, who are all struggling to have faith and believe in Jesus. As we know from previous lessons, Jesus' disciples continue to struggle to understand His true authority and buy into His vision of saving the world through His death. Now, His disciples are struggling to perform miracles that Jesus has given them the authority to perform. As we see throughout the gospel and here with the boy's father, Jesus explains to those He is healing, that it comes down to faith in order to be healed.

As leaders, we can take away from Jesus that it is okay to become frustrated and to communicate your concerns with your team's lack of faith in what the organization is doing. We see in this story Jesus expressing His frustration by being very stern with His disciples, saying, "How long shall I put up with you?" (Mark 9:19). There may be times, as leaders, that we must be very direct and stern with our team to wake them up and get them motivated. Being stern or direct at times does not mean we do not love our team; it just shows our passion and concern for their performance. Lastly, Jesus ends up healing the boy from the evil spirit (something His disciples couldn't do). As leaders, we must ensure we are able to do the hard things that we ask our own team to do. In the military, we say, "Lead from the front and by example!" We must be willing and able to do anything we ask our team to do.

Be prepared to do anything you ask of your team and discern when it is appropriate to be stern and direct with them.

Application: Are you prepared to do anything that you ask of your team? Does your team believe this? Examine yourself and what you've asked of your team. Have you made the sacrifices you've asked them to make or more? Have you accomplished individual tasks that you are asking your team to do? Do you supervise from a position of desiring your team's success and not out of your own comfort and convenience? Reflect today on what leading from the front looks like for you.

MAKE YOURSELF THE VERY LEAST *JA*

> "Sitting down, Jesus called the Twelve and said, 'If anyone wants to be first, he must be the very last, and the servant of all.'"
>
> −Mark 9:35

Read: Mark 9:33–37 "Who Is the Greatest"
To teach His disciples about servant leadership, Jesus uses the illustration of a "little child." Taking the child in His arms, Jesus tells His disciples that whoever welcomes a child in His name welcomes Him and the One who sent Him. This teaching comes after the disciples had been arguing about who was the greatest among them. Jesus gathers them, explaining that the greatest must be the servant of all, and illustrates this with the example of a small, innocent child.

This passage is a clear demonstration of why Jesus is the quintessential servant leader and the best teacher of servant leadership. Servant leadership is not merely a style or form of leadership; it is the essence of true leadership. Leaders may need to give orders, exert authority, and make unpopular decisions, but they must never abandon their responsibility to serve those they lead. In challenging times, a leader's service to their team should be at its peak. Leaders must prioritize the welfare of their team above their own while exercising their authority.

Leadership is not position and privilege; it's service and sacrifice.

Application: How well do you serve your team? Do you make yourself the least and focus on crediting your team and exalting their accomplishments over your own? Write down three ways you can praise your team to outsiders without pointing toward your own efforts as the leader. Be specific and even praise people by name when appropriate.

EXPANDING INFLUENCE *JA*

"I tell you the truth, anyone who gives you a cup of water in My name because you belong to Christ will certainly not lose his reward."

—Mark 9:41

Read: Mark 9:38–41 "Whoever Is Not Against Us Is for Us"
The disciples rebuke a man for driving out demons in the name of Jesus because he was not part of their group. They likely believed they were the only ones with the authority to perform such acts. However, Jesus responds that they should not stop anyone from doing miracles in His name, as these individuals are advancing the kingdom of heaven. He further teaches that even the smallest acts of love and kindness shown to His followers, such as giving a cup of water, will be recognized by Him.

Jesus is instructing the Twelve not to isolate themselves or adopt an "us vs. them" mentality. This is a vital concept for leaders to instill in their teams. Teams should seek opportunities to collaborate and support those who are not directly opposing them. Additionally, leaders should cultivate a team culture that prioritizes taking the first step in showing love and kindness to others, and being grateful when such gestures are reciprocated.

Leaders do not restrict their team's influence, they expand it.

Application: Have you ever restricted your team's influence because you wanted to retain the success your team was having as their own? Rid yourself of that mentality today. Adopted a mentality to collaborate rather than compete. Write down three ways you can expand your team's influence.

PRESERVE GOOD *JA*

> "Salt is good, but if it loses its saltiness, how can you make it salty again? Have salt in yourselves and be at peace with each other."
>
> —Mark 9:50

Read: Mark 9:42–50 "Causing to Sin"

Jesus provides a stern warning about the gravity of our actions and their potential to lead others, especially new believers, into sin. He emphasizes that causing someone to sin is so serious that it would be better for us to be thrown into the sea than to be responsible for such an offense. Jesus insists that whatever is causing us to sin, or causing others to sin, must be cut off immediately, highlighting the severe consequences of sin and the necessity for ruthless accountability.

He teaches us to have "salt" in ourselves, meaning we should preserve what is good by remaining close to Him. He concludes by instructing us to "be at peace with each other" (Mark 9:50), emphasizing the importance of maintaining harmony and integrity within the community of believers.

Sin always stems from selfishness, where we fail to consider others or the broader impact of our actions. Recognizing our own sin is difficult enough but acknowledging that our words or deeds may lead others to sin requires even greater humility. It is crucial to examine ourselves and identify where our actions may have caused harm or led someone into sin. Reflect on your behavior today and consider where your words or deeds might have contributed to another's stumbling.

Leaders must recognize the severity of actions that lead others into sin and take immediate steps to eliminate the sources of such behavior.

Application: Do you accept that your actions as a leader are even more severe than those of your teammates? Leaders hold themselves to a higher standard and welcome others to hold them accountable. What steps are you taking today to be accountable?

THE MARRIAGE VOW *JA*

"But at the beginning of creation God 'made them male and female.' 'For this reason a man will leave his father and mother and be united to his wife, and the two will become one flesh.' So they are no longer two, but one."

—Mark 10:6–8

Read: Mark 10:1–12 "Divorce"

Today, our world is deeply confused about gender and sexual orientation. Jesus makes it clear, quoting Genesis 1:27 and 5:2, that God created mankind as 'male and female' (Mark 10:6). We cannot selectively believe parts of God's word and discard others that do not align with our personal agendas. Jesus further explains that God created them male and female to complement each other in marriage. A father is not complete in his son nor a mother in her daughter. When a son leaves his mother and father, and a daughter leaves her mother and father, they are to complete each other in marriage. This divine structure allows humanity to "be fruitful and increase in number" (Gen 1:28). Any deviation from this godly design is a sin and leads to destruction.

Churches and denominations are splitting over this fundamental concept, not because they misunderstand Jesus, but because they interpret God's word to fit their desires. Viewing God's word in this selfish manner means seeking it to serve our flesh rather than to transform our hearts. This selfish pursuit is often masked as unselfishness and virtuous, pretending to align with God's Holy standard of love.

Husbands must lead their wives in the commitment they have made. When the Pharisees questioned Jesus about divorce, they sought affirmation of their custom that allowed men to divorce their wives easily. Jesus corrects their misunderstanding, teaching that God forms the marital union, and neither man nor woman has the authority to dissolve it.

> **Divorce destroys. A man must lead his wife in the marriage commitment and leading means serving and sacrificing, not dominating.**

<u>Application</u>: Unfortunately, men who have little leadership intelligence think they need to lead their wives with their dominance. That couldn't be further from the truth and will ruin marriages. Do you know anyone like this? Husbands and wives must fulfill their roles according to God's word for both spouses to lead well.

A FREE GIFT *JA*

"I tell you the truth, anyone who will not receive the kingdom of God like a little child will never enter it."

—Mark 10:15

Read: Mark 10:13–16 "The Little Children and Jesus"
In verse 14, Jesus was "indignant" when His disciples rebuked people for bringing children to Him. The disciples likely thought Jesus' status and responsibilities made Him too important to engage with little children. However, Jesus immediately corrected this misconception, clearly stating that the kingdom of God belongs to such as these.

Jesus' statement that we must "receive the kingdom of God like a little child" or we "will never enter it" (Mark 10:15) highlights a profound spiritual truth. A child receives a gift from their parents without any notion of earning it—it is given unconditionally. The only requirement for the child is to accept it. Jesus uses this analogy to teach that we can do nothing to earn the kingdom of God; it is a gift bestowed upon us through the unconditional love of the Father, made possible by the sacrifice of His Son.

As leaders, we are called to serve those who are young in faith or age without expecting anything in return. This does not diminish the younger person's responsibility to respect their elders but rather mandates that we, who are mature in our faith, be approachable and willing to bless those who are younger. We should share our experiences and resources generously, fostering growth and understanding.

> **Mature leaders must be approachable and willing to invest in those who are younger in age or faith, providing guidance and support through shared experiences and resources.**

Application: If you consider yourself a mature leader, how do you invest in younger leaders? Consider being a mentor, teaching Sunday school (for adults or children), or serving in your community as a way to influence younger leaders and share your experiences.

"GOOD" IS NOT "GOOD" WITHOUT THE KING *JA*

> "Jesus looked at them and said, 'With man this is impossible, but not with God; all things are possible with God.'"
>
> —Mark 10:27

Read: Mark 10:17–31 "The Rich Young Man"
Jesus tests the willingness and devotion of a young rich man to follow Him. This young man was diligent in doing all the "good" things he knew to secure eternal life, but found that his efforts were insufficient. Despite obeying the commandments, he lived primarily to serve himself. When Jesus challenged him to sell his possessions, give to the poor, and follow Him, the man was unable to concede.

Our success can easily trap us into thinking we achieved it solely by our power and abilities. This mindset makes us more reluctant to follow Christ when He calls us away from our success in a different direction. What we often fail to realize, due to our lack of faith, is that Jesus wants to bless us with a far greater return on investment than we could manage for ourselves if only we will follow Him for the sake of the Gospel.

We tend to think in terms of what we understand, but faith requires us to think in terms we don't understand. When the disciples wondered who could be saved (Mark 10:26), Jesus replied that it is impossible for man to enter eternal life on their own accord, but not with God. Entering the kingdom of heaven is about a relationship with the kingdom's King.

When we have a relationship with the King, then and only then can we do good. If we don't have a relationship with the King, then we can only just do.

Application: Do you think you can do "good" without Christ? I'd argue that you can't. To be truly good, it must originate from what is truly good and God is the only source of what is truly good. Adopt this mindset of what defines "good" today and commit to leading others to do good.

AMID TERRIBLE EXPERIENCES, LEAD *JA*

> *"'We are going up to Jerusalem,' He said, 'and the Son of Man will be betrayed to the chief priests and teachers of the law. They will condemn Him to death and will hand Him over to the Gentiles, who will mock Him and spit on Him, flog Him and kill Him. Three days later He will rise.'"*
>
> *—Mark 10:33–34*

Read: Mark 10:32–34 "Jesus Again Predicts His Death"

Jesus once again predicts His death, pulling the twelve disciples aside to explain what will happen in Jerusalem. He is preparing His disciples for the difficult and uncomfortable situation ahead.

How do you prepare your team for an upcoming difficult and uncomfortable situation? James 1 tells us that we will all face trials and temptations of many kinds. Often, we might think that such terrible things shouldn't happen to followers of Christ. Certainly, Peter thought this the first time Jesus predicted His death, and Jesus sternly rebuked him by even calling him "Satan" (Mark 8:31–38).

We live in a fallen world and must constantly anticipate and prepare ourselves and our teams for trials to come. One of John Maxwell's *15 Invaluable Laws of Growth* is the Law of Pain, which states, "Good management of bad experiences leads to great growth."[7] Jesus was preparing His team for a very bad experience so that they would be prepared to manage the situation well. And did they? Not at first, but when they saw their risen Savior, they built the Church.

War provides a forum where leaders rise who handle great trials and terrible experiences well. One great example came from the battle for Tarawa in 1943. Tarawa is a small atoll in the Pacific and was heavily defended by the Japanese when the Marines landed. So fiercely defended that one Japanese commander stated that it would take one million men one hundred years to take Tarawa. The 2d Marine Regiment secured it in 72 hours. The commander of that regiment sent a short report during the battle which demonstrates a leader who is handling a terrible situation well, with a positive attitude. Colonel David Shoup reported to his higher headquarters on November 21, 1943, "Casualties many; Percentage of dead not known; Combat efficiency; we are winning." Short, clear, concise communication to report that the situation is terrible, but that the team is moving forward to secure the objective. And Americans continue to live in freedom because of leaders who managed terrible situations well.

Reinforce the importance of resilience and perseverance, helping your team see beyond immediate difficulties to the greater purpose and potential growth that can follow.

Application: How have you handled bad experiences lately? Leaders must pause in the chaotic, uncertain, and uncomfortable situations. They must not be overwhelmed. Preparing in advance for bad experiences is the best way to be confident that you will handle them well. Leaders owe that to their teams. Reflect on how you handled your last bad experience. Write down what you could have done differently to manage and even lead through it well.

ATTAINING GREATNESS JA

"'We can,' they answered. Jesus said to them, 'You will drink the cup I drink and be baptized with the baptism I am baptized with, but to sit at My right

> or left is not for Me to grant. These places belong to those for whom they have been prepared.'"
> –Mark 10:39–40

Read: Mark 10:35–45 "The Request of James and John"
James and John must have misunderstood Jesus' point from earlier when He used a little child to illustrate that whoever "wants to be first must be the very last, and the servant of all" (Mark 9:35). In Matthew's account, it is not James and John who request to sit at Jesus' right and left, but their mother who makes the request on their behalf. Jesus used this opportunity to reiterate what it means to serve as a leader. Earlier, He used a child to illustrate this concept, and later, at The Last Supper, He will wash the disciples' feet to emphasize the point before giving Himself up for the sins of the world.

Our key verse here is not merely to remind us that we must be "slave to all," or that if we want to be great, we must first be a servant (Mark 10:43–44). Instead, it emphasizes that when we act as servant-leaders, we should not automatically expect greatness in the form of wealth, status, or promotion. When Jesus asked James and John if they could drink from the cup He drinks, they answered, "We can," and Jesus affirmed that they would (Mark 10:39). But then Jesus pointed out that it is not for Him to grant such positions as sitting at His right or left, as those "places belong to those for whom they have been prepared" (Mark 10:40). These positions are already assigned and do not define true greatness.

Our sin of pride has diluted what "greatness" in Jesus' eyes really means. As did His disciples; we think greatness equates to wealth, status, or holding a position of significant authority over others. Those things are not "greatness." They are gifts from God to be stewarded appropriately by the one to whom they are given. We attain greatness in God's eyes when we love, serve, and sacrifice with the gifts He has given us.

We are great when we use God's gifts to serve others. When we are great, we advance the kingdom of God.

<u>Application</u>: Do you agree that greatness can only be achieved in the spiritual realm? Many of Jesus' words throughout the Gospels allude to this fact. When we make ourselves the least, when we put others before us, when we trade the things of this world for the things of God, that is when we become great. How can you put others before yourself today? Do you want to be great and especially, a great leader? Then set your own dreams and ambitions aside for God's will in your life.

NEVER GIVE UP *JA*

> "Many rebuked him and told him to be quiet, but he shouted all the more, 'Son of David, have mercy on me!' Jesus stopped and said, 'Call him.'"
> —Mark 10:48–49

<u>Read</u>: Mark 10:46–52 "Blind Bartimaeus Receives His Sight"
On other occasions, Jesus healed a blind man by spitting in his eyes and placing His hands on them, and another by placing mud on the man's eyes and telling him to wash in a local pool. In this instance, Jesus tells the man that his faith has healed him. Nothing more was required on Jesus' part; the man's faith in who Jesus is healed him. In the other instances, Jesus' contact with the blind men were chance meetings (see, Mark 8:22–26 and John 9). But in this passage, it is the blind man who initiates his pursuit of Jesus.

Although he was told to "be quiet...he shouted all the more" (Mark 10:48). This blind man believed what he heard about Jesus. Many people during Jesus' day saw yet did not believe. Many today see God's hand and yet do not believe. This blind man never witnessed a miracle of God until one was performed on him.

The prophet Jeremiah, speaking on behalf of God, writes in Jeremiah 29:13, "You will seek me and find me when you seek me with all your heart." When the crowds rebuked this blind man, he shouted louder and sought Jesus harder.

Never give up on the great potential God has placed inside of you and never give in to those who say you can't.

Application: Do you give up easily when the naysayers tell you to be quiet? Do you quit when the going gets tough and a little uncomfortable? Do you run away from uncertainty because you worry too much rather than embrace it and create your own opportunities with the potential God has given you? Commit to persevering through the trials today and creating opportunities where God has directed you.

DO GOOD WITH CONFIDENCE *JA*

> "Blessed is the coming kingdom of our father David! Hosanna in the highest!"
>
> —Mark 11:10

Read: Mark 11:1–11 "The Triumphal Entry"
Jesus knew that riding a colt into Jerusalem from the Mount of Olives would be a symbolic claim to the throne of David, declaring Himself the Messiah (see, Zech 9:9). He also understood that this peaceful act would provoke the religious leaders in Jerusalem, who would then want Him dead for making such a claim. By the end of the week, the same crowd that hailed Him as the Messiah would be calling for His crucifixion.

Do we hold back from doing good because we fear how people will react or how it might make us look? In this fallen world, what is good will sometimes be confrontational. We must not provoke for the sake of provoking, but we also must not avoid doing what is right to sidestep confrontation.

Jesus' disciples knew who He was, even though one of them would betray Him later in the week. As a leader, Jesus connected with the Twelve, coaching and mentoring them into a team of men who would build the Church after His ascension.

We shouldn't be concerned with those who oppose the good we do when our team is confident and steadfast under our leadership.

Application: Reflect on a time when you were doing God's work and knew it was good. Did you face any opposition? Write down what the opposition was and how you handled it. How could you have handled it better? Did it affect your leadership and how you interacted with your team? Consider how you will respond next time you face opposition when walking in God's will. Choose to respond with love, grace, and humility, but be steadfast in doing good.

DEFY EVIL JA

"The chief priests and the teachers of the law heard this and began looking for a way to kill Him, for they feared Him, because the whole crowd was amazed at His teaching."
—Mark 11:18

Read: Mark 11:12–19 "Jesus Clears the Temple"
After entering Jerusalem as the Messiah, the previous day, Jesus and His disciples left the city and spent the night in Bethany. His reentry into Jerusalem was less ceremonious than the day before. Feeling hungry and seeing a fig tree with no fruit, as it was not in season, Jesus cursed it, and it withered. He then reached the temple courts and cleared out the money changers and merchants.

Why was the crowd amazed at this? I believe it was due to His boldness in defying a long-established, money-making practice. People were using the Law of Moses, given by God, to make money. It was a lucrative market: if everyone is a sinner, and you can profit from people seeking forgiveness, there's always demand. Jesus wasn't having it. The temple was not meant to profit from the people; rather, the people were supposed to give their tithe to the temple from their first fruits in obedience to God (see, Mal 3:6–18).

While the people feared the power and judgment of the chief priests and the teachers of the law, Jesus did not. He was not afraid of what mortal men could do to Him (Ps 56:3–4), because His kingdom is not of this world. There is a time for tact, a time to rationalize, and a time to debate. But there is also a time to be bold and take action to defy evil.

One quote that stirred my heart to a life in special operations was by an 18th Century English politician named Edmund Burke. He said, "The only thing necessary for the triumph of evil is for a good man to do nothing." If you are covered by the blood of Jesus, you are good. Do something.

> **Leaders must be bold. They must stand in the gap against evil. God has given each of us strengths for such a time.**

<u>Application</u>: It is imperative that leaders boldly defy evil. This doesn't mean treating someone who has sinned as less than us, but it does mean treating sin as sin and acknowledging that Satan is public enemy #1. He is the true enemy. Where in your life, workplace, or community, do you need to boldly address evil? Write down what may oppose the advancement of God's kingdom within the different environments you live. Then pray for guidance and make a plan to address the opposition appropriately.

DECLARE IT *JA*

"Therefore I tell you, whatever you ask for in prayer, believe that you have received it, and it will be yours. And when you stand praying, if you hold anything against anyone, forgive him, so that your Father in heaven may forgive you your sins."

—Mark 11:24–25

Read: Mark 11:20–26 "The Withered Fig Tree"
Jesus again displays His authority over creation when He curses the fig tree, and it immediately withers. Peter was amazed. Jesus responded to Peter's amazement by telling him that he has the same authority through faith in God.

I wondered why Jesus cursed the fig tree for not producing fruit when He was hungry. Mark even records that it was not the season for the tree to produce figs. It seems kind of humorous and ironic. Jesus condemns His own creation for doing what He created it to do in the first place. I think the reason behind Jesus' curse is so that He could make this point to Peter and the disciples: "Whatever you ask for in prayer, believe that you have received it, and it will be yours" (Mark 11:24).

Some who know me best are aware of my hidden talent for being able to sleep while driving. Unfortunately, when I do, my talent for driving diminishes rapidly. When I would leave home after visiting for a few days, my dad would always cover my trip in prayer. It is nothing short of a miracle that I haven't had worse accidents.

A month ago, my wife mentioned that she wanted new living room furniture. The furniture we had was uncomfortable, but I said, "We're not getting new furniture until we move." Well, she prayed one Friday in early May that God would bless us with furniture. The next day, she found a couch and loveseat on Facebook, both with reclining seats, advertised as "free." We thought, "What's the catch?" Well, the next day, we drove 10 minutes to pick them up, and there was no catch. It's the best living room furniture we've owned, even better than the brand-new set we bought 12 years ago.

I could go on, and you may think I must not lack faith, but I certainly do. Though I have no excuse for a lack of faith, I'm a wretched sinner who too often turns toward Satan's lies instead of God's promises. This passage is a promise of God: believe it, declare it, and have it.

> **Leaders do not worry about what tomorrow will bring. They declare it and move forward as if they already have it.**

<u>Application</u>: Where do you need God's hand in your life? Do you need to declare His providence for His move within your team? Or maybe you just want God to show up and put a smile on your face reminding you that He is here. He'll do that, and it is a great joy when He does. Take your requests to Him and declare them in Jesus' name.

NO RESPONSE NECESSARY JA

> "So they answered Jesus, 'We don't know.'
> Jesus said, 'Neither will I tell you by what authority I am doing these things.'"
>
> Mark 11:33

<u>Read</u>: Mark 11:27–33 "The Authority of Jesus Questioned"
The chief priests, the teachers of the law, and the elders found themselves in a difficult position when trying to answer Jesus' questions because they had put themselves there. They did so by living lives devoid of integrity and faith. Jesus had just finished telling His disciples that they could ask for whatever they wanted, and it would be given to them. However, when they arrived in the

temple courts, Jesus wouldn't even give the chief priests and other religious leaders the simple answer they asked for. Instead, He tested their integrity.

For most of the three years of Jesus' ministry, religious leaders throughout the region tried to trap Him. Now, Jesus was the one trapping them. He knew their hearts were hardened because they wanted to retain their power and control over the populace. In this brief interaction, Jesus showed them that they had no power or control over Him, and it enraged them.

We do not always owe people an answer. You will get nowhere with someone whose heart is hardened to what you will say. In these situations, deescalate the conversation by refraining from feeding it. Jesus knew that the religious leaders rejected Him, His example, and His mission. He prioritized His time, spending it with those who accepted His leadership, not those who rejected it.

Do not waste your words and time on those who do not care what you have to say.

Application: It would be arrogant to think that we are always the ones with some truth to speak and it is everyone else who is hardened to hear it. Examine yourself first. How might you be hardened to hearing truth from others? Ask God to soften your heart to hear and be open to His truth regardless of who He speaks through. Also ask God for discernment for when it is best for you to refrain from answering someone who is only seeking to argue.

DROP YOUR PRIDE *JA*

"He had one left to send, a son, whom he loved. He sent him last of all, saying, 'They will respect my son.'"

—Mark 12:6

Read: Mark 12:1–12 "The Parable of the Tenants"
Following Jesus' refusal to answer the chief priests and teachers of the law in the previous passage, He begins to speak to them in a parable. Despite their hardened hearts and lack of conviction, the religious leaders realize that the parable is about them and start planning how to arrest Him.

In this parable, Jesus is the last prophet sent to the Jews and represents the son of the owner of the vineyard. The religious leaders understand that He is speaking against them, yet they are too stubborn to humble themselves to Jesus' message. What prevents them from receiving Jesus' message? I believe it is the simple sin of pride, which leads us to crave power, wealth, and control over others.

It is often easy for us to become prideful as we accumulate more possessions, achieve more accomplishments, and gain more control. In such times, it may seem ridiculous to humble ourselves before someone with less power, wealth, and control. However, as leaders, this humility is, may be, exactly what we need.

Leaders must take full responsibility while empowering their teams. By relinquishing centralized control and decentralizing it to the team a healthier culture emerges, the team and its members experience greater growth, and the mission is accomplished with higher proficiency. The team's failures are the leader's failures, and their successes are the team's successes, which the leaders should acknowledge. A leader's success is ultimately a byproduct of their team's success.

Relinquish your pride and take full responsibility for the failures of your team.

Application: Do you take full responsibility for the failures of your team? Or does your pride stand in your way causing you to ask, 'why should I take responsibility for something a member of my team did?' If this is you, I challenge you to ask yourself what you, as the leader, could have done better to empower your team, set them up for success, coach or mentor them, etc. We must hold our teammates accountable, but we must first hold ourselves accountable for what we could have done better. Drop your pride.

SLAVES TO GOD *JA*

> "Then Jesus said to them, 'Give to Caesar what is Caesar's and to God what is God's.'"
>
> —Mark 12:17

<u>Read</u>: Mark 12:13–17 "Paying Taxes to Caesar"

So, what is God's? "The earth is the LORD's and everything in it; the world, and all who live in it" (Ps 24:1). What Caesar demands is God's, what God demands is God's, and what we keep is God's. A rather simple formula: nothing belongs to us nor any governing agency. It is all God's.

In verse 13, we read that some of the Pharisees and Herodians were sent to try to catch Jesus in His words. These groups consisted of Jewish religious leaders (Pharisees) and Jews who supported Roman rule (Herodians). Their goal was to trap Jesus into saying that the people shouldn't pay taxes to Caesar, thereby giving them grounds to accuse Him of inciting unrest against the governing authorities.

How does Jesus handle their trap? With the truth of God's word. We are to submit to both governing authorities and God's authority. Caesar demands people pay taxes. God demands much more—He demands our hearts. When we give our hearts to God, the rest of our being follows. Our strength, minds, spirits, time, talents, and resources all follow. However, submitting our hearts to Him is a daily, hourly, and sometimes even minute-to-minute intentional effort.

I heard this sobering thought from a friend. "I often want to get my 'orders' from God and then go off and operate alone, reporting back when the mission is complete, or I need resources. Clearly that isn't what a righteous man like Job was up to. Staying in communion with God and staying with God while He sets the path and pace (Job 23:11, 14)—those are the ways of a righteous leader." God wants all of us, all the time.

Though nobody likes to pay taxes, we all benefit from public resources. Similarly, we all benefit when we give our hearts to God. Our relationships benefit, our finances benefit, our time management benefits, our productivity benefits—our life becomes more fulfilled, and we achieve God's promise of an abundant life. Leaders set this example in their personal lifestyles with their money and resources, with the decisions they make, in their character, and in many other ways. As God lightens our load, we should replicate Him and help lighten the load of others.

Lead by lightening the load for others—take on your team's burdens so they can succeed in the mission.

Application: Do you commit all of yourself to God—your full physical, mental, emotional, and spiritual being? When we do, it is freeing, and we increase the effectiveness of our purpose. In the same way, as a leader, do you offer to take some of the burden your teammates face? Write down three ways that you can better commit aspects of your life to God and three opportunities you have to take some burdens off your teammates. It may be something as simple as doing the dishes or laundry for your spouse.

HE IS THE GOD OF THE LIVING *EA*

"Now about the dead rising—have you not read in the Book of Moses, in the account of the burning

> bush, how God said to him, 'I am the God of Abraham, the God of Isaac, and the God of Jacob'?"
>
> —Mark 12:26

Read: Mark 12:18–27 "Marriage at the Resurrection"

The Sadducees challenge Jesus with a complex question about marriage in the resurrection, attempting to trap Him. As usual, Jesus rebukes their trappings and provides a wise lesson on who God is while offering invaluable insights into Old Testament teachings.

This passage serves as a powerful reminder that we are the bride of Christ. In life, we often encounter self-help advice suggesting that to achieve a happy, healthy marriage we should 'put our spouses first.' However, the flaw in this approach is that, as imperfect beings, we are likely to disappoint each other. In _contrast, if we keep Christ at the center of our marriage and strive to follow His design for us, we will naturally grow closer as a couple.

Consider the Carry the Load foundation, a veterans' charity that supports and honors fallen servicemembers. During 'Memorial May,' participants walk from five different locations across the country, covering over 20,000 miles and 48 states, converging in Dallas, Texas, on Memorial Day. Applying this analogy to marriage, just as Dallas is the destination for Carry the Load, a Christ-centered life should be our daily goal. As a husband and wife who start from different places at the beginning of their marriage, if both walk toward the same goal—a Christ-centered life—they will inevitably draw closer to one another. Conversely, if they focus solely on walking toward each other and not toward Christ, they risk moving further away from Him as their central focus.

Maintaining a central, unifying goal (like Christ in marriage) helps align and strengthen collective efforts toward a common purpose.

Application: Does your team have a clear, unifying goal? Does everyone on the team understand and take ownership of the team's common purpose? Consider how you can be clearer with your team about its common purpose. If your team (whether family, work, or community) does not have a common purpose, write down a plan to establish one with input from your team and ensure everyone is communicating clearly, openly, and honestly.

MISSION-TYPE ORDERS EA

> "'Love the Lord your God with all your heart and with all your soul and with all your mind and with all your strength.' The second is this: 'Love your neighbor as yourself.' There is no commandment greater than these."
>
> —Mark 12:30–31

Read: Mark 12:28–35 "The Greatest Commandment"
Jesus is asked to identify the most important commandment. His response is profound and succinct, summarizing all Ten Commandments and the entire Jewish Law into two commands: to love God completely (Commandments 1–4) and to love others as oneself (Commandments 5–10).

In the Marine Corps, we often discuss 'mission tactics' and 'mission-type orders.' Marine Corps Doctrinal Publication 1 describes this as the tactics of assigning a subordinate a mission without specifying how it must be accomplished. Similarly, Jesus provides His 'mission tactics' by condensing the Ten Commandments into two core directives: Love God (Commandments 1–4) and Love People (Commandments 5–10). Jesus begins to reveal to the Jewish people that their traditional laws are no longer required in the same way, as He has come to fulfill and replace The Law. While the Ten Commandments remain applicable, Jesus is teaching them to understand the Law differently, focusing on the principles of love rather than the letter of the law.

In application, we can take Jesus' mission-type orders to love God, love people, and use it in our daily walk. If we love God and lead with the compassion and ideals He has imbued in us through the Holy Spirit, we only stand to exemplify that love and compassion for those we lead, which is exactly what a Christ-centered leadership approach should look like.

> **Simplifying complex directives into clear, mission-focused principles can guide teams effectively, as demonstrated by Jesus' concise summary of the commandments.**

<u>Application</u>: Once your team has a common purpose, a unifying goal, like we discussed in the previous lesson, then it is up to you as the leader to issue clear "mission-type" orders. If the Bible was a two-page book that gave a clear description of God, a clear description of the troubles we will face with other people, and then the commands to 'love God' and 'love other people,' would that change how we are supposed to serve God? No. But by the grace of God, He gives us over 1500 years of knowing Him and learning about human behavior and then gives us the Holy Spirit to continue our learning and understanding. His orders are simple. So should ours be with our team. How can you simplify the directives you give to your team so that they are empowered to accomplish any task?

BEWARE OF THE 'TEACHERS OF THE LAW' *EA*

"As He taught, Jesus said, 'Watch out for the teachers of the law. They like to walk around in flowing robes and be greeted with respect in the marketplaces...'"

—Mark 12:38

Read: Mark 12:35–40 "Whose Son Is the Christ"

Jesus warns His followers to beware of the ill intentions of some high leaders of the Jewish faith. He highlights how these leaders are disingenuous to their faith, acting in their own best interests, seeking money and accolades, and exploiting widows under the guise of piety.

Do the actions of these scribes remind you of anyone? Do they ever remind you of yourself? Much like the lesson Jesus is teaching here, it is imperative that we remain grounded as organizational leaders. When in charge of a team, it is incredibly easy to let power and influence go to our heads. When this happens, it can lead to corruption, arrogance, servitude, a toxic work environment, and other undesirable and unproductive outcomes.

I once worked for an extremely toxic leader who created an environment where favoritism, corruption, and arrogance ran rampant due to a mindset that "we existed to serve him." It was a miserable place to work, and his presence continues to negatively impact those who worked for him to this day.

To avoid this in your own organizations, remember to stay humble, lead from an ethical foundation, and remain true to the principles of Jesus' teachings as applied to leadership. Leading with humility and integrity will foster a positive and productive environment, aligning your leadership style with the values Jesus emphasized.

Leaders must be humble, avoid self-serving behaviors, and ensure their actions genuinely align with the values and principles they profess.

Application: Examine yourself now and write down two self-serving behaviors that you currently have or have had in the past. How can you rectify those behaviors and reassure your team that you exist to serve them? Write down two steps you can take to serve your team and foster a positive and productive environment for them.

GIVING MUCH WHEN YOU HAVE LITTLE *EA*

"They all gave out of their wealth; but she, out of her poverty, put in everything—all she had to live on."

—Mark 12:44

<u>Read</u>: Mark 12:41–44 "The Widow's Offering"
In this brief but powerful passage, Jesus highlights the true nature of generosity and sacrifice. As He observes people giving to the temple treasury, He contrasts the large donations from the wealthy with the humble offering of a poor widow. Despite the small monetary value of her contribution, Jesus points out that her gift is far greater because she gave out of her poverty, offering all she had.

What are we giving to the teams we lead today? How much time are we spending developing those we serve? Are we carving out time in our schedules to teach, coach, and mentor them, or are we too busy to offer them advice?

Often, we get so bogged down with daily tasks that we forget leaders exist to serve the led. We can easily worry more about what we owe the boss than what we owe our subordinates. Let's challenge ourselves to take time today for those we lead, always maintaining an open door and an open ear. Prioritizing the development and well-being of our teams not only honors their contributions but also reflects the true spirit of leadership exemplified by Jesus.

True leadership requires genuine sacrifice and giving from the heart, prioritizing our time for the development of those we serve over our own abundance.

<u>Application</u>: Write down three tasks you owe leaders above you. What is the timeline for completing those tasks? Now, write down three tasks that you owe your team as their leader. Consider how you are prioritizing their development and empowering them to

carry out the mission of the team. Prioritize these tasks above those you owe your superiors while also not missing your deadlines.

EXPECT TURBULENCE *EA*

> "Whenever you are arrested and brought to trial, do not worry beforehand about what to say. Just say whatever is given you at the time, for it is not you speaking, but the Holy Spirit."
>
> —Mark 13:11

Read: Mark 13:1–31 "Signs of the End of the Age"
Jesus explains the events that will occur following His death and prior to His return. He encourages Peter, James, John, and Andrew to rely on the Holy Spirit, which they do not yet fully understand, to find the right words to say when they face trials.

As leaders, what do we lean on to help us mentor or debrief the team? Are we speaking the truth in love, as Paul mentions in Ephesians? One technique I've developed over the years when counseling or debriefing team members is to first ask them how they thought the observation period or event went. This approach provides them an opportunity to self-reflect while allowing me to formulate my feedback based on their self-perception. Using this technique, a debrief can be tailored to an individual's perception of the events rather than solely my own perception of their performance.

When debriefing members of your team, don't worry beforehand about what to say. First, ask for their perspective. Then, respond with truth in love, relating to their own opinions and allowing them an opportunity to self-critique. This method fosters personal growth and creates a more constructive and supportive environment for development.

Encouraging self-reflection and self-assessment among team members fosters their personal growth and helps tailor feedback to be more impactful and relevant.

Application: Do you take time to hear from your team? Do you create an environment to debrief situations and encourage feedback from your team? Just like your perspective offers great insight, so do the perspectives from each of your teammates. Fit in one-on-one and team debriefs within the routine of your team and encourage their input and self-assessment.

DAILY DISCIPLINES *EA*

"Therefore keep watch because you do not know when the owner of the house will come back—whether in the evening, or at midnight, or when the rooster crows, or at dawn."

—Mark 13:35

Read: Mark 13:32–37 "The Day and the Hour Unknown"
Jesus underscores the importance of remaining vigilant, prepared for His imminent return. As we anticipate His coming, we must reflect on how we are stewarding the responsibilities He has entrusted to us and what condition they will be in, upon His arrival.

To maintain order in His house, let us examine our daily routines and disciplines. Reflecting on my own experience, during my time in flight school, I used to commute from Pensacola to Milton, FL, often listening to political talk radio along the way. However, I noticed a detrimental effect on my mood throughout the day, realizing that, starting the day with such negativity influenced my mindset.

Now, I choose to begin my mornings with 30 minutes of reading Scripture instead. This intentional practice has led to a profound shift in my outlook, fostering peace and clarity as I face the challenges of each day. Importantly, this positive mindset extends to my interactions in the workplace, nurturing genuine and wholesome relationships with my coworkers over time.

Leaders should maintain constant vigilance and discipline, ensuring their actions and mindset are consistently aligned with positive values and preparedness, as demonstrated by starting the day with constructive habits.

<u>Application</u>: How do you prepare? Do you have daily disciplines each day to prepare your body, mind, heart, and soul for future situations? If you are reading through the Gospels with these lessons each day, you are already being disciplined with your mind and soul. Examine where you need to be more disciplined and start with developing one habit before moving to a second one. It takes about 30 repetitions of doing something before it starts to be a habit. Start today with a new healthy habit.

IDOL WORSHIP *EA*

"Then Judas Iscariot, one of the Twelve, went to the chief priests to betray Jesus to them. They were delighted to hear this and promised to give him money. So he watched for an opportunity to hand Him over."
—Mark 14:10–11

<u>Read</u>: Mark 14:1–11 "Jesus Anointed at Bethany"
One of the most renowned narratives in the New Testament, pivotal to the events leading to the crucifixion, recounts Judas' betrayal of Jesus. In this poignant tale, Judas' greed for money eclipses his loyalty to Jesus.

In essence, money becomes an irresistible idol for Judas. Reflecting on this narrative in a contemporary context prompts us to examine our own lives: What idols do we prioritize over our relationship with Jesus?

For many modern American men, common idols include wealth, sports, recreation, among others. While these pursuits are not inherently negative, when they overshadow Jesus in our lives, they become objects of worship. A morning tee time or youth sports practice may subtly draw us away from attending Sunday services.

While we may not replicate Judas' betrayal of Jesus, our devotion to these idols may betray other commitments in our lives—neglecting family dinners, postponing date nights with our spouses, or reneging on promises to loved ones.

Let us collectively commit to setting aside temptations and idols when they threaten to obscure our devotion to Jesus, refocusing on the pursuits that draw us nearer to His divine presence.

Leaders must be vigilant about identifying and avoiding personal temptations and idols, ensuring their priorities remain aligned with their core values and mission.

Application: What idols are standing in the way of you and your team from aligning with God's will? Is it the revenue you must bring in? Is it certain goals and ambitions you have? Focus on aligning with God's will and commit to trusting His providence in your life.

MOVING FORWARD WITH FAITH AND INITIATIVE BH

"So He sent two of His disciples, telling them, 'Go into the city, and a man carrying a jar of water will meet you. Follow him. Say to the owner of the house he enters, The Teacher asks: Where is My guest room,

> where I may eat the Passover with My disciples: he will show you a large room upstairs, furnished and ready. Make preparations for us there.' **The disciples left, went into the city and found things just as Jesus had told them. So they prepared the Passover."**
>
> —Mark 14:13–16

<u>Read</u>: Mark 14:12–26 "The Last Supper"

In this passage, we witness Jesus giving His disciples precise and seemingly unusual instructions. Despite the strangeness of the task, the disciples don't question; they trust and act. They follow Jesus' guidance, and everything unfolds exactly as He described. This scenario mirrors a powerful leadership principle: leaders must inspire trust and the willingness to act, even when the path isn't entirely clear.

As leaders, it is crucial to communicate our vision and instructions with clarity. This not only builds trust but also empowers our teams to take action confidently. Reflect on how you communicate with your team. Are your directives clear? Do your team members feel empowered and trusted to execute their tasks without excessive oversight? Remember, clarity in communication can significantly influence the effectiveness and morale of your team.

Additionally, as leaders, sometimes we need to step into the role of a follower, executing tasks with confidence and resolve, even when we don't have all the answers. This approach not only demonstrates trust in the mission but also models decisive action for our teams.

Leadership is built on clear communication and the willingness to take decisive action, even when the path is uncertain.

<u>Application</u>: Do you wait to have all the answers before taking action? Do you fear uncertainty? When we align our will with God's, we will trust Him in the midst of uncertainty. As a leader,

how can you communicate with more clarity so that your team will trust you when the future is uncertain?

PREPARING FOR TRIALS *BH*

> "'You will all fall away,' Jesus told them, 'For it is written: I will strike the shepherd, and the sheep will be scattered. But after I have risen, I will go ahead of you into Galilee.' Peter declared, 'Even if all fall away, I will not.'"
> —Mark 14:27–29

Read: Mark 14:27–31 "Jesus Predicts Peter's Denial"
Jesus openly acknowledges the impending struggles and failures of His followers. He foresees their moment of weakness but reassures them of His continued leadership and guidance after His resurrection.

Jesus doesn't shield His disciples from the reality of upcoming trials. Instead, He prepares them, fostering resilience and a deeper understanding of their journey ahead. As leaders, we should be proactive in acknowledging potential difficulties and equipping our teams with the mindset and tools to face them.

Even as He predicts their scattering, Jesus reassures His disciples of His resurrection and continued presence. This promise of hope and guidance encourages them to persevere through the forthcoming trials. Leaders should similarly offer a vision of the future that instills hope and motivation, even in difficult times.

Leaders anticipate challenges and prepare their teams with resilience and hope for the future.

Application: Recall a trial that you were not prepared for. In hindsight, how could you have prepared for it? In the military, we are trained to anticipate the enemy's actions before he makes them. We must do that with any opposition that we face. Write down three trials that you can anticipate in your personal and professional life and consider how you will prepare yourself and your team to face those trials.

THE POWER OF VULNERABILITY AND ACCOUNTABILITY BH

"They went to a place called Gethsemane, and Jesus said to His disciples, *'Sit here while I pray.'* He took Peter, James and John along with Him, and He began to be deeply distressed and troubled. *'My soul is overwhelmed with sorrow to the point of death,'* He said to them. *'Stay here and keep watch.'* Then He returned to His disciples and found them sleeping. *'Simon,'* He said to Peter, *'are you asleep? Couldn't you keep watch for one hour? Watch and pray so that you will not fall into temptation. The spirit is willing, but the flesh is weak.'"*

—Mark 14:32-34 & 37–38

Read: Mark 14:32–42 "Gethsemane"
We observe Jesus in the Garden of Gethsemane, deeply distressed and seeking solace in prayer. He invites Peter, James, and John to support Him during this critical time. This moment illuminates essential leadership principles: understanding your team, leading with authenticity, and ensuring accountability. Jesus selects Peter, James, and John, demonstrating His awareness of their unique roles and the support He needs. As leaders, recognizing the strengths and capabilities of team members is crucial to involving them effectively in mission-critical tasks. Assess the unique strengths and skills of your team members.

In a moment of profound emotional distress, Jesus is open about His sorrow. This vulnerability strengthens His bond with His disciples, showing that even the strongest leaders face challenges.

Being genuine about our struggles builds deeper connections and fosters a supportive team environment. Upon returning, Jesus finds His disciples sleeping and expresses His disappointment, urging them to stay vigilant. This highlights the importance of accountability in leadership, ensuring that team members are committed and focused on their responsibilities.

In the Army, there's a saying: "Trust but verify." We must have confidence in our team's abilities and intentions, but also be willing to verify that they are meeting the standards and fulfilling their roles effectively. Jesus exemplifies this by trusting His disciples to keep watch, but checking back to ensure they remain vigilant.

Great leaders understand their team's strengths, lead with vulnerability, hold everyone accountable, and practice 'trust but verify' to ensure collective success.

Application: Are you vulnerable with your team? Do you admit when you are struggling or stressed out? This is tough for all of us, but Jesus gives us a great example of the stress He is experiencing and how He opens up to those closest to Him. Find a close mentor/accountability partner that you can trust and be vulnerable with them. Also, commit to being vulnerable with those you lead as appropriate.

RESPONDING WITH CALMNESS IN CRISIS BH

"Going at once to Jesus, Judas said, 'Rabbi!' and kissed Him. The men seized Jesus and arrested Him. Then one of those standing near drew his sword and struck the servant of the high priest, cutting off his ear. A young man, wearing nothing but a linen garment, was following Jesus. When they seized Him, he fled naked, leaving his garment behind."
—Mark 14:45–47 and 51–52

Read: Mark 14:43–52 "Jesus Arrested"

We witness the dramatic moment of Jesus' betrayal and arrest. Despite the chaos and treachery, Jesus remains composed and serene, setting a powerful example of leadership in the face of crisis. The reactions of those around Him—the disciple who fights and the young man who flees—highlight the diverse ways people respond to pressure.

Amid the turmoil of His arrest, Jesus maintains a calm and composed demeanor. His steady presence amidst the chaos demonstrates the importance of remaining collected and clear-headed in challenging situations. This trait is vital for leaders, as it provides reassurance and stability for their teams during crises.

The contrasting reactions of Jesus' followers provide insight into different responses to stress. One disciple resorts to violence, striking out in defense, while another flees in fear, abandoning everything. As leaders, understanding our natural tendencies—whether to confront or avoid difficulties—can shape our approach to conflict resolution and crisis management.

Jesus' example encourages us to foster resilience within ourselves and our teams. Whether facing betrayal, conflict, or fear, maintaining a sense of purpose and composure is crucial. Leaders should strive to cultivate an environment where calm and thoughtful responses are valued over impulsive actions.

Leaders remain calm under pressure, understand their instinctive responses to conflict, and foster resilience in their teams.

Application: Recall a recent tense situation or a conflict that you experience with and/or within your team. Did you remain calm? How was your response to the pressure you experienced? Your response will overflow to your team. Prepare now so that you are capable of remaining calm in tense situations. Write down how you could have responded better in a recent conflict.

EMBRACING PURPOSE WITH COURAGE AND RESOLVE BH

"Again the high priest asked Him, 'Are you the Messiah, the Son of the Blessed One?' 'I am,' said Jesus. 'And you will see the Son of Man sitting at the right hand of the Mighty One and coming on the clouds of heaven.'"

—Mark 14: 61–62

Read: Mark 14:53–65 "Jesus Before the Sanhedrin"

Jesus stands before the high priest, fully aware of the fate that awaits Him. Despite the dire consequences, He courageously affirms His identity as the Messiah. This profound moment reveals Jesus' unwavering commitment to His purpose, exemplifying the strength and resolve needed to fulfill one's calling, even when it comes at the greatest cost.

Jesus knew that His mission would lead to suffering and death, yet He remained steadfast in His purpose. This ultimate sacrifice underscores the importance of embracing our calling with unwavering commitment, even when faced with daunting challenges or personal sacrifices.

When asked if He is the Messiah, Jesus boldly affirms His identity, knowing it will lead to His condemnation. His example teaches us the importance of standing firm in our values and beliefs, even when doing so might bring about difficult or adverse consequences.

Jesus' declaration to the high priest also points to a greater vision beyond His immediate suffering—the promise of His return in glory. Leaders must hold onto a vision that transcends present difficulties, guiding their actions and providing hope for the future.

True leadership requires embracing your purpose with unwavering courage and resolve, standing firm in your values, and maintaining a vision that guides you through adversity.

Application: Do you embrace your purpose with courage and resolve, or are you timid and think that your purpose is too big for you? God has placed great potential in each of us. But it is for us to use that potential, and we must do so boldly because Satan wants each of us to fail. Where have you been timid with your purpose? What next step do you need to take to be more intentional about serving your purpose?

THE VALUE OF MENTORSHIP AND HUMILITY *BH*

> "Immediately the rooster crowed the second time. Then Peter remembered the word Jesus had spoken to him: 'Before the rooster crows twice you will disown me three times.' And he broke down and wept."
> —Mark 14:72

Read: Mark 14:66–72 "Peter Disowns Jesus"
Peter's heart-wrenching moment of realization comes to fruition as he remembers Jesus' prediction of his denial. Despite his earlier confidence, Peter's fear leads him to disown Jesus three times. This poignant episode offers profound insights into the importance of mentorship, humility, and self-awareness in leadership.

Peter's denial highlights a fundamental truth: we may not always understand how we will react in times of crisis. Despite his firm belief that he would never deny Jesus, the pressure and fear at the moment led him to do exactly that. This serves as a reminder that as leaders, we must acknowledge our vulnerabilities and be aware that our reactions under stress can surprise us.

Jesus, knowing what lay ahead, tried to prepare Peter for the difficult reality he would face. As the perfect mentor, Jesus offered insights based on His deep understanding and foresight. This illustrates the vital role that mentors play in guiding us through challenges we may not yet foresee.

Peter's experience underscores the importance of trusting and heeding the advice of mentors, even when their guidance seems out of sync with our current perceptions or beliefs. Jesus warned Peter of his upcoming denial, but Peter did not grasp the gravity of the warning until it was too late. This teaches us the value of listening closely and trusting those who see beyond our immediate understanding.

Leaders recognize their vulnerabilities, seek and trust mentorship, and listen to wisdom even when it challenges their expectations and original intentions.

Application: Do you identify wisdom when you hear it? Whether from a mentor or a teammate, do you listen to wisdom from others and allow it to challenge your own thoughts, beliefs, and conclusions? John Maxwell says, "good leaders are great listeners." But they are only good leaders because they examine what they hear and are open to challenging their own thoughts. Reflect on a recent disagreement you've had and consider where there may be wisdom in the opposing view.

INTEGRITY OVER POPULARITY JA

> "Wanting to satisfy the crowd, Pilate released Barabbas to them. He had Jesus flogged, and handed Him over to be crucified."
>
> —Mark 15:15

Read: Mark 15:1–15 "Jesus Before Pilate"
In the fulfillment of Scripture, we witness a pivotal moment of weakness and compromise from Pilate. Despite recognizing Jesus'

innocence in verse 14, Pilate capitulates to the crowd's demands, releasing Barabbas and condemning Jesus to be flogged and crucified. Pilate's decision was driven by a desire to satisfy the crowd rather than to uphold justice and righteousness.

As leaders, we often face immense pressure from various stakeholders, whether it's a team, organization, or community. The temptation to please others and avoid conflict can be overwhelming. However, true leadership calls for unwavering integrity and the courage to stand by our convictions, even in the face of opposition.

Pilate's failure serves as a stark reminder that leadership is not about seeking approval or popularity, but about doing what is right. Integrity must be the cornerstone of our leadership. This means making difficult decisions based on principles and values, rather than succumbing to external pressures.

Consider Dietrich Bonhoeffer, a German Lutheran pastor who was a determined opponent of the Nazis in Germany. When the Nazis came to power in 1933, he emphatically opposed their persecution of the Jews and called on all Christians to do the same. History tells us that many professing Christians did not follow Bonhoeffer's stance out of fear of Nazi retribution. He urged the Church not only to "bandage the victims under the wheel, but jam a spoke in the wheel itself." After being accused of conspiring to kill Hitler, he was arrested in April 1943 and held until his execution by hanging on April 9, 1945, as the Third Reich saw its demise approaching.

Integrity is the foundation of strong character upon which the leader creates a healthy culture.

Application: How does your integrity hold up in the face of opposition? Do you show your character to be the same regardless of the environment or the adversity you face? Commit to resolute integrity today and prepare yourself to not succumb to what is popular. Your integrity will be the foundation for a healthy culture within your team.

SACRIFICE, NEVER COMPROMISE JA

> "And when they had mocked Him, they took off the purple robe and put His own clothes on Him. Then they led Him out to crucify Him."
> —Mark 15:20

Read: Mark 15:16–20 "The Soldiers Mock Jesus"
With Pilate's capitulation to the crowd and orders to have Jesus flogged and crucified, a young band of Roman soldiers enjoyed an opportunity for entertainment at Jesus' expense. The whole company of soldiers gathered to mock Jesus. This was not a procedural handling of a prisoner, but rather an opportunity for some young men to get their rocks off. Jesus, the Savior and Creator God, mocked by those He came to save.

When the standards of justice collapse, the mob rules. Our Founding Fathers understood this principle well. They meticulously crafted a system of government in the United States that would be governed by law, not by the whims of any individual or the rule of the mob. The rule of law in America has been a pillar promoting liberty and justice for all.

Consider how you can uphold justice and integrity in your leadership. Are there areas where you feel pressured to compromise your values? Reflect on the importance of maintaining principles in the face of opposition, remembering the example of Jesus, who, despite being mocked and crucified, remained faithful to His mission.

Leaders must lead according to their personal values in submission to God's will rather than follow the crowd.

Application: Similarly to the previous lesson, this one underscores the importance of upholding our values and integrity in the face of opposition. Do you allow your values and foundational beliefs to guide you, or do allow your situations to manipulate your values and integrity? Write down a recent situation where you compromised your values and how you would act differently to uphold your values if faced with the same situation again.

BEARING THE CONSEQUENCES *JA*

> "In the same way the chief priests and the teachers of the law mocked Him among themselves. 'He saved others,' they said, 'but He can't save Himself! Let this Christ, this King of Israel, come down now from the cross, that we may see and believe.' Those crucified with Him also heaped insults on Him."
>
> —Mark 15:31–32

Read: Mark 15:21–32 "The Crucifixion"
How demoralizing and embarrassing for Jesus to hang naked on a cross while the chief priests, passersby, and even the criminals crucified alongside Him hurled insults at Him for His claim to be the Messiah.

For three years, Jesus taught in the synagogues, healed the sick, made the blind see, the deaf hear, and the lame walk, and even raised several people from the dead. He claimed to be *"gentle and humble in heart"* (Matt 11:29), and taught that the kingdom of heaven is ushered in through man's heart. His only fault, according to the religious leaders, was that He did not conform to their rules. At His crucifixion, they claimed they would believe Him if He saved Himself. Yet, even when He rose from His grave, they did not believe.

A few weeks ago, I was working out in the garage with my two oldest sons, and one of them was listening to a sermon. The pastor mentioned how Islam considers Jesus a prophet, but cannot accept that God would ever become human. The pastor shared how Muslims could never accept that God could be brutally flogged, dragged through the streets of Jerusalem, and then executed by crucifixion. No one can do that to God. And I thought...that's right. No one can do that to God. But God can do that for us...and He did.

God was tried unjustly, beaten, mocked, flogged, insulted, crucified, and killed by man because He allowed it to happen without supernaturally intervening. He came to bear the punishment of sin, not to remove the punishment. Though the crowds and the justice system were unjust toward Him, God was just with sin. He never excused it, nor does He today. Instead, He bore its consequence.

Leaders assume the risk and are willing to bear the consequences of their team's mistakes.

Application: How well do you bear the responsibilities of your collective team's mistakes or of individual's mistakes within your team? Do you take ownership of the consequences that may fall out from it? Strong leaders take ownership and work through their team's failures to develop their teammates and create a strong team culture.

RESTORING THE TEAM JA

"The curtain of the temple was torn
in two from top to bottom."
—Mark 15:38

Read: Mark 15:33–41 "The Death of Jesus"
While Christ's death secures our victory over sin, His resurrection gives us faith that the victory is for us, enabling us to live and walk in that victory. When Jesus took His last breath, the veil that

separated the Holy Place in the temple from the Most Holy Place, which housed the presence of God, was torn from top to bottom (Mark 15:38). This event signifies that no further animal sacrifices are needed for our sins to be atoned for, allowing us to enter the presence of God. Jesus fulfilled the requirements of God's Law, receiving the punishment that was rightly ours.

Every time a sinner humbles themselves and seeks God's forgiveness, He freely gives it. This is possible because of His only begotten Son's willing sacrifice and the unconditional love that sacrifice displays, satisfying any anger or displeasure from the Holy, Eternal God.

Unconditional love and the forgiveness that we can give through that love will restore relationships, mend broken hearts, and reconstitute a team to be a formidable force for advancing the kingdom of God. Leaders are to "lead from the front" and "set the example." Leaders must exemplify forgiveness. We must hold our teammates accountable to maintain the standards of the team, but this does not eliminate the need to forgive. Forgiveness acknowledges that a wrong was done or a mistake was made, and it recognizes that there must be an accounting. More damage is done to a team when leaders and teammates focus on the hurt caused and the betrayal committed rather than on the accounting and forgiveness.

Effective leaders demonstrate forgiveness, fostering a team environment where accountability and grace coexist, paving the way for restoration and unity.

Application: When was the last time you were truly hurt or even felt betrayed? Have you forgiven the person who hurt you? When you do, it will be freeing for you and for all others aware of the hurt you experienced. Decide now to forgive any hurt against you because it will grow you and restore your team.

STAND AND BE COUNTED JA

> "Joseph of Arimathea, a prominent member of the Council, who was himself waiting for the kingdom of God, went boldly to Pilate and asked for Jesus' body."
> —Mark 15:43

<u>Read</u>: Mark 15:42–47 "The Burial of Jesus"
The "Council" refers to the Sanhedrin, the body of religious leaders who had Jesus arrested and brought charges against Him. Joseph of Arimathea, a prominent member of this council, may have participated in the accusations against Jesus not 24 hours before asking for Jesus' body to bury it. According to Mark 14:55, "the whole Sanhedrin were looking for evidence against Jesus so that they could put Him to death, but they did not find any." So why did Joseph now personally go to Pilate to ask for Jesus' body and use his own tomb to place it?

Is it possible that witnessing how Jesus behaved as false accusations were hurled at Him, as Pilate acknowledged finding no fault in Jesus, as the chief priests rallied the crowd to demand Jesus' crucifixion, and as Pilate ordered Jesus' execution and flogging, Joseph of Arimathea humbled himself to the fact that Jesus was the awaited Messiah—the Son of God? As a prominent Jew who studied the Scriptures, Joseph certainly had ample time and opportunity to investigate if Jesus met the descriptions of the coming Messiah. Even the commander of the soldiers tasked with carrying out Jesus' flogging and execution, likely unfamiliar with Jewish Scriptures, declared that Jesus "surely...was the Son of God" (Mark 15:39).

Could Joseph have faced reprimand for caring for this 'criminal' who his own association of religious leaders had brought charges against? Likely. But he acted anyway. Regardless of whether the leaders above us or the team we are a part of honor God, we are still responsible for our own faith and how we answer Jesus' question: "Who do you say I am?" (Mark 8:29). Our association does not prevent us from having freedom in Christ. As followers of Jesus Christ in a team of unbelievers or a culture where Christ is not acknowledged, we are called to sacrifice as Jesus sacrificed and serve as He served. Our responsibility to love God and love others (Mark 12:30–31) is not voided when we are in a toxic team environment surrounded by enemies of God.

> **True leaders exhibit courageous faith, standing up for what is right and demonstrating Christ-like love and service, even in the face of opposition and a toxic team environment.**

Application: Do you belong to any organizations that are at odds with your faith or have an overall toxic team environment? How do you maintain your faith and your integrity within those organizations? Write down three ways you can uphold your morals and maintain the integrity of your faith within your role in those organizations.

RESTORING CONFIDENCE JA

> "Later Jesus appeared to the Eleven as they were eating; He rebuked them for their lack of faith and their stubborn refusal to believe those who had seen Him after He had risen."
> —Mark 16:14

Read: Mark 16:1–20 "The Resurrection"

Despite the eyewitness accounts of several women (Mark 16:1) and two men (Mark 16:12), Jesus' disciples did not believe He had risen. But then He personally stood among them while they were eating and rebuked them for their unbelief.

This was not only a lack of faith that Jesus could raise Himself from the dead under His own authority, but also a disbelief and distrust in Jesus' own words. On multiple occasions, Jesus told His disciples that He would suffer and die, but then rise again. His words were true; He backed them up with His actions and gained followers. However, when adversity came, the great deceiver himself—the devil—sowed seeds of doubt in the minds of Jesus' closest followers, just as he had done since the fall of man.

The lack of faith the disciples exhibited did not surprise Jesus. He knew the heart of man, yet pursued them anyway. He did not excuse their lack of faith but rather rebuked it, restored it, and then empowered them to spread the Gospel to the world.

When our team doesn't immediately buy into our vision, decisions, or actions, do we become defensive and angry, or do we move to restore their confidence and empower them to act and serve the common purpose? "Be quick to listen, slow to speak, and slow to become angry" (James 1:19). As leaders, and with the availability of time, we must listen to the dissenting opinions of our teammates, offer clarity to any vision or decision in question, and then give clear mission-type orders (see Red Letter Leadership Lesson for Mark 12:28–35) with our weight of authority and committed support behind the team.

Effective leaders address doubt with understanding, provide clarity, and empower their teams to overcome challenges and fulfill their mission.

Application: Have you experienced doubting teammates? How did you address their doubts? If you haven't, think about when you have doubted. Write down three ways that you can overcome your doubts, address challenges, and fulfill your mission.

THE BOOK OF LUKE

THE HISTORICAL ACCOUNT *JA*

> "Therefore, since I myself have carefully investigated everything from the beginning, it seemed good also to me to write an orderly account for you, most excellent Theophilus, so that you may know the certainty of the things you have been taught."
>
> –Luke 1:3–4

Read: Luke 1:1–4 "Introduction"

I love history, specifically military history. I earned my BA in History from Penn State University and my MA in History from Millersville University. I enjoy studying history and pulling leadership lessons from the past. Because of my passion for studying history, I'd venture to say the Book of Luke is my favorite of the four Gospel accounts. Why? Because Luke is written from the perspective of a historian. Luke may have met Jesus or heard Him speak. We don't know. But we do know that he was not one of the Twelve, so much of what he writes was not his own firsthand experiences with Jesus. He "carefully investigated everything," and wanted to provide an "orderly account" of the events surrounding the life, death, and resurrection of Jesus, the Christ (Luke 1:3–4).

Luke addresses his Gospel account to a man named Theophilus. The name Theophilus is a Greek name meaning "lover of God" or "friend of God." This could be interpreted to mean that Luke is addressing his work to those who claim to "love God." Biblical scholars believe that this was an actual man since Luke addresses him as "most excellent Theophilus" in verse 3, and it was common at the time to address writings to the publisher, with Theophilus believed to be the one who would publish Luke's Gospel to the public.

Biblical introductions to the Book of Luke suggest that he was a close companion of the Apostle Paul, and that he may have been a Gentile by birth and well-educated in Greek culture.

Like Paul's letters to the many churches he traveled to or Luke's Gospel addressed to Theophilus, we can read these writings and learn timeless principles that will change the trajectory of our lives if we only humble ourselves to the truth. Similarly, just as we read historical accounts of the founding of America, the Civil War, the Civil Rights Movement, or other significant events in history to gain insights and learn what history proves right or wrong; we can read the Holy Bible in the same manner and learn from the past to apply to our future. The one key difference between the Bible and any other historical writings is that the Bible gives the account of when God walked among us, took the punishment for our sin upon Himself, humbled Himself to death on a cross, and then walked out of His own grave under His own power. No other historical accounts besides those contained in the Bible provide a clearer and more believable understanding of things that are otherwise unbelievable.

Leaders heed the lessons of Scripture because they are God-breathed, God-ordained, and testify to the truest form of love to ever enter the heart of man.

Application: How do you study the past so that you can be prepared for the future? When you complete the reading of these lessons and have accomplished your goal to read through all four Gospels, choose one book of the Bible or choose another study to take you through other parts of the Bible. Seek to see different perspectives of the leadership lessons you've learned in the Gospels from varying characters and circumstances throughout all Scripture.

GOD DEFINES US *JA*

> "'The Lord has done this for me,' she said.
> 'In these days He has shown His favor and taken
> away my disgrace among the people.'"
>
> —Luke 1:25

<u>Read</u>: Luke 1:5–25 "The Birth of John the Baptist Foretold"

Before Elizabeth became pregnant with John the Baptist, her womb was barren. During this time in Jewish culture, a barren woman was said to have disfavor with God. Children not only brought the mother happiness, but not having any children brought her social reproach. However, we read in the text that both Elizabeth and her husband Zechariah, "were upright in the sight of God, observing all the Lord's commandments and regulations blamelessly" (Luke 1:6). Elizabeth's barren womb was not an indication that she lacked favor with God. On the contrary, her barren womb was to bring a miracle from God that would usher in the miracle of the coming Messiah.

My wife's womb was "barren" when we started trying to become pregnant in the fall of 2009. Friends were becoming pregnant within months of trying. Nearly a year later, in July 2010, my wife came to me and told me that she had been wrestling with God over a desire to adopt. She honestly confided to me that she did not want to adopt when God first put the idea in her mind, but for over six months, He worked on her heart, and she came to me with a clear inclination that we should. So, we prayed, and I was quickly on board. We believed that God gave us the ability to do so, and therefore He was placing on us the responsibility. About nine months later, we adopted a sibling group of four—one boy and three girls—from the Pennsylvania Foster Care System and then were off to Virginia for the next year for my initial officer training in the Marine Corps.

Again, in the fall of 2012, God gave us the opportunity to pursue another adoption. I grew up with brothers and knew I wanted my son to have brothers, especially given the fact that I was often away from home for training or deployments. In November 2013, we brought home two older brothers from Ethiopia. They quickly fit in and became the best big brothers to their younger siblings. Our family was complete. Six children were our max for parenting, considering that my wife often parented our children on her own while I was away.

But God had other plans. Following my wife's obedience to donate a portion of her liver to a young 11-month-old boy who was dying of biliary atresia, God miraculously opened her womb. As her liver regenerated in the healing process, it very literally opened her womb, allowing her to bear children. She became pregnant with our seventh child about 10 months after her liver surgery.

Our circumstances do not define us. God defines us. Leaders must lead with that in mind, lest we judge others wrongly, become arrogant in our circumstances, or miss an opportunity to see a mighty move of God.

Lead where God has placed you. He put you there for a reason; it's not by your own doing.

<u>Application</u>: Are you a determined trailblazer of your own future, or do you trust God to blaze your trail in the direction He wants to take you? "In his hearts a man plans his course, but the LORD establishes his steps" (Prov 16:9). It is good for us to have a vision, follow our purpose and the dreams God has placed on our hearts, and to do so with sound plans. However, we must always be committed to trusting Him with our steps. Let God define you. Write down three areas across the environments in which you live and work, where you need to trust God more with your steps.

DEFINING REALITY *JA*

"'For nothing is impossible with God.' 'I am the Lord's servant,' Mary answered. 'May it be to me as you have said.' Then the angel left her."
—Luke 1:37–38

Read: Luke 1:26–38 "The Birth of Jesus Foretold"

Six months after the angel Gabriel visits Elizabeth, he comes to Mary. He tells Mary that she is "highly favored" (Luke 1:28) and will give birth to "the Son of the Most High" (Luke 1:32). Mary asked Gabriel how it will happen since she is a virgin (Luke 1:34). She trusted the words of the angel Gabriel rather than asking for confirmation. She only asked for the plan. While Zechariah doubted that his wife, Elizabeth, would be pregnant, Mary believed and asked for God's plan as it would be in her life.

How often does God want to use us as part of His big plan, but we are too stubborn to believe it as Zechariah was? In his book, *Leadership Gold*, John Maxwell writes that "A leader's first responsibility is to define reality."[14] How will our team operate together under a common vision if the leader of that team does not define the reality in which the team must work? Zechariah questioned reality. Mary defined it.

"Nothing is impossible with God" (Luke 1:37). This means God's supernatural works, though unbelievable and unrealistic to us, are in fact truth and reality. As leaders, we must seek God's reality and ask Him to define it for us so that we can lead our team well in it. We must not question reality with an attitude of 'How do I know this is reality?' which expresses doubt. Rather, we should do as Mary did and ask God to define the reality He gives us. Effective leaders define reality by trusting God's plan and seeking His guidance, fostering unity and clarity within their teams.

Define reality, don't doubt it.

Application: Do you find yourself too often doubting the reality that God wants to speak into your life? Commit to trusting His will. Ask Him to define your reality and trust Him to guide your steps as you lead those He's placed in your life to lead.

THE INFLUENCE OF A GODLY WOMAN *JA*

> "Blessed is she who has believed that what the Lord has said to her will be accomplished."
> —Luke 1:45

Read: Luke 1:39–45 "Mary Visits Elizabeth"
Mary went to visit her older cousin, Elizabeth, and upon seeing her, Elizabeth was filled with the Holy Spirit. Elizabeth then proceeded to pronounce blessings on Mary, acknowledging that Mary is carrying the Lord in her womb (Luke 1:43). These two women are arguably the matriarchs of the Christian faith. One bore a son who prepared the way for the Savior of mankind, and the other bore a Son who saved mankind and restored us to the Father.

In first-century Judean culture, women did not serve in leadership positions. They bore children and cared for the home. Many cultures throughout history, and even today, keep women out of leadership positions. But that has never meant that women do not, cannot, or should not lead. God has used and continues to use women to break, tame, and mend the heart of man. Women can see and understand emotions that men might miss. I've learned this as a husband and as a father. My wife has helped me understand what my daughters are feeling and how my words may have been received when I was unaware.

Though a man and woman may share the exact same personality style, they will be completely different according to the gender identity God has given them—male or female (Gen 1:27). For the women, recognize and acknowledge the unique strengths God has stamped on you as a female, and then grow and leverage those strengths to have a profound influence on other women and the men in your life and on your team.

Effective leaders recognize and leverage the unique strengths of both men and women, fostering a culture of mutual respect and profound influence.

Application: For the women, have you submitted to the role God has for you and the influence He wants you to have toward other women and men in your life? For men, have you submitted to the great asset that God has placed in women and the influence they can have on you? Reflect on your specific strengths today and especially how they are manifested in your gender. God did not make a mistake with you, and He has commissioned all of us to lead.

AN ATTITUDE OF HUMILITY JA

> "He has brought down rulers from their
> thrones but has lifted up the humble."
> —Luke 1:52

Read: Luke 1:46–56 "Mary's Song"
Similar to Hannah's Prayer in 1 Samuel 2:1–10, "Mary's Song" as recorded in Luke, is praise and worship to a God who sees the heart and rewards the humble. Jesus' upbringing within a family of lowly, humble origin and social status speaks to the truest form of leadership. Jesus did not come to display His power and authority through worldly

success and status. He came to display it through His humility, love, and gentleness. He ushered in the kingdom of God and showed the world His power and authority devoid of worldly contamination. A company may promote people to leadership positions, a government may give authority to judges and legislators, but there was no earthly authority that gave Jesus any power or status.

This concept underscores the fact that we can possess tremendous influence without position or status. When we stop trying to achieve dominance over someone whom we are trying to influence but rather approach them with a humble attitude, we place ourselves in a better position to lead them to action and influence them for good.

Humble leaders recognize that their influence is not in their position or status but in their attitude.

Application: What would those you lead say about your attitude? Would they say you are humble, open to learning, open to other perspectives, and recognize that you may not have all the best solutions? Or, might they say you are someone who never asks for your team's input? Are you a leader who uses your position as affirmation that you have the best solutions, clearest perspective, and worthy vision? Consider how you can open up more with those you lead and humble yourself to their perspectives and input.

SUFFERINGS AS GOD'S GRACE JA

"He asked for a writing tablet, and to everyone's astonishment he wrote, 'His name is John.' Immediately his mouth was opened and his tongue was loosed, and he began to speak, praising God."
—Luke 1:63–64

Read: Luke 1:57–66 "The Birth of John the Baptist"

The last words Zechariah uttered before the angel Gabriel struck him with muteness were words of doubt that his wife Elizabeth would become pregnant. After nine months of silence, Zechariah's first words were to name his son. Why was such a consequence necessary? One might think he would start believing once Elizabeth showed symptoms of pregnancy.

Zechariah's muteness was a manifestation of God's grace upon him and his family. Though he couldn't share Gabriel's message or explain to Elizabeth that she would be with child, his silence also prevented him from spreading his doubt to his fellow priests and his wife, Elizabeth. God shielded him from the repercussions of his lack of faith. When he finally regained his speech, Zechariah was humbled and excited to acknowledge his previous doubts, now able to testify to God's truth through his newborn son.

Reflect on the consequences you've endured that, in hindsight, you can humbly acknowledge God's grace. We all have them because God is good and gracious, and we are sinners in need of a savior. When you view your sufferings as God's grace, you gain a powerful testimony.

Recognize and embrace the consequences of your doubts and failures as opportunities for growth and testimony.

Application: Think back to a time when you faced suffering and hardship. In hindsight, can you see where some of your hardship may have been God's grace? God doesn't promise that our lives will lack any hardship, but He does promise to walk through the terrible circumstances that this fallen world throws at us. List three hardships that you have faced where you can now see God's grace through the suffering.

EMBRACING OUR UNIQUE ROLES *JA*

> "And you, my child, will be called a prophet of the Most High; for you will go on before the Lord to prepare the way for Him, to give His people the knowledge of salvation through the forgiveness of their sins."
> —Luke 1:76–77

<u>Read</u>: Luke 1:67–80 "Zechariah's Song"

In 1 Corinthians 12, the Apostle Paul explains how the Body of Christ, the Church, functions as one body with many parts. Each part has a unique role, serving the whole through differing functions and abilities. Paul illustrates this with the analogy of a human body, emphasizing that the Church is composed of individuals with varied strengths, abilities, and resources, all serving in their respective God-given capacities for the mission of the Body of Christ. In 1 Corinthians 12:28, Paul writes, "God has appointed first of all apostles, second prophets, third teachers," highlighting the diversity of roles within the Church. We see that Zechariah's son, John, was appointed as a prophet to "prepare the way for [the Lord]" (Luke 1:76).

In my journey into leadership development, I've discovered the value of the DISC behavior assessment, especially the Maxwell DISC Method as a Maxwell DISC Trainer and Consultant. Each DISC style has unique strengths, and what amazes me is how these styles complement each other. Just as John the Baptist's life was ordained by God to prepare the way for the Lord, each of us has God-given strengths and abilities with corresponding responsibilities.

Reflect on the unique strengths and abilities God has given you. Recognize the role you play in the larger mission and how your contributions support the Body of Christ in the confines of your team(s). Embrace the diversity of roles within your community and appreciate how each part works together to achieve a common purpose.

Effective leadership recognizes and leverages the unique strengths and abilities of each individual, understanding that our diverse roles collectively contribute to the greater mission.

Application: Have you embraced the roles God has placed you in and the strengths He's given you to serve in those roles? It's easy to wish we were in a different role or wish we had some other gift, but the truth is, if we had that attitude, we would always be wishing. Write down three ways that you can grow your strengths within the roles God has placed you. Then, be intentional about allowing God to use you in those roles and stop wishing He would send you somewhere else. Bloom where you are planted!

WAY MAKER *JA*

> "In those days Caesar Augustus issued a decree that a census should be taken of the entire Roman world."
> —Luke 2:1

Read: Luke 2:1–7 "The Birth of Jesus"
Caesar Augustus, the first Roman emperor, ruled from 31 B.C. to A.D. 14. He transitioned the government from a republic—an inspiration for America's Founding Fathers when forming the U.S. Constitution—to an imperial system. He issued a census that required Joseph and Mary to travel to Bethlehem to register since Joseph was of the line of David and Bethlehem was the town of the house of David. Bethlehem was about a three day walk from Nazareth.

In the United States, a census occurs approximately every ten years. Similarly, in the Roman Empire, censuses were routine but infrequent. Augustus had been emperor for about 30 years by this time, so this was likely not his first census. This census occurred precisely when Mary was due to deliver Jesus, illustrating how God used a government, which had formerly given their citizens representation before turning to dictatorial rule, to fulfill His divine plan for redeeming mankind at the exact time and place He intended.

God is at work amid the world's evil. Don't be swayed by those who worry about the future. Instead, embrace God's will and follow Him. God remains sovereign, and your Savior sits at His right hand, interceding for you. No evil can ultimately harm you. This doesn't mean we won't face suffering, but when we align our will with God's, no pain or evil can separate us from His love. Encourage someone today with this truth.

> **Adopt God's will as your own and be the change others are waiting for.**

Application: There is nothing in this world that will keep God from fulfilling His plan. Have you submitted to His will and made it your own or are you hoping He'll make your will His own? Trust that He will chart the path and make the way.

FAITH LIKE A SHEPHERD *EA*

> "...and the shepherds returned, glorifying and praising God for all the things they had heard and seen, which were just as they had been told."
> —Luke 2:20

Read: Luke 2:8–20 "The Shepherds and the Angels"
Witnessing the beginning of the most incredible miracle in the history of mankind, the story of the shepherds is one of both faith

and trust. When the angel appeared to the shepherds at night while they were tending to their flock, they were immediately filled with great fear. However, their fears were quickly allayed by the angel's affirmation of good news. The angel went on to tell the shepherds the greatest news in world history: the birth of Christ the Lord, who was the Lord God Himself (although the shepherds likely did not fully grasp this at the time). In response to their angelic encounter, Luke's text does not mention a whisper of hesitation among them; they trust that what they have been told is a word directly from God and begin their journey to Bethlehem as directed.

As we attempt to apply this text to our lives today, how can we display the trust the shepherds showed in this passage? Is it trust in our current circumstances, trust in the planning or trajectory of a small business, or maybe trust that we can lean on His help in dealing with a difficult employee or coworker?

There are many ways we can display our faith in His plan and what He calls us to do, but one of the most important attributes is to have trust in the plan He has for us, be comfortable with it, and execute it with the same vigor displayed by the shepherds when called to see the birth of the Savior of the World.

Leaders must emulate the shepherds' unwavering trust and immediate action in response to divine guidance by demonstrating faith and decisiveness in our roles as decision-makers.

Application: Are you decisive in your faith? I know I can struggle with decisiveness. The military has improved my ability to be decisive but I know it is still lacking. How do you trust God's intervention in areas in your life and work that need your decisions? Write down three decisions you must make and commit to going to God each day this week to seek His direction.

LEADERSHIP HAS NO BANK ACCOUNT EA

> "And to offer a sacrifice in keeping with what is said in the Law of the Lord: 'a pair of doves or two young pigeons.'"
> –Luke 2:24

Read: Luke 2:21–40 "Jesus Presented in the Temple"
As outlined in Leviticus 12:8, new mothers were to offer a lamb as part of their post-childbirth cleansing rituals, "But if she cannot afford a lamb, she is to bring two doves or two young pigeons, one for a burnt offering and the other for a sin offering." Luke 2:24, in this passage tells us that Joseph and Mary offered up doves or pigeons as part of their sacrifice, not a lamb, indicating they were poor, or of modest means.

Jesus coming from humble beginnings is a great illustration that leadership has no bank account. He didn't need wealth, fame, or fortune for people to believe and follow Him. He came to serve and left through sacrifice, with people innately following Him along the way, often with no questions asked and at the drop of a hat.

For us, this text demonstrates that we aren't required to be born with special privilege or social status to lead people effectively. Some of the basic tenets of successful leadership are humility, a servant's heart, and treating people with dignity and respect, as we remember to "...love your neighbor as yourself." (Matt 22:39). Challenge yourself to lead people effectively through a humble servant's heart today.

> **Leadership has no bank account. It is independent of wealth and prosperity. It is first derived from a place of humility and a servant's mindset, then developed through experience.**

Application: Are you waiting for more wealth or status to influence others the way you believe God wants you to? Regardless of how wealthy you are or are not, God has placed you at this moment in history and surrounded you with the people that He has for you to influence them in a way that brings Him glory. Don't wait for your situation to be how you think it should. God wants you to multiply your talents now (Matt 25:14–30).

RIGHT WHERE I'M SUPPOSED TO BE EA

> "'Why were you searching for Me?' He asked. 'Didn't you know I had to be in My Father's house?'"
> —Luke 2:49

Read: Matthew 5:1–12 "The Beatitudes"
When Jesus' parents accidentally left their 12-year-old behind in the temple for three days, it must have been incredibly distressing for them. However, upon return they found Him sitting and listening to the teachers while asking them questions. The text goes on to tell us that "...all who heard Him were amazed at His understanding and His answers, and when His parents saw him, they were astonished." Upon being confronted by His parents, Jesus' response when challenged gives us continued indication that He was unlike any other child; "Didn't you know I had to be in My Father's house?"

If someone we haven't seen in a while were to drop in on us at work, what would they find us doing and how would they find us acting? Would we be living out our Christ centered ideals in the way we are treating people, or would they find us stressed out and agitated?

What if that same person were to drop in on us in our house unknowingly? Would we be proud of what they found us doing? Proud of how we are treating our family?

While none of us are perfect or even close to it, strive today to live out His ideals by demonstrating the fruits of the Spirit found in Galatians 5:22–23, "...love, joy, peace, patience, kindness, goodness, faithfulness, gentleness, and self-control."

Leaders embody their values consistently, inspiring others through authenticity and integrity.

<u>Application</u>: If Jesus were to drop in on you today, what would He find you doing and how would He find you treating people? Does your leadership embody your values and how you would want to be led? Consider one thing that you value in a leader that you can honestly say you are not doing as a leader.

PREPARE THE WAY EA

> "As it is written in the book of the words of Isaiah the prophet: 'A voice of one calling in the wilderness, "Prepare the way for the Lord, make straight paths for Him. Every valley shall be filled in, every mountain and hill made low. The crooked roads shall become straight, the rough ways smooth. And all people will see God's salvation."'"
> –Luke 3:4–6

<u>Read</u>: Luke 3:1–20 "John the Baptist Prepares the Way"
When the word of God came to John, the son of Zechariah, in the wilderness (Isa 40:3), it was the first time in 460 years, since the prophet Malachai, that God spoke to His people. John began traveling the entire Jordan region proclaiming a baptism of repentance for the forgiveness of sins. John goes on to state "...I baptize you with water. But one who is more powerful than I will come, the straps of whose sandals I am not worthy to untie. He will baptize you with the Holy Spirit and fire." (Luke 3:16)

Of course, John is talking about Jesus and the beginning of His ministry. In Acts 2, we see exactly what John is talking about,

"When the day of Pentecost came...they saw what seemed to be tongues of fire that separated and came to rest on each of them. All of them were filled with the Holy Spirit and began to speak in other tongues as the Spirit enabled them." (Acts 2:1–4) For the first time in history, the Holy Spirit will now live within followers of Christ, in a temple not made by hands, should we choose to repent for our sins and be baptized.

John goes further in showing us what living a life filled with the Holy Spirit might look like, "'What should we do then?' the crowd asked. John answered, 'Anyone who has two shirts should share with the one who has none, and anyone who has food should do the same.' Even tax collectors came to be baptized. 'Teacher,' they asked, 'What should we do?' 'Don't collect any more than you are required to,' he told them. Then some soldiers asked him, 'And what should we do?' He replied, 'Don't extort money and don't accuse people falsely—be content with your pay'" (Luke 3:10–14). As we can see, when questioned, John didn't require his examiners to do anything immediate or radical, he simply instructed them to adopt Christ-like principles in their already prescribed daily duties.

> **Lead today through the principles of generosity, integrity, and fairness, as demonstrated by John the Baptist's guidance to the crowds, tax collectors, and soldiers.**

Application: Do you lead fairly? This doesn't mean you treat everyone the same and give everyone the same things. This means, do you show the same respect to everyone without favoring one over another? There are many times we must discriminate and are selective as leaders, but that doesn't mean we show favoritism. It means that our selection was based on merit, performance, actions, behavior, not our favor or disfavor with someone.

DIVINE APPOINTMENT EA

> "...and the Holy Spirit descended on Him in bodily form like a dove. And a voice came from heaven: 'You are my Son, whom I love; with You I am well pleased.'"
> –Luke 3:22

<u>Read</u>: Luke 3:21–38 "The Baptism and Genealogy of Jesus"
John the Baptist marks the end of his ministry with the baptism of Jesus, which then marks the beginning of Jesus' ministry. Immediately following His baptism and while He was praying, the heavens opened up and the Holy Spirit descended upon Jesus like a dove, with a voice from heaven stating, "You are my Son, whom I love; with You I am well pleased."

From the very beginning of His ministry, we can see the divinity that surrounds Jesus. God the Father marks the occasion by sending both the Holy Spirit and His exhortations to complete the Holy Trinity in the sight of man. Luke follows this account in the text with the genealogy of Jesus, which finishes with Him being the 'Son of God,' further adding to His divine credibility.

We also see from this passage that God loved Jesus in the same way Jesus later describes loving us. In this case, of the four Greek words for love, Luke is using the Greek verb 'agapao,' or an unconditional, sacrificial love. John's gospel also tells us that, "God so loved the world that He gave His one and only Son..." using the same 'agapao' type of love. Because we know the end of the story, we can see why the 'agapao' variant is used, with the beginning of Jesus' ministry marked by unconditional love as described by the Father, and the end of His ministry marked by sacrificial love as Jesus was the final sacrifice for the sins of all humanity.

Christ-centered leaders demonstrate unconditional and sacrificial love, following the example set by Jesus, whose ministry was marked by divine approval and ultimate selflessness.

Application: How do you need to be unconditional in your love, your service, and your sacrifice for your team? Leaders demonstrate such love, service, and sacrifice for their teammates so that their teammates are comfortable expressing it to each other and those they serve. This will greatly enhance your team's efficiency and effectiveness, and it will take a consistent and intentional daily effort to attain.

JESUS FACE TEMPTATION EA

> "Jesus, full of the Holy Spirit, left the Jordan and was led by the Spirit into the wilderness, where for forty days He was tempted by the devil. He ate nothing during those days, and at the end of them He was hungry"
> —Luke 4:1–2

Read: Luke 4:1–13 "The Temptation of Jesus"
Following His anointment and baptism, Jesus is led by Spirit to face Satan in the wilderness for 40 days. During this time, Jesus faces a myriad of temptations, culminating in the final three temptations outlined by Luke. These temptations are a diabolical attempt to subvert God's plan for human redemption by causing Jesus to fall into sin and disobedience, thus disqualifying Him as the sinless Savior. As expected, Jesus is triumphant over Satan's schemes, and He leaves the wilderness prepared to begin His earthly ministry, having once again proven God's power is greater than the schemes of The Deceiver.

Extrapolated to our lives, if God allowed Jesus to be tempted, then we can be absolutely sure that we will be tempted at some point in our lives, which many of us will admit occurs on a daily basis. There are many temptations men face in executing their daily responsibilities both inside and outside the home. Some common examples include wealth, power, money, recognition, and acceptance.

What are you leaning on to help you deal with the specific temptations in your life? Using the model from this passage, we see that following each of the temptations Jesus faces, He quotes the book of Deuteronomy. We can use this example to demonstrate that when we are tempted, prudence dictates that we lean on Scripture and faith to help us overcome those temptations.

In times of temptation and challenge, leaders should rely on their foundational principles and values, just as Jesus relied on Scripture and faith to overcome Satan's temptations in the wilderness.

<u>Application</u>: Facing temptation is certain. Therefore, we must prepare now to face temptations and challenges tomorrow. We all have opposition against us; and those we lead and we must prepare to lead our teams through it. Are your personal core values identified and in place? Is your faith rooted in Christ and in the truth of His word so you are prepared to stand when the opposition mounts against you? Anticipate three ways in which you or your team will be challenged, opposed, or tempted in the next 90 days. Then take time for how to prepare for it.

THINK OUTSIDE THE BOX *EA*

"'Truly I tell you,' He continued, 'no prophet is accepted in his hometown.'"

—Luke 4:24

<u>Read</u>: Luke 4:14–30 "Jesus Rejected at Nazareth"
Immediately following His return from the wilderness, Jesus begins His ministry in His hometown of Nazareth. However, upon hearing Him preach out of the book of Isaiah, and then referencing how God treated His people when they rejected the prophets He

sent, His hometown mob becomes angry and attempts to kill Him. However, Jesus miraculously escapes through the mob as His time had not yet come.

During this event, Jesus makes the statement "no prophet is accepted in his hometown." Beyond its literal meaning, this lesson can be extrapolated to include the common leadership practice of "getting out of your comfort zone." Many times, getting out of our comfort zone requires us to overcome the primary driving factor that prevents us from doing so...fear. Many call this practice "thinking outside the box." Once we overcome our fears and begin living outside the comfort zone/outside the box, true growth begins to occur. Akin to a workout where muscle fibers must be stretched, causing micro tears, to be rebuilt and grow back stronger, we also experience growth when we stretch our thinking and explore new ways of problem solving.

Over the last 12 months in attempting to describe the daily approach I'd like the junior officers to adopt when solving complex problems, I've developed a pictorial chart that shows what it's like to live outside one's comfort zone and think outside the box. Thinking outside the box doesn't mean that we operate in areas that are unethical, immoral, or illegal. Rather, we need to learn to live in the area between the edge of our comfort zone and the edge of the box, often exploring the outer limits, called the gray zone, without crossing that illegal, unethical, or immoral line. In my experience, if we can inculcate a culture that teaches our young leaders to challenge the norms, live outside their comfort zone, and be willing to operate in areas that are sometimes in the gray (without crossing the line), I have found it develops a much more effective organization. As a result, young leaders take ownership of their billet responsibilities while building confidence to work independently.

Challenge yourself today to create a culture that emphasizes independent, outside-the-box thinking.

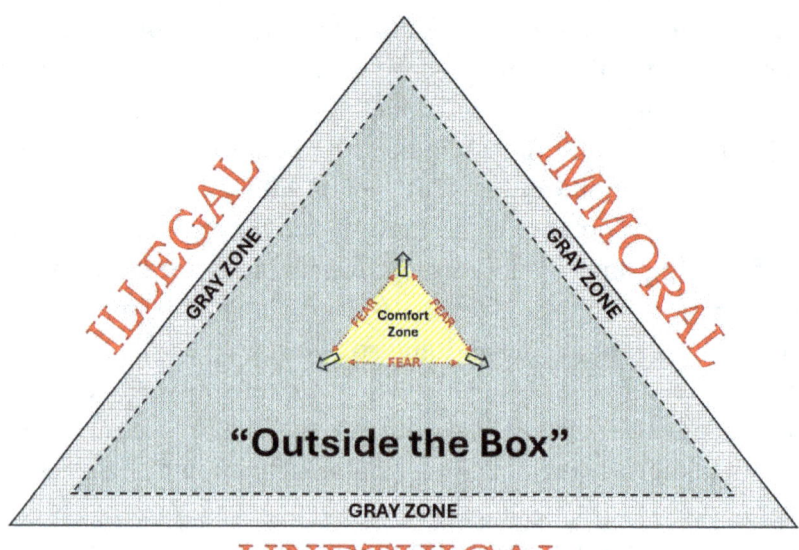

Application: How will you challenge yourself today to think outside the box? Think beyond your current comfort zone. Maybe task a member of your team with something that you haven't been willing to empower them with yet. Take, 'that can't be done,' out of your vocabulary, and start saying to your team, 'how can we get that done?' Challenge your team to push beyond their comfort zones too. Select one way to think outside the box this week.

LEADING WITH AUTHORITY AND ACTION *BH*

> "All the people were amazed and said to each other, 'What is this teaching? With authority and power He gives orders to evil spirits and they come out!' And the news about Him spread throughout the surrounding area."
>
> –Luke 4:36–37

Read: Luke 4:31–37 "Jesus Drives Out an Impure Spirit"
We witness Jesus in Capernaum, teaching with such authority and power that people are amazed. His words not only inspire but also command action, as seen when He drives out an impure spirit. This passage highlights Jesus' role as a leader who speaks and acts with authority, setting an example for us to follow.

Jesus' teachings were compelling because He spoke with authority. His words were not just informative, they were transformative. When faced with the man possessed by an evil spirit, Jesus didn't hesitate—He rebuked the spirit and commanded it to leave. This decisive action demonstrates the importance of speaking and acting with conviction and confidence.

Jesus' authoritative teaching and powerful actions earned Him a reputation that spread far and wide. People recognized His ability to lead, protect, and heal, which drew them to Him. As leaders, building a strong reputation based on our actions and integrity is crucial for gaining trust and influence.

Jesus didn't stand by when confronted with evil—He stepped up and took action. Effective leaders recognize when they need to step forward and address issues directly. This proactive approach not only resolves problems, but also sets a standard for others to follow.

Effective leaders speak and act with authority, build a strong reputation through their actions, and step up when leadership is needed.

Application: Some of us are more decisive than others. It is important to know the unique style of our behaviors. Regardless, leaders must be able to take action. They must discern when action is necessary and when increased patience is necessary. Examine yourself. Are you the one to be quick to take action or too patient when action is necessary?

BALANCING SERVICE WITH SOLITUDE *BH*

> "At daybreak, Jesus went out to a solitary place. The people were looking for Him and when they came to where He was, they tried to keep Him from leaving them. But He said, 'I must preach the good news of the kingdom of God to the other towns also, because that is why I was sent.'"
> —Luke 4:42–43

Read: Luke 4:38–44 "Jesus Heals Many"
We see Jesus healing many people, including Simon's mother-in-law. His miraculous acts draw attention and admiration, yet, Jesus balances His ministry with moments of solitude and reflection. This passage offers essential lessons on the importance of servant leadership, the need for solitude, and the clarity of purpose.

Jesus heals the sick and drives out demons, exemplifying the qualities of a servant leader. His actions reflect a deep commitment to serving others, providing healing and relief from suffering. Reflect on how you serve your team. Are you meeting their needs and helping them overcome challenges? Embrace the servant leadership model by prioritizing the well-being and development of those you lead.

Despite His demanding ministry, Jesus frequently withdrew to solitary places to rest and connect with God. This practice highlights the importance of balancing active service with moments of reflection and spiritual renewal. Do you take time to retreat and recharge? Schedule regular moments of solitude and prayer to maintain your spiritual health and leadership effectiveness.

When the people tried to keep Jesus from leaving, He remained focused on His mission to proclaim the good news to other towns. Jesus knew His purpose and stayed committed to it, even when faced with the desire of others to keep Him in one place. Are you staying true to your mission, even when it's tempting to remain where you are? Maintain clarity and commitment to your purpose, ensuring that your actions align with your long-term vision.

Leaders serve others with compassion, prioritize moments of solitude for spiritual renewal, and stay focused on their greater purpose.

<u>Application</u>: Write down several ways in which you serve your team and help them overcome challenges; and how you could improve in your service to them. Do you get burned out in serving? Consider how you can rest and recharge so that you can stay focused on the greater purpose of your team, your role, and God's will in it all.

TALENT MANAGEMENT AND SURRENDER *BH*

"When Simon Peter saw this, he fell at Jesus' knees and said, 'Go away from me, Lord; I am a sinful man!' For he and all his companions were astonished at the catch of fish they had taken, and so were James and John, the sons of Zebedee, Simon's partners. Then Jesus said to Simon, 'Don't be afraid; from now on you will catch men.' So, they pulled their boats up on shore, left everything and followed Him."
—Luke 5:8–11

<u>Read</u>: Luke 5:1–11 "Jesus Calls His First Disciples"
Jesus calls His first disciples, illustrating key principles of leadership and discipleship. This story provides us with valuable lessons on the importance of talent management and the profound act of surrendering to divine guidance.

Jesus understood the importance of having the right people on His team to fulfill His mission. By choosing Simon Peter, James, and John, He exemplified strategic talent management, ensuring

He had the right individuals to carry out His work. Evaluate your team and ensure you have the right people in the right positions. Reflect on Jim Collins' principle from *Good to Great:* "first who, then what."[15] Identify who needs to be on your team before deciding what tasks to tackle, and be willing to make necessary changes to achieve your mission.

Simon Peter provides profoundly strong leadership through surrendering to Jesus' guidance. This act of faith leads to an overwhelming reward, demonstrating the power of surrendering to divine direction. Reflect on areas where you might be resisting guidance or direction from the Holy Spirit. Create an environment to listen to God daily and submit to what He is telling you, even when it challenges your current understanding or feels uncomfortable, trusting that it will lead to greater outcomes.

The disciples' constant willingness to leave everything behind and follow Jesus highlights the level of commitment and sacrifice required to pursue a higher calling. This dedication is essential for achieving great leadership and impactful results.

Leaders must know their teammates' talents to develop them and grow the team around them.

Application: Do you have the right people in the right roles on your team? What could improve the collective talent and strength of the team? When considering promotion or another form of advancing an individual, don't promote off tenure but rather off performance. Leaders must be excellent talent managers.

THE WILL TO ACT *BH*

"While Jesus was in one of the towns, a man came along who was covered with leprosy. When he saw Jesus, he fell with his face to the ground and begged Him, 'Lord, if

You are willing, You can make me clean.' Jesus reached out His hand and touched the man. 'I am willing,' He said. 'Be clean!' And immediately the leprosy left him."

–Luke 5:12–13

Read: Luke 5:12–16 "Jesus Heals a Man with Leprosy"
Jesus heals a man with leprosy, demonstrating not only His divine power but also His willingness to act. This story offers essential insights into the qualities of determination, motivation, and purpose that are vital for effective leadership.

Jesus' response, "I am willing," highlights His readiness and determination to act. His willingness to heal the leper reflects a strong sense of purpose and commitment to doing what is necessary. Reflect on your own willingness to act as a leader. Do you have the determination to take necessary actions, even when they are challenging? Cultivate a mindset of readiness and commitment to addressing the needs of your team and achieving your goals.

Jesus not only declared His willingness but also took immediate action by reaching out and healing the man. His compassion drove Him to act decisively and make a tangible difference in the man's life. Consider how you can combine compassion with decisive action in your leadership. Strive to be a leader who acts with both heart and resolve, making a positive impact on those you lead.

Jesus' actions were driven by a clear sense of His mission and purpose. His commitment to healing and helping others was rooted in His understanding of His divine calling. Ensure that your leadership is guided by a clear and compelling purpose, motivating you to take necessary actions, and make sacrifices to achieve your goals.

Leaders possess the will to act, demonstrate compassion through decisive action, and are driven by a strong sense of purpose.

Application: Do you have a bias for action? Are you willing to take the necessary actions regardless of how challenging they may seem? Reflect on your own sense of purpose as a leader. Are your actions and you drive/willingness to act aligned with your core mission and values? Lastly, does your bias for action put the needs of your teammates and the mission above your own? Reflect and journal your thoughts.

CONFIDENCE, EMPATHY, AND AUTHORITY *BH*

"When Jesus saw their faith, He said, 'Friend, your sins are forgiven.' The Pharisees and the teachers of the law began thinking to themselves, 'Who is this fellow who speaks blasphemy? Who can forgive sins but God alone?' Jesus knew what they were thinking and asked, 'Why are you thinking these things in your hearts? Which is easier: to say, "Your sins are forgiven," or to say, "Get up and walk"? But I want you to know that the Son of Man has authority on earth to forgive sins.' So, He said to the paralyzed man, 'I tell you, get up, take your mat and go home.'"

–Luke 5:20–24

Read: Luke 5:17–26 "Jesus Forgives and Heals a Paralyzed Man"
Jesus demonstrates exceptional leadership qualities in His interactions with the paralyzed man and the Pharisees. This passage provides us with valuable lessons on confidence, empathy, and authority in leadership.

Jesus' reaction to the paralyzed man being lowered in front of Him while teaching is a powerful example of empathy and patience. Instead of being frustrated by the interruption, Jesus addresses the man's needs with compassion. This is a reminder to us that we must strive to lead with a heart that understands and responds to the challenges our team faces.

Jesus confidently asserts His authority to forgive sins and heal the paralyzed man, challenging the doubts and thoughts of the Pharisees. His confidence reinforces His leadership and authority. Consider how you demonstrate confidence in your leadership and decisions. Lead with confidence, clearly communicating your decisions and the rationale behind them to your team.

When questioned by the Pharisees, Jesus responds decisively, proving His authority and silencing their doubts. This strong response showcases His ability to handle challenges effectively. We must follow Jesus' example by responding to challenges with confidence and decisiveness, reinforcing your leadership.

Leaders must lead with empathy and patience, demonstrate confidence in their authority, and respond to challenges with strength and clarity.

Application: Reflect on your response the last time you experienced an unexpected disruption or need within your team. Were you patient and empathetic, addressing the needs of your team members with compassion? Reflect on how you handle challenges or questions about your leadership. Do you respond with strength and clarity, addressing concerns head-on? Are you assured in your authority and capable of addressing doubts or challenges?

DIVERSIFYING YOUR TEAM AND PRIORITIZING *BH*

"Then Levi held a great banquet for Jesus at his house, and a large crowd of tax collectors and others were eating with them. But the Pharisees and the teachers of the law who belonged to their sect complained to His disciples, 'Why do you eat and drink with tax collectors and sinners?' Jesus answered them, 'It is not the healthy who

> need a doctor, but the sick. I have not come to call the righteous, but sinners to repentance.'"
>
> –Luke 5:29–32

Read: Luke 5:27–32 "Jesus Calls Levi and Eats with Sinners"
Jesus calls Levi, a tax collector, to follow Him and then attends a banquet at Levi's house. This passage illustrates important leadership lessons on team diversity and prioritizing those who need leadership the most.

Jesus recruits Levi, a tax collector, demonstrating His willingness to include individuals who may not be widely accepted but possess unique value. Despite societal prejudices, Jesus recognizes Levi's potential and brings him onto His team. Embrace diversity to build a team that is rich in talent and varied in viewpoints, enhancing creativity and problem-solving.

Jesus spends time with tax collectors and sinners, prioritizing those who are in need of guidance and direction. He understands that His mission is to reach out to those who need Him the most, regardless of societal judgments. We must follow Jesus' example by prioritizing the needs of those who require our guidance and support the most, helping them reach their full potential.

Jesus' response to the Pharisees highlights His unwavering commitment to His mission. He remains focused on His purpose, regardless of external criticism or societal expectations.

Leaders embrace diversity in their teams, prioritize those who need guidance the most, and stay focused on their mission regardless of external criticism.

Application: Are you dedicating time and resources to support and mentor those who are struggling? Do you embrace the diversity of your team so that you can leverage every teammates' strengths? Write three names of people that you need to support and mentor, and approach them this week with encouragement for how you see their potential and how you want to help them grow. If you don't have a mentor, carefully select a person to approach and ask if they will mentor you.

UNDERSTAND THE *WHY* BH

> "They said to Him, 'John's disciples often fast and pray, and so do the disciples of the Pharisees, but Yours go on eating and drinking.' Jesus answered, 'Can you make the friends of the bridegroom fast while he is with them? But the time will come when the bridegroom will be taken from them; in those days they will fast.'"
>
> —Luke 5:33–35

<u>Read</u>: Luke 5:33–39 "Jesus Questioned about Fasting"

Jesus is questioned about why His disciples do not fast like the disciples of John and the Pharisees. His response encourages a deeper understanding of the reasons behind certain traditions and practices. This passage provides important insights for leaders on questioning the status quo and understanding the purpose behind actions.

Jesus challenges the Pharisees' expectations by questioning the necessity of fasting while He, the Messiah, is present. He prompts them to think critically about their practices and the reasons behind them. Leaders should encourage their team to question the status quo and seek to understand the underlying reasons for their actions.

Jesus highlights that the purpose of fasting is to seek closeness with God, a practice that was not necessary while He, God incarnate, was among them. His presence changed the context and the need for the practice. As leaders, we need to focus on and understand the *why*. We must ensure that every action has a clear and meaningful purpose, aligning with the present needs and goals of your team or organization.

Leaders question the status quo, understand the purpose behind actions, and adapt to changing circumstances.

Application: Reflect on the traditions and practices within your organization or team. Are there actions or routines that are followed without a clear understanding of their purpose? Consider the purpose behind the actions and traditions in your leadership. Are they still relevant and necessary in the current context? Write down three actions of your team that may not follow the vision, mission, or greater purpose of the team. Consider how you can make changes to remove these actions and how that may improve the effectiveness of your team.

EXALT THE SPIRIT JA

"Then Jesus said to them, 'I ask you, which is lawful on the Sabbath: to do good or to do evil, to save life or to destroy it?'"

—Luke 6:9

Read: Luke 6:1–11 "Lord of the Sabbath"
The fourth of The Ten Commandments, given by God to Moses and relayed to the Israelite community, commands us to keep the Sabbath day holy. In reverence to God, who set apart a full day after creating the heavens and the earth and everything in them, we are also to set aside time to rest and reflect (Gen 2:1–3; Exo 20:8–11). If we focus solely on work, we fail to rest and reflect on the value and production of our efforts.

By the time Jesus arrived, Jewish religious leaders had twisted this commandment to repress the people. They determined what constituted "work," and used their interpretations of the Scriptures to exert control over the populace rather than to serve them. They rebuked Jesus' disciples for picking wheat and crushing grain to eat on the Sabbath, and closely watched to see if Jesus would heal on this holy day. Their concern was not for restoration and healing, but for maintaining their grip on power.

Before Jesus, the Law was inscribed where it could be read. After Jesus, the Law was written in our hearts. Jesus demonstrated that God's Law is meant to magnify His goodness among His people, not to prevent us from loving Him and others in word and deed. When facing a difficult decision about whether a text, spoken word, or deed is good, ask yourself, "Will it gratify my flesh or the Spirit of God?" When you can affirm the latter, move forward confidently. When you deny your flesh, you make room to exalt the Spirit.

Good leaders conduct precise cost-benefit analyses. Christ-centered leaders also conduct flesh–Spirit analyses.

Application: Where may your flesh be in the way of the Spirit? What areas of your life only gratify yourself? Give yourself an honest "flesh–Spirit" analysis and consider all the environments in which you live. Find areas that gratify yourself over the Spirit and ask God to work you through removing that desire for self-gratification.

SELECTION CRITERIA *JA*

"When morning came, He called His disciples to Him and chose twelve of them, whom He also designated apostles."
–Luke 6:13

Read: Luke 6:12–16 "The Twelve Apostles"

It is often said that Jesus does not call the qualified; He qualifies the called. Praise God! Reflecting on my life, I've undertaken many roles and responsibilities for which I felt unqualified.

Jesus did not start His ministry by seeking followers. He began by proclaiming that the kingdom of God is near, demonstrating its nearness through His words and actions. This quickly earned Him credibility and followers. Although He specifically commissioned only twelve as "apostles," there were likely dozens more "disciples" — dedicated followers. From His large following, Jesus chose twelve individuals and qualified them to establish His Church.

As leaders, we must consistently pursue our own development while also fostering the growth of our teams. Jesus calls us all to follow Him, but He does not commission everyone as "apostles." For every task He assigns, He also qualifies and equips us. Are you seeking only the best, most qualified individuals for your team? Or are you looking for those with the potential to become the best? Sometimes that individual is one in the same. The choice is easy. Other times, the choice is less defined. My experience as a candidate and as an instructor in MARSOC's Assessment and Selection Course has shown me that the Marine Corps' elite unit seeks candidates with the most potential to thrive, not necessarily those with the most apparent talent.

Effective leaders build a team with unlimited potential and then train the team in the skills necessary to accomplish the mission.

Application: What criteria do you use when selecting team members? Are you only looking for the most talented, stand-out performer or are you seeking the person who best fits your team, who is coachable, and who has the strengths and talents that align well with your team and its mission?

THE COST OF CHRIST *JA*

"Rejoice in that day and leap for joy, because great is your reward in heaven. For that is how their fathers treated the prophets. But woe to you who are rich, for you have already received your comfort."
—Luke 6:23–24

Read: Luke 6:17–26 "Blessings and Woes"
During the Last Supper, John records that Jesus taught His disciples: *"If the world hates you, keep in mind that it hated me first. If you belonged to the world, it would love you as its own"* (John 15:18–19). In this passage, Jesus encourages those who may be downtrodden with worries and struggles, those who may think they do not measure up to be in the kingdom of heaven because of their low social status or the oppression of religious leaders who treat them as outcasts. In the culture of the day, and even in cultures around the world today, people who were born with disabilities, born into poor families, and those whose lives may have been destroyed by the consequences of circumstances beyond their control, were considered to have God's judgment against them, and their life was seen as the consequence of their own sin.

Jesus comes on the scene and offers blessing and relief to the poor and lowly. Not only does He offer blessings to the poor, but He also cautions those in the crowd who are rich, well-fed, and whose lives are filled with smiles. The poor need help and when they seek God, they will find it. Their financial status may not change, their social status may not change, and people may still look down on them, but they know their inheritance is heaven and they are co-heirs with Christ (Rom 8:17). Those defined by their full bank accounts, full bellies, and full social life have no desire for the work of Christ. They have their "reward in full" (Matt 6:2) and cannot see the tremendous riches of God.

Two lessons earlier, we reflected on how our decisions exalt the flesh versus the Spirit. This passage helps us reflect on how we are categorizing the "cost." If our decisions at home or in business are focused on increasing happiness in our lives, then our trust is in ourselves, and we have no need for the riches of God. If our decisions are focused on increasing holiness in our lives, then we will focus on the cost of Christ because He alone is holy. Whether you are rich or poor, embrace the cost of Christ.

Let the words of the Apostle Paul resonate with you: "But whatever was to my profit, I now consider loss for the sake of Christ. What is more, I consider everything a loss compared to the surpassing greatness of knowing Christ Jesus my Lord, for whose sake I have lost all things. I consider them rubbish, that I may gain Christ" (Phil 3:7–8). The cost of Christ is worth the gain of heaven.

Christ-centered leaders consider the cost of Christ over the cost of wealth creation.

Application: What cost have you already bore to serve Christ? Do not be discouraged in it, but be blessed. Do you embrace the cost of serving Christ over embracing the things of this world and your own financial and professional ambitions? Write two ways how you can lean you and your team into embracing the cost of serving Christ more deliberately.

OUR MOST POWERFUL WEAPON JA

"Be merciful, just as your Father is merciful."
—Luke 6:36

Read: Luke 6:27–36 "Love for Enemies"
In Matthew's Gospel account, Jesus says, "Be perfect, therefore, as your Heavenly Father is perfect" (Matt 5:48). In this context,

being merciful can be seen as synonymous with being perfect. So, what does it mean to "be merciful?" If we understand mercy as 'not receiving what we deserve,' then God's mercy is not issuing us punishment for our sins against Him. The context of this passage is that we are to show mercy to those who have hurt us, hate us, stolen from us, and who have no intention of repaying money lent to them. There is no greater form of love than to love those who hate you.

This challenging lesson is the standard of true love that Christ demonstrated for us (see, Rom 5:8). Reflect on how you can take the first step in leading with this kind of love in your circumstances. Let me share a short story about a man who demonstrated this love.

Haytham, a young Iraqi Christian in his late twenties living in Lebanon, felt God's call to return to Iraq to preach the Gospel. In 2003, after the fall of Saddam Hussein's regime, Haytham moved with his wife, Mary, to Mosul in the Iraqi province of Nineveh. They immediately faced persecution, being shunned by neighbors, spied on, and followed when they left their house. As their ministry grew and new believers were baptized, the local mosque's sheikh issued a fatwa against Haytham, demanding that Christians be expelled from the community.

In the summer/fall of 2004, Haytham and his family moved to another location in Mosul. Violence increased as the insurgency grew. One day, Haytham asked his wife how she would cope if he were martyred. She did not want to consider such a tragedy, but he insisted. The next day, as Haytham and his mother were driving to pick up some church members, they were ambushed by gunmen. Haytham was shot several times, with one bullet partially severing his spinal cord.

At the hospital, Haytham began praying. When the doctor treating him heard his prayer, he asked if Haytham was cursing the men who had shot him. Haytham answered, "I wish I could meet them and tell them about the salvation of the Lord so that they would not die in their sins and go to hell." The doctor was baffled and asked why Haytham would pray such a thing. Haytham explained, "God, who is love, abides in my heart, and He gave me love for all, even for my enemies."[16]

Most of us reading this, and most Americans, have never had our love tested to this extent. When we consider persecution in America, it often involves hurt feelings, being taken advantage of, or complaints about political corruption. If we are honest, we have not witnessed nor experienced the level of persecution that many of our brothers and sisters around the world endure daily.

When American leaders in families, small businesses, large corporations, church communities, and government agencies set an example of love following immense hurt and turmoil, and continue to do so amidst ongoing challenges, we will witness an outpouring of God's grace and mercy to heal our land.

True leadership embodies mercy and unconditional love, especially toward those who have wronged us, demonstrating the transformative power of Christ's love and fostering healing and unity.

Application: If you ever found yourself in the same situation as Haytham, do you think you could love like him? Whether you experience such turmoil or not, consider what that could be like in your life and ask God to prepare you to love unconditionally.

RIGHT THE SHIP JA

"How can you say to your brother, 'Brother let me take the speck out of your eye,' when you yourself fail to see the plank in your own eye? You hypocrite, first take the plank out of your eye, and then you will see clearly to remove the speck from your brother's eye."

–Luke 6:42

Read: Luke 6:37–42 "Judging Others"
When Jesus calls someone a hypocrite, He often addresses the religious leaders of His time. However, in this instance, He is teaching the crowd and characterizing anyone as a hypocrite who judges their brother before humbling themselves and addressing their own flaws.

I find myself realizing more and more that I often jump to conclusions about someone or a situation before clearing out the cobwebs in my life and the planks in my own eye. It is very easy to see a wrongdoing, a mistake made by someone else, or a poor decision by another leader, and either think condemning thoughts about that person or even approach them to point it out—because, well, we need to hold our brothers and sisters accountable. Agreed. But let me offer a different approach.

What if we first examined our own lives, identifying the mistakes we've made that are similar to what we have witnessed by our brother or sister in Christ, our neighbor, or our teammate, and then meditated on it for a day or even a few hours before approaching the one we feel obligated to hold accountable? When we approach that individual, we can first acknowledge where we have fallen short in the same regard, and then offer to share our own experiences. I believe people will be much more willing to listen and accept that they have made a mistake when you approach them with humility and empathy. Of course, we must consider our relationship and connection with that person while applying good tact.

As I write this, I am convicted. I hope you are too. Conviction handled appropriately will grow your ability to lead and be a team collaborator. Be humble.

Leaders:
1. <u>Reflect</u> on your own flaws
2. <u>Approach</u> your teammate who's made the mistake
3. <u>Hold accountable</u> through empathy and encouragement
4. <u>Provide</u> for their development
5. <u>Repeat</u>

Application: Consider the five-step approach when passing judgment on a teammate. Pick one person who needs to be held accountable for their actions or someone who you think needs to make specific improvements as a member of your team. Rehearse using this five-step approach with that person and then approach them with love and grace.

OUT OF YOUR OVERFLOW *JA*

> "The good man brings good things out of the good stored up in his heart, and the evil man brings evil things out of the evil stored up in his heart. For out of the overflow of his heart, his mouth speaks."
>
> −Luke 6:45

Read: Luke 6:43–45 "A Tree and Its Fruit"
As human beings, we are inherently evil when compared to God's perfect standard. So, how do we ensure that our hearts are good and that we are capable of bringing forth 'good things?'

First, we must have Jesus. Only Jesus can remedy the evil of the human heart. Second, we must adopt healthy, disciplined habits to ensure we develop and maintain our physical, spiritual, mental, and emotional health. When we struggle in any of these four aspects, we slip into our sinful nature.

We are not robots that can be recharged by plugging into a wall each night. We must take the time to do certain things or abstain from others, spend time with people we love and who love us, and focus on recharging our batteries and filling our cup. We must prioritize our own personal growth over the growth of our team. If we do not, our cup will run dry, our battery power will be depleted, and as leaders, we will fail our teammates. When we ensure our own health and personal growth, we are able to overflow our physical, spiritual, mental, and emotional health to our team.

Effective leadership begins with our commitment to consistent personal development, so that we are fully charged and capable of developing our teams.

Application: How do you rest, refit, and recharge your "batteries?" God implemented rest into His plan for us. However, we must be intentional about resting and recharging so that we can sustain ourselves for our teammates. Examine your daily and weekly routines. If you don't deliberately rest and recharge yourself physically, mentally, emotionally, and spiritually commit today to being intentional about building those habits.

LEADERSHIP FOUNDATION JA

> "He is like a man building a house, who dug down deep and laid the foundation on rock. When a flood came, the torrent struck that house but could not shake it because it was well built."
>
> —Luke 6:48

Read: Luke 6:46–49 "The Wise and Foolish Builders"
Why do humility and commitment to discipline lead to proficiency in any skill? Because they are foundational elements of personal and team development that provide stability and resilience.

Jesus illustrates this principle by comparing those who listen to His teachings and put them into practice to a well-built house that withstands a strong flood. Conversely, those who hear but do not apply His teachings are likened to a house with no solid foundation, which is destroyed when the floodwaters rise.

The foundation of our leadership must be built on humility and solid character growth. No one values a leader who is merely the fastest, smartest, or most experienced over one with strong character. Regardless of competence, a leader's effectiveness will crumble if undermined by dishonesty and lack of integrity, which is not easily restored.

As a Marine Special Operations Team (MSOT) Commander, I faced critical performance failures during training exercises, which led to a loss of confidence from some of the Marine Raiders I led. I believe I restored their confidence by taking full responsibility for those failures. While this did not instantly improve my competency, it demonstrated that my character was intact and firmly rooted, reassuring the MSOT of my commitment to navigate any challenges that lay ahead.

Reflect on how your team perceives the quality of your character. Are their perceptions accurate? If not, why might they hold that view? Remember, you are not the leader because of being the fastest, smartest, or most experienced; you are the leader because you influence the team and guide their efforts toward mission accomplishment. Are you someone they want to follow?

Before leaders seek to develop competency in skill, they must adopt an attitude of humility and seek their own character growth.

Application: We write a lot about humility. That's no accident. Much of who Jesus was, He was a humble leader. Can you classify yourself as a humble leader? Do you believe that humility is foundational to becoming a great leader? Consider two areas where you need to humble yourself and make yourself vulnerable to someone that can help you illuminate where you must be more humble.

YOUR INFLUENCE IS NOT INFINITE *JA*

"He was not far from the house when the centurion sent friends to say to Him: 'Lord, don't trouble Yourself, for I do not deserve to have You come under my roof. That

is why I did not even consider myself worthy to come to You. But say the word, and my servant will be healed.'"
—Luke 7:6–7

Read: Luke 7:1–10 "The Faith of the Centurion"
A centurion in the Roman military commanded about 100 soldiers. In the United States military, this is equivalent to a small company of infantrymen or a battery of artillery. This military commander clearly understood authority and the power that comes with it. Following Jesus' "Sermon on the Mount," as Matthew's Gospel describes it, and the many healings Jesus had performed in the area, the centurion heard about Jesus' reputation and may have even been in the crowd when Jesus taught and healed people.

The "elders of the Jews," whom the centurion sent to summon Jesus, said to Jesus that the centurion "deserves to have You" heal his servant (Luke 7:5). I can see them now, acting very pompously as if they somehow share the centurion's authority at this moment. Given what we know about how religious leaders acted at this time, my assumption isn't far off. However, the elders may also think that Jesus wants nothing to do with the Romans, because He is a Jew from a poor area under Roman oppression, so they are only trying to convince Jesus of the good nature of this Roman commander. In either case, the centurion speaks contrary to what the elders said and claims that he is undeserving of Jesus coming to him. His humble attitude shows his true character and causes Jesus to proclaim that He has "not found such great faith even in Israel" (Luke 7:9).

Throughout the events depicted in this passage, Jesus and the centurion never spoke directly to each other and never saw each other. Yet, the centurion humbled himself to Jesus' authority, and Jesus recognized the man's faith as even greater than any in Israel. The centurion could have been arrogant, thinking that he would never stoop so low as to ask for help from a poor Jew. In this passage, however, he demonstrates impeccable leadership—the ability and awareness to recognize where his own authority, power, and influence are limited. Then he seeks the One whose authority, power, and influence can affect his own situation, and he empowers that person, Jesus, through faith, to act.

Teamwork occurs when leaders can submit themselves to another's influence when theirs has reached its limits.

Application: Have you recognized times when your influence seems to have reached its limits? Consider shifting your influence in an indirect approach. Write three names of people that you could seek out and partner with to expand your influence when yours reaches its limits. It could be teammates or people outside your team, who will help propel your mission and vision forward through their influence.

VISION THROUGH COMPASSION JA

> "Then He went up and touched the coffin,
> and those carrying it stood still. He said,
> 'Young man, I say to you, get up!'"
>
> —Luke 7:14

Read: Luke 7:11–17 "Jesus Raises a Widow's Son"

Before Jesus walked out of His own grave, He personally raised the dead back to life on several occasions as documented in the Gospels. Additionally, when He took His last breath on the cross, many people who had died were raised to life and appeared to people around Jerusalem (Matt 27:51–53).

In this passage, we see Jesus' heart for a widow who lost her only son. In the 1st Century AD Jewish culture, a woman without a male protector was seen as cursed, as was a barren womb. Jesus likely walked by, attended, and witnessed many funerals during His three year ministry. For whatever reason, this funeral would not end in the burial of the dead, but in celebration of "The Resurrection" and "The Life."

Beyond returning life to this young man, Jesus returned hope to the widow and blessings to her life and to those of the town. With this act of compassion, Jesus demonstrates that His power to heal has no limits. Jesus' compassion instills confidence, hope, and belief, showing that death is not the end.

Compassionate leaders can ignite the soul of man because they see and believe what others do not.

Application: In what situations do you or your team face where compassion can revive despair? Jesus' compassion for others caused Him to act, to serve, and to bring life to those in utter despair. How can you influence the revival of someone suffering from despair and bring them overflowing joy? Can you offer notes of encouragement, a text, a card, a phone call, and support them through your compassionate concern and inspire them to live the life God has intended them to live?

RESOLUTE LEADERSHIP JA

> "For John the Baptist came neither eating bread nor drinking wine, and you say, 'He has a demon.' The Son of Man came eating and drinking, and you say, 'Here is a glutton and a drunkard, a friend of tax collectors and 'sinners.'"
> —Luke 7:33–34

Read: Luke 7:18–35 "Jesus and John the Baptist"
Though John the Baptist had already humbled himself to Jesus, recognizing Him as greater, at this early point in Jesus' ministry, John was still uncertain if Jesus was the coming Messiah. When

John's disciples questioned Him, Jesus didn't give a direct answer but instead told them to report what they had "seen and heard: The blind receive sight, the lame walk, those who have leprosy are cured, the deaf hear, the dead are raised, and the good news is preached to the poor" (Luke 7:22). Jesus pointed to His actions and teachings as evidence of His identity and proclaimed that those who do not fall away on account of Him will be blessed (Luke 7:23).

The religious leaders of the time, trusting more in their social and political status than in the word of God, had hardened hearts and were blind to the good news that John and Jesus brought. As Jesus comments in verses 33 and 34, they viewed John the Baptist as demon-possessed because he lived in the wilderness and saw Jesus as a glutton, drunkard, and a friend of sinners because He ate and drank with them.

Leaders must be resolute against the attacks that come at them from all sides. They must build their foundation on the solid rock of Jesus Christ—the Cornerstone. Without this foundation, they risk becoming like the Pharisees in this passage, making contradictory accusations to suit their own agenda, unable to see the perspective of truth. A leader's strength lies in their ability to remain resolute and focused on truth, even in the face of doubt and criticism. This strength must be anchored in a solid foundation, ensuring clarity of purpose and unwavering integrity.

> **When Christ-centered leaders face attacks for doing what is right, they stand firm in the face of opposition and courageously choose not to retaliate.**

<u>Application</u>: Are you confident enough in the leader that you are that you will stand resolute when criticism and rejection comes? If not, how can you grow in your confidence? Seek out a confident leader that you know and ask them how they lead with such confidence. Prepare now to have unwavering resolve later.

VALUING THOSE WE SERVE *JA*

"Therefore, I tell you, her many sins have been forgiven—for she loved much. But he who has been forgiven little loves little."

—Luke 7:47

Read: Luke 7:36–50 "Jesus Anointed by a Sinful Woman"
When one of the Pharisees invited Jesus to dinner, likely intrigued by His wisdom, the Pharisee still harbored doubts about Jesus' status as a prophet. The Pharisee's skepticism is revealed in verse 39, where he questions Jesus' discernment because Jesus allowed a sinful woman to approach Him. However, what followed was an unexpected lesson in humility.

Jesus shared a short parable with the Pharisee, highlighting the sinful condition of the woman and presenting Himself as the merciful Savior. Through this parable, Jesus exposed the woman as a great sinner, but then, recognizing her heartfelt worship and repentance, He forgave her sins. Jesus explained that those who have been forgiven much will love much, while those who think they need little forgiveness will love little. It's not that those forgiven little are incapable of deep love, but rather, those who fail to recognize their need for forgiveness struggle to express profound love.

This passage challenges us to examine the attitude of our hearts. Are we like the Pharisee, who saw himself as more worthy of Jesus' attention than the sinner, or are we like the woman, deeply aware of our sin and pouring out our love in humble worship?

In leadership, this principle is crucial. Do we arrogantly act as if we are more deserving of our position than those several rungs down the line and block chart, or do we recognize that we all have different strengths and weaknesses? A humble leader understands that their role is to serve those they lead, acknowledging that many of them possess strengths the leader may lack. By valuing and utilizing these strengths, a leader can build a high-performing team.

When we see our own value and our identity in Christ, then we will see the value in others and be able to leverage others' strengths to build formidable, high-performing teams.

<u>Application</u>: Do you value yourself? Do you recognize your value and your identity in Christ? How do you show value to others whether they are your close teammates or people you pass by from day to day? Write three ways you can show value to your team.

SEEK UNDERSTANDING *JA*

"When He said this, He called out, 'He who has ears to hear, let him hear.'"

–Luke 8:8

<u>Read</u>: Luke 8:1–15 "The Parable of the Sower"
Throughout His ministry, Jesus often concluded His teachings with the phrase, "He who has ears, let him hear." This was not just a poetic ending but a profound challenge. In verses 9 and 10, Jesus explains the meaning behind this statement. The kingdom of God, in its purest form, is beyond human comprehension due to our sinful nature. Jesus, knowing the hearts of men, understands who will reject His truth and who will humble themselves to accept it. His truth is revealed to all through acts of grace, mercy, and supernatural power. He heals, He resurrects, and He forgives. Yet, only those who seek understanding will truly grasp it, while those who resist will remain in darkness.

As leaders, this concept is critical. Are we genuinely seeking understanding, or do we only listen to what we want to hear? The

Apostle Paul warns in 2 Timothy 4:3–4 of a time when people will reject sound doctrine and instead gather themselves around teachers who say what their "itching ears want to hear." This was evident during Jesus' ministry when most religious leaders listened to Him not to learn but to criticize and ensnare Him in His words. They failed every time because His words are the truth.

To lead effectively, we must first seek understanding of God's word and His principles. Only then can we discern what is good, true, noble, right, pure, lovely, admirable, and praiseworthy (Phil 4:8). Reflect on how you seek understanding. When dealing with a competitor or someone you perceive as an adversary, do you listen with a genuine desire to understand, or are you only looking for an opportunity to criticize and trap them in their words?

True leaders listen not to criticize, but to learn and discern the truth. This approach fosters wisdom and builds trust, both of which are essential for effective leadership.

Application: Do you seek to understand, or do you seek to be understood? One perspective is the selfless attitude to consider what others are saying and what they are thinking while the other is the selfish attitude that is more concerned with people understanding them. When we seek to understand, we build trust with our teammates.

LISTEN TO UNDERSTAD *JA*

"Therefore consider carefully how you listen. Whoever has will be given more; whoever does not have, even what he thinks he has will be taken from him."

–Luke 8:18

Read: Luke 8:16–18 "A Lamp on a Stand"

Though the secrets of the kingdom of God are difficult for our sinful nature to understand, Jesus declares that He will not hide anything from us. He has come to proclaim His truth and the kingdom of God, not to keep it hidden.

After explaining the Parable of the Sower in the previous passage, Jesus offers a powerful caution about how we listen. He emphasizes that those who listen carefully and seek understanding will be blessed with more insight and wisdom, while those who listen superficially or with a critical spirit will lose even the little understanding they might have.

Jesus isn't talking about material possessions in this passage. Instead, He's focusing on spiritual growth and understanding. Those who approach His teachings with an open heart and a genuine desire to learn will be rewarded with deeper knowledge and insight. "Whoever has will be given more" (Luke 8:18) refers to the spiritual wealth that comes from a heart open to God's truth. When we listen with intention and humility, we not only retain what we learn but also build upon it, receiving even more wisdom and understanding over time.

On the other hand, those who listen with a critical or self-righteous attitude, seeking to find fault rather than truth, will find that their understanding diminishes. "Whoever does not have, even what he thinks he has will be taken from him" (Luke 8:18). This warning illustrates the spiritual danger of pride and a closed mind. Such an attitude prevents growth and leads to self-deception, where what little truth one possesses is gradually lost, leaving them more vulnerable to the devil's deceptions.

As leaders, this teaching is a reminder of the importance of how we listen—whether to God's word, our team members, or others around us. Are we listening to gain understanding, or are we listening only to criticize or confirm our own biases? The way we listen directly impacts our growth as leaders and our ability to lead others effectively.

In his book, *Leadership Gold*, one of John Maxwell's top leadership lessons that he has learned over decades of leading and being a student of leadership is that "the best leaders are listeners."[17] He states, "great leaders are good listeners." I'd like to share with you the five points he makes to argue why listeners are more effective leaders:

1. Understanding people precedes leading them.
2. Listening is the best way to learn.
3. Listening can keep problems from escalating.
4. Listening establishes trust.
5. Listening can improve the organization.

Leaders who listen with humility and an open heart will continue to grow in wisdom and influence, while those who listen only to criticize will find their understanding—and their leadership—diminishing over time.

Application: Examine your listening skills. Like our previous lesson, do you listen to understand or do you listen to know when you can start talking again? Make a concerted effort this week to listen intently to your team without feeling like you must respond.

OUR FIRST ALLEGIANCE JA

> "He replied, 'My mother and brothers are those who hear God's word and put it into practice.'"
>
> —Luke 8:21

Read: Luke 8:19–21 "Jesus' Mother and Brothers"
Jesus emphasizes that His primary identity is the Son of God, not merely as a son to Mary or a brother to His siblings. This distinction highlights the eternal and spiritual focus that Jesus maintained

throughout His ministry. While He loved His family, His first allegiance was always to His Heavenly Father and to fulfilling God's will.

Jesus teaches us that the most important aspect of our lives is not our earthly relationships, but our commitment to hearing God's word and putting it into practice. This can be challenging, especially when those closest to us—our parents, siblings, or friends—do not share our commitment to Christ. However, Jesus shows us that our ultimate loyalty must be to God and His kingdom.

This does not mean that we should distance ourselves from or neglect our loved ones. On the contrary, we are called to love them, serve them, and be a witness to them, even if they do not share our faith. We may need to set boundaries when their influence could lead us away from God's will, but our love for them should remain steadfast.

Reflect on those close to you who may not know Christ or are not fully committed to living for Him. How can you demonstrate the love of Christ to them, even as you prioritize your relationship with God? Perhaps it involves being patient, offering a listening ear, or gently sharing your faith when the opportunity arises. Remember, actions often speak louder than words, and living out your faith can be a powerful testimony to those who are watching.

Remaining in God's will takes precedence over the wills of our closest teammates.

Application: Where are your will and values aligned? We must start with ensuring your purpose, will, and values are nested within God's, before adopting the values and vision of any other team or teammate. Examine your beliefs, values, and the purposes you serve. How are you aligning those with God's will? What about them that need adjusted?

CONFRONT YOUR DOUBT JA

"The disciples went and woke Him, saying, 'Master, Master, we're going to drown!' He got up and rebuked the wind and the raging waters; the storm subsided, and all was calm. 'Where is your faith?' He asked His disciples."
—Luke 8:24–25

Read: Luke 8:22–25 "Jesus Calms the Storm"
The story of Jesus calming the storm is a well-known and powerful illustration of faith in the midst of fear. For many who grew up in the church, this narrative is a familiar part of Sunday school teachings. The fact that this event is recorded in all three synoptic Gospels—Matthew, Mark, and Luke—underscores its significance. Unlike the many healings Jesus performed, calming a storm is an extraordinary act, likely only performed once, making it unforgettable for those who witnessed it.

By the time this event occurred, Jesus' disciples had been with Him for several months, possibly even years. They had left behind their previous lives to follow Him, witnessed numerous healings, and even saw Him raise someone from the dead. Despite all this, they still succumbed to fear when a storm threatened their lives, even with Jesus right there in the boat with them, calmly sleeping.

This reaction is a powerful reminder that even the most devout followers of Christ can struggle with fear. Fear is a natural human response, but how we choose to confront it reveals the depth of our faith. The disciples' fear, despite all they had seen and experienced, highlights the challenge of truly trusting Jesus in every situation.

The question isn't about eliminating fear—fear is a part of the human experience. The real question is how we confront our fears. Do we face them with doubt, questioning God's presence and power in our lives? Or do we confront them with determination, anchored in the faith that Jesus is with us, even in the most turbulent storms?

Just as Jesus rebuked the wind and waves, bringing calm to the storm, He calls us to trust in His power and presence in our lives. When we face our fears with determination and faith, we allow Jesus to bring peace to our hearts, no matter the circumstances.

Even when the storms of life seem overwhelming, a leader must remain determined, trusting in God's presence and power to bring peace and calm.

Application: What doubts and fears are you facing today? Are there fears that spring up from uncertainty in your family or workplace? Remain calm and seek the one who brings peace in the midst of the storm. Right now, take 5 minutes and list your fears to God. Ask Him to walk with you through the storms when they rage and the eerie quiet of uncertainty that creates fear and doubt. Pray now that you will trust His will and providence in your life and move forward with the peace He will give you.

"D.W.J.D" JA

> "The man from whom the demons had gone out begged to go with Him, but Jesus sent him away, saying, 'Return home and tell how much God has done for you.' So, the man went away and told all over town how much Jesus had done for Him."
>
> –Luke 8:38–39

Read: Luke 8:26–39 "The Healing of a Demon-Possessed Man"
In the summer of 2024, I attended the International Maxwell Conference (IMC) in Orlando, FL, where I completed my certification as a Maxwell Leadership Certified Team (MLCT) Member. During the worship service, John Maxwell delivered a message rooted in his latest book, *Jesus, the High Road Leader*. Maxwell defines an MLCT Member as "a person of value, who values people,

and adds value to people." He epitomizes this definition daily, drawing directly from the example of Jesus.[18]

This passage is a striking example of how Jesus valued someone whom society had utterly rejected. After crossing the Sea of Galilee, Jesus confronted a man possessed by many demons—a man who had been bound in chains and cast out to live among the tombs. The townspeople saw him as worthless, dangerous, and beyond hope. But Jesus saw his inherent worth, setting him free from the demons that tormented him. Despite this miraculous act, the townspeople wanted nothing to do with Jesus and asked Him to leave (Luke 8:37). Jesus complied because He does not stay where He is not welcome.

Do we value people the way Jesus did, or do we value them as the crowd does?

Halfway through Maxwell's message, he distributed bracelets inscribed with "D.W.J.D."—an evolution of the "W.W.J.D." (What Would Jesus Do?) bracelets popular in the late 1990s. Maxwell's point in his book is that we should stop merely asking what Jesus would do and instead start doing what Jesus did—"Do What Jesus Did." Jesus valued people because they were made in the image of His Father.

You can never influence someone that you don't value.

<u>Application</u>: What does it look like for you to show value to one person today? Write three ways that you can show value to someone and do it for at least one person today.

OUR LARGEST STEP *JA*

"Then He said to her, 'Daughter, your faith has healed you. Go in peace.'" "But He took her by the hand and said, 'My child, get up!'"

—Luke 8:48 and 54

Read: Luke 8:40–56 "A Dead Girl and a Sick Woman"
In this miraculous display of His compassion, power, and peace, Jesus heals a woman who had suffered from hemorrhaging for years and raises to life a young girl who had just died of an illness. In both cases, His power is activated by the faith of those who sought Him.

When Jairus' daughter died before Jesus arrived at the house, Jesus simply told him, "Don't be afraid; just believe, and she will be healed" (Luke 8:50). Despite the mourners wailing outside, Jesus told them to stop, saying the girl was only asleep (Luke 8:52). Their reaction was to laugh at Him. Jesus then chose only the girl's parents, Peter, James, and John to enter the house with Him to witness the miracle. Why did He exclude the others? One reason could be the strength of Jairus' faith, which brought Jesus to the house in the first place. Another reason might be that Peter, James, and John had greater faith than the other disciples, as these three were often selected by Jesus to witness His most profound displays of power. A more practical reason could be the size of the house—only a few could fit inside. All the explanations are reasonable.

Can we, as humans, empower an all-powerful God? Yes! We do so through our faith. Jesus doesn't force us to love or believe in Him, but when we do, it unlocks His infinite power. Do you want to experience that power in your life? Then trust and believe that He is able.

We all face struggles—whether physical illness, relational stress, emotional brokenness, mental blocks, or spiritual weaknesses. This passage encourages us to believe, and we will be healed. Healing doesn't always come in the form we desire, but understand this: your struggles are not meant to weigh you down. They are there to build you up, to shape you into more than a conqueror, so that the glory of God will be revealed in your life and to those around you.

Leaders move forward in courageous faith with a clear vision of the end state even when they do not fully understand the ways or means.

Application: God is waiting for your faith to catapult the potential He has placed in your life. He wants to influence many people through you. Will you decide to have courage in your faith to move forward with a clear vision even when you don't know how you will achieve it? Find a mentor or an accountability partner to encourage you to stay the course when your faith is weak.

CONSIDER YOUR APPROACH JA

"If people do not welcome you, shake the dust off your feet when you leave their town, as a testimony against them."
—Luke 9:5

Read: Luke 9:1–9 "Jesus Sends out the Twelve"
Matthew, Mark, and Luke all record the event when Jesus commissions the Twelve with authority to heal, drive out demons, and preach the kingdom of God. Although each account offers a different perspective, all three make a point to include Jesus' instruction to "shake the dust off your feet," if they are not welcomed.

A leader's vision, energy, or approach is not always welcomed. It may be embraced by some while rejected by others. In some cases, leaders must shake the dust off their feet and depart the situation or environment altogether. In other cases, they must do so and then reapproach the situation from a different angle. However, before leaving, a leader must first examine themselves to determine whether their approach or delivery was the cause of the rejection.

My good friend and Red Letter Leadership teammate, Eric "Spaz" Albright, flew over 250 combat missions in the single-seat cockpit of the Marine Corps' AV-8B Harrier attack jet. Although I haven't spoken with him much about those missions, I assume he had to circle back and reattack on more than one occasion. Whether his own approach was off, preventing effective targeting, or he was waived off by the terminal air controller on the ground, he likely had to reattack enemy targets multiple times.

Consider your approach. Your decision or course of action may be what the situation needs, but is your delivery and approach the best way to handle it? Before shaking the dust off your feet when you are not welcomed, consider approaching your team and the situation from another angle. This may require you to apologize and seek forgiveness from your teammates, but it could also lead to the breakthrough you seek.

Effective leadership requires both the wisdom to know when to persist and the humility to reassess and adjust your approach when necessary.

Application: When was the last time that you felt like how you handled or approached a situation was not welcomed by your team? Think back to that time and consider how you could adjust your approach? What angles or perspectives of the situation might you have missed? In a short paragraph, journal how you could have handled the situation better and commit to doing so the next time you are faced with a similar situation.

BLOOM WHERE YOU ARE PLANTED *JA*

> "He replied, 'You give them something to eat.' They answered, 'We have only five loaves of bread and two fish—unless we go and buy food for all this crowd.'"
>
> —Luke 9:13

Read: Luke 9:10–17 "Jesus Feeds the Five Thousand"
The disciples returned from their mission of driving out demons, healing the sick, and preaching the kingdom of God, eager to report

their successes to Jesus. Recognizing their need for rest and emotional recharge, Jesus decided to take them to a remote place. However, the crowds followed them even there. As the day wore on, the disciples, concerned for the people's well-being, suggested sending the crowd away to find food and shelter—a reasonable consideration. But Jesus responded, "You give them something to eat" (Luke 9:13). He was challenging the disciples to see themselves as the solution to the problem at hand.

Often, we look elsewhere for solutions when the answer lies within us. God gifts us with specific strengths and talents, and He places us in particular locations, surrounded by certain networks and support groups. These are not coincidences; they are part of God's plan to equip us to solve problems and bring His kingdom to earth through our actions. Words alone will not draw people to Jesus, but our actions—rooted in faith and empowered by God—can make a profound impact.

Instead of making excuses or complaining about the enormity of the challenges we face, we should have faith that God has placed us exactly where we are needed to be the solution. He placed us right here, right now to be the solution to the problem. Bloom where He has placed you to bloom.

> **Leaders are problem solvers. Believe that God has equipped you to be the solution to the challenges around you.**

<u>Application</u>: Where has God placed you? Physically: In the family, geographic location, and work that He has placed you? Write down where He has placed you. Instead of wishing He placed you here or there, commit to using the talents He's given you and serving Him right where He placed you. Surrender to His will in your life because He will use you in ways you never thought possible.

DENY SELF *JA*

> "Then He said to them all: 'If anyone would come after Me, he must deny himself and take up his cross daily and follow Me.'"
>
> —Luke 9:23

Read: Luke 9:18–27 "Peter's Confession of Christ"
In this passage, Jesus deliberately asks His disciples, particularly the Twelve, who they believe He is. Simon Peter, often the most vocal of the group, boldly declares, "The Christ of God." Jesus then instructs them not to tell anyone and proceeds to explain the true cost of following Him.

If we truly believe that Jesus Christ is the greatest leader to have ever walked the earth, and that He is indeed "The Christ of God," then we must be prepared to "deny [ourselves] and take up [our] cross daily" (Luke 9:23) in order to follow Him in leadership. Christ-centered leadership is not for the faint of heart; it requires a willingness to deny oneself.

One of Red Letter Leadership's Seven Pillars is "Leadership is a daily effort." We also emphasize that the first step in leading yourself and others is to adopt an attitude of humility. True humility means denying our own will, ambitions, and agenda for the sake of the team—especially the ultimate team, the Body of Christ. If we are to be Christ-centered leaders, we must prioritize the advancement of God's kingdom through the teamwork of the Body of Christ, with Christ as the head, above all other endeavors.

> **Leadership requires daily humility and self-denial, prioritizing the advancement of the team over personal ambitions.**

Application: What about yourself must you deny today? What are you hoping to accomplish that does not serve anything other than your own ambitions? Ask God to show you the great potential He has for you, and where you stand in your own way of growth.

AFFIRM ONE ANOTHER *JA*

> "A voice came from the cloud, saying, 'This is My Son, whom I have chosen; listen to Him.'"
>
> —Luke 9:35

Read: Luke 9:28–36 "The Transfiguration"

Jesus' miraculous actions—healing the sick, raising the dead, driving out demons, giving sight to the blind—along with His teachings, all give evidence that He is the Messiah, the One foretold by the ancient prophets. Yet, despite these extraordinary acts, He was also a human being and a close friend to His twelve disciples, especially Peter, John, and James. It's natural to imagine that anyone walking with the Messiah might occasionally struggle with doubts, wondering if He truly was the Chosen One.

In the account of the Transfiguration, God the Father directly addresses Peter, John, and James, affirming that Jesus is His Chosen One. Although Jesus always spoke the truth because He is the truth, He didn't go around boasting about His identity as the Messiah. Instead, He allowed His actions, His compassion, and the fulfillment of prophecy to point to Him. He also gave space for the Father to affirm Him before His closest friends and followers.

As leaders, no matter our competencies, strengths, or impressive resumes, we will still encounter those who doubt our abilities. This is why it's essential to consistently encourage and affirm one another. We should not let pride prevent us from receiving praise and affirmation from those around us—a brother, sister, spouse, mentor, or boss. Remember, "It is more blessed to give than to receive" (Acts 20:35). Today, make it a point to offer praise and affirmation to someone in your life.

Leaders do not seek their own affirmation, but rather seek to affirm those on their team and those who influence their team.

Application: Do you appreciate encouragement and affirmation? Of course you do. Who in your life needs some today? List at least one member of your family, one coworker, and someone in your church or community and something that you can encourage each one for. Then commit to giving that encouragement to at least one of them today.

DEMONS EA

> "Even while the boy was coming, the demon threw him to the ground in a convulsion. But Jesus rebuked the impure spirit, healed the boy and gave him back to his father."
> —Luke 9:42

Read: Luke 9:37–45 "The Healing of a Boy with an Evil Spirit"
Following one of the most unique events in Jesus' story, the Transfiguration, He comes down off the mountain to continue His ministry. Word has spread far and wide regarding His miraculous abilities, so anywhere He goes people find Him and ask for healing. In this lesson, we find a father bringing his son to Jesus to cast out a demon causing convulsions, screaming, and foaming at the mouth. Upon bringing the boy to Jesus, He immediately rebukes and casts out the demon, curing the boy's ailment.

While Jesus quite literally dealt with demons, many of us have heard the phrase, "I'm dealing with a demon" in the metaphorical sense. What demons are you dealing with? What roadblocks are preventing progress for you? Is it difficulty with a coworker or an employee? Is it the prospect of changing jobs or positions within your organization? Are you wrestling with the thought of how/when to expand your business? Regardless of the "demons" you might be dealing with, as the text shows us, you can bring it to the feet of Jesus. Using prayer, reflection, and Scripture to help you solve a problem not only provides clarity and foresight, but it will also bring you closer in relationship with Him in the process.

For me, deliberate prayer and reflection time has been a skill I've had to learn over time. However, what I've found is that starting my day with at least 30 minutes of solitary, personal prayer and study, greatly increases the clarity from which I can begin my day. The time spent before the world wakes up and gets moving is a great opportunity to clear my head, think through the challenges I might face, and grow in relationship with Christ through both prayer and Scripture. Frankly, this has become the part of the day I most look forward to. I challenge you today to deliberately carve out time to do the same over the next month and let us know how it goes.

Find personal time to bring your "demons" to Jesus with prayer.

<u>Application</u>: The time it takes you to read this lesson and the associated Scripture passage is probably about 10 minutes. If you don't spend time reflecting on these readings or other readings you do and recording your reflections, consider incorporating that time into your daily routine.

OUTSIDE INFLUENCE *EA*

> "Then He said to them, 'Whoever welcomes this little child in My name welcomes Me; and whoever welcomes Me welcomes the One who sent Me. For he who is least among you all—he is the greatest.'"
> —Luke 9:48

<u>Read</u>: Luke 9:46–50 "Who Will be the Greatest"
Once again, we find the disciples bewildered and bickering amongst themselves. In this lesson, they are arguing about who among them

is the greatest, prompting Jesus to teach them a profound lesson on true greatness. Jesus places a child beside Him and explains that whoever welcomes a child in His name welcomes Him, and whoever welcomes Him welcomes the One who sent Him. He emphasizes that true greatness lies in humility and service to others, not in seeking personal glory or status. Furthermore, Jesus is not only unfazed by the news of others casting out demons in His name, He encourages it, "for whoever is not against you is for you." (Luke 9:50)

From this passage, leaders can draw a crucial lesson about humility and inclusivity. Jesus emphasizes that greatness in the kingdom of God is not about status or power, but about humility and service. Welcoming and valuing those who are considered least, such as children, reflects a heart aligned with God's values. In leadership, this means prioritizing the well-being and contributions of all team members, regardless of their position or perceived importance. A leader who practices humility fosters a culture of respect and unity, which can enhance collaboration and morale within the organization.

Additionally, the passage teaches the importance of inclusivity and collaboration. When John expresses concern about someone driving out demons in Jesus' name but not being part of their group, Jesus' response underscores that the mission is greater than group boundaries. Leaders should recognize and support those working toward the same goals, even if they are outside the immediate team or organization. This inclusive mindset encourages broader cooperation and helps break down silos, enabling more effective and comprehensive approaches to achieving common objectives. Embracing humility and inclusivity can significantly enhance a leader's ability to inspire and unify their team.

The least among us is sometimes the greatest. Value and welcome everyone, and recognize that collaboration with those outside your immediate group can advance common goals.

Application: Do you remember a team that you were/are a part of where its hierarchy cause people to think they are "better" than those below them in the organization? This is a toxic culture and can be changed with attitude. When we value everyone else we increase our efforts to collaborate and work together. Commit today to ensuring you have the right attitude to value others and collaborate with others in order to strengthen your team and encourage collaboration with others outside your team.

POSITION OR INFLUENCE? *EA*

> "...but the people there did not welcome Him, because He was heading for Jerusalem. When the disciples James and John saw this, they asked, 'Lord, do you want us to call fire down from heaven to destroy them?' But Jesus turned and rebuked them."
> —Luke 9:53–55

Read: Luke 9:51–56 "Samaritan Opposition"
After completing His work in southern Galilee, Jesus begins His journey to Jerusalem, passing through the Samaritan region. Although Jesus sent messengers ahead to prepare the local people for His arrival, He is not received well in this region. Luke explains that this rejection is because Jesus' focus was on His impending death, burial, and resurrection—the fulfillment of His earthly ministry. However, when two of the disciples ask if He would like them to destroy the city that rejected Him, Jesus sharply rebukes them, wanting no part of such retaliation.

When our leadership style or presence is unwelcome or poorly perceived, how do we respond? Do we rebuke those who reject us? Do we expect people to follow us just because of our position? John Maxwell labels this 'positional leadership,' the most basic form of leadership, where authority is granted simply because of the job or title one holds. This level of leadership requires no ability or effort to achieve. As Maxwell states, a position is a poor substitute for influence.[19]

Leadership through influence, rather than authority, calls for a deep understanding of the power of example. Effective leaders like Jesus navigate rejection and resistance not with force (like the two disciples sought), but with persuasion and moral authority. Such influence is powerful and enduring, capable of inspiring change and dedication even in the most challenging circumstances. By focusing on influence over authority, leaders can create a more dynamic, engaged, and committed team.

> **"A position is a poor substitute for influence." –John Maxwell**

<u>Application</u>: Take a few minutes to reflect and examine yourself. Do you carry out your leadership duties because of the position you hold or the influence you wield? Your influence will carry you and your team much further than your position. Commit to leading through your influence, not your position. Write down three ways the health of a team and its culture can improve with a leader who is committed to leading through influence.

FUTURE IS THE FOCUS *EA*

"He said to another man, 'Follow me.' But he replied, 'Lord, first let me go and bury my father.' Jesus said to him, 'Let the dead bury their own dead, but you go and proclaim the kingdom of God.'"
—Luke 9: 59–60

<u>Read</u>: Luke 9:57–62 "The Cost of Following Jesus"

At first glance, Jesus directing a young man to forgo the burial of his father and follow Him into Jerusalem may come off as crass or paint Jesus' words as unempathetic. However, upon deeper analysis, Jesus' words in this instance are deliberate and intentionally symbolic. Upon accepting Jesus as our own Lord and Savior, an intentional, deliberate heart change must occur. As such, we must leave our past behind and focus on future glory and what is to come, which is exactly what Jesus is portraying to the young man in this passage; let the things that happened yesterday be handled by those still living with the dead (either spiritually, figuratively, or literally), and focus on Him and the future He will provide you.

As applied to leaders, this passage serves as an excellent reminder that while good leaders focus on today's tasks at hand, great leaders also focus on developing the organization and its people for future endeavors and initiatives. We have a saying in my current unit, 'Your last command's job was to prepare you for today, our job is to prepare you for five years from now.' The point of that assertion is that we cannot spend an abundance of time teaching our senior enlisted leaders and commissioned officers how to do their current job; they should already know how to do their job, and do it well. As a command leadership team, our focus needs to be on building and refining the leadership skills of our mid-level leadership team so they're ready to lead a larger, more complex unit as they continue to gain rank and garner more responsibility with a bigger impact. If we focus on deliberately addressing with them the building blocks required for positions of higher authority, they will be far better prepared with a far higher likelihood of success when they reach those positions. Conversely, if we don't spend time focusing on developing those mid-level leaders for future responsibilities, they will be 'learning on the job,' or 'building the airplane as they fly it,' once they reach that point in their careers, and that isn't fair to them or their future commands.

Great leaders focus not only on present tasks but also on preparing their teams for future responsibilities and greater challenges.

<u>Application</u>: What are you doing today to ensure you are not only managing current tasks effectively, but also deliberately preparing your team members for future roles and responsibilities? How are you mentoring, coaching, and developing them for future roles within the team or outside your team? If you don't have monthly or at least quarterly 1:1 meetings with your teammates, consider how you can incorporate that to ensure a personal connection with them and your involvement in their future.

DON'T BE A WOLF EA

> "After this the Lord appointed seventy-two others and sent them two by two ahead of Him to every town and place where He was about to go. He told them, 'The harvest is plentiful, but the workers are few. Ask the Lord of the harvest, therefore, to send out workers into His harvest field. Go! I am sending you out like lambs among wolves.'"
> —Luke 10: 1–3

<u>Read</u>: Luke 10:1–24 "Jesus Sends out the Seventy-Two"
As Jesus prepared for His final days, He sent seventy-two disciples ahead of Him into towns and cities to proclaim the good news that "The kingdom of God is near you" (Luke 10:9). He instructed them to heal the sick in towns that welcomed them. However, in towns that rejected them, they were to publicly declare, "Even the dust of your town that sticks to our feet we wipe off against you. Yet be sure of this: The kingdom of God is near" (Luke 10:11). Jesus warned that for such towns, the judgment would be more severe than for Sodom.

This account from Luke prompts us to reflect organizationally on how we would receive help if it were offered today. What if 'messengers' arrived offering personal assistance or improvement? Would we recognize and welcome these messengers, or dismiss them as intruders, akin to the wolves Jesus mentions?

In the spirit of Proverbs 27:17, which advocates for mutual iron on iron sharpening, leaders must actively seek comprehensive, 360-degree feedback. While feedback often comes from colleagues or friends, as Jesus demonstrates, it can also come unexpectedly from outside our immediate network or 'circle of trust.'

> **Embrace assistance from unexpected sources. Avoid being the wolf when a sheep from another herd comes to help.**

Application: Be vulnerable. Have an open mind. Be humble to accept constructive criticism and encouraging feedback regardless of where it resides. Be willing to accept any criticism even when it is offered inappropriately or in a mean-spirited way. Receive it and then discern whether or not you should heed it. Be consistently open to your own growth and commit to encouraging the growth of your team.

BE NEIGHBORLY EA

"In reply Jesus said: 'A man was going down from Jerusalem to Jericho, when he was attacked by robbers. They stripped him of his clothes, beat him and went away, leaving him half dead. A priest happened to be going down the same road, and when he saw the man, he passed by on the other side. So too, a Levite, when he came to the place and saw him, passed by on the other side. But a Samaritan, as he traveled, came where the

> man was; and when he saw him, he took pity on him. He went to him and bandaged his wounds, pouring on oil and wine. Then he put the man on his own donkey, brought him to an inn and took care of him. The next day he took out two denarii and gave them to the innkeeper. "Look after him," he said, "and when I return, I will reimburse you for any extra expense you may have.""
>
> –Luke 10:30–35

Read: Luke 10:25–37 "The Parable of the Good Samaritan"
The verses in question were spoken by Jesus in response to a probing question from a lawyer who was seeking self-justification. Jesus, known for communicating through parables, illustrates His point by describing three different responses to a man who was robbed on the road. Through The Parable of the Good Samaritan, He clarifies the concept of 'who is a neighbor' by showing that sometimes, help comes from the most unexpected sources.

Applying this to a leadership context, it prompts us to reflect: Am I being neighborly today? When we look around at teams and organizations similar to ours, we should evaluate what we are doing to assist those teams or the individuals within them. Are we so consumed with our own agendas that we overlook those who may be struggling, missing opportunities to extend an olive branch of support, much like the Samaritan did for the Jew on the road?

Recently, I started having lunch with a peer from a sister unit who holds the same position as I do. These meetings, which began by chance, have evolved into a constructive relationship. We are now actively and intentionally seeking ways to enhance our respective units through mutual support and collaboration. Often, being a good neighbor involves consciously choosing to communicate, start conversations, and build relationships that foster mutual growth and support with individuals we might not have initially intended to or expected to engage with.

> **The question is not only "who is my neighbor" but "how can I be a neighbor" today?**

Application: It is easy to want everyone to see us as a friend and neighbor, but it is imperative that we value you everyone and see them as friends and neighbors. How will we respond in our words and actions differently when we do? Think of someone, or another team, that seems more like the opposition than a supporter or friend. Without compromising your own team's integrity or values, how can you serve the person or team that you consider the opposition? How will your service improve relations, collaboration, and help shape the bigger picture of your environment more favorable to all.

BE PRESENT *EA*

> *"'Martha, Martha,' the Lord answered, 'you are worried and upset about many things, but few things are needed—or indeed only one. Mary has chosen what is better, and it will not be taken away from her.'"*
>
> –Luke 10: 41–42

Read: Luke 10:38–42 "At the Home of Mary and Martha"
When Jesus entered a village and sat down for dinner with Martha and her sister Mary, Martha became agitated because she was busy in the kitchen preparing the meal, while her sister Mary sat at the feet of Jesus, fully engaged and present in the moment. Jesus responded by pointing out to Martha that Mary's approach should be emulated, as she was free from distractions and anxiety, fully appreciating the time at hand.

In my day-to-day interactions at work, I often find myself in the same position as Martha. As a leader, I have many visitors and folks who stop by my office for direction or discussion throughout the day. Like Martha, I am frequently distracted by the tasks I was working on before someone stopped in, and I often fail to give those who are seeking advice the attention they deserve.

A lesson we all can learn from Luke's account of Jesus visiting Mary and Martha's is the importance of being present in the moment. Whether it's being preoccupied with a previous task when a coworker stops by the office or scrolling through social media while our spouses are trying to converse with us, many of us can admit that we struggle with being truly present. Let's make a concerted effort today to set aside distractions when opportunities to engage in meaningful conversations with spouses, coworkers, or anyone else arise.

Be present and free of distractions.

Application: In the information age, this is likely a convicting lesson for all of us. Reflect today on your past week. When have you been physically present at home or with your team but the distractions of this world, whether that be social media, TV, or something else, intercept your attention from those who deserve it?

LEADING THROUGH PERSISTENT PRAYER BH

> "So I say to you: Ask and it will be given to you; seek and you will find; knock and the door will be opened to you. For everyone who asks receives; the one who seeks finds; and to the one who knocks, the door will be opened."
> —Luke 11:9–10

Read: Luke 11:1–13 "Jesus' Teaching on Prayer"
Jesus' disciples approach Him with a simple yet profound request: "Lord, teach us to pray." In response, Jesus provides them with the

Lord's Prayer, setting a clear and timeless standard for how to communicate with God. He doesn't stop there; He further emphasizes the importance of persistence and faith in prayer by encouraging them to ask, seek, and knock, assuring them that God responds to those who earnestly pursue Him.

As leaders, we learn from Jesus the significance of establishing clear guidelines and models for our teams to follow. Providing a standard, like the Lord's Prayer, equips those we lead with the tools they need to navigate challenges and stay aligned with core values and purposes. Additionally, Jesus teaches us that leadership involves acknowledging our limitations and encouraging reliance on a higher source of wisdom and strength. Just as Jesus directed His disciples to seek God's guidance through persistent prayer, we too should foster an environment where seeking insight beyond our understanding is valued and practiced.

This approach aligns with leadership principles highlighted by thinkers like Simon Sinek, who stresses understanding and communicating the "Why" behind our actions. By encouraging our teams to connect deeply with their purpose and seek guidance through prayer, we empower them to act with intention and resilience, especially in the face of uncertainty and obstacles.

Effective leadership involves setting clear standards and encouraging persistent pursuit of wisdom and guidance beyond ourselves through prayer.

Application: Do you have a core group of close confidants that you can seek wisdom and guidance? God wants His Body to work together as a team. Though we must be persistent in prayer, we must also seek wisdom from others within the Body of Christ. Commit to being a mentee and seek out someone from whom you can gain wisdom.

LEADERSHIP AND UNITY BH

> "Whoever is not with Me is against Me, and whoever does not gather with Me scatters."
>
> —Luke 11:23

<u>Read</u>: Luke 11:14–28 "Jesus and Beelzebul"

Jesus performs a significant miracle by driving out an evil spirit from a man, demonstrating His divine power. Instead of recognizing Him as the Messiah, some people begin to spread rumors that Jesus' power comes from Beelzebul, the prince of demons. Jesus addresses this accusation with wisdom, pointing out that a kingdom divided against itself cannot stand. He also states a profound truth: "Whoever is not with Me is against Me, and whoever does not gather with Me scatters" (Luke 11:23).

As leaders, we can draw several lessons from this encounter. Jesus shows us the importance of maintaining unity within our teams. Just as He emphasized the need for alignment and unity, we must ensure that our team members are on board with the mission and vision we are pursuing. When a team is united, it moves forward with strength and purpose. However, when division creeps in, it weakens the team, leading to disarray and confusion.

Moreover, Jesus' response to those who doubted and criticized Him teaches us how to handle opposition. As leaders, we will inevitably face criticism, especially when making difficult decisions or taking bold actions. Like Jesus, we must respond with wisdom and maintain our focus on the bigger picture. Instead of getting sidetracked by negativity, we should address it directly, reaffirm our commitment to the mission, and encourage our team to stay united.

Finally, the idea of gathering versus scattering is crucial in leadership. A leader's role is not just to guide but to bring people together, creating a cohesive unit that works toward a common goal. When a leader fails to do this, the team becomes fragmented, and its effectiveness diminishes. Ensuring that every team member is aligned and working toward the same objectives is essential for achieving success.

Effective leaders maintain unity within their teams, handle opposition with wisdom, and ensure that everyone is working toward a common goal.

Application: Do you do a good job uniting your team? First, is your team working toward a common goal nested in a unified vision? Do you incorporate them into your strategic and tactical planning? Do you give your team buy-in? These are only a few ways in which leaders unify their teams. Write down three ways that you can strengthen the unity of your current team(s).

THE CHALLENGE OF UNBELIEF *BH*

"For as Jonah was a sign to the Ninevites, so also will the Son of Man be to this generation."
—Luke 11:30

Read: Luke 11:29–32 "The Sign of Jonah"
Jesus expresses His frustration with those who still refuse to believe He is the Messiah, despite the many signs and miracles He had performed. He compares Himself to Jonah, who was a sign to the Ninevites when he emerged from the belly of the whale after three days and nights. Just as Jonah's experience was a call for the people of Nineveh to repent, Jesus foreshadows His own death and resurrection, which will serve as the ultimate sign of His divine identity and purpose. Jesus is not just a prophet, He is God in the flesh, offering the greatest proof of His mission.

As leaders, we often face similar frustrations when our team members fail to buy into our vision or doubt our abilities, even when our track record speaks for itself. No matter how much we demonstrate our competence and commitment, there will always be those who resist or refuse to fully support our leadership.

It's important to recognize that not everyone will be persuaded, no matter how compelling our evidence or how clear our direction is. We must remain steadfast in our mission, understanding that some will simply not embrace our leadership or the path we are trying to take the organization.

Not everyone will embrace your leadership, but stay committed to your mission and vision, leading with confidence and integrity.

Application: Reflect on a time when your team did not embrace your leadership or a path you wanted to take them. How did you adjust? Did you remain committed to the vision? Were you able to move forward with the support you did receive? If not, how did you garner more support?

GUARDING THE LIGHT WITHIN BH

"Your eye is the lamp of your body. When your eyes are healthy, your whole body also is full of light. But when they are unhealthy, your body also is full of darkness. See it, then, that the light within you is not darkness."
—Luke 11:34–35

Read: Luke 11:33–36 "The Lamp of the Body"
Jesus emphasizes the importance of maintaining purity and holiness. Our eyes serve as the gateway to our soul, and what we choose to see can either fill us with light or lead us into darkness. As leaders, what we take in through our eyes shapes our beliefs and directly impacts our strength and influence.

It's crucial to be mindful of what we expose ourselves to—whether it's what we watch, read, or engage in. As Christian leaders, our responsibility is to protect our minds and souls so that we can be a positive light to those we lead, whether at home, in our community, or within our organization.

By being intentional about what we allow our eyes to see, we can ensure that the light within us remains strong and shines brightly for others.

Leaders must guard their hearts and minds to ensure they maintain their character of integrity and live above reproach.

Application: Consider your daily routines: Do they help you start the day with blessings and positivity? Are there habits or influences that allow darkness to creep in? Leaders must be vigilant in guarding their minds and souls, ensuring that what they take in through their eyes fills them with light, not darkness.

AUTHENTIC INFLUENCE BH

"Then the Lord said to him, 'Now then, you Pharisees clean the outside of the cup and dish, but inside you are full of greed and wickedness. You foolish people! Did not the One who made the outside make the inside also?'"

—Luke 11:39–40

Read: Luke 11:37–54 "Woes on the Pharisees and the Experts in the Law"

Jesus confronts a Pharisee, who was surprised when Jesus did not wash His hands before eating. Knowing the Pharisee's thoughts, Jesus uses the moment to teach a powerful lesson: it is more important to be clean on the inside than merely to appear clean on the outside. The Pharisees, known for their elaborate outward displays of piety and importance, were often inwardly full of greed and wickedness.

Jesus emphasizes the value of inner purity over external appearances. As leaders, we can apply this lesson by focusing on our internal development—cultivating a pure heart, loving thoughts, and sincere intentions—rather than just maintaining an outward facade of perfection. Too often, leaders fall into the trap of portraying a "do as I say, not as I do" attitude, which can undermine their credibility and influence.

True leadership is rooted in authenticity. When we prioritize our internal growth, it reflects in our actions, decisions, and relationships. Jesus teaches that if we neglect our inner self, it will eventually manifest outwardly, exposing a lack of sincerity. To lead effectively, we must deliberately develop ourselves from the inside out, ensuring that our leadership is grounded in genuine character and integrity.

> **True leadership starts from within; cultivating a pure heart and sincere intentions is essential for authentic influence.**

Application: Do you replicate the leadership that you want your team to follow? Do you prioritize leading yourself over leading others? Reflect on how well you lead yourself today? Do you have a sound personal development plan? Do you have close confidants that can hold you accountable to set the example for your team?

LEADING WITH THE HOLY SPIRIT BH

"When you are brought before synagogues, rulers and authorities, do not worry about how you will defend

> yourselves or what you will say, for the Holy Spirit will teach you at the time what you should say."
>
> —Luke 12:11-12

Read: Luke 12:1-12 "Warnings and Encouragements"
Jesus provides crucial guidance to His disciples, urging them to be wary of hypocrisy and to rely on the Holy Spirit when they face trials or need to speak before those in authority. As leaders, we often prepare extensively for important meetings, speeches, or presentations, relying on our knowledge, experience, and rehearsals to ensure success. However, Jesus teaches us a deeper truth—while preparation is essential, we must also recognize the power and presence of the Holy Spirit in our lives.

Jesus' words, "the Holy Spirit will teach you at the time what you should say," remind us that our abilities alone are not enough (Luke 12:12). Once we have done our part in preparing, it's vital to surrender to the Holy Spirit, allowing Him to guide our thoughts, words, and actions. This doesn't mean we neglect preparation, but rather that we acknowledge the limit of our own control and invite the Holy Spirit to take over where our efforts end.

As leaders, this lesson is particularly important when we find ourselves in challenging situations—whether addressing our team, speaking to leaders in positions over us, or navigating difficult decisions. By pausing to recognize God's sovereignty and inviting His Spirit to lead, we not only ease the burden on ourselves, but also align our leadership with His divine wisdom.

Before your next significant task, take a moment to pray, asking the Holy Spirit to guide your speech, heart, and mind. Trust that, in those moments when you feel uncertain or inadequate, God's Spirit will provide the words and direction you need.

Christ-centered leaders prepare diligently but ultimately rely on the Holy Spirit for guidance and wisdom in critical moments

<u>Application</u>: This is a very convicting lesson. How often do you pray before a very important task? Think of the priority tasks you have this week. Offer a 1–2 sentence prayer for each task and ask God to show Himself to you in His answer. He loves to answer prayer.

THE HEART OF LEADERSHIP *BH*

> "But God said to him, 'You fool! This very night your life will be demanded from you. Then who will get what you have prepared for yourself?' This is how it will be with whoever stores up things for themselves but is not rich toward God."
>
> —Luke 12:20–21

<u>Read</u>: Luke 12:13–21 "The Parable of the Rich Fool"

In this parable, Jesus delivers a powerful lesson about the dangers of greed and the importance of generosity. The rich man in the story is fixated on accumulating wealth, convinced that his riches will secure his future. However, Jesus points out the futility of this mindset—life is unpredictable, and material wealth is temporary. The man's greed blinds him to the true purpose of life, which is to be "rich toward God," by using our resources to help others and fulfill God's will.

As leaders, this lesson is particularly relevant. A leader driven by greed is focused solely on personal gain, often at the expense of others. This self-serving attitude can alienate team members and create an environment of distrust and resentment. On the other hand, a generous leader—one who practices servant leadership—sees beyond personal ambitions and prioritizes the well-being of their team. Generosity in leadership means investing in others, sharing knowledge, resources, and opportunities to help them grow and succeed.

In our personal lives, especially within our families, we are called to model this generosity. It's important to remember that the blessings we have are not just for our benefit, but are given to us so we can bless others. By adopting a biblical perspective, we shift our focus from what we can accumulate to how we can serve and uplift those around us.

True leadership is marked by a heart of generosity, where the focus is on serving others rather than self-gain.

Application: Where is your heart? Are you more focused on what you can give than what you can have? God's heart is that we serve one another and think of others before ourselves. Is your heart focused on others?

LET GO JA

> "And do not set your heart on what you will eat or drink; do not worry about it. For the pagan world runs after all such things, and your Father knows that you need them. But seek His kingdom, and these things will be given to you as well."
>
> —Luke 12:29–31

Read: Luke 12:22–34 "Do Not Worry"
Why do we worry? The answer often lies in our desire for control. When we worry about things like what we will eat or drink, we are, in essence, displaying a distrust in our Heavenly Father to meet our needs. This distrust stems from our desire to dictate how our needs are met, believing that our way is the best way.

When we insist on controlling everything, we often deceive ourselves into thinking that we are the most capable person for the task. This mindset stifles initiative, creates friction between leaders and their teams, and ultimately leads to a decline in productivity. Those who struggle with control often have strengths in being independent, decisive, and dependable. However, their fear of losing control can lead to defensive behavior and a refusal to trust others, which hinders team success.

In a previous lesson, I wrote that our influence is not infinite. No one person has all the answers, all the power, or all the strength to handle every situation. I concluded that, "Teamwork occurs when leaders can submit themselves to another's influence when theirs has reached its limits." Leaders are teammates as much as they are leaders, and they must recognize where their influence is limited.

Throughout my military service, I served under both empowering leaders and those who controlled every move. The difference in the health and culture of those teams was like night and day. When controlling and dominating leaders learn to trust their teams and empower them to thrive, the potential of that team knows no bounds.

Effective leaders recognize that control is an illusion. By trusting and empowering their teams, they unlock potential that far exceeds what they could accomplish alone.

Application: Do you tend to want more control over how your team executes the mission or are you confident in your empowerment of them? If you are a worrier, chances are you prefer to control things. But that is generally not the right answer and hasn't been since the dawn of creation. Choose today to trust your team and drive their potential through how you commit to empowering them. Calculate the risk. Mistakes are ok.

DO MUCH MORE JA

"From everyone who has been given much, much will be demanded; and from the one who has been entrusted with much, much more will be asked."

–Luke 12:48b

Read: Luke 12:35–48 "Watchfulness"

"The earth is the LORD's and everything in it; the world and all who dwell in it" (Ps 24:1). This verse reminds us that everything we have belongs to God. Jesus can demand much from us because what we have is not truly ours—it is His. The real question is, what value are you adding to others with what He has given you? What service and support are you offering to those around you?

In American culture, it's easy to covet our accomplishments and strive for more success. But are we solely responsible for our achievements? Of course not. Many people have supported us along the way, and our Heavenly Father has provided the health, abilities, and opportunities to us to reach where we are today. There is no such thing as a self-made man or woman.

Since retiring from the Marine Corps, I have often found myself coveting my identity as a Marine Raider following my service in the Marine Corps' most elite force. But this mindset is wrong. My identity is in Christ. He blessed me with the opportunity to serve as a Marine Raider so that I could use that experience to add value to others. He has given me much, and He demands much in return. I must follow His lead.

So, how do we keep our lamps full of oil as we wait for our Master to return? We do it by using the great talents and resources with which He has blessed us to pour out so much value and love onto others that they are inspired to stand with us in anticipation of our expectant King.

When you think you've done enough with the blessing of your time, talents, and resources, do more.

Application: Do you have an accomplishment or identity that you covet and overly lean on like I shared in this lesson? God gives us experiences and allows us achievements so that we use them for His glory. Do not stop serving Him because you've accomplished much. Commit today that you will always seek to advance His kingdom with the talents and resources He's given you as long as He keeps breath in your lungs.

THE TRUTH DIVIDES *JA*

"Do you think I came to bring peace on earth? No, I tell you, but division."

—Luke 12:51

Read: Luke 12:49–53 "Not Peace but Division"

Jesus' words in this passage might seem contradictory to His message of peace. But they aren't. Jesus did come to bring peace, but not the kind of worldly peace that many expected. In this passage, He is clarifying that His mission wasn't to overthrow earthly oppressors or establish an earthly kingdom of peace. Instead, He came to bring a deeper, more profound peace—the peace that passes all understanding, a peace that endures through the severest divisions and chaos, and a peace of the heart.

Jesus knew that His truth would ultimately lead Him to the cross, and that following Him would lead many to martyrdom and cause division and violence across the globe. Yet, He spoke the truth and lived it, setting an example for all of us.

As leaders, we must recognize that truth—especially biblically sound truth—may not be popular. It will often cause division and may come with significant consequences. Leading in truth requires a willingness to face these challenges head-on. We are not promised an easy path on this side of heaven. When we lead our families, communities, and businesses in the truth of Jesus Christ, we will encounter suffering. But we can endure, knowing that our ultimate reward awaits us in eternity.

Leadership grounded in truth may lead to division and conflict, but true leaders stand firm, knowing that their commitment to truth is a reflection of their faith and integrity.

Application: Are you committed to the truth knowing that it will bring division and cause friction within your team? What are you doing today to prepare for that friction? How are you preparing yourself and your team to maintain their integrity, their vision, and their commitment when the storms of division come? Write three ways in which you will commit to maintaining a connection with each member of your team and strengthen your bond of trust with them.

CRITICALLY THINK *JA*

"Hypocrites! You know how to interpret the appearance of the earth and the sky. How is it that you don't know how to interpret this present time?"
—Luke 12:56

Read: Luke 12:54–59 "Interpreting the Times"
In today's world, we see people hesitating to put their trust in Jesus, yet they readily place their faith in flawed institutions such as government and churches. We know that governments are often plagued by corrupt, low-road leaders. And many churches across America are compromising the truth of God's Word for the sake of political correctness. Despite living in an age where information is more accessible than ever, we are hypocritical if we aren't willing to trust Christ and surrender fully to His will.

We wait for signs, for a calling, or for God to intervene more directly in our lives. But this is hypocrisy. God has already given us everything we need and is always ready to reveal Himself to us if we're willing to look. Yet, we often sit idly, questioning where God is, or why He isn't fixing the problems we see in our society. We've become so focused on worldly things that we believe we are entitled to God's blessings.

The evidence of His truth is all around us. Instead of asking, "Where is God?" we should be asking, "Where am I not looking for Him?" Instead of questioning why God allows moral decay in society, we should ask, "What has God given me that I can use to bless others?" Rather than seeking success and comfort on earth, we should aim for significance in heaven.

Christ-centered leaders are critical thinkers who can lead amid the chaos of uncertain times because they are firmly established on the truth of God's word.

Application: Do you consider yourself a critical thinker? Do you challenge your own thoughts as fiercely as you challenge others'? With a foundation firmly rooted in God's word, we must be challenging every notion to ensure it aligns with His word. When we don't, we risk being deceived by Satan. What ideas must you challenge to test that they align with Scripture? That is your responsibility as a leader.

EXPECT TRAGEDIES *JA*

> "Jesus answered, 'Do you think that these Galileans were worse sinners than all the other Galileans because they suffer this way? I tell you, no! But unless you repent, you too will all perish.'"
>
> —Luke 13:2–3

Read: Luke 13:1–9 "Repent or Perish"
In ancient times, people often believed that calamities were direct punishments for sin. While it's true that "all have sinned and fallen short of the glory of God" (Rom 3:23), this doesn't mean that every tragedy is a result of personal wrongdoing. If we are honest, none of us are exempt from suffering—we all deserve the consequences of our sin. Yet, God's grace often shields us from the full weight of what we deserve.

Recently, two Marine Raiders I served with tragically took their own lives, and another was diagnosed with stage four brain cancer. These men have wives and children who love them. Why does such suffering occur?

Success and accomplishments don't make us immune to tragedy. None of us are entitled to a life free from hardship. Jesus reminds us that "to whom much is given, much is expected" (Luke 12:48b). And what is expected of all of us is repentance. Without repentance, we perish.

A fellow Marine Raider and Christ follower reminded me today that "everything – Jesus = nothing" and "nothing + Jesus = everything." When we fully grasp this truth, we understand that even in the midst of calamity, dissent, and the fiercest storms, we must stay the course. Our teams need us most during these times of crisis, and our steadfastness as leaders is critical.

Christ-centered leaders prepare for the storms because they are expectant, and then they lead their teams through them.

Application: Have you ever felt entitled to live a comfortable life free of tragedies and unexpected chaos? Remember, we live in a fallen world. We must expect tragedies. What should set Christ-centered leaders apart is how we handle them when they come. We must constantly seek our growth in Christ and set a climate for our teammates to grow too.

THE VOICE OF TRUTH *JA*

"Then should not this woman, a daughter of Abraham, whom Satan has kept bound for eighteen long years, be set free on the Sabbath day from what bound her?"

–Luke 13:16

Read: Luke 13:10–17 "A Crippled Woman Healed on the Sabbath"
Jesus heals a woman who had been crippled for eighteen years. Yet, instead of celebrating this miraculous healing, the synagogue ruler scolded Jesus because He performed the healing on the Sabbath, a day when work was prohibited (Luke 13:14). Imagine that—a woman is freed from nearly two decades of suffering, and the response is criticism over the timing. This hypocrisy reveals just how out of touch this generation was with the Spirit of God.

But before we judge the synagogue ruler too harshly, perhaps we should first examine ourselves. When was the last time we criticized the good someone did simply because we disagreed with how they did it?

I enjoy a glass of bourbon, and my wife loves dry red wine. Some in the Body of Christ believe that Christians shouldn't drink alcohol. While I respect their perspective, I, of course, disagree. It saddens me that the American church can be so critical of those that drink alcohol while ignoring the sin of gluttony which has plagued the comfortable, lazy American Church for decades.

My wife's commitment to maintaining her physical health played a critical role in a miraculous healing. In March 2015, we donated blood at our church blood drive in Sneads Ferry, NC, and agreed to be put on the National Donor Registry. A month and a half later, Duke University's Liver Transplant department contacted my wife, asking if she would be tested as a potential match for an 11-month-old boy in desperate need of a liver transplant.

The testing revealed she was a match, and she agreed to donate about a third of her liver. The doctors told us they might need to take some veins from her leg to connect her liver to the boy's body. However, when the doctors at Duke University—the top liver transplant hospital in the nation—performed the surgery, they discovered that her liver matched the boy's body perfectly, down to the veins. They had never seen such a flawless match before. My wife literally gave that baby boy life, and he just celebrated his 10th birthday this past summer. This was a miraculous healing that

Jesus still delivers today, and it wouldn't have been possible if my wife hadn't taken care of her physical body.

Miracles come through obedience, and we must not let our own biases or traditions prevent us from recognizing the power of God at work.

<u>Application</u>: Have you ever criticized, or been criticized, for a good deed because how you carried out the deed was contrary to established traditions or practices? Maybe what you did wasn't "politically correct." Commit to honoring God's word over traditions which have been developed by human minds.

INFLUENCE TAKES TIME *JA*

"It is like a mustard seed, which a man took and planted in his garden. It grew and became a tree, and the birds of the air perched in its branches."
—Luke 13:19

<u>Read</u>: Luke 13:18–21 "The Parables of the Mustard Seed and the Yeast"

Leadership and influence can often be perceived as a direct science—do "x," and you'll achieve "y." However, anyone who has led knows that this couldn't be further from the truth. Gaining influence, especially within a team, takes time and persistence. There will be days when we fail as leaders, setting back our progress. Likewise, when team members fail in their responsibilities, the entire team can regress. Leadership is about influencing people, and dealing with people involves an infinite number of variables.

Leadership development is a lifelong process. To believe you've "arrived" as a leader or that there's no more room for growth is the beginning of your downfall. Leadership requires continual learning, self-awareness, and effort. We must all be perpetual students of leadership.

Influence doesn't happen by chance or osmosis. Like the mustard seed that grows into a large tree or the yeast that causes dough to rise, intentional effort is required. The starting point for effective leadership is humility and the intentional effort to know and lead ourselves first. Only then will we be truly equipped to lead others.

> **Growing your influence is a daily effort in a lifelong process that is bound to have setbacks. Stay the course and be intentional about your growth and those you are developing.**

Application: Do you become frustrated when you know you are leading the right way, but you're not seeing the results in the people whom you are trying to influence? I know I do. Stay the course and know that the results will come. Pray for those you influence and constantly re-evaluate and grow your own leadership capacity. What do you do each day to grow as a leader?

FOLLOWERSHIP *JA*

"Then you will say, 'We ate and drank with You, and You taught in our streets.'"

–Luke 13:26

Read: Luke 13:22–30 "The Narrow Door"
As Jesus continued teaching in towns and villages, He addressed a question about who would be saved. His response calls us to examine ourselves: are we merely going through the motions of religion, or do we truly know Jesus as our Savior and friend, and know His Father as our Father?

Jesus desires our close companionship and loyalty. He is our leader, and we are His followers. In this passage, He makes it clear that simply being in His presence—eating, drinking, or associating with Him as equals or mere acquaintances—will not grant us access to the Father or make us heirs of the kingdom of God. Our relationship with Jesus must be deeper and more intimate than any other relationship we have.

In the same way, as leaders, we must first be committed followers. If we cannot fully commit to following another leader, we are in no position to expect others to follow us. Christ-centered leaders must be completely devoted to following Christ above all else. Even leaders who do not follow Christ must commit to following someone if they hope to be effective in leadership. A 'follower' is a term that has become a negative characteristic of someone. However, a committed follower to a leader, wise counsel or someone with much more experience than you is the only direct path to growing as a leader yourself.

> **Leaders learn a great deal about leadership through committed, subservient followership.**

Application: When you think of being a follower, do you consider that as a negative connotation? We should all seek people to follow. John Maxwell says, "if you are the smartest one in the room, find another room."[20] It's healthy to follow as long as you're following someone who is following Jesus. Write three people who you see as mentors in your life or who you think could be mentors for you. Consider having a conversation with them about mentoring you.

FEARLESS FOCUS JA

"He replied, 'Go tell that fox, I will drive out demons and heal people today and tomorrow, and on the third day I will reach my goal.'"

—Luke 13:32

Read: Luke 13:31–35 "Jesus' Sorrow for Jerusalem"
When a Pharisee warns Jesus to leave the area because Herod seeks to kill Him, Jesus remains completely unfazed by the threat. He knows that no mortal can deter Him from His purpose, as He alone has the authority to lay down His life and take it back up again.

At this moment, Jesus expresses profound sorrow for the people of Jerusalem. He longed to offer them the same security, confidence, and peace that He possessed, but they were unwilling. Why? Fear. When we fear God, we have nothing else to fear, but when we do not, we find ourselves fearing everything. Fear leads to worry, and worry leads us to hold tightly to control, preventing us from trusting in the safety and security of Almighty God.

Jesus was secure in His identity and His purpose. His focus was razor-sharp, and nothing—not even the threat of death—could derail Him from completing the task He came to do.

As leaders, we face distractions constantly. Some distractions may tempt us to stray from what is morally right, while others are rooted in fears that cause us to worry, leading to poor decisions driven by anxiety. Yet, when we model the fierce commitment Jesus displayed, we become a source of inspiration and motivation for our teams, who grow in confidence under our leadership.

Fearless commitment to our purpose not only keeps us on course but also empowers those we lead to trust and grow in confidence alongside us.

Application: Does fear grip you and distract you from your purpose? Jesus wants to refocus you and get you back on track with the purpose He's placed in you. Return your fear to God only, and let Him address your other fears. Admit the fears/concerns you may have to your accountability partner or a mentor. God wants to move you forward with a renewed focus, but you can't do that if you are letting your fears/concerns weigh you down.

REACHING DOWN *JA*

"For everyone who exalts himself will be humbled, and he who humbles himself will be exalted."
—Luke 14:11

Read: Luke 14:1–14 "Jesus at a Pharisee's House"

In American culture, we are inundated with the pursuit of wealth, status, and the illusion of success. Our flesh naturally sees what others have, and we desire to reach their level or surpass it. We are often focused on climbing the ladder of accomplishment and prestige, striving to elevate ourselves above others. But Jesus presents a radically different perspective: He calls us to descend the ladder, to humble ourselves and help others with their climb.

Jesus makes it clear that we should view ourselves as the least in the room and be content with that position. We are not to assume we've reached some lofty status but rather to embrace humility, positioning ourselves at a lowly place. Isn't this the heart of true leadership? Would you want to follow someone who is arrogant and self-absorbed, boasting about their position and accomplishments? Certainly not.

If you are a leader who has achieved great success, it's important to remember that you didn't climb to the top alone. Someone valued you enough to help you along the way, offering guidance and support. Leadership is not about reaching the top by yourself—it's about ensuring that you reach down the ladder to bring others up. When we humble ourselves, we invite others to do the same, and we foster a culture of mutual support and growth.

True leadership is not about how high you can climb, but how many people you can bring with you.

Application: Who are you helping today with their climb? Your children? Your teammates in the work environment? It takes our humble attitude to even remember to look down before we can begin to help others with their climb. If you are at a point in your life where you are in a valley, then first focus on leading yourself out of the valley and seek good mentors and accountability partners to do that. If you are currently on the mountain top, then turn around and help someone with their climb.

LEADERSHIP ENDURANCE *JA*

> "I tell you, not one of those men who were invited will get a taste of my banquet."
>
> –Luke 14:24

Read: Luke 14:15–24 "The Parable of the Great Banquet"
In the parable of the Great Banquet, Jesus paints a vivid picture of what happens when invited guests prioritize their worldly possessions and tasks over the invitation to God's kingdom. The lesson is clear: though all are invited into the kingdom of God, many will cling to their earthly wealth and pursuits, missing out on the far greater riches of His kingdom.

As leaders, this passage invites us to examine where our focus lies. Leadership, by definition, revolves around relationships with people. In fact, if one word could sum up the entire Bible, it would be "relationship." God desires a deep, enduring relationship with us, and He calls us to foster the same with others.

Yes, the tasks we lead our teams to accomplish are important. But tasks are temporary; relationships are eternal. If we neglect building strong, lasting relationships, especially those that can weather the storms of life, we risk failing at every other task we set out to complete.

We need people on our teams who are focused on tasks, but we also need those who are people-oriented to strike a healthy balance.

If you're someone who naturally leans toward being task-oriented, perhaps it's time to shift your focus slightly. Consider making it a priority to invest in the people around you. Write down on your to-do list, "Have coffee with a team member," or "Send a note of encouragement." Place that task at the top of your list—because investing in people is the most important task you'll ever accomplish.

Lasting success in leadership comes not from completing tasks, but from investing in relationships that stand the test of time.

Application: Do you need to take a short pause from your task list and nurture a current relationship? Maybe you even need to be more intentional about it like making specific dates and times that you and your spouse spend time together. Or maybe you need to plan monthly 1:1 mentoring sessions with your teammates. Whatever your environment, commit to ensuring you invest more in people than you do in your tasks.

COMMITMENT *JA*

"And anyone who does not carry his cross and follow Me cannot be My disciple"

–Luke 14:27

Read: Luke 14:25–35 "The Cost of Being a Disciple"
By this point in His ministry, Jesus had attracted a large following. People were eager to hear Him teach and witness His miraculous healings. However, in this passage from Luke, Jesus reminds the crowd that truly following Him requires more than curiosity or

admiration—it requires deep commitment. To drive this point home, He uses strong language, urging His listeners to "hate" those closest to them, even their own lives, in comparison to their commitment to Him. He wasn't calling for literal hatred, but for an understanding that following Him would demand total devotion, above all else.

Marriage is a union of two imperfect people. A family is when those two imperfect people have imperfect children. Our communities are a gathering of imperfect people. Our workplaces are an environment of imperfect people, trying to work together under the leadership of an imperfect person. This is why our first and greatest commitment must be to follow the One who is perfect—Jesus. When we prioritize following Him, we are better equipped to lead and love the imperfect people around us.

Christ-centered leadership demands a firm and unwavering commitment to follow Jesus. In today's world, we see moral decay affecting many facets of society—the family, education systems, churches, government, and culture. If we are to reverse this decline, we need strong leaders who are deeply reliant on Christ and fully committed to Him, no matter the cost.

> **You cannot lead the commitment of others if you are not committed yourself.**

Application: Take a moment to reflect: where have distractions or lesser commitments weakened your devotion to Christ? We must be His disciples before we can "go and make disciples" as He commanded us. Can you honestly say that you are His disciple in how you are currently living and prioritizing each day He has given you. Recommit yourself today to following Him with the same focus and determination that He calls for in this passage.

DEVELOP A CONNECTION *JA*

> "Suppose one of you has a hundred sheep and loses one of them. Does he not leave the ninety-nine in the open country and go after the lost sheep until he finds it?"
> –Luke 15:4

Read: Luke 15:1–7 "The Parable of the Lost Sheep"
The Pharisees and teachers of the law grumbled about how Jesus, a respected Rabbi, welcomed and ate with sinners. But Jesus made His mission clear—it's not the righteous who need to be found, but the lost. It's not the healthy who need a doctor, but the sick. Likewise, it's not the believer who needs to believe, but the unbeliever. Jesus' example challenges us to seek out those who are spiritually lost and lead them to salvation.

While this passage speaks to spiritual lostness, it also reminds us that we are surrounded by people in need, both physically and spiritually. Our fallen world is full of opportunities to meet others' natural needs, opening the door to share the Gospel. We can give food or donate clothing, but sometimes God calls us to take extra steps—to make a personal connection before delivering His message.

In one leadership training session I facilitated, a participant shared his experience as a missionary in China. Due to the government's sensitivity to Christianity, he couldn't openly evangelize. Instead, he had to focus on building relationships first, earning trust through genuine care and connection. Only then did opportunities arise to share the Gospel through his actions and words.

A relational connection opens lines of communication that can lead to changing lives.

Application: God often calls us to serve in deeper ways. Consider how you can go beyond meeting immediate needs to form meaningful connections. It is great to provide meals or donate money, but where might God be leading you to go further, to reach someone who is lost by building trust and a relationship first?

RE-ESTABLISHING YOUR VALUES *JA*

> "Or suppose a woman has ten silver coins and loses one. Does she not light a lamp, sweep the house and search carefully until she finds it?"
>
> –Luke 14:8

<u>Read</u>: Luke 15:8–10 "The Parable of the Lost Coin"
Jesus continues His teaching on seeking the lost, this time through the parable of a woman who loses one of her ten silver coins. In the First century Judea, a silver coin represented a full day's wages. Losing a coin would be a serious matter for her family, potentially causing financial strain and marital tension. The woman's desperation to find the coin illustrates the lengths to which we go when we lose something valuable.

The value of what is lost determines the effort we put into finding it. Jesus uses this parable to remind us of how precious the lost are in the kingdom of God and how much effort should be exerted to bring them back. But it also makes us reflect on what we value in our own lives.

In the previous lesson, I emphasized the importance of building relational connections as a means to lead others to Christ. In my personal life, I've been convicted of the need to strengthen my connection with my own family. After 21 years of active military service, I had assumed that holding the titles of "husband" and "father" automatically meant I was connected with my wife and children. Recently, I've realized that assumption was misguided. A title does not equal a connection—I must be intentional about nurturing those relationships if I want to positively influence my family.

This lesson can apply to all areas of our lives. Whether we are thinking about our family teams, workplaces, or communities, we need to ask ourselves: What do we truly value? And are we willing to put in the effort to nurture and find what may be lost?

Leaders identify what is most valuable (core values) and then are intentional about establishing them.

Application: Do you know what your personal core values are? Do you know what the collective core values are for each of the teams you are a member of? Are you willing to put in the effort to re-establish or re-define those values if you or your team may be off track?

FOSTERING A GROWTH ENVIRONMENT *EA*

> "So he got up and went to his father. But while he was still a long way off, his father saw him and was filled with compassion for him; he ran to his son, threw his arms around him and kissed him. The son said to him, 'Father, I have sinned against heaven and against you. I am no longer worthy to be called your son.' But the father said to his servants, 'Quick! Bring the best robe and put it on him. Put a ring on his finger and sandals on his feet. Bring the fattened calf and kill it. Let's have a feast and celebrate.'"
> —Luke 15:20–23

Read: Luke 15:11–32 "The Parable of the Lost Son" (Part 1)
This and the next lessons will explore the Parable of the Lost Son. In this lesson, we will delve into the father's role and his response to the return of his lost son.

In this parable, the father, who has two sons, faces a request from his youngest son for an early inheritance to leave the family and strike out on his own. The father reluctantly grants this request. Unfortunately, the son soon squanders his wealth on reckless living and, finding himself destitute and working in deplorable conditions, longs to eat as well as the pigs he tends. Eventually, he decides to return home, planning to ask his father for forgiveness and acknowledge his sins against both heaven and his family.

Upon his return, the father, instead of condemning the son for his actions or focusing on how he wasted his inheritance, welcomes him warmly. Far from treating him as a servant, which the son expected and believed he deserved, the father restores his status within the family, giving him the best seat at the table, fine robes, a ring, and even celebrating with the choicest food.

As we reflect on the practical application of this lesson, consider how we would react in a similar situation. If someone who has wronged us shows genuine remorse and seeks forgiveness, would we respond with open arms as our Father would do for us, or would we insist on retributive justice? This parable challenges us to evaluate our capacity for forgiveness and grace. Now, let's apply the lesson of compassion and forgiveness from the Parable of the Lost Son in our leadership roles.

Embrace the opportunity to support and restore those who acknowledge their mistakes, fostering an environment where growth and learning from past actions are encouraged and celebrated.

Application: None of our teammates will be perfect. A few passages ago, we explored how we love and lead imperfect people and to do so, we must be fully committed to Christ-centered leadership. The lesson in this parable puts it into real practice. How will you foster a culture in your team which supports growth and be able to restore a teammate when they have made a mistake?

COLLABORATE TO EXCEED STANDARDS *EA*

"'Your brother has come,' he replied, 'and your father has killed the fattened calf because he has him back safe and sound.' The older brother became angry and refused to go in. So his father went out and pleaded with him. But he answered his father, 'Look! All these years I've been slaving for you and never disobeyed your orders. Yet you never gave me even a young goat so I could celebrate with my friends.'"

—Luke 15: 27–29

Read: Luke 15:11–32 "The Parable of the Lost Son" (Part 2)
In the last passage, we discussed the father's response in the Parable of the Prodigal Son. Now, let's examine the brother's reaction.

Upon learning of the celebration his father held for his brother who had taken his inheritance, left the family, and quickly squandered it, the elder brother faced two choices: embrace or reject his returning sibling. In the parable, he opts for rejection, jealous as to how his long-standing obedience and service to his father never earned him the recognition that his wayward brother received. The father goes on to explain to his son that it is fitting to celebrate and be glad, for his brother was dead but is now alive, he was lost but is now found (Luke 15:32).

How do we react when colleagues succeed in the workplace, especially if we doubt the validity of their achievements? The older brother's reaction in this parable reminds us that, despite occasionally disagreeing with leadership's decisions, our role is to collaborate with peers rather than compete against them, particularly in terms of organizational outcomes.

For three years, I served as the chief instructor at a school focused on leadership development for young Marine officers. The instructors under my leadership were all hand selected, high-level performers with promising futures. It would have been easy to fall into a peer-competitive atmosphere as they competed for favorable evaluations. However, we collectively decided to measure ourselves against a set standard, prioritizing the improvement of our students over personal accolades. I encourage you to adopt this collaborative mindset in your workplace, promoting an environment that values collective success and personal growth.

Lead your team to collectively strive to exceed a common standard rather than compete against each other.

<u>Application</u>: How can you improve collaboration amongst your teammates and even with other teams? It is good to compete, but leaders must promote healthy competition and suppress unhealthy competition that results in jealousy, rejection, and destroyed relationships. Focus on exceeding a common standard and not on reducing your competition.

HARD RIGHT vs. EASY WRONG *EA*

> "No one can serve two masters. Either you will hate the one and love the other, or you will be devoted to the one and despise the other. You cannot serve both God and money."
>
> –Luke 16: 13

<u>Read</u>: Luke 16:1–13 "The Parable of the Shrewd Manager"
This lesson addresses both the fleshly desires of man and the duplicity of his character. When a manager of a wealthy man's accounts faces the prospect of losing his job, he does not choose to leave quietly, but instead resorts to swindling money from both the clients and his boss. Rather than taking the moral high ground, he opts for the fleshly path and finds a way to scam the clients and

cheat his employer. Jesus uses this parable to illustrate that a person can serve either money or God, but not both.

Often in our own lives, we face a choice of priorities. We must decide between storing up treasures in our bank account or storing up treasures in heaven. While we generally know the right choice, we often opt for the easier path, because it seems more tangible at the time. Beyond money, the real dilemma here is the struggle with serving earthly idols, with money being just one of them.

Be challenged today to find ways to maintain the moral high ground when faced with a choice between earthly and heavenly treasures. Be encouraged to make the hard right decision instead of the easy wrong one. Be determined to put faith first in your life and the lives of your family.

When faced with difficult choices, true leadership involves prioritizing integrity and long-term values over immediate gains.

Application: Reflect on your values which hold eternal rewards. Do you prioritize those over the values that only hold earthly rewards? Reflect on your team's values. Do they support the growth of the team and its desire to exceed high standards over the long term? Ensure your values drive your team's efforts for long-term success and not short-term greed and gratification.

ULTIMATE ACCOUNTABILITY *EA*

> "The Pharisees, who loved money, heard all this and were sneering at Jesus."
> —Luke 16:14

Read: Luke 16:14–18 "Additional Teachings"
In a continuation of the previous parable on the inability to serve both God and money, Jesus confronts the Pharisees, who were

lovers of money, for justifying themselves in the eyes of men rather than seeking approval from God. He challenges their hypocrisy, reminding them that what is highly esteemed among men is often detestable in God's sight. As leaders, we must be vigilant not to fall into the trap of seeking validation through worldly success or the admiration of others, but instead focus on what truly matters—integrity, humility, and righteousness in God's eyes.

Leadership often comes with temptations to compromise on our values in favor of what seems immediately beneficial. The Pharisees' desire for wealth and status clouded their judgment, leading them to mock Jesus rather than reflect on the truth of His words. Similarly, in our roles, the pursuit of power, recognition, or financial gain can lead us away from the principles that should guide our leadership. Jesus' words remind us that true leadership is not about how we are perceived by others, but about how closely we adhere to God's standards of justice, mercy, and faithfulness.

As leaders, let us commit to leading with authenticity and a clear conscience before God. Let us reject the allure of worldly success that conflicts with our spiritual values. Instead, let's seek to honor God in all our decisions, knowing that our ultimate accountability is to Him, and not to the shifting opinions of the world. In doing so, we align our leadership with the eternal truths that Jesus taught and thus create a positive, Christ-centered ideals type of work environment.

> **True integrity in leadership means aligning our actions with God's values, even when it goes against the expectations of others.**

Application: Do you live according to Jesus' standards? Do you accept Him as your ultimate accountability partner? Our accountability partners should be of the same gender and be a committed follower of Christ.

DO YOU SEE IT *EA*

"He answered, 'Then I beg you, father, send Lazarus to my family, for I have five brothers. Let him warn them, so that they will not also come to this place of torment.' Abraham replied, 'They have Moses and the Prophets; let them listen to them.' 'No, father Abraham,' he said, 'but if someone from the dead goes to them, they will repent.' He said to him, 'If they do not listen to Moses and the Prophets, they will not be convinced even if someone rises from the dead.'"

—Luke 16:27-31

Read: Luke 16:19-31 "The Rich Man and Lazarus"
In yet another rebuke of those focused on earthly wealth, Jesus teaches through this parable that true value lies not in material possessions but in the condition of the heart. The rich man, highly esteemed and influential during his life, finds himself in Hades after his death, while Lazarus, a beggar of the lowest societal rank, is seated beside Abraham in the afterlife.

After realizing his eternal fate, the rich man pleads to have Lazarus sent back to warn his brothers to repent, so they don't suffer the same punishment. However, Abraham explains that they have already been given the teachings of Moses and the prophets, and if they don't listen to them, they wouldn't believe even if someone returned from the dead.

From a leadership perspective, are there obvious truths we've been given that we fail to acknowledge? Is there someone in our organization who has consistently performed well but remains unrecognized or unpromoted? Are we ignoring a clear direction the organization needs to take, even though it has already been laid out for us?

Leaders must recognize and act on clear truths and opportunities within their organization, rather than ignoring them until it's too late.

Application: Reflect today on clear truths that apply to your team. A good tactician in the military will exploit the success of his command in battle. He will reinforce his lines that are winning against the enemy to ensure victory. Consider the truth of God's word, the truths about your team's mission and your teammates. Don't reinforce what you may hope but reinforce the truth and the opportunities God has given you and your team before they are gone.

LEADERSHIP TRHOUGH INFLUENCE EA

"Jesus said to His disciples: 'Things that cause people to sin are bound to come, but woe to anyone through whom they come. It would be better for them to be thrown into the sea with a millstone tied around their neck than to cause one of these little ones to stumble'...
He replied, 'If you have faith as small as a mustard seed, you can say to this mulberry tree, "Be uprooted and planted in the sea," and it will obey you.'"
—Luke 17:1–2,6

Read: Luke 17:1–10 "Sin, Faith, Duty"
In one of the parables from this passage, Jesus compares faith to a mustard seed. As seen in other Gospels, the mustard seed symbolizes how faith, though starting small and seemingly insignificant, can grow into something extraordinary when nurtured. Additionally, the passage warns of the serious consequences of leading others astray, teaching that influencing someone to sin is even more grievous than sinning yourself.

While these parables highlight the dangers of negative influence, they also underscore the powerful potential of positive influence.

Often, we are unaware of the backgrounds or experiences of those we lead and how much positive leadership can impact their lives. A small act of encouragement, optimism, or hope could be the spark that transforms someone's life. Just as a mustard seed grows into a strong tree when cared for, so too can a person's potential flourish with the right guidance and support.

Reflect on those within your sphere of influence today. Who among them has untapped potential? Seek out opportunities to recognize and nurture that potential. Someone in your life has abilities they have yet to discover—be the one to help them find it.

A small act of positive influence, like nurturing a mustard seed, can inspire and unlock the potential in others, creating lasting and impactful growth.

Application: How do you influence those you are responsible to lead? Do you influence them in a way that causes them to desire more of you or in a way that causes them to avoid you? John Maxwell notably stated, "Leadership is influence; nothing more, nothing less."[21] Your leadership will be defined by how you influence. Reflect and journal on your influence today.

HUMBLE GRATITUDE EA

"Jesus asked, 'Were not all ten cleansed? Where are the other nine? Has no one returned to give praise to God except this foreigner?' Then He said to him, 'Rise and go; your faith has made you well.'"
−Luke 17:17−19

Read: Luke 17:11–19 "Ten Healed of Leprosy"
As Jesus was walking to Jerusalem, He instructed the ten lepers to go show themselves to the priest. On their way, they were healed

of their boils, but only one returned to give thanks and praise to Jesus. In response, Jesus asked, "Where are the other nine?"

This serves as a powerful reminder to show gratitude to those who have helped us along our journey. We often forget that we didn't achieve success on our own—someone mentored us, extended grace when we stumbled, or provided an opportunity that helped us move forward. Recognizing the contributions of others is essential.

Today's challenge is to reach out to a mentor or someone who has positively influenced your life. Thank them for the role they've played in your growth, both personally and professionally, and express your gratitude. Additionally, encourage someone in your circle to do the same, spreading the spirit of thankfulness.

Humble leadership involves recognizing and expressing gratitude to those who have supported us, while encouraging others to cultivate the same attitude of thankfulness.

Application: Do you take the time to say thank you? When we humble ourselves to the truth that we are not self-made men and women and that our team needed help, we begin to see the help we received. It is important for leaders to set the example of expressing gratitude and create a culture and mindset in their teammates that seek to express gratitude to those who have influenced them and supported them in some way.

EMPOWER YOUR GREATNESS JA

"The kingdom of God does not come with your careful observation, nor will people say, 'Here it is,' or 'There it is,' because the kingdom of God is within you."

—Luke 17:20–21

Read: Luke 17:20–37 "The Coming of the Kingdom of God"
When asked by the Pharisees when the kingdom of God will come, Jesus tells them that it is ignorant to think about the kingdom of God coming because it is "within you" (Luke 17:21). Jesus then proceeds to teach His closet circle—His Twelve disciples.

He teaches them by explaining natural examples of spiritual realities as He often does with parables. Jesus explains that people will be going about their daily lives—eating, drinking, buying, and selling. He contrasts those prepared to meet Him with those absorbed in self-gratification, unaware of the spiritual realities around them.

In The Lord's Prayer, Jesus prays, "Your Kingdom come" (Luke 11:2). In this reading, He teaches that God's kingdom is within us. And in Matthew 11:12, He claims that, "From the days of John the Baptist until now, the kingdom of heaven has been forcefully advancing, and forceful men lay hold of it." If we replace "forceful" with "intentional," we see the importance of being deliberate about advancing God's kingdom both within us and in our world.

Are you "intentional" about advancing the kingdom of God? It begins with your submission to His will, allowing His kingdom to grow in you, like a mustard seed that expands and touches others (Luke 13:19). This growth requires both our willingness to let God work in us and our proactive engagement to influence those around us.

> **We empower our greatness when we submit to Jesus as Lord of our life. Our greatest influence is when our commitment to the Savior changes the lives of those around us.**

Application: Submitting to God's will is not something that we only say we do in our hearts and then go on to live gratifying our own desires and ambitions. Submitting to His will is an intentional, daily effort to seek Him and to offer ourselves as "living sacrifices" (Rom 12:1)—sacrificing our dreams, our goals, our ambitions—and aligning them with His for the lives He gave us. Are you intentional about submitting to Jesus today? Ask Him to show you where you haven't been intentional. Ask for self-discipline to become more intentional. Seek His word and direction in your life daily.

THE POWER OF PERSISTENCE BH

> "And will not God bring about justice for His chosen ones, who cry out to Him day and night? Will He keep putting them off? I tell you, He will see that they get justice, and quickly."
>
> —Luke 18:7–8

Read: Luke 18:1–8 "The Parable of the Persistent Widow"
Jesus shares the story of a widow who persistently petitions a judge for justice. Despite the judge's initial reluctance, her relentless pursuit eventually leads him to grant her request. Jesus uses this parable to teach about the importance of persistence, especially in prayer. The widow's unwavering determination exemplifies the power of steadfastness in the face of adversity.

As leaders, we often face challenges that require perseverance. This parable reminds us that persistence is a crucial trait for effective leadership. Whether advocating for our team, pursuing organizational goals, or seeking guidance, persistence can lead to breakthroughs where initial efforts may fail. Just as the widow did not give up, leaders must remain steadfast, trusting that their dedication will yield results in due time.

Moreover, the parable teaches us about the character of God. If an unjust judge can be moved by persistence, how much more will a just and loving God respond to the cries of His people? As leaders, we must cultivate a deep trust in God's timing and justice, knowing that our efforts, combined with faith, will bring about the right outcomes.

> **Leaders understand the power of persistence and trust in God's justice, remaining steadfast in their efforts and prayers.**

Application: How are you persevering through trials and remaining a persistent leader? If you've humbled yourself and examined the decisions you've made and the actions you and your team are taking, and you are certain it is the right path, then persist. Prepare yourself and your team to face opposition in many forms but persist in your efforts to achieve the objectives you are seeking.

LEADING WITH HUMILITY *BH*

> "For all those who exalt themselves will be humbled, and those who humble themselves will be exalted."
> —Luke 18:14

Read: Luke 18:9–14 "The Parable of the Pharisee and the Tax Collector"

The Gospels provide numerous lessons to stress the importance of humility in leaders. Here, Jesus shares a parable that contrasts the prayers of a Pharisee and a tax collector. The Pharisee, full of pride, boasts of his righteousness and looks down on others, while the tax collector humbly acknowledges his sins and seeks God's mercy. Jesus emphasizes that it is the tax collector, not the Pharisee, who leaves justified before God.

This parable highlights a crucial aspect of leadership: humility. The Pharisee's attitude represents the dangers of arrogance and self-righteousness in leadership. When leaders focus too much on their own accomplishments and moral superiority, they lose sight of the needs of others and fail to foster genuine connections with their team.

On the other hand, the tax collector's humility allows him to recognize his shortcomings and seek guidance and forgiveness. As leaders, it's essential to approach our roles with a similar mindset. A humble leader is open to feedback, willing to admit mistakes, and focused on the growth and well-being of their team rather than their own ego.

In leadership, humility fosters trust, respect, and collaboration. It creates an environment where team members feel valued and supported, leading to stronger, more effective teams. By humbling ourselves, we position ourselves to learn, grow, and lead in a way that honors both God and those we serve.

Humble leadership fosters trust and collaboration, enabling teams to thrive and grow.

<u>Application</u>: As we have observed through studying Jesus, humility must be in the heart of the leader. It is foundational for the leader to grow themselves and to develop a healthy team culture. Reflect on when you started reading these lessons. How has your attitude toward the importance of humility evolved since the beginning in Matthew 1? Have you tried to be more humble in all environments in your life? Write down three reflections that you have regarding how you have grown in humility.

LEADING WITH CHILDLIKE FAITH BH

"Truly I tell you, anyone who will not receive the kingdom of God like a little child will never enter it."

—Luke 18:17

Read: Luke 18:15–17 "The Little Children and Jesus"
In this passage, people were bringing their little children to Jesus so that He might touch them and bless them. However, the disciples rebuked them, thinking that Jesus had more important matters to attend to. Jesus, however, called the children to Him and used the moment to teach a vital lesson on humility and faith. He emphasized that the kingdom of God belongs to those who receive it with the openness and trust of a child.

This story highlights an essential quality for leaders: the ability to maintain a sense of childlike faith and humility. Childlike faith is characterized by trust, openness, and a willingness to learn and grow. As leaders, it's easy to become hardened by the challenges we face and the responsibilities we bear. However, Jesus teaches that true leadership requires us to maintain a heart that is open to God's guidance and willing to embrace new perspectives.

A childlike attitude in leadership doesn't mean being naive or inexperienced; rather, it means being open, adaptable, and approachable. It's about leading with a spirit that values trust over skepticism, and faith over doubt. This kind of leadership encourages a culture where creativity, innovation, and genuine collaboration can flourish.

In a world where leaders are often expected to have all the answers, Jesus reminds us of the importance of humility and faith. By leading with the heart of a child, we create a space where others feel safe to express their ideas, take risks, and grow alongside us.

Leaders embrace childlike faith and humility, fostering a culture of trust, openness, and growth.

Application: Like young children who put their trust in their parents, people will trust you when you humble yourself to God as your Father and they see the integrity of your faith. There are many people in the military who do not share the same faith as us but who trusted us and respected us when they saw the integrity of our faith. Walk forward today with integrity and let no one turn your faith to the left or to the right.

THE CHALLENGE OF LEADING WITHOUT ATTACHMENTS BH

"When Jesus heard this, He said to him, 'You still lack one thing. Sell everything you have and give to the poor, and you will have treasure in heaven. Then come, follow Me.'"

–Luke 18:22

Read: Luke 18:18–30 "The Rich Ruler"
A rich ruler approaches Jesus, asking what he must do to inherit eternal life. The ruler, who has diligently followed the commandments, is confident in his righteousness. However, when Jesus challenges him to sell everything he has and give to the poor, the ruler becomes sorrowful, for he is very wealthy. This encounter reveals the ruler's deep attachment to his wealth and his reluctance to let go in order to fully follow Jesus.

For leaders, this story is a powerful reminder of the dangers of attachment—whether it be to wealth, status, or power. Leadership often comes with its own set of challenges, and one of the greatest is the temptation to hold on to what gives us a sense of security and identity. The rich ruler's sorrowful reaction exposes how tightly we can cling to our possessions or achievements, even when they hinder our ability to grow as leaders and followers of Christ.

Jesus' response to the ruler also highlights the principle that true leadership often requires sacrifice. To lead effectively, we must be willing to let go of personal attachments that can cloud our judgment or hold us back from making decisions that benefit others. The call to "sell everything" is not just about wealth—it's about being willing to release anything that competes with our commitment to our higher purpose and to those we serve.

This passage challenges us to examine our own attachments and consider how they might be affecting our leadership. Are there things we're holding on to that prevent us from fully embracing our calling? As leaders, we are invited to lead with open hands and hearts, ready to release what is necessary to follow the path that God has set before us.

> **True leadership requires the willingness to let go of attachments that hinder our ability to serve and follow God's calling.**

Application: Take time to reflect on areas in your life where your attachment to a personal dream, goal, ambition, social status, etc. is standing in your way of growing. Ask a close friend or accountability partner what attachments they see are hindering your growth. What areas in your life do you need to relinquish control and let God be God in your life?

LEADING THROUGH SACRIFICE BH

> "Jesus took the Twelve aside and told them, 'We are going up to Jerusalem, and everything that is written by the prophets about the Son of Man will be fulfilled. He will be delivered over to the Gentiles. They will mock Him, insult Him and spit on Him; they will flog Him and kill Him. On the third day He will rise again.'"
>
> –Luke 18:31–33

Read: Luke 18:31–34 "Jesus Again Predicts His Death"
Jesus gathers His disciples to deliver a difficult and somber message—He will soon face suffering, death, and ultimately resurrection. Despite the clarity of His words, the disciples do not fully understand what He is telling them. This moment underscores

a crucial aspect of leadership: the willingness to face personal sacrifice for the greater good, even when those we lead may not fully comprehend the path we must take.

Jesus' prediction of His death is a powerful example of servant leadership. He knows the pain and suffering that lie ahead, yet, He moves forward with unwavering resolve, understanding that His sacrifice is essential for the salvation of humanity. This teaches us that leadership often requires stepping into situations where the outcome involves personal loss or hardship, but the benefit to others far outweighs the cost to ourselves.

As leaders, we may find ourselves in positions where we must make difficult decisions that involve sacrifice—whether it's time, resources, or even personal comfort. These moments define us and our leadership. They test our commitment to our mission and the people we serve. Jesus' example reminds us that true leadership is not about avoiding hardship but embracing it when it serves a greater purpose.

Moreover, Jesus' openness in sharing His impending sacrifice with His disciples highlights the importance of transparency in leadership. While the disciples did not fully grasp what was coming, Jesus did not withhold the truth from them. As leaders, being honest and transparent about challenges, even when they are difficult, builds trust and prepares our teams for what lies ahead.

> **True leadership embraces sacrifice for the greater good and requires transparency, even in the face of difficult truths.**

Application: Do you tell the truth even when you know that your team does not want to hear it? Are you willing to step out of your comfort zone in large and small ways for the greater good of your team? Any growth, whether personal or collective, will take sacrificing something and stepping out of our comfort zone.

LEADING WITH COMPASSION *BH*

> "Jesus stopped and ordered the man to be brought to Him. When he came near, Jesus asked him, 'What do you want Me to do for you?' 'Lord, I want to see,' he replied. Jesus said to him, 'Receive your sight; your faith has healed you.'"
> —Luke 18:40–42

Read: Luke 18:35–43 "A Blind Beggar Receives His Sight"
Jesus encounters a blind beggar on the roadside who cries out to Him for mercy. Despite the crowd's attempt to silence the beggar, Jesus stops, listens, and responds with compassion, restoring the man's sight. This story demonstrates the power of compassionate leadership and the importance of being attentive to the needs of those who might be overlooked by others.

Jesus' response to the blind beggar teaches us that effective leaders must be willing to pause and truly see the people they lead. The crowd tried to dismiss the man, seeing him as an interruption or a distraction. However, Jesus recognized the man's worth and need, showing that leadership is not just about guiding the majority but also about caring for the individual, especially those in distress.

Compassionate leadership involves being present and responsive to the needs of those around us. It requires us to look beyond the surface, and see the true struggles and desires of our team members. By doing so, we not only meet their immediate needs but also inspire faith and trust, as Jesus did with the blind beggar.

Moreover, Jesus' question, "What do you want me to do for you?" highlights the importance of clear communication in leadership. Rather than assuming what the man needed, Jesus asked directly, giving the man the dignity of voicing his own needs. As leaders, we should follow this example by engaging in open dialogue with our team, seeking to understand their needs and how we can best support them.

> **Compassionate leadership involves being present, listening to the needs of others, and responding with care and understanding.**

Application: Consider those in whom you have influence. Do you lead them with compassion? Are you present and listening to their needs? If you feel there are people under your leadership who you need to connect with, start with an attitude of compassion toward them. Pick at least one person to be more present with this week and listen to their needs.

TRANSFORMATIVE ENCOUNTERS BH

"For the Son of Man came to seek and to save the lost."
—Luke 19:10

Read: Luke 19:1–10 "Zacchaeus the Tax Collector"
In this passage, we encounter Zacchaeus, a tax collector who is despised by his community. His desire to see Jesus leads him to climb a sycamore tree, demonstrating both his determination and the lengths he is willing to go to encounter the Savior. When Jesus sees him, He calls Zacchaeus by name, saying He must stay at his house. This encounter with Jesus sparks a profound transformation in Zacchaeus' life.

This story teaches us about the power of recognition and acceptance in leadership. Jesus saw beyond Zacchaeus' profession and reputation; He recognized the man's potential for change and redemption. As leaders, we should strive to see the individuals behind the titles or roles they hold. Everyone has a story, and by acknowledging their value, we can inspire growth and transformation.

Zacchaeus' response to Jesus is immediate and transformative. His encounter with Christ leads him to repent and pledge to give half of his possessions to the poor and repay anyone he has cheated four times the amount. This radical change reflects how impactful genuine encounters can be. As leaders, we have the opportunity to foster environments where such transformative encounters can occur, whether through mentorship, encouragement, or simply by being present and available to our teams.

Furthermore, Jesus' mission is clear: He came to seek and save the lost. This should be a guiding principle for us as leaders. We must actively seek out those who may feel marginalized, overlooked, or in need of support. By cultivating an environment of belonging and understanding, we can empower others to experience their own transformative moments.

Leadership involves recognizing the potential in others, fostering transformative encounters, and actively seeking those who need support and guidance.

Application: Are you focused on simply driving your team to complete the mission, or are you investing in developing leaders who can accomplish the mission and more? While urgency can sometimes take precedence, challenge yourself today to prioritize mentorship and consistent support, shaping teammates into capable leaders for the future.

WHATCHA YA GONNA DO WITH WHATCHA GOT? *JA*

"Why then didn't you put my money on deposit, so that when I came back, I could have collected it with interest?"
—Luke 19:23

Read: Luke 19:11–27 "The Parable of the Ten Minas"
God's gift to us is the potential we have through the talents, abilities, and strengths He's given us, married with the moment in history, location, and networks of people in which He's placed us. Our gift to God is what we do with that potential.

When I was stationed at Camp Lejeune, North Carolina, my family and I attended a church right outside the back gate of the base named New River Community Church of God. We loved our church family. I remember one sermon series the pastor, Pastor Steve, preached on "stewardship" titled, "Whatcha Ya Gonna Do With Whatcha Got?" You don't need to hear his sermon or read this parable from Jesus to answer that question. However, the sermon series and this parable bring clarity and insight to that question to allow us to seek God's will and remind us that all we have belongs to Him.

The parable is clear that those who do nothing with what belongs to the King will forfeit the little bit they have left when the King comes to collect. The parable paints a harsh reality, but it is only harsh for those who think their gifts, talents, abilities, power, status, wealth, etc., belong to them. God can remove any of those characteristics in an instant.

So, the question remains, in a little better grammar, 'What are we doing with what God has given us?'

Leaders are stewards of the talents God has given them while also divinely positioned to steward the talents of others.

Application: Take inventory of the talents, resources, and relationships God has entrusted to you. Ask yourself, "Am I using these for His glory?" This week, identify one specific way to better steward what you've been given and take action to make an impact.

WALK IN YOUR PURPOSE *JA*

"'I tell you,' He replied, 'if they keep quiet, the stones will cry out.'"

—Luke 19:40

Read: Luke 19:28–44 "The Triumphal Entry"

As Jesus descended the Mount of Olives, fulfilling prophecy by riding on a colt, the crowd of disciples worshiped Him, recognizing Him as the long-awaited Messiah. The Pharisees, however, were displeased and blinded by their religious arrogance. They demanded Jesus to rebuke His disciples for their adoration, unable to recognize the truth of who Jesus really was.

At first glance, one might think this passage portrays Jesus as arrogant, demanding worship. But the real arrogance lies with the Pharisees, who consistently opposed Jesus throughout His ministry. Despite witnessing His miracles, they refused to acknowledge His divine authority. Their hearts were hardened, preventing them from seeing that the very One they were waiting for was in front of them.

Jesus doesn't need our worship to validate His identity. As Colossians 1:15–16 reminds us, "He is the image of the invisible God, the firstborn over all creation," and all things were created through and for Him. He is worthy, not because we worship Him, but because of who He is—God incarnate, the Creator and Sustainer of all things.

The beauty of this passage is that Jesus desires our praise, not out of His need for affirmation, but out of His love for us. If we choose not to worship, creation itself will cry out, for all of creation exists to glorify its Creator.

True leaders don't seek recognition to validate their worth; they lead out of their purpose and identity.

Application: Reflect on your motivations—are you seeking affirmation from others, or are you leading from a place of purpose and conviction? This week, strive to lead in a way that honors your God-given identity, letting your actions glorify Him, even when others fail to acknowledge your efforts.

FIRM LEADERSHIP *JA*

"'It is written,' **He said to them,** *'My house will be a house of prayer;' but you have made it 'a den of robbers.'"*

—Luke 19:46

Read: Luke 19:45–48 "Jesus at the Temple"

Jesus steps into the temple and immediately addresses the gross misuse of what was supposed to be the place where all of God's people came as sinners to be made right with Him. Because of the evil of man and our love for money, the religious leaders and merchants teamed together to make a profit from God's requirement of them to offer sacrifices.

The very sins Jesus confronted that day were among the sins that would send Him to the cross. Yet, instead of exacting punishment, He took on the penalty Himself. His righteous anger in the temple foreshadowed the greater act of love and sacrifice that was to come just days later. Jesus, as the ultimate leader, would lay down His life for those He rebuked, offering them—and all of us—a chance to be reconciled with God.

Jesus embodies the perfect balance between firmness and grace. He never compromises God's standards, but He also provides a way for us to return to God when we fail. As leaders, we must take this to heart. We are called to hold high standards, but we must also be ready to forgive, to sacrifice, and to serve those we lead.

Great leaders stand firm on principles while extending grace, ensuring that those who falter are not cast aside but are given a path to redemption.

Application: Examine how you lead others—are you upholding high standards while extending grace when failures occur? This week, identify a situation where you can demonstrate both firmness and forgiveness, reflecting Christ's example in your leadership.

THE WISDOM TO ENGAGE OR DISENGAGE *JA*

"Jesus said, 'Neither will I tell you by what authority I am doing these things.'"
—Luke 20:8

Read: Luke 20:1–8 "The Authority of Jesus Questioned"
In this scene, the chief priests and teachers of the law, blinded by arrogance and ignorance, questioned the authority by which Jesus performed His miracles, cleansed the temple of money changers, and taught the truths of God's kingdom. As religious authorities, they saw Jesus as a threat—a rogue figure circumventing their rule and undermining their power. But their hardened hearts, deaf ears, and blind eyes prevented them from recognizing the truth that Jesus embodied and proclaimed.

The religious leaders attempted to trap Jesus, knowing that His authority did not come from them. Their goal was not to genuinely seek understanding but to force Jesus into an answer they could use against Him. In response, Jesus, with remarkable wisdom, did not engage in their argument. Instead, He posed a question that exposed their lack of sincerity. When they refused to answer, Jesus declined to engage further, shutting down their attempt to trap Him.

In this interaction, Jesus models an important leadership principle: wisdom in responding to confrontations, especially those driven by arrogance and an unwillingness to learn. Rather than feeding into the antagonistic behavior of the chief priests, Jesus de-escalated the situation. He did not argue with those who were not open to the truth, knowing that engaging in a fruitless debate would only fuel their pride and opposition.

True wisdom in leadership is knowing when to engage and when to disengage. Rather than feeding into arguments driven by pride or ignorance, wise leaders redirect the conversation or choose silence, allowing truth to speak for itself.

Leaders have the wisdom to hold their tongue when speech would only exacerbate the situation.

Application: Reflect on how you respond to opposition—do you strive to win arguments or to lead with wisdom and grace? This week, practice the discipline of silence or redirection in a confrontation, ensuring your actions reflect both truth and humility.

GREED JA

> "But when the tenants saw him, they talked the matter over. 'This is the heir,' they said. 'Let's kill him, and the inheritance will be ours.'"
>
> —Luke 20:14

Read: Luke 20:9–19 "The Parable of the Tenants"
In this parable, the tenants acted as if their deceit and mistreatment of the owner's servants were unnoticed, eventually leading them to think they could also kill the owner's son without consequence. At the core of their evil actions was greed—an insatiable desire for more. "For the love of money (not money itself) is a root of all kinds of evil" (1 Tim 6:10). The tenants' love for personal gain drove them to commit increasingly worse sins, ultimately leading to their downfall.

This parable is a stark reminder of how greed distorts our thinking. Like the tenants, people today often make decisions primarily based on how they impact finances. When greed becomes the driving force, it can lead to sinful decisions and behaviors. Although we are called to be wise stewards of the resources God provides, we must remember that those resources are not meant for merely our personal gratification. They are entrusted to us to multiply and to bless others.

As leaders, we must be vigilant about the role of finances in our decision-making. It is easy to fall into the trap of making choices based on how they benefit us financially. However, God calls us to use what He has given us for the advancement of His kingdom and the benefit of others. True stewardship is about aligning our resources with God's purposes, not simply seeking personal gain.

It is also important not to become disheartened when we see others, like the tenants in the parable, seemingly getting away with greed or corruption. Whether in business, ministry, or personal life, we may encounter individuals or groups who appear to prosper through dishonest or immoral means. However, God's justice is sure. Our responsibility is to remain faithful stewards of what God has blessed us with, trusting Him to provide and protect as we work for His kingdom.

Leaders must align financial decisions with God's kingdom purposes, resisting the temptation to prioritize personal gain over serving others.

Application: Take time this week to assess your motivations in financial and leadership decisions—are they driven by greed or by stewardship for God's Kingdom? Commit to one action that reflects faithfulness and generosity, trusting in God's justice and provision.

EXPRESS YOUR VALUE IN GOD'S WAY *JA*

"They were unable to trap Him in what He said there in public. And astonished by His answer, they became silent."
−Luke 20:26

Read: Luke 20:20–26 "Paying Taxes to Caesar"
In Luke 20:1–8, we learned the wisdom of disengaging from conversations that only serve to fuel unnecessary arguments. In verses 20–26, we see Jesus again demonstrate His wisdom in the face of a trap set by the chief priests. These priests sent spies with the intent of catching Jesus saying something incriminating, hoping to hand Him over to Pontius Pilate. However, their hearts and minds were preoccupied with the things of this world, not the things of God.

When they asked Jesus about paying taxes to Caesar, His response, *"Then give to Caesar what is Caesar's, and to God what is God's,"* was both profound and disarming (Luke 20:25). Jesus revealed a critical truth: while we may live under earthly authorities, God's authority is paramount. Jesus affirmed the necessity of paying taxes in the natural world, but He shifted the focus to a deeper reality—that God demands a return on what He has given us, not in worldly currency, but in the value of our hearts, our worship, and our lives.

Caesar's coin, the denarius, had value in the Roman Empire, just as the dollar or any other currency does today. But these are merely expressions of value—not true value itself. Worldly currency allows us to assign a price to things, but God's value system transcends human measures of worth. God owns everything, including the very source of all wealth and power. What He seeks is not our money, but our devotion, our stewardship, and our willingness to live in alignment with His purposes.

As followers of Christ, we are called to see beyond earthly value systems and to allow God's true value to flow through us. When we view money, possessions, and status as temporary and secondary to God's eternal purposes, we can free ourselves from being trapped by the constraints of finances. We become vessels through which God's love, generosity, and provision flow to bless others.

When we align our lives with what God values, we become conduits of His blessings, allowing His purposes to flow through us and into the lives of others.

Application: Evaluate your perspective on money, possessions, and status—are they tools for God's Kingdom or ends in themselves? This week, make a deliberate choice to use what you've been given to serve God's purposes and bless someone. Allow His value in your life to flow through you.

HIS WAYS ARE HIGHER *JA*

"But those who are considered worthy of taking part in that age and in the resurrection from the dead will neither marry nor be given in marriage."

—Luke 20:35

Read: Luke 20:27–40 "The Resurrection and Marriage"
The Sadducees, who denied the resurrection, came to Jesus with a question aimed at discrediting Him. They referenced a hypothetical scenario about marriage in the afterlife, attempting to trap Jesus into a theological debate. But Jesus responded with wisdom, explaining that marriage is an institution for this age, not the age to come. Furthermore, He emphasized that only those *"considered worthy"* will participate in the resurrection, implying a separation between this life and the life to come.

    The Sadducees were deeply entrenched in their belief that there is no resurrection. They were more concerned with maintaining their earthly estates, legacy, and status than seeking an understanding of the eternal life Jesus was describing. However, rather than dismissing their question, Jesus gave them an opportunity to learn and believe in the resurrection, offering truth even in the face of their unbelief. If their hearts had been open, they could have seen that their limited understanding was flawed.

    This encounter teaches us a valuable lesson about how we approach God. Often, we want to see and understand Him on our own terms, expecting Him to fit within the constraints of our human logic and beliefs. However, as Jesus demonstrated, God's ways are far beyond our own (Isa 55:9). He will not conform to our limited understanding, but He will always reveal Himself to those willing to see and believe. Just as the Sadducees had the chance to expand their vision and grasp the truth of resurrection, so too we have the opportunity to embrace God's bigger picture. When we open our hearts and minds to His wisdom, we gain access to His vast provisions, guidance, and sovereignty, allowing us to address our challenges with a divine perspective.

Leaders must be open to God's greater plan, recognizing that His ways surpass our human understanding.

<u>Application</u>: Reflect on areas where you may be limiting your understanding of God's will based on personal beliefs or experiences. This week, seek God's perspective on a current challenge, being open to insights that may expand your vision beyond your own constraints.

BEWARE OF LOW ROAD LEADERS *JA*

> "Beware of the teachers of the law. They like to walk around in flowing robes and love to be greeted in the marketplaces and have the most important seats in the synagogues and the places of honor at banquets."
>
> –Luke 20:46

<u>Read</u>: Luke 20:41–47 "Whose Son is the Christ"
It's hard not to draw a parallel between the teachers of the law whom Jesus warns us to "beware of" and the current state of American politics and leadership. Just as the teachers of the law in Jesus' day held positions of influence and power, but failed to serve with humility, we see similar trends in modern politicians and

celebrities. Many, despite their high platforms, have succumbed to what John Maxwell calls "low road leadership."

In his book *High Road Leadership*, Maxwell outlines 12 attributes of leaders who choose the higher path.[22] I'd like to highlight two of these attributes in light of the warning from Jesus. First, a high road leader **values all people**. This is in stark contrast to the teachers of the law, who used their positions for personal gain, seeking admiration rather than truly valuing others. We might ask ourselves the same about our current leaders: do they genuinely value all people, or are they seeking their own elevation?

The second attribute Maxwell emphasizes is that a high road leader **develops emotional capacity**. Maxwell teaches that "the key to developing greater emotional capacity is resilience, which is the ability to recover or adjust easily to misfortune or change." High road leaders don't allow failures or challenges to harden their hearts or derail their purpose. Instead, they learn and grow from setbacks. Again, we must ask, do we see this resilience in our modern-day politicians, or do we see defensiveness and an unwillingness to learn from their mistakes?

True greatness in leadership doesn't come from holding a high position or accumulating years of experience. It arises from humility, valuing people, and developing the resilience to grow through challenges. Jesus' warning should prompt us to discern the leaders we follow, ensuring that they embody the principles of high road leadership. Great leaders are not born into greatness—they arise through their humility to recognize they aren't great yet, and their discipline to strive for it.

Great leaders value all people, develop resilience through adversity, and humbly strive for growth—choosing the high road over the low road in every aspect of leadership.

Application: Take a moment to evaluate your own leadership approach—are you seeking personal gain, or are you valuing others and growing through challenges? Do you embrace adversity or dodge it? This week, intentionally practice humility in your leadership and respond to a setback with resilience, learning from the experience to move forward stronger.

GIVING IS THE BEST FORM OF GAINING *JA*

> *"'I tell you the truth,'* He said, *'this poor widow has put in more than all the others.'"*
>
> –Luke 21:3

Read: Luke 21:1–4 "The Widow's Offering"
Jesus observes a widow offering two small copper coins at the temple treasury while the rich were also placing their gifts. He doesn't dismiss the offerings of the rich but draws attention to the widow's contribution because she gave all she had to live on. While the rich gave from their abundance, the widow gave from her poverty, and in doing so, her gift carried greater value in the eyes of God.

This passage highlights the importance of giving not just based on what we have but based on the condition of our hearts. Our giving is more about how valuable it is to us than about how much we can give to God. The widow in this passage had a valid argument to withhold her giving—she needed it to sustain life. But she gave anyway. Our giving should not be limited to what is comfortable or convenient.

Leaders are less concerned about how much they can keep for themselves and more concerned about the value they can add to others.

Application: Reflect on your approach to giving—are you giving out of abundance or sacrifice? This week, challenge yourself to give in a way that stretches your comfort zone, ensuring your gift reflects a heart of genuine devotion. Are you seeking to add value to others or hoard value for yourself?

TRIALS AND TRIBULATIONS FOR ALL *JA*

"But make up your mind not to worry beforehand how you will defend yourselves."
—Luke 21:14

<u>Read</u>: Luke 21:5–38 "Signs of the End of the Age"
Jesus warns of wars, disasters, and persecution, urging His followers to stay vigilant and not let their hearts be weighed down by the anxieties of life. His teachings remind us that these events are not new—they have been happening for centuries. Today, we witness wars, natural disasters, and societal unrest, as well as the ongoing persecution of Christians around the world. From the Middle East conflict to devastating hurricanes, it can feel overwhelming, yet Jesus calls us not to despair but to prepare.

Our world is filled with anxiety, whether through political unrest, natural calamities, or personal struggles. Many choose to drown these worries with indulgence or live in denial, consumed by the pleasures of the moment. But Jesus cautions us to "be careful," lest we fall into spiritual complacency, allowing these anxieties to distract us from our purpose and faith. His words in verse 34, challenge us to be ready for His return, living with our eyes fixed on eternity, not merely on the troubles of this world.

As Christians, we are not promised immunity from these trials, but we are promised hope beyond them. The key is to anchor our faith in Christ, preparing ourselves mentally and spiritually for when disaster strikes. We must remember that, unlike the world, our hope is rooted not in this life but in the promise of resurrection and eternal life with Christ. Calamities will come, but how we respond in faith will set us apart.

Leaders prepare for challenges without being consumed by fear, standing firm in faith and hope, knowing that ultimate victory lies in Christ, not in avoiding adversity.

Application: When facing opposition or adversity, resist the temptation to succumb to fear or frustration. Instead, stand firm in your purpose, keep your focus on your faith, and lead with resilience, knowing that your response will define your leadership. Take a step back and identify the trial, opposition, adversity you are dealing with. Then, plan effectively, with support from those around you, to handle it in a Christ-centered manner.

ACCOUNTABILITY STRUCTURE JA

> "He consented and watched for an opportunity to hand Jesus over to them when no crowd was present."
> —Luke 22:6

Read: Luke 22:1–6 "Judas Agrees to Betray Jesus"
In Luke 22:3, we are told that "Satan entered Judas," marking the beginning of his betrayal of Jesus. This passage reminds us that none of us are immune to Satan's deception; and Judas' tragic downfall serves as a stark warning to leaders today. Paul's exhortation to "work out your salvation with fear and trembling" (Phil 2:12) is a call to vigilance, urging us to stay spiritually grounded and accountable, knowing that even those closest to Christ can fall prey to temptation.

Judas' failure wasn't just in the act of betrayal—it began when he allowed his selfish agenda to override truth. When truth doesn't fit our desires, we face a dangerous temptation to manipulate or oppose it. Judas, rather than confessing his sin and seeking restoration, fell deeper into deceit, isolating himself from both truth and accountability. This path of isolation led him to despair, culminating in the ultimate tragedy of taking his own life (Matt 27:5).

As leaders, we are often given positions of influence where it is easy to shape situations to fit our own plans. But Judas' story warns us that if we don't cultivate an attitude of humility and establish systems of accountability, we open ourselves up to the same dangers. It is critical to have checks and balances, not just in external systems but within our own hearts. Humility requires us to be vulnerable, to admit when we are wrong, and to seek restoration before it's too late.

Leaders must maintain humility and create accountability structures to resist selfishness and deception, ensuring they remain aligned with truth rather than their personal agendas.

Application: Reflect on your leadership decisions and ensure you're not driven by selfish desires or isolated from accountability. Seek wisdom and humility, remain grounded in truth, and build systems of support to guard against the subtle dangers of self-deception. Be vulnerable and seek the accountability of others.

BE THE GREATEST *JA*

> "But you are not to be like that. Instead, the greatest among you should be like the youngest, and the one who rules like the one who serves."
>
> —Luke 22:26

Read: Luke 22:7–38 "The Last Supper"

At the Last Supper, Jesus offers us the most powerful and timeless example of servant leadership. Chapter 13 of John's Gospel is the only account of Jesus washing His disciples' feet and it likely occurred shortly before or after Jesus taught this lesson from Luke 22. The image of God incarnate, kneeling to wash His disciples' feet, serves as a profound reminder that leadership begins with service. Over the past two decades, the concept of servant leadership has gained significant traction not only in faith-based communities but also in the secular world. Yet, despite the countless seminars and books, no example surpasses that of Jesus, the King who came to serve and ultimately sacrifice Himself "while we were still sinners" (Rom 5:8).

True leadership is impossible without adopting a servant's heart. While decision-making, taking responsibility, and owning outcomes are vital aspects of leadership, none of these can be performed effectively without first embracing humility. The leader who seeks to serve, who places the needs and growth of their team above their own pride or position, is the leader who excels in creating lasting impact.

Paul's charge to "consider others better than yourselves" (Phil 2:3) is central to this model. It takes humility to lead well, as it requires putting others' needs first and recognizing that leadership is not about being served but about serving. As leaders, we must understand that we do not deserve to lead unless we first become servants to those we guide.

> **Leaders must humble themselves by valuing the needs and development of others above their own desires or status.**

<u>Application</u>: Reflect on your leadership approach and evaluate how you can serve those you lead. Prioritize their growth, needs, and development, remembering that leadership begins with a servant's heart.

BE DISCIPLINED IN PRAYER *JA*

"'Why are you sleeping?' He asked them. *'Get up and pray so that you will not fall into temptation.'"*
—Luke 22:46

Read: Luke 22:39–46 "Jesus Prays on the Mount of Olives"
As Jesus and His disciples left the Passover meal and walked to the familiar Mount of Olives, a pivotal moment unfolded in the Garden of Gethsemane. Jesus, fully aware of the suffering to come, stopped to pray, asking His disciples to join Him in seeking God's strength. Yet, Luke tells us the disciples fell asleep, "exhausted from sorrow" (Luke 22:45). In contrast, after Jesus prayed, "yet not My will, but Yours be done," an angel came to strengthen Him (Luke 22:42–43). God did not remove the burden from Jesus, but He provided the strength to endure it.

The disciples, overwhelmed with sorrow and exhaustion, missed the opportunity to receive that same divine strength. What if they had chosen to pray rather than sleep? Perhaps Peter would have had the fortitude to avoid denying Jesus in His darkest hour.

This passage teaches us a vital lesson: when we are physically, mentally, spiritually, and emotionally drained, we must turn to God in prayer. Physical sleep, while essential, cannot restore our spirit in the way prayer can. Prayer connects us to the divine source of strength that empowers us to face challenges we would otherwise collapse under.

Those who know me well, know I fall asleep easily. I might have been the first disciple to fall asleep in that moment. But it's important to recognize that prayer does what sleep cannot—it refreshes our spirit, steadies our emotions, and grants us the resilience to endure our greatest trials.

When leaders face exhaustion, prayer is the key to receiving the strength to persevere through spiritual and emotional trials, equipping us to overcome challenges that mere physical rest cannot resolve.

Application: When faced with overwhelming challenges, prioritize prayer over escape or distractions. Seek God's strength to sustain you, knowing that He will empower you to endure when you turn to Him in faith.

INFLUENCE YOUR ENEMIES JA

"But Jesus answered, 'No more of this!' And He touched the man's ear and healed him."
—Luke 22:51

Read: Luke 22:47–53 "Jesus Arrested"

Late at night, under the cover of darkness, the chief priests, temple officers, and Judas Iscariot came to arrest Jesus. Darkness often shrouds the evil deeds of humanity, and this night was no different. The religious leaders, seeking to avoid public outcry from the crowds who loved Jesus, orchestrated a covert operation to seize Him, knowing they could not openly do so in daylight. Jesus, who had brought truth, love, and hope to the people, was now being captured by those who rejected Him. A false trial would soon follow, and by morning, no one would want to be associated with Him.

Despite this betrayal, Jesus responded with peace, healing the ear of one of the men who came to arrest Him (Luke 22:51). This act of compassion highlights the depth of Jesus' love—not only for His followers but for His enemies. He extended the same grace and care to those who sought to harm Him as He did to the poor and oppressed.

When leaders embody Christ-centered leadership, they do not resort to forceful or oppressive means to assert control. Instead, they de-escalate tension, foster connection, and inspire trust. Jesus demonstrated this by responding with humility and healing in a moment of violence. He lived out the very words He taught.

James 1:22 calls us to action: "Do not merely listen to the word, and so deceive yourselves. Do what it says." Leaders do not only speak of peace, love, and humility, but also live it out in every interaction, even when faced with betrayal and opposition.

Leadership is not only leading your team but influencing your enemies as well.

Application: When faced with conflict, betrayal, or other forms of opposition and adversity, choose the path of grace and humility, responding as Jesus did—with peace and healing—knowing that true leadership is shown through actions, not just words.

INTEGRITY AGAINST OPPOSITION *JA*

"The Lord turned and looked straight at Peter. Then Peter remembered the word the Lord had spoken to him: 'Before the rooster crows today, you will disown Me three times.'"

—Luke 22:61

Read: Luke 22:54–62 "Peter Disowns Jesus"
In just a few hours, Peter experienced a drastic shift in behavior. Earlier, surrounded by his fellow disciples in the garden, he was ready to defend Jesus with a sword (Luke 22:50). Yet, when faced with the opposition of those who sought to harm Jesus, Peter denied ever knowing Him, not once, but three times (Luke 22:61). This stark contrast in Peter's actions reveals how dramatically our behavior can change based on the environment we find ourselves in. When he was in the presence of his friends, Peter was bold, but in the presence of his enemies, fear and self-preservation led him to abandon his integrity.

As leaders, we often face similar challenges. It is easy to maintain integrity and conviction when we are in a safe and supportive environment. However, when we are surrounded by opposition or potential harm, the temptation to compromise can become overwhelming. Peter's denial illustrates how fear and pressure can cause even the most devoted followers of Christ to falter in their integrity.

The integrity of a leader should not be contingent on the environment or the circumstances they face. Leaders who trade their integrity for comfort or self-protection, like Peter did in that moment of weakness, are not fit to lead. Integrity that crumbles under pressure is not true integrity. Christ-centered leaders are called to a higher standard, one where their character remains steadfast, no matter the external pressures.

True leadership demands consistency in both conviction and action, even when surrounded by opposition or danger.

<u>Application</u>: Take a moment today to reflect on your personal integrity as a leader. Are there areas in your life where fear or pressure have led you to compromise? This week, commit to standing firm in your values, even when facing opposition. Find one opportunity to act with unwavering integrity, regardless of the circumstances.

WALK QUIETLY THROUGH THE CROWD JA

> "But with loud shouts they insistently demanded that He be crucified, and their shouts prevailed."
> —Luke 23:23

<u>Read</u>: Luke 22:63—23:25 "The Guards Mock Jesus" and "Jesus Before Pilate and Herod"

This passage displays a sad reality that often repeats itself in society—where the loudest voices overpower the truth. Jesus is brought before religious leaders, Pilate, and Herod, but none of these authorities can find any reason for the accusations against Him. Despite this, the chief priests and the crowds continue to shout for His crucifixion. Pilate, instead of standing up for what is right, gives in to the pressure of the mob and orders Jesus' death, not because of justice, but to satisfy the crowd's demands.

This situation reflects what we often see today in American politics and culture. Many times, the loudest voices, even if they're wrong, get more attention than quiet, steadfast truth. The truth can be drowned out in a world full of noise, arguments, and biased opinions. Just as Jesus remained calm and silent in front of His accusers, the truth often stands firm, even when it goes unnoticed or unheard by those too caught up in the noise.

Jesus didn't give in to the crowd's demands or the leaders' mockery. He knew who He was and held His ground in the face of false accusations and hatred. His example shows us how we must stand firm in the truth, even when the world chooses to follow false and loud voices. Like Pilate, leaders today can fall into the trap of making decisions based on pressure instead of what's right, allowing injustice to prevail.

Christ-centered leaders walk quietly through the crowd holding firm to what is right, even when the noise around them demands otherwise.

Application: This week, evaluate areas where you may be tempted to compromise or follow the loudest voices around you. Instead, choose to stand firm in your convictions, seek justice, and make decisions based on truth rather than popularity.

INSPIRE THE CHANGE YOUR WANT TO SEE *JA*

"Then he said, 'Jesus, remember me when You come into Your kingdom.'"

—Luke 23:42

Read: Luke 23:26–43 "The Crucifixion"
On the day of Jesus' crucifixion, the self-righteous leaders and religious authorities condemned the Son of God to death. Yet, a criminal, who was receiving just punishment, experienced a radical transformation following his connection with the Savior. He humbled himself before Jesus, acknowledging Christ's true righteousness, and was promised entry into paradise. This story reminds us that we cannot enter heaven by simply claiming to be right or convincing others of our righteousness. Salvation comes only through Jesus, who makes us right before God.

Leaders, how are you sanctifying those you lead and helping them become "right?" Matthew and Mark's Gospels tell us that initially, both criminals mocked Jesus. But one of them changed his heart. This transformation suggests that Jesus' words and actions—His humility and selflessness even in the face of unimaginable suffering—made a lasting impact. Jesus connected with this criminal not through a grand display of power, but through His selfless example, putting others before Himself, even forgiving those who crucified Him.

As leaders, we should reflect on how our actions and attitudes impact those around us. Are we demonstrating humility and grace, helping others to grow and become "right" in their actions and attitudes? True leadership requires sacrifice, connection, and the willingness to put others' needs before our own.

The humility and selflessness of a leader can inspire profound transformation in others.

Application: This week, reflect on how your leadership is helping others grow in righteousness. Are you modeling humility and grace in a way that fosters transformation in those you lead? Take action by putting their needs before your own and demonstrating Christlike love through sacrifice.

BALANCED STRENGTH *JA*

"Jesus called out with a loud voice, 'Father, into Your hands I commit My spirit.' When He had said this, He breathed His last."
—Luke 23:46

Read: Luke 23:44–49 "Jesus' Death"

Jesus was in complete control of His spirit, and after taking the full weight of God's wrath for us, He willingly gave up His spirit. From His birth to His final breath, He followed His Father's will perfectly. In His last moment of life, He demonstrated His authority by choosing to lay down His life, and soon after, He would display His authority to take it up again through His resurrection.

Through every moment of suffering—His arrest, trials, beatings, and eventual execution—Jesus remained true to the character of God. His integrity and strength were unwavering. He never lost control, even under immense pressure. This is an extraordinary example of balanced strength, where His divine power was perfectly aligned with His purpose and mission.

As a consultant for The Maxwell DISC Method, I've learned that our strengths, especially in leadership, can become obstacles when out of balance. Stress, difficult days, or focusing on ourselves can turn our strengths into stumbling blocks. God created us in His image, and our personalities reflect His design. But when the enemy tempts us, we may misuse those strengths to stir conflict, provoke anger, or lead others away from Christ instead of toward Him.

Keep your strengths balanced by maintaining your integrity, even under pressure, and remaining committed to God's will with the purpose He has given you.

Application: Reflect on your leadership strengths this week and assess if any of them are out of balance. Are you using them to align with God's purpose, or are they becoming obstacles in your leadership? Take action today by identifying one area where you can adjust your approach to bring balance and alignment with your strengths and purpose.

UPHOLD YOUR VALUES JA

> "Going to Pilate, he asked for Jesus' body."
> –Luke 23:52

Read: Luke 23:50–56 "Jesus' Burial"

Joseph of Arimathea was a member of the Sanhedrin, the council that unjustly condemned Jesus. Yet, when the council sought Jesus' execution, Joseph did not agree with their decision or actions (Luke 23:51). After Jesus' death, Joseph courageously approached Pilate to request His body, a risky move that could have cost him his reputation and standing. His actions demonstrate that even when the environment around us—whether in our culture, workplace, or social circles—goes against our beliefs, we still have a responsibility to stay true to our values.

Joseph's example shows that integrity is not shaped by external pressures but by an internal commitment to what is right. Despite the Sanhedrin's decision, he remained firm in his convictions, demonstrating courage and loyalty to his beliefs. Maintaining our values can sometimes come at a personal cost, but leaders who remain steadfast in their principles inspire others to do the same.

Leaders must stand by their values, even when it's difficult or unpopular.

Application: Are you firm enough in your relationship with Christ, that you will uphold your values at all costs? Examine yourself today and be honest. Do you think that you could stand up against political correctness, cultural norms, and the otherwise direct hate from the world to uphold the truth of God's word? Our world needs more men and women that can.

YOUR TESTIMONY HAS VALUE *JA*

> "When they came back from the tomb, they told all these things to the Eleven and to all the others."
> —Luke 24:9

Read: Luke 24:1–12 "The Resurrection"
In first-century Judea, a woman's testimony held little legal or cultural weight. Yet in Luke's account of the resurrection, it was women who first witnessed and proclaimed the risen Christ. Despite Jesus' promises to rise again and His previous miracles of raising the dead, the remaining 11 disciples didn't initially believe the women's testimony—except for Peter, who ran to the tomb to see for himself.

Like these women, we are called to share our testimony, even when others may dismiss or doubt it. Recently, I attended Pete Vargas' *Your Message Matters Bootcamp*, where Pete outlined four steps to effectively share your message with others. When I heard him speak live in August 2024, in Orlando, FL, he emphasized the power of personal testimony, referring to Revelation 12:11: "They overcame him by the blood of the Lamb and by the word of their testimony." We are to embrace this same boldness, sharing the unique story God has given us, no matter how it's received by others.

Nearly 12 years ago, my wife was doing routine things around the house when she heard Jesus speak to her and tell her that one of her best friends was pregnant with her second child. My wife also claims that Jesus told her to call her friend and tell her this as a testimony. So she did. When she called her friend, who was an unbeliever, her friend surprisingly responded, "I haven't even told my husband yet!" My wife's testimony, no doubt, had a profound effect on her friend that day.

Boldly sharing your testimony, even in the face of doubt or opposition, can lead others to experience truth.

Application: Reflect on your own testimony and consider how you can boldly share it this week. Even if others may doubt, trust that your story has the power to inspire, heal, and lead others to Christ. Step out of your comfort zone today by sharing your testimony.

WHAT AREN'T WE SEEING? *EA*

"When He was at the table with them, He took bread, gave thanks, broke it, and began to give it to them. Then their eyes were opened, and they recognized Him, and He disappeared from their sight."
—Luke 24:30–31

Read: Luke 24:13–35 "On the Road to Emmaus"
In what is the first appearance of Jesus post-resurrection, two men encounter the risen Lord on the road to Emmaus as they return from the Passover. While discussing the events of the day and the Scriptures with Jesus, they fail to recognize Him. It is only later, when they break bread together, that their eyes are opened, and they realize who He is—just as He vanishes from their sight.

How often has Jesus been walking alongside us in our lives, and we haven't recognized it? How many times have we dismissed situations or challenges, not realizing they were actually the work of His hand? Have there been difficult moments in your personal life or workplace that you viewed as a burden, when they may have been a blessing in disguise?

During my 20 years as a Marine officer, I had the privilege of working under some exceptional leaders and, at times, with those who fell short of that description. Working with the positive, influential leaders was an enriching experience, and I learned a great deal. Conversely, working with less effective leaders was often difficult, but even in those times, there were valuable lessons to be gained—sometimes learning what not to do. Early in my career, I resented these tough environments. However, with time and maturity, I've come to realize that many of the challenges we face aren't just for us, they're opportunities to learn lessons that will allow us to help others and improve their lives.

Take every opportunity to recognize and evaluate the situations in your life, whether on the mountain top or in the valley, and gain insight to advance your personal development.

Application: Reflect on a current challenge or situation in your life. Ask God to open your eyes to the lessons He may be teaching you through it, and trust that even in difficulties, there is a purpose. Take the opportunity this week to embrace the lessons and use them to help others grow as well.

TIMING MATTERS *EA*

"You are witnesses of these things. I am going to send you what My Father has promised; but stay in the city until you have been clothed with power from on high."

—Luke 24:48–49

Read: Luke 24:36–53 "Jesus Appears to the Disciples" and "The Ascension"

After His resurrection, Jesus appears to His disciples and reveals the truth of His victory over death. He opens their minds to understand the Scriptures and explains how His suffering, death, and resurrection were necessary for the fulfillment of God's plan. Though the disciples now know the truth and are eager to share the Good News, Jesus instructs them to wait in Jerusalem until they are "clothed with power from on high"–a clear indication that while they are aware of their mission, the timing to move forward is not yet right.

This passage highlights the importance of God's timing in our lives. Just because we are made aware of a new opportunity, a calling, or an area where we feel led to act, doesn't always mean that the time to move is immediate. The disciples had received the most life-changing news—their Savior had risen—but Jesus reminded them to wait for the promised Holy Spirit to equip them for the work ahead. Similarly, there are moments in our own lives when we may feel ready to act, but God calls us to be patient and wait for His perfect timing.

Is there an area in either your personal or professional life where you feel called to move, but the timing doesn't feel quite right? Trust that God's plan is not only about what He wants you to do, but when He wants you to do it. Seek His guidance and trust that, in His timing, He will provide everything you need to fulfill the task before you.

Effective leadership requires not only understanding the mission, but also exercising patience and waiting for the right timing to act, trusting that the necessary resources and guidance will come when needed.

Application: Take time this week to reflect on a decision or opportunity you're eager to pursue. Pray for discernment and patience, and ask God to show you the right timing. Trust that when the time is right, He will equip you with everything you need to move forward with confidence.

THE BOOK OF JOHN

THE FATE OF THE APOSTLES *EA*

"For it seems to me that God has put us apostles on display at the end of the procession, like those condemned to die in the arena. We have been made a spectacle to the whole universe, to angels as well as to human beings. We are fools for Christ, but you are so wise in Christ! We are weak, but you are strong! You are honored, we are dishonored! To this very hour we go hungry and thirsty, we are in rags, we are brutally treated, we are homeless. We work hard with our own hands. When we are cursed, we bless; when we are persecuted, we endure it; when we are slandered, we answer kindly. We have become the scum of the earth, the garbage of the world—right up to this moment."
—1 Corinthians 4:9–13

Read: 1 Corinthians 4:9–13

As we begin the book of John, let's take a moment to reflect upon who he was and the fate he and some of the disciples endured. As the only disciple to die of natural causes, even John wasn't free from persecution during his life. Late in the first century, John was brought to Rome and condemned to death by being thrown into a vat of boiling oil. Miraculously, he was unharmed by the boiling oil and emerged from the ordeal alive and unscathed. This miraculous survival led to the belief that God was protecting John, and because of this, Domitian ultimately decided to exile John to the island of Patmos instead of executing him. It was during his exile on Patmos that John is believed to have received the visions recorded in the Book of Revelation. Here is a short list of the fate of all twelve of the original disciples:

Peter: Crucified upside down in Rome.
Andrew: Crucified on an X-shaped cross in Patras, Greece.
James (son of Zebedee): Beheaded by King Herod Agrippa I in Jerusalem (Acts 12:2).

John: Died of old age after miraculously surviving death by boiling oil.

Philip: Crucified in Hierapolis (modern Turkey).

Bartholomew (Nathanael): Flayed alive and then beheaded in Armenia.

Matthew (Levi): Slain with a sword in Ethiopia.

Thomas: Speared to death in India for spreading the Gospel.

James (son of Alphaeus): Thrown from a tower in Jerusalem, then stoned and clubbed by an angry mob, which he miraculously survived; later mutilated with saws.

Simon the Zealot: Fatally attacked by a mob near the Persian Gulf.

Judas (Son of James): Shot to death with arrows in Mesopotamia.

Judas Iscariot: After betraying Jesus, hanged himself (Matt 27:5).

As we reflect on the sacrifices made by the disciples to preach the Gospel after Jesus' resurrection, let's take a moment today to consider the sacrifice we are personally willing to make to defend the Gospel and share the Good News.

Application: Today, set aside a few quiet minutes to ask yourself: 'What am I truly willing to sacrifice for the sake of the Gospel?' What do you have in time, talents, and resources, that God may be calling you to sacrifice in obedience to His will? Be intentional about seeking Him and obeying.

THE LIGHT, FULL OF GRACE AND TRUTH *EA*

"The Word became flesh and made His dwelling among us. We have seen His glory,

> the glory of the One and only Son, who came
> from the Father, full of grace and truth."
>
> —John 1:14

<u>Read</u>: John 1:1–18 "The Word became Flesh"

John introduces us to Jesus as the Word, who existed with God from the beginning and through whom all things were made. John describes Jesus as the light of the world, shining in the darkness, bringing life to all who receive Him. He also emphasizes that Jesus came full of grace and truth, showing us the way to live and revealing God's love to us. This passage reminds us that Jesus is the ultimate example of how we should live, embodying both grace and truth in everything He did.

As we reflect on this passage, we must ask ourselves, "Am I being a light to those around me at home or in the workplace? Do I embody the grace and truth that Jesus showed us?" Just as Jesus brought light into the world, we too are called to be a source of light in the lives of others—offering kindness, wisdom, and truth in all our interactions. The challenge for us is to ensure that our actions and words reflect the ideals that John speaks of in these verses, being living examples of the love and grace Jesus offers.

> **Christ-like leadership involves being a light
> to those around us by embodying grace,
> truth, and integrity in our actions.**

<u>Application</u>: Reflect on one specific way you can embody Christ's grace and truth today—perhaps by offering kindness, speaking encouragement, or addressing a situation with integrity. Identify an area in your life—at home, work, or in your community—where you can be a light and take intentional action to demonstrate God's love. Pray for guidance and strength to shine His light in all your interactions, trusting Him to work through you.

BE TRUE TO YOURSELF AND YOUR STYLE EA

> "John replied in the words of Isaiah the prophet,
> 'I am the voice of one calling in the wilderness,'
> 'Make straight the way for the Lord.'"
> —John 1:19–23

Read: John 1:19–28 "John the Baptist Denies being the Christ"
In this passage, we see the Pharisees questioning John the Baptist about his identity, asking if he is the Messiah, Elijah, or the Prophet. John, firmly knowing his purpose, responds with humility and clarity, saying he is not any of these figures but simply "the voice of one crying in the wilderness," as prophesied. John never pretends to be someone he is not, but remains true to his calling to prepare the way for the Lord. His clear sense of identity and purpose stands as a powerful example of authenticity and leadership.

This idea reminds me of my time teaching at the Expeditionary Warfare School. As alluded to in a previous lesson, instructors would often ask me what teaching style they should adopt, especially newer ones who assumed there was a standard way they were expected to teach or act. They were always surprised when I told them, "An instructor at the schoolhouse looks just like you do." My point was to emphasize that they needed to be themselves, not imitate what they thought someone else was. Like John's response to the Pharisees, we must be clear and true about who we are and our leadership style, without pretending to be someone we're not.

As we lead in our daily lives, it's important to embrace the unique gifts and style God has given us. Authenticity allows us to lead with integrity and effectiveness. Take a moment today to reflect on whether you are being true to who you are, or if you are trying to fit into someone else's mold. Remember, God has called you to be yourself, and that's exactly what those you lead need from you.

Authentic leadership comes from embracing your true self and identifying and leading with your unique strengths, rather than trying to fit someone else's mold.

Application: Reflect on whether you are leading with authenticity or trying to fit into someone else's mold. Identify one way you can embrace your unique strengths and leadership style today, trusting that God has equipped you to fulfill your purpose. Commit to leading with integrity and being true to the person God created you to be, knowing that authenticity fosters trust and effectiveness.

EMPHATIC CREDIT EA

"The next day John saw Jesus coming toward him and said, 'Look, the Lamb of God, who takes away the sin of the world! This is the One I meant when I said, "A man who comes after me has surpassed me because He was before me."'"
—John 1:29–30

Read: John 1:29–34 "Jesus the Lamb of God"
John the Baptist sees Jesus approaching and declares, "Look, the Lamb of God, who takes away the sin of the world!" John had been preparing the way for the Messiah, but when Jesus appears, he steps aside and humbly points others to Christ. John doesn't seek to take credit for his ministry or elevate himself. Instead, he acknowledges that his role was to reveal Jesus to the world, testifying that Jesus is the Son of God. John's humility in lifting up Jesus is a powerful reminder of the importance of directing praise and attention to others when it's deserved.

This attitude of humility is crucial in our own lives and leadership style. It can be tempting to seek recognition for our contributions, especially if it is deserved, but John's example teaches us to find more satisfaction in supporting and lifting up others. A leader's greatest impact often comes not from personal accolades, but from how they empower those around them to shine. I noticed a significant shift in my performance appraisals when I transitioned from focusing on my individual achievements to prioritizing the team's success. Once I stopped worrying about how I was perceived, and instead focused on doing the right thing for the right reasons, the appraisals naturally improved, regardless of the outcome.

Reflect today on how you respond when someone else deserves the recognition. Are you quick to give them the credit, or do you find yourself wanting to keep the spotlight on your own efforts? Consider how you can lift others up in your workplace or community, allowing their strengths to be seen while still fulfilling your role with grace and humility.

Emphatic credit is always better than self-recognition.

Application: Reflect on a recent success in your workplace or community and identify someone whose contributions made it possible. Make it a priority today to give them emphatic and sincere credit, either publicly or privately, demonstrating humility and lifting them up. By shifting the focus away from yourself, you not only build others up but also strengthen trust and teamwork.

COME AND SEE *EA*

"The first thing Andrew did was to find his brother Simon and tell him, 'We have found the Messiah' (that is, the Christ)."

–John 1:41

Read: John 1:35–42 "Jesus' First Disciples"
One of the most important turning points in biblical history occurs in these few verses, where Jesus is seen calling His first disciples to follow Him in His new ministry as the Christ. According to John's account, Andrew was one of the first disciples called (the other was probably John, the author of today's gospel teaching). Immediately upon being called, Andrew runs and finds his brother, Simon, whom Jesus promptly renames Cephas, which means Peter.

What do we do when we have good news that needs to be shared? When we become aware of others' accolades, do we keep them to ourselves, or do we actively seek to recognize those who deserve it?

Much like the previous lesson when we talked about giving credit, it is not only important to acknowledge others for what they deserve, but it is also crucial to publicly recognize those who merit it. As leaders, it can be very easy to say things like, "they were just doing their job," or offer a private pat on the back. However, giving others credit in public not only acknowledges the accomplishments of an individual worthy of praise, but it also shows others the value of positive behavior and influences the way they carry themselves on a day-to-day basis by highlighting the organization's values.

Don't stop at privately praising someone when public recognition will serve a far greater purpose.

Application: Identify someone in your workplace, community, or family who has demonstrated exceptional effort or achievement. Take a step beyond private acknowledgment by recognizing their contribution publicly, whether in a team meeting, social gathering, or even on social media. Highlighting their success not only honors them but also inspires others to emulate the values and behaviors that lead to excellence.

THE POWER OF PERSONAL INVITATION *BH*

> "Then Nathanael declared, 'Rabbi, You are the Son of God; You are the king of Israel.'"
> —John 1:49

<u>Read</u>: John 1:43–51 "Jesus Calls Philip and Nathanael"

In this passage, we see how Jesus personally calls Philip, who, in turn, invites Nathanael to meet Jesus. Although Nathanael initially doubts, questioning if anything good can come from Nazareth, he follows Philip's encouragement to "come and see." This simple invitation changes Nathanael's life as he encounters Jesus and believes.

As leaders, we often have the privilege of inviting others to new roles, responsibilities, or ways of thinking. Philip's example of "come and see" reminds us that personal invitations can open doors to opportunities that others might not have considered on their own. In leadership, our encouragement and invitations have the power to help others overcome doubt and uncertainty. Just as Nathanael's skepticism was overcome by meeting Jesus, our belief in someone's potential can inspire them to believe in themselves.

Jesus' approach also teaches us about meeting people where they are. He recognizes Nathanael's integrity and speaks to his character, which shifts Nathanael's perception entirely. As leaders, we are called to see people as they are and affirm their strengths and abilities. By acknowledging the unique qualities in others, we encourage them to embrace their roles with confidence.

Philip's invitation and Jesus' recognition of Nathanael show us that when we see and affirm the potential in others, we become a catalyst for growth. This type of leadership, based on personal connection and encouragement, has a lasting impact.

Leaders extend personal invitations that open doors to growth, helping others overcome doubts and embrace their full potential.

Application: This week, take a moment to personally invite someone to step into a new opportunity or perspective they might not have considered. Be intentional in affirming their strengths and potential, helping them to see what they might not yet recognize in themselves. Your words of encouragement could be the spark that inspires growth and confidence in their journey.

MIRACLES IN THE ORDINARY BH

> "His mother said to the servants,
> 'Do whatever He tells you.'"
>
> –John 2:5

Read: John 2:1–11 "Jesus Changes Water to Wine"
Jesus performs His first miracle, turning water into wine at a wedding in Cana. When the wine runs out, Mary brings the concern to Jesus, showing her confidence in His power. Although Jesus initially seems hesitant, Mary instructs the servants to follow His directions. When they do, water is miraculously turned into wine, saving the wedding from potential embarrassment and revealing Jesus' glory to those present.

This passage reveals several important leadership lessons. First, it highlights the power of faith in others. Mary's trust in Jesus' ability to help demonstrates the influence of someone who believes in our potential, even when we feel uncertain. Her encouragement to "do whatever He tells you," also reflects a crucial aspect of leadership: empowering others to act with confidence.

Jesus' miracle shows us that extraordinary things often happen through ordinary means. He didn't use elaborate resources—just simple water jars. Similarly, effective leaders recognize the potential in everyday tools, resources, and people to achieve significant outcomes. By using what is readily available, we can inspire transformation, seeing potential where others might overlook it.

Finally, Jesus didn't seek attention or recognition for His miracle, emphasizing humility in leadership. His action was purely out of compassion and service, without a desire for acclaim. This attitude of humility is essential for leaders, reminding us that genuine acts of service often make the greatest impact.

Leadership is about recognizing potential in others, empowering them to act, and embracing humility as we seek to serve those around us.

Application: Look for an opportunity this week to encourage someone to step into their potential, just as Mary did for Jesus. Use the resources and tools you already have at hand to make a meaningful impact, and do so with humility, focusing on serving others rather than seeking recognition. Your faith and actions can lead to extraordinary results.

A ZEAL FOR INTEGRITY *BH*

"To those who sold doves, He said, 'Get these out of here! Stop turning my Father's house into a market!'"

—John 2:16

Read: John 2:12–25 "Jesus Clears the Temple"
Jesus visits the temple in Jerusalem and sees it being used for commerce rather than worship. The temple courts, intended for prayer and communion with God, have become a place of business

and exploitation. Angered by this misuse, Jesus drives out the merchants and money changers, overturning their tables and commanding them to respect the sacredness of God's house.

This event shows us a powerful example of Jesus' zeal for integrity and respect for God's purposes. As leaders, maintaining integrity is essential—not only in our actions but in the environments we cultivate. Just as Jesus acted to cleanse the temple, leaders are called to uphold principles, foster accountability, and ensure that places of work and influence align with their core values and mission.

Jesus' boldness here challenges us not to shy away from addressing issues when our values or our team's values are compromised. Even if uncomfortable, standing up for what's right is a key responsibility of leadership. Jesus didn't act out of personal gain; His actions were rooted in a desire to restore purity and purpose. This teaches us that integrity-driven leadership prioritizes the greater good and often involves making difficult decisions for the benefit of those we serve.

Finally, Jesus' righteous anger in the temple reminds us that passion for what is right—when controlled and directed—can be a powerful force for change. Passion with purpose enables leaders to influence and impact their environments, helping create a culture that reflects their values.

Leadership calls us to act with integrity, creating environments that reflect our values and advancing positive change, even when it's difficult.

Application: Take time this week to evaluate the environments you lead—whether at work, home, or in your community—and identify areas that may need alignment with your core values and mission. Be bold in addressing any inconsistencies, fostering a culture of integrity and purpose. Lead with passion and humility, prioritizing what is right for the benefit of those you serve.

THE CALL TO LEAD WITH HUMILITY AND TRUTH *BH*

"Jesus answered, 'Very truly I tell you, no one can see the kingdom of God unless they are born again.'"

—John 3:3

Read: John 3:1–21 "Jesus Teaches Nicodemus"

Nicodemus, a respected Pharisee and teacher, comes to Jesus by night to learn more about Him and His teachings. Jesus explains the need for spiritual rebirth—a new life that begins by believing in Him. Nicodemus struggles to understand this profound truth, revealing that even those with significant knowledge and status may have blind spots when it comes to spiritual insight. Jesus gently guides him, speaking with both authority and compassion.

Through this conversation, Jesus teaches us that spiritual rebirth is central to understanding God's kingdom. Nicodemus, though a leader himself, shows humility in seeking Jesus' wisdom, even if it means admitting what he doesn't know. As leaders, we should be open to learning and willing to question our own assumptions, especially when deeper insights are at stake. True leadership does not come from status or intellect alone but from a heart ready to grow and receive truth.

Moreover, Jesus' approach with Nicodemus highlights the importance of patience and discernment when we lead others. When team members or colleagues struggle to grasp new ideas or perspectives, leading with compassion and clarity can make all the difference. Just as Jesus met Nicodemus in his confusion, effective leaders meet people where they are, helping them grow in understanding while upholding truth.

Lastly, the passage reminds us that leadership is rooted in love. In John 3:16, Jesus says, "For God so loved the world that He gave His one and only Son." This powerful statement calls us to lead with love as our driving force. A heart grounded in love and humility impacts others far beyond our words and actions, creating a lasting legacy of care and integrity.

Humility, truth, and love are foundational to effective leadership. Be open to learning, patient with others, and always guided by love.

Application: Approach your leadership this week with humility, being open to learning from others and questioning your own assumptions. When guiding someone who is struggling to understand or grow, lead with patience and compassion, meeting them where they are. Let love be your motivation, ensuring that your words and actions reflect care and truth in every interaction.

THE PATH OF DEFERENCE *BH*

"He must become greater; I must become less."
—John 3:30

Read: John 3:22–36 "John the Baptist's Testimony about Jesus"
John the Baptist, a powerful teacher in his own right, encounters a moment of potential rivalry when people begin to compare his ministry with that of Jesus. Rather than being competitive or defensive, John sets a profound example by acknowledging his role in God's larger plan. He explains that Jesus is from above, the true authority, and that his own role is simply to prepare the way. John's response reveals the deep, intentional humility that recognizes and celebrates the roles others play in God's work without seeking self-elevation.

For leaders, John's perspective is a powerful example of deference. Effective leadership often requires the ability to step aside or uplift others to achieve the greater goal. Rather than focusing on how to gain recognition, it is more productive to focus on how we can contribute to the mission in a way that serves others. When we empower and recognize those around us, we create a culture where everyone's strengths can shine and elevate the overall purpose.

Do you make room for others to contribute, and do you celebrate their growth? Like John the Baptist, consider how you can embody selflessness, which ultimately builds greater respect, trust, and unity within a team.

> **True leadership celebrates others and supports a greater purpose beyond self.**

<u>Application</u>: Intentionally recognize and celebrate someone else's contributions to your team or mission. Look for ways to step back and create space for others to shine, demonstrating humility and selflessness. By uplifting those around you, you build trust, unity, and a culture that values every role in achieving the greater purpose.

BREAKING BARRIERS IN LEADERSHIP BH

> "But whoever drinks the water I give them will never thirst. Indeed, the water I give them will become in them a spring of water welling up to eternal life."
> —John 4:14

<u>Read</u>: John 4:1–26 "Jesus Talks with a Samaritan Woman"
Jesus breaks social and cultural barriers by speaking to a Samaritan woman at a well—a bold move in a time when Jews and Samaritans did not interact and women were not often addressed directly in public. Jesus, however, sees beyond these divides, approaching the woman with compassion and offering her the transformative "living water" of eternal life. His approach reveals the importance

of treating every individual as valuable and worth investing in, regardless of societal expectations or prejudices.

As leaders, we can learn from Jesus' example of inclusive and empathetic leadership. Breaking through social or workplace barriers enables us to connect authentically with those we lead and serve. It can be easy to overlook or underestimate certain team members based on assumptions, but true leadership seeks to understand each individual's unique value. By treating others with respect and encouraging open communication, we foster a culture of trust and inclusivity where everyone feels empowered to contribute fully.

Consider the barriers you may encounter in your leadership role. Are there people you may unintentionally overlook, or situations where greater empathy is needed? Approach these with intentionality, remembering that leadership often calls us to reach beyond comfort zones to build bridges and foster genuine connections.

Leadership that transcends barriers paves the way for true connection and empowers others to thrive.

Application: Identify someone you may have unintentionally overlooked or underestimated and take a step to connect with them authentically. Break down any barriers by showing empathy, respect, and a willingness to listen. By fostering inclusivity, you can inspire trust and unlock the unique value each person brings to your team or mission.

THE HARVEST IS PLENTIFUL *BH*

"'My food,' said Jesus, 'is to do the will of Him who sent Me and to finish His work.'"

—John 4:34

Read: John 4:27–38 "The Disciples Rejoin Jesus"
Jesus shifts the disciples' perspective on priorities. While they focus on physical needs, Jesus emphasizes the greater importance of fulfilling God's mission. As the disciples rejoin Him and see the crowd of Samaritans approaching, Jesus uses the moment to teach them about the spiritual "harvest"—the people ready to receive God's truth and love. He reminds them that, while one person may plant the seed of faith, others help it grow, and together, they all share in the rewards.

Leadership, too, is about sowing seeds for future growth, even if we may not always see immediate results. As leaders, we must stay focused on our larger purpose and remember that our work often prepares the way for those who come after us. Whether it's setting up long-term goals, mentoring team members, or making small but consistent investments in others, each act of leadership can be part of a greater harvest.

Consider where you can plant seeds within your team or organization. Is there a vision you can cast that others can help bring to fruition? Are there people you can mentor to carry on the mission long after you're gone? Embracing this perspective helps us focus on a legacy that reaches beyond immediate outcomes and aligns with a greater purpose.

True leadership invests in a lasting legacy, preparing others to continue the mission and reap the rewards.

Application: Invest in someone by mentoring, encouraging, or equipping them to grow in their role or purpose. Cast a vision that inspires your team to see the bigger picture and their part in it, even if the results aren't immediate. Remember, each seed you plant today contributes to a harvest far greater than what you might witness alone.

BY THE WORD OF YOUR TESTIMONY *JA*

"And because of His words many more became believers."
—John 4:41

Read: John 4:39–42 "Many Samaritans Believe"

In John 4:9, we're reminded that Jews typically avoided Samaritans, based on religious customs that deemed them "unclean." According to some scholars, Jewish leaders had taught their people that using even a drinking vessel touched by a Samaritan would make them unfit for worship (NIV footnote, John 4:9). Yet, Jesus defied this barrier when He spoke with a Samaritan woman at the well, showing His willingness to break cultural boundaries to reach individuals with His message.

This encounter became a turning point, not only for the woman, whose life was transformed, but for the many others she influenced. After her life-changing experience, she went into her town to tell others what she had witnessed, sparking curiosity and leading others to come to Jesus. Her testimony set the stage for many to believe in Him. This is a small glimpse of the Great Commission in action: Jesus transforms an individual, who then shares their story, drawing others to faith.

For us as leaders, this account speaks to the impact of our personal testimony. If we want to be Christ-centered leaders, we cannot overlook the power of sharing our journey with Him. Our testimony isn't just about how we first encountered Jesus but it is the ongoing story of transformation, victory, and growth through Him. It matters—it can inspire, uplift, and guide others toward faith. Don't shy away from sharing; let your story be a living testimony of Christ's work in you.

> **Sharing your story can lead others to Christ, inspiring transformation far beyond your personal experience.**

Application: Share a personal story of how Jesus has transformed your life with someone who needs encouragement or hope. Be intentional about using your testimony to point them toward God's love and grace. Your willingness to share could spark a life-changing moment for someone else, just as the Samaritan woman's story did.

REDIRECT *JA*

"When He arrived in Galilee, the Galileans welcomed Him. They had seen all that He had done in Jerusalem at the Passover Feast, for they also had been there."
—John 4:45

Read: John 4:43–54 "Jesus Heals the Official's Son"
As Jesus left for Jerusalem, He remarked that *"a prophet has no honor in his own country"* (John 4:44). This statement proved true as He returned to perform two significant miracles, each directed at non-Jews. First, He transformed the life of the Samaritan woman at the well, whose testimony later led many in her town to faith (John 4:39). Then, He healed a royal official's son, leading the official and his entire household to believe (John 4:53). When Jesus was rejected by some, He continued His mission elsewhere, reaching those willing to receive Him.

We all have unique value, being designed in God's image with a specific purpose that fits into His plan for expanding His kingdom. Yet, sometimes we face rejection—our message, products, services, or even leadership might not be accepted. When this happens, don't let discouragement settle in. First, take time for self-examination. Pray and seek God's guidance, asking Him to reveal any adjustments needed in your approach. If you're confident that you're in step with His will, then perhaps it's time to explore other places or groups that may be more receptive to your message.

Jesus demonstrated patience and grace in how He pursued His mission. He didn't react angrily or forcefully when people turned away; instead, He allowed space for others who were ready to receive His message. Be encouraged by His example—when we stay faithful to God's purpose, the right opportunities will come, even if we have to pivot our focus temporarily.

> **Rejection is often redirection—stay patient, remain faithful, and God will open new doors for your unique purpose.**

Application: When faced with rejection, pause to seek God's guidance and reassess your approach. If your message or efforts align with His purpose, look for new opportunities or audiences where you can make a meaningful impact. Stay faithful, knowing that God's plan often leads us to those who are ready to receive.

BEHIND THE SCENES *JA*

"The man who was healed had no idea who it was, for Jesus had slipped away into the crowd that was there."
—John 5:13

Read: John 5:1–15 "The Healing at the Pool"
Jesus miraculously heals a man who had been an invalid for 38 years. Without the strength to move to the healing pool on his own, this man had no way to find Jesus. But Jesus came to him. Notably, this healing happened in Jerusalem, surrounded by religious leaders who cared more about traditions than helping those in need. In a city teeming with rules and restrictions, Jesus moved toward the brokenness—meeting this man right where he was.

There are times when advancing the kingdom of God requires us to work in the "gray area" or "behind the scenes." Some places in the world—and even in parts of America—make it challenging or even dangerous to openly share the gospel. Here, creativity and discretion become essential. Just as Jesus went to the man quietly, addressing the need without drawing attention to Himself, we may sometimes need to work strategically to advance God's kingdom in challenging spaces. He wants us to step out of our comfort zone and take risks to advance His kingdom. He will give us the tools, resources, and other support to do so.

US special operations forces are notorious for operating in the "gray area," and conducting low-visibility missions. They are trained to find ways to accomplish their missions without ever being detected. Sometimes detection is mission failure. I've conducted many training and real-world missions operating this way. The simplest things become difficult because failing to do them correctly could have devastating results. Like walking across a 2x6 board lying on the ground or walking across the same board 100 feet in the air. Same task but the consequences change drastically if you lose your footing.

Not every task we must accomplish, whether personally or professionally, will have a clear, unobstructed path to completion. We will often need to take an indirect approach to accomplishing our mission.

> **Effective leaders stay mission-focused and work creatively, behind the scenes to accomplish the mission.**

Application: This week, identify an area where you may need to take an indirect or creative approach to accomplish your mission or goal. Whether it's in your personal life, professional work, or faith journey, step out of your comfort zone and use strategic thinking to overcome obstacles. Trust that God will equip you with the tools and resources needed to succeed, even in the challenging or "gray area" situations.

EMPOWER WITH JUDGMENT *JA*

"By Myself I can do nothing; I judge only as I hear, and My judgment is just, for I seek not to please Myself but Him who sent Me."

–John 5:30

<u>Read</u>: John 5:16–30 "Life through the Son"

Jesus explains His relationship to Father God to the Jews, likely many of the religious leaders and teachers of the law in Jerusalem. He had just healed a man who had been lame for 38 years and began to explain to the Jews who were persecuting Him for doing work on the Sabbath, where His authority and ability comes from. This, of course, caused them to become even more indignant and so they likely were not listening to Him with ears to hear. They simply wanted to kill Him for saying that He is one with the Father, rather bear witness to His miraculous and gracious deeds.

In verse 22, He states that the Father *"has entrusted all judgment to the Son."* Then at the end of this passage in verse 30, Jesus states that He can do nothing by Himself and He judges only what He hears from the Father. This passage is a vivid picture of how the Son and the Father of the Triune God work together to carry His character and intent. He continues in verse 30 to claim that His judgment is just because He does not seek to please Himself but the Father who sent Him.

The teaching from Jesus is a clear picture of submission to authority, empowerment, and righteous judgment. Jesus submits to His Father and through that humble submission, the Father empowers Jesus through full trust and confidence by giving Him all authority. With His authority, Jesus states that His judgment is just only because He does not seek to please Himself. When a team submits to their leader and the leader exercises their judgment from a position of not seeking to please themselves, then a culture of empowerment is created, and the team thrives. It often begins with getting out of our own way.

Leaders first submit to a higher authority then empower their team through sound judgment.

Application: Examine areas where your leadership could benefit from greater humility and submission to authority. In your decision-making, focus on seeking the greater good, not personal gain. Encourage your team to submit to one another and to your leadership, fostering an environment where empowerment and trust lead to thriving collaboration.

ASSESS BEHAVIOR JA

"You diligently study the Scriptures because you think that by them you possess eternal life. These are the Scriptures that testify about Me, yet you refuse to come to Me to have life."

—John 5:39–40

Read: John 5:31–47 "Testimonies about Jesus"
Jesus brought the truth, He lived the truth, and He spoke the truth; and the Jews rejected Him. They prided themselves on knowing the Scriptures, but they missed Jesus' fulfillment of them. Jesus wasn't trying to provoke them. He was simply assessing their behavior and calling a spade a spade. Their eyes were closed to the truth standing in front of them because they were more concerned about maintaining their authority over what they decided is the truth for the rest of their culture and religion. Jesus called them out by exposing their errant behavior.

We are not God and so we don't know people's hearts or what they are thinking like Jesus did, but we can make accurate judgments based on people's behavior and communication. Jesus states in Luke 6:45, "For the mouth speaks what the heart is full of." If a person's words and actions show hate, anger, and malicious intentions, like the Jews in this passage, then we can make an accurate judgment that they are not being led by the Spirit or submitting to God. We all certainly have lapses of not following the Spirit and that is why it is so important to be humble and to seek forgiveness from those we've wronged while also forgiving the wrong done to us.

I have really enjoyed training leaders and teams in the Maxwell DISC Method. The DISC methodology provides a clear assessment of our behavior and communication styles, as well as our strengths in seven areas of leadership. When we understand ourselves and identify the unique design God has placed on each of our lives, we will be better equipped to examine ourselves, our teammates, and people who may oppose us like Jesus did.

Leaders who assess behavior are capable of making sound judgments about people rather than foolish assumptions.

Application: Reflect on your own behavior and communication, asking if it aligns with the Spirit. Use tools like the DISC assessment to better understand your own leadership style and the styles of those you lead. Look for opportunities to practice humility by seeking forgiveness or offering it, and examine how you can respond to opposition with grace while staying true to the truth.

PROBLEM-SOLVING JA

"When Jesus looked up and saw a great crowd coming toward Him, He said to Philip, 'Where shall we buy bread for these people to eat?'"

–John 6:5

Read: John 6:1–15 "Jesus Feeds the Five Thousand"

Jesus identifies a real problem to Philip. Crowds gathered from the countryside to come to hear Jesus speak. It was late in the day, and they were hungry (Matt 14:15). Philip gave a direct response to Jesus' question about purchasing food, "eight months wages would not buy enough" (John 6:7). Philip only considered the question that Jesus asked, not the problem that needed solved.

As leaders, sometimes we are distracted by a concern or fear that is staring us in the face, and we lose sight of the greater problem. We start to play that arcade game, "Whack-A-Mole," and we lose focus on the source of the problem. John writes that Jesus asked Philip this question only to test him (John 6:6). Jesus already knew how He was going to solve the problem of a hungry crowd.

Problems arise daily in our lives. When we feel like we just climbed out of the valley, there's another mountain staring at us in the face. Sometimes, the problems are mere obstacles to address while others are direct and aggressive opposition against us. In either case, we must look at the problem from different angles. Taking a narrow-minded approach to solving problems will leave us stuck and paralyze us from moving forward. By stepping back to consider the full picture, we can see different angles and develop more effective solutions that lead our teams forward. Leaders are expected to move their teams forward.

Effective leaders analyze the problem and address root causes rather than only the symptoms.

Application: Take a step back when faced with a problem and consider it from multiple angles. Avoid getting stuck by focusing only on immediate concerns. Instead, look for a broader perspective to find more effective solutions. Encourage your team to do the same, fostering a mindset that drives progress forward.

FEAR NOT *JA*

"But He said to them, 'It is I; don't be afraid.'"
—John 6:20

Read: John 6:16–24 "Jesus Walks on the Water"

The disciples set off across the lake without Jesus. Night came and with it strong winds and rough seas. By the time they saw Jesus, they had already been rowing over three miles which likely spanned several hours. When they saw Jesus, they were terrified because their only rationale for seeing a man out in the middle of the lake, walking on water, was that it must be a ghost. Jesus calms their fears by assuring them that, "It is I."

We all face storms in our own lives. When God shows up, does that terrify us or comfort us? It should bring immediate comfort, but sometimes, we aren't expecting Him and He shows up in ways that may seem terrifying and uncomfortable. We must remember that His plans for us are good. He may not always calm our storms or move our mountains, but we can be assured that He will calm our fears and provide a solution if we only humble ourselves to recognize and fear Him alone and not our circumstances.

Leadership is burdensome and we can easily be sucked into fearing failure. Jesus wants us to fear Him and conquer failure. In reverence to Him, He wants us to take our fears, failures, storms, and mountains to Him to solve. We are designed to need God. Our storms rage because we are not created to deal with them on our own. Embracing reverence for God above all else frees us from being captive to our circumstances.

Christ-centered leaders overcome fear with faith, understanding that God is enthroned above all our circumstances.

Application: When facing a storm or difficult situation this week, shift your focus from fear of the circumstances to reverence for

God. Remember that He shows up, not to add fear, but to offer comfort and solutions. Humble yourself to trust His presence and let that shift in perspective guide you through the challenges.

MISSION OVER ME *JA*

"Do not work for food that spoils, but for food that endures to eternal life, which the Son of Man will give you. On Him God the Father has placed His seal of approval."
—John 6:27

<u>Read</u>: John 6:25–59 "Jesus the Bread of Life"
After walking on the Sea of Galilee to meet His disciples, Jesus returns to Capernaum and delivers a profound teaching in the synagogue. He explains that eternal life requires *"eating His body and drinking His blood,"* a teaching the crowd takes literally, failing to grasp its spiritual significance. Despite the miraculous feeding of thousands just days before, the crowd still demands a sign, seeking more physical provision rather than understanding Jesus' deeper purpose.

Jesus confronts their misplaced desires, saying they seek Him not because of the miracles pointing to God's glory, but because they want more bread (John 6:26). He redirects their focus, urging them to work for eternal rewards rather than temporary satisfaction (John 6:27). Jesus wants His followers to prioritize kingdom purposes, trusting Him to meet their physical needs as they align their lives with His mission.

This lesson convicts me because 2024 has been a tough year, personally and professionally. I have often found myself more concerned with the business of Red Letter Leadership, than its kingdom purpose. I often view my own personal financial goals as my needs, and I miss the tremendous blessings and provisions God has given me and my family along the way. I am like the Jews in this story, who were one of the thousands fed by Jesus' miracle and they return to Him wanting more from Him, not more of Him.

Effective leaders remain focused on their higher purpose, trusting that prioritizing mission over personal gain brings lasting impact.

Application: Reflect this week on your own desires—are you seeking more from God or more of God? Re-align your focus with kingdom priorities, trusting that He will provide for your physical needs as you pursue His greater purpose.

COMMITTED FOLLOWERS FOLLOW CHARACTER *JA*

> "Simon Peter answered Him, 'Lord, to whom shall we go? You have the words of eternal life.'"
> —John 6:68

Read: John 6:60–71 "Many Disciples Desert Jesus"
After Jesus taught about "eating His body and drinking His blood," many of His disciples chose to walk away, unable to reconcile this difficult teaching with their expectations. They sought a wise teacher to deepen their understanding of Scripture, not realizing Jesus was the fulfillment of those very Scriptures. Peter, however, affirmed his commitment, declaring, "You have the words of eternal life," and recognizing Jesus as the Holy One of God (John 6:68). Peter's trust in Jesus was rooted in His character, which had been demonstrated through His words and deeds.

  A leader's character is the foundation of trust and connection with their team. When a leader's actions or decisions confuse or challenge those they lead, it is their proven character that sustains their influence. While Jesus was perfect, the rest of us are not.

We can sometimes confuse or mislead those who count on us to lead them. When we make these mistakes, we must humble ourselves and ensure that our character remains intact. Like Peter's recognition that Jesus has the words of eternal life and is the Holy One of God, our character will drive people to want to follow us even when we have an off day.

A leader's character is the anchor that sustains trust and loyalty.

<u>Application</u>: Reflect on your leadership journey and identify a recent situation where your actions may have confused or challenged those you lead. How can you restore trust by humbling yourself and reaffirming your character to your team this week?

INVESTING YOUR INFLUENCE JA

"Therefore, Jesus told them, 'The right time for Me has not yet come; for you any time is right.'"

—John 7:6

<u>Read</u>: John 7:1–13 "Jesus Goes to the Feast of Tabernacles"
Jesus' brothers, not yet believers, urged Him to go to Judea for the Feast of Tabernacles, assuming He sought public recognition and a large following. However, Jesus understood that His mission and message would not win Him widespread approval but would provoke opposition because it testified against the world's evil (John 7:7). Unlike Peter, who declared Jesus the "Holy One of God" (John 6:68–69), His brothers misunderstood His purpose and saw His growing influence through a worldly lens.

Sometimes, when we believe we have a message to share, we consider how we can be heard rather than considering if those we are wanting to speak to want to hear our message. For example, social media is a platform to be heard, not necessarily to listen. It certainly can be useful to grab people's attention to a message that you have, but it is often used more heavily by those looking to be heard.

Jesus was not focused on His following. He was focused on speaking the truth. Unfortunately, the truth exposed the world's evil, and rather than examining themselves, many who heard Jesus speak were critical of His message even to the point of wanting Him dead. Jesus is arguably the most influential person in world history. Yet, when He lived, He was not concerned about gaining a following. He invested in a small group of men (The Twelve), who would go on to grow His church.

Great leaders focus on truth and meaningful investment in others rather than chasing widespread recognition or approval.

Application: Consider your approach to sharing your message. Are you focused on being heard, or are you more concerned with whether your message is truly being received and understood? This week, seek opportunities to listen first, then speak, ensuring that your message is delivered with clarity and purpose, not for the sake of recognition.

RED LETTER LEADERSHIP JA

> "He who speaks on his own does so to gain honor for himself, but he who works for the honor of the one who sent him is a man of truth; there is nothing false about him."
>
> —John 7:18

Read: John 7:14–24 "Jesus Teaches at the Feast"
To the Jews, Jesus appeared to be a wise teacher who studied under another teacher. But Jesus corrects their false notion and states

that His "teaching is not [His] own. It comes from Him who sent Me" (John 7:16). In essence, Jesus speaks the truth of the Word of God. Since He is the Word, He needs no teacher. However, He never spoke like that. He always directed His listeners to the Father when they questioned where He came from or where He learned.

This is a good reminder that all leaders are followers first. We all gain wisdom when we are humble and open to learning. When leaders stop learning, they stop being the leaders that their teams deserve. The question is: from whom are we learning? I had the vision to write lessons from Matthew 1 through John 21 to bring the reader to the wisdom from the greatest leader that ever lived. Why should leaders turn anywhere else for leadership insight? I believe the lessons in the Gospels can lead us to address any problem we experience whether the problem is in our family, at work, in our community, or another environment we occupy. I elicited help from Ben Hunter and Eric Albright because writing these lessons for the same purpose would hold much more value if there were other perspectives in the writings. I can speak for Ben and Eric when I say, we hope that by now in your journey through the Gospels, you've realized that there is no greater source of leadership instruction than the red letters.

I can say with confidence that although I have no business, human resource, public management, or organizational leadership degree, I have worked in all of those domains and I can assure you, the account of Jesus and the words attributed to Him can speak into any leadership challenge.

As leaders, let's not speak on our own, but let's be dedicated students of the greatest leader to have lived and speak "for the honor of the one who sent [us]" (John 7:18).

> **The best leaders remain humble learners, speaking and leading with wisdom drawn from the ultimate source—Jesus Christ.**

Application: Reflect on how His wisdom addresses your current leadership challenges. Commit to being a lifelong learner, continually drawing from the source of the greatest leadership model—Jesus—so you can lead with the same humility and wisdom He demonstrated.

PRIORITIZE PERFORMANCE JA

> "Still, many in the crowd put their faith in Him. They said, 'When the Christ comes, will He do more miraculous signs than this man?'"
>
> —John 7:31

Read: John 7:25-44 "Is Jesus the Christ?"

At the beginning of this passage, John records the people, who were listening to Jesus speak, state that, "when the Christ comes, no one will know where He is from" (John 7:27). Then, at the close of the passage, he records that others in the crowd said, "How can the Christ come from Galilee? Does not the Scripture say that the Christ will come from David's family and from Bethlehem, the town where David lived?" (John 7:41-42). Even when we read, we will hear what we want to hear if our minds are not open to receiving and critically thinking on information. If the people would have sought the truth, they would have found it.

Jesus fulfilled all the prophecies foretold about the coming Messiah, but His familial lineage and location of His hometown was never what He talked about. His teaching was always directing the audience to the Father. He operated in the spiritual realm and His actions were manifested in the natural to display the truth of the kingdom of God.

Several passages ago, I wrote a lesson about how Jesus assessed behavior and how we would be wise to do the same. Unfortunately, many of the crowds in this passage were more concerned with Jesus' worldly heritage, than they were His spiritual one. If they would have assessed His behavior and asked how He is capable of such miracles, they may have been more open to believing that

He is the Christ. Verse 31 tells us that many put their faith in Him because of His miracles.

I was at the chiropractor a few days ago and the place looked like a dysfunctional business and worse, an illegitimate medical practice. Between the receptionist, the doctor's assistant, and all the patients around me, I thought, 'this is my first and last visit here.' But then the doctor saw me and spoke in ways that made complete sense. He did an examination, showed me where and why I was having issues with the concerned area, and then treated it. Following a short 15-minute treatment, he tested me again and I showed definitive improvement. It was like night and day for the joint I was having issues with. His office wasn't pretty. It wasn't aesthetic, certainly wasn't what I was looking for, and a big turn-off for me as the patient. But I listened to him and gave him a chance, and the man delivered!

Despite Jesus' earthly heritage, He performed miracles and gave teachings that only the Son of God could do.

Exceptional leaders uncover potential and prioritize performance over appearance to drive meaningful results.

<u>Application</u>: This week, take a moment to step back and reassess the situations or people in your leadership environment. Are you focused on outward appearances or worldly credentials, or are you looking deeper into the actions and character that reveal true potential and impact?

DROP YOUR STONE *JA*

"When they kept on questioning Him, He straightened up and said to them, 'If any one of your is without sin, let him be the first to throw a stone at her.'"

–John 8:7

Read: John 7:45–8:11 "Unbelief of the Jewish Leaders"
In one of Scripture's most profound moments on judgment, Jesus confronts the hypocrisy of the Pharisees, who bring before Him a woman caught in adultery. They cite the Law of Moses as justification for her stoning. Yet, the same law requires that both the man and the woman be punished (Lev 20:10; Deut 22:22–24). Notably absent is the man involved, highlighting the Pharisees' selective application of justice.

Rather than delve into the technicalities of the law, Jesus addresses the deeper issue—the condition of their hearts. His actions forced them to confront their own guilt. One by one, they dropped their stones and walked away, realizing they were no more righteous than the woman they condemned.

This passage highlights the transformative power of forgiveness. Jesus doesn't deny the reality of sin—if sin weren't real, forgiveness wouldn't be necessary. Instead, He models how forgiveness breathes life into individuals and communities. As leaders, embracing forgiveness can restore relationships, strengthen teams, and disrupt cycles of condemnation and resentment. Forgiveness is a profound act of grace that cannot be forced to offer nor prevented from giving, and its impact extends beyond the individual to transform entire groups.

I met a gentleman who founded and leads an organization in Uganda that is committed to fight against child sacrifice and trafficking in Uganda. He shared some gruesome, heinous stories with me about how evil witch doctors are. He also shared how he's been able to lead some of these witch doctors to Christ, while they've sat in prison, and the ones that became Christ followers turn to support his work as informants. But what struck me the most was when he told me that, "I could be a witch doctor, but only by the grace of God, I'm not." This is a man that understands the human heart is inherently evil. He understands that his sin has separated him from God as much as the witch doctor's has, but it's by God's grace that he was raised well, met Jesus, and is hunting down the witch doctors instead of being one. Men like that will change their communities for Christ. They will not be overcome by evil but will overcome evil with good (Rom 12:21).

Forgiveness is a life-giving act of leadership that restores relationships, transforms teams, and unleashes the power of grace to disrupt evil and foster unity.

Application: Reflect on any judgments or resentment you may be holding toward others in your life or work. This week, practice forgiveness—whether it's forgiving someone else or seeking forgiveness yourself. Take a moment to remind yourself that we all stand in need of grace, and embrace the opportunity to disrupt cycles of condemnation with the transformative power of grace. Just as Jesus modeled, offer forgiveness freely, knowing it has the potential to restore relationships and bring healing to individuals and communities.

DRAW ME CLOSE JA

"I am one who testifies to Myself; My other witness is the Father, who sent Me."

–John 8:18

Read: John 8:12–30 "The Validity of Jesus' Testimony"
The Pharisees challenge Jesus that His testimony is not valid because He speaks for Himself. Jesus corrects them by stating that the Father is His witness. So then to validate Jesus' testimony, we must know who the Father is and what He says regarding Jesus. The irony of this scene is that Jesus is speaking with the Pharisees—the experts of the Law, who are to know it better than any of the common people. If anyone should be an expert in the

Father's testimony about Jesus, it should be these religious leaders. Sadly, they have mistaken hearing the Father's testimony about Jesus with their religious traditions.

The one theme of the entire Bible is relationships: first, our relationship with God and then our relationships with each other. The Bible was written so that we can know the true character of God and have an intimate relationship with Him. Jesus' testimony to the Pharisees in this passage declares that His words and actions (His testimony) matches up with the Scriptures (the Father's testimony). If the Pharisees were truly seeking to know and understand who Jesus was—and a few of them were—they would have learned and believed.

We get ourselves in trouble when we use the word of God to first judge others before using it to know God and draw us closer to Him. True leadership begins with connection—with God and with others. A leader cannot guide or influence effectively without genuine relationships. Leadership is not leadership if establishing relationships is not part of the process. When we study the Bible to know the heart of God, we learn the Spirit of Jesus that is behind His words and actions. When we can understand Jesus, we can understand real leadership.

Christ-centered leaders do not simply take Jesus' words at face value, but rather seek to understand the true nature of His heart.

Application: This week, examine your approach to studying Scripture. Are you using it to judge others or to deepen your relationship with God? Shift your focus to using the Bible as a tool to grow closer to God, allowing His heart and character to shape your leadership. Strengthen your relationships with those you lead by first cultivating a deeper understanding of Jesus and His ways. Lead by example, embracing the spirit of Jesus in both word and action.

THE TRUTH WILL SET YOU FREE EA

"If you hold My teaching, you are really My disciples. Then you will know the truth, and the truth will set you free."
—John 8:31–32

Read: John 8:31–41 "The Children of Abraham"
As the Jews surrounding Jesus continue to dispute His purpose, His calling, and His identity, and how they follow their father Abraham, Jesus patiently explains to them who He is and why He came there. He impresses upon them that He is sent by the Father and that once they repent and accept this new truth, they will be free from the bondage of the law that has enslaved them since their time wandering in the desert.

Similarly, how do you handle speaking the truth when it may be unpopular, especially if it is rejected by a vast majority, and even more so if it is a new reality that some may not have heard of or understand? When we face hard truths, are we more likely to go with the crowd or stand on our principles?

I can remember a time when I was required to speak truth to power, and blow the whistle on an incoming commander for whom I had previously worked. He was wildly unpopular with most of the community I came from, primarily due to fear of retribution. However, I chose to stand on moral principle and do the right thing, even if it was unpopular. I let the truth be known about that individual's toxic abuse and the climate he created when I had previously worked for him when he was the commanding officer. In that instance, being truthful about my previous experience was far greater than maintaining popularity, and even though it changed the trajectory of my career, I look back now completely confident that it was the right decision.

Morally sound leadership requires the courage to speak unpopular truths and uphold moral principles, even in the face of fear and potential backlash.

Application: Reflect on a situation where you may have avoided speaking an unpopular truth due to fear of backlash, or maybe an area of unpopular truth regarding self-awareness and self-improvement you have had a hard time admitting. Commit today to stand on moral principles, even when it's difficult or unpopular. Identify one area in your life where truth needs to be spoken with courage and integrity, and take a step toward addressing it with grace and humility.

FRAGILE, BUT FOUNDATIONAL *EA*

"Yet because I tell you the truth, you do not believe Me."
–John 8:45

Read: John 8:42–47 "The Children of the Devil"
Continuing from the previous lesson, where Jesus chastises the Jewish followers for claiming Abraham as their father, He takes it further by asserting that their true father is not God, which it should be, but rather the devil. Jesus challenges them to prove Him guilty of sin, which they cannot do; and He equates their disbelief with alignment to Satan's playbook, as he is the father of lies. Their unwillingness to hear the truth reveals their failure to recognize God's message, highlighting the spiritual blindness that prevents them from accepting His word.

This passage emphasizes the importance of trust in relationships. Just as the Jews needed to trust and believe Jesus when He claimed to be sent from God, we often find ourselves needing to trust those we work for or those who work for us. Trust is one of the hardest qualities to build, the easiest to lose, and one of the most challenging aspects of leadership to embrace.

I remember when I was a young leader, I often took tasks off my subordinates' plates and put them on my own, primarily due to a lack of trust, although I didn't recognize it at the time. As my leadership style matured, I realized I couldn't do everything myself and learned that it was okay to trust others with tasks, even if they might fail. I began not only to become comfortable with trusting others but also to embrace it. When used properly, trust can be a powerful tool for developing those around you. If subordinates truly believe you, trust them and have confidence in their abilities to complete a task, it will result in empowerment, confidence, and growth. Moreover, if you aren't the one teaching your subordinates to focus on trust in relation to mission accomplishment, who else will teach them?

> **Effective leadership hinges on the ability to build and nurture trust, empowering others to take on responsibilities and grow, even in the face of potential failure.**

Application: Identify at least one task or project this week that you can delegate to a team member. Clearly communicate your trust in their ability to handle it and provide any necessary guidance. After completion, review the results together, offering constructive feedback to reinforce their confidence and further build trust. Track the outcomes of this delegation to measure the impact on their growth and team morale.

BEFORE ABRAHAM WAS, I AM *EA*

> *"'I tell you the truth,' Jesus answered, 'before Abraham was, I am.'"*
>
> *—John 8:58*

Read: John 8:48–59 "The Claims of Jesus about Himself"
As Jesus continues His heated discussion with the Jews present, He strives to explain not only that He knows the Father, but that

He was sent by the Father. Going even further, He tells them that He was present before Abraham was born, claiming a transcendence over time that could only be true of God. As expected, the Jews do not understand, and this leads to an angry revolt, with them picking up stones to throw at Him, while Jesus hides Himself and leaves the temple.

Much like Jesus, the God of "I AM," who transcends space and time, many foundational leadership principles He teaches us are also timeless. Specifically, servant leadership is a role we can all take on in many different areas of our lives, and it will never wear out or grow irrelevant. Selfless sacrifice, with the effort to improve others' lives or help them grow in specific areas, will always be received positively and can never be a wrong approach to any event or situation.

The second lesson from this passage is that, despite being pressed, Jesus remains steadfast in His commitment to foundational truths, even when they are not fully understood by others. Through this, He shows us that even when working with difficult individuals becomes exasperating, it is imperative to stick to the principles by which we stand and the truth that supports those principles.

Effective leadership requires unwavering commitment to foundational principles, even in the face of misunderstanding or opposition, and the ability to serve selflessly for the benefit of others.

Application: Identify one foundational principle or truth that guides your leadership or personal interactions and tell someone. This week, commit to upholding that principle in a challenging situation, even if it's misunderstood or opposed, and ask the person you shared it with to follow up in a week to see if you have accomplished the task. Additionally, find one opportunity to practice servant leadership by selflessly helping someone in your team or in your community, and track how this act positively impacts their growth or situation.

TURNING A CURSE INTO A GIFT *EA*

> *"'Neither this man nor his parents sinned,'* said Jesus, *'but this happened so that the works of God might be displayed in him.'"*
>
> –John 9:3

Read: John 9:1–12 "Jesus Heals a Man Born Blind"

How many times have we found ourselves in situations where we ask, "Why me?" How many times have we faced tough decisions, unsure of why we are the ones making them or if we are even qualified to do so?

Similar to the account of Jesus healing the blind man in this passage, many times the situations we face are being used for His good, even though we may not see it at the time. As Romans 8:28 reminds us, "...we know that in all things God works for the good of those who love Him...," even when we don't always understand how or why. There are moments when the challenges we face can seem overwhelming, but those very challenges may be the ones that shape us and others in unexpected ways.

I can remember a particular situation my wife and I went through several years ago, a time when we were in an incredibly challenging season of our lives and often found ourselves asking, "Why us?" However, through that hardship and a close friend inviting us back to church, we reconnected with Christ, leading to the salvation and baptism of our entire family. Even though we didn't understand why we had to face that situation at the time, we now use it as an opportunity to help others grow. What once seemed like a curse, we now view as a gift—something only possible through the power of God.

On this Thanksgiving Day, 2024, I am deeply grateful for the everlasting gift of grace that Jesus has given our family and for the salvation He provided through Christ's sacrifice, for which I will be eternally thankful.

Faithful leadership involves trusting that even difficult situations can be used for greater good, and embracing the opportunity to grow and help others, even when the purpose isn't immediately clear.

Application: Reflect on a current or recent challenge in your life and identify at least one way it could be used to grow yourself or positively impact others. Set a measurable goal this week to share your experience with at least two people who might benefit from your insights or encouragement. Additionally, journal three specific ways this challenge may be working for good in your life or others', focusing on gratitude for the lessons learned.

THE IRONY OF DISBELIEF EA

"'Nobody has ever heard of opening the eyes of a man born blind. If this man were not from God, he could do nothing.' To this they replied, 'You were steeped in sin at birth; how dare you lecture us!' And they threw him out."
—John 9:32–34

Read: John 9:13–34 "The Pharisees Investigate the Healing"
In the continuation of the miracle where Jesus heals a man blind from birth, the Pharisees question the man about his account of the situation in an attempt to better understand who Jesus is. However, even after thorough interrogation, the Pharisees still refuse to believe that Jesus is who He says He is. When the healed man tells them, "If Jesus weren't from God, He could do nothing," the Pharisees chastise him for daring to teach them, as they considered themselves the experts of Scripture.

How many times have we encountered situations that seemed unreasonable or illogical? When faced with these situations, how do we respond? Do we work through them to reach a logical conclusion, asking questions to better understand, or do we dismiss them and leave the issue for someone else to handle?

There is much we can learn from the Pharisees' behavior in this situation. First, they refused to believe that there could be an answer beyond what they already knew. Second, they were outraged that a man they considered a 'common sinner' might be able to explain scriptural teachings more clearly than they could. The irony is that while the "common sinner" was once physically blind and received his sight, the real blindness lay with the Pharisees, whose arrogance kept them spiritually blind and, ironically, beyond the reach of healing.

Leadership requires humility and openness to learning from others, even those we may perceive as less experienced or qualified, rather than holding onto rigid, preconceived beliefs.

Application: This week, intentionally seek feedback or insight from at least three people whose perspectives or experiences differ from your own, particularly in an area where you feel confident or knowledgeable. Reflect on what you learn from these interactions and identify one specific change you can make in your approach or understanding. Document these lessons and commit to applying them in your leadership or decision-making processes.

DOES OUR SIGHT BLIND US? *EA*

"Jesus said, 'If you were blind, you would not be guilty of sin; but now that you claim you can see, your guilt remains.'"

–John 9:41

Read: John 9:35–41 "Spiritual Blindness"

After the blind man is cast out by the Pharisees, Jesus learns of this and seeks him out, revealing His true identity to him. Upon hearing this, the blind man immediately professes Jesus to be the Son of Man. Jesus further explains, saying, "I have come into this world so that the blind will see, and those who see will become blind" (John 9:39). Upon hearing this, the Pharisees ask, "What? Are we blind too?" Jesus replies, "If you were blind, you would not be guilty of sin; but now that you claim you can see, your guilt remains" (John 9:40–41).

If we were to apply this analogy to our own lives, do we more closely align with the blind man or the Pharisees? Do we feel as though we have all the answers, potentially becoming overconfident in our assumptions, or are we humble and willing to hear a different opinion or truth and respond with immediate, profound belief?

As we reflect on this story of the blind man and his interactions with both Jesus and the Pharisees, we learn about trust, faith, arrogance, and lack of humility. The first two virtues are closely aligned with the fruit of the Spirit, while the last two are works of the flesh. As part of a healthy, ongoing introspection, take a moment today to reflect on your leadership style. Write down the attributes you see in yourself—both the positive and the negative. Then, ask two or three close coworkers whom you trust to provide honest feedback, creating a similar list as they perceive you. Compare the lists for similarities and differences, but brace yourself, as the results may surprise you. Once you've completed this, ask yourself again: Do you align more closely with the blind man or the Pharisees?

Effective leadership requires self-awareness and the ability to recognize when our own vision is clouded, allowing us to seek clarity and truth from others in order to lead with greater understanding.

Application: This week, write down at least three attributes—both strengths and weaknesses—you believe define your leadership style. Then, ask at least two trusted colleagues for their honest feedback on your leadership qualities, requesting them to share three attributes they observe in you. Compare your self-assessment with their input, noting any differences. Identify one specific area for improvement and commit to taking measurable steps to address it, fostering greater self-awareness and growth.

CONSISTENCY IS KEY EA

> "The watchman opens the gate for him, and the sheep listen to his voice. He calls his own sheep by name and leads them out. When he has brought out all his own, he goes on ahead of them, and his sheep follow him because they know his voice."
>
> —John 10:3–4

Read: John 10:1–21 "The Shepherd and His Flock"
In a continuation of his conversation with the Jews and the Pharisees following the healing of the man blind from birth, Jesus shares the parable of the Good Shepherd, emphasizing the familiar relationship between the shepherd and his sheep. The sheep know the voice of their shepherd and follow him willingly, trusting that he will lead them to safety and provision. Unlike thieves and robbers who come to harm them, the sheep recognize their shepherd's voice and follow him because they have developed a bond of trust over time. Jesus compares Himself to the shepherd, highlighting that His followers, like the sheep, are able to recognize His voice and follow Him because they trust Him due to consistent guidance and care.

As leaders, we must ask ourselves tough questions about consistency in the way we lead others. Is our leadership style consistent enough that our subordinates recognize it like the sheep recognize the shepherd's voice in the dark? Are we providing clear, consistent direction, or do we waver when challenges arise? Do we speak with a voice our team can trust, or do we send mixed signals that undermine their confidence? Consistency is vital for building trust, but it requires us to lead with conviction and resilience, no matter the circumstances.

When we think about building cohesion and efficiency within a team, consistency is one of the most important traits a leader can exhibit. A consistent leader is someone others can rely on; someone whose values and actions align with the vision they've set for their team. To lead with consistency, we must first be clear on our values and expectations, ensuring that our decisions, especially tough ones, align with the organization's core principles. In the military, a common way commanders express their vision is through a "Command Philosophy." This philosophy provides commanders with a codified way to articulate their priorities and vision for the unit. Once established and communicated, it serves as a guide in decision-making. By consistently applying this philosophy, subordinates will come to anticipate a commander's decisions, reducing anxiety and fostering greater cohesion within the team.

Consistency in decision-making builds trust, allowing your team to recognize and follow your direction with confidence, even in challenging times.

Application: Write down three core values or principles that guide your leadership. Share these with your team during your next meeting or communication, clearly articulating how they influence your decisions. Over the next two weeks, consciously apply these values consistently in your leadership actions, and ask two team members for feedback on whether your decisions align with the principles you've shared. Use their feedback to adjust and strengthen your consistency.

LEADING WITH CONVICTION *BH*

"The works I do in My Father's name testify about Me, but you do not believe because you are not My sheep."
—John 10:25–26

Read: John 10:22–42 "Further Conflict over Jesus' Claims"
Jesus faces growing opposition from religious leaders questioning His identity and authority. Despite their hostility, He remains steadfast in His mission and speaks with unwavering confidence about His relationship with the Father. Jesus emphasizes that His works testify to His divine authority and that those who belong to Him—His sheep—hear His voice and follow Him.

This moment teaches leaders the importance of standing firm in their convictions, especially when facing criticism or resistance. As leaders, there will always be times when our decisions or visions are challenged. Like Jesus, our actions should align with our values and speak louder than our words. When others question our integrity or doubt our motives, our consistency and commitment to doing what is right will serve as our strongest testimony.

Leadership rooted in conviction doesn't waver in the face of adversity. It also prioritizes those who truly follow and support the mission. Jesus reminds us that not everyone will understand or agree with our leadership, but our responsibility is to lead faithfully, ensuring our actions reflect the mission and values we uphold.

Leadership rooted in conviction stands firm in the face of opposition and lets actions speak louder than words.

Application: Today, take time to reflect on your leadership values and the mission you are pursuing. Are your actions consistently aligned with your core beliefs? When faced with criticism or resistance, how do you stay steadfast in your convictions? Choose to lead with unwavering commitment and integrity, ensuring that your actions speak louder than your words, and prioritize those who truly support and follow the mission. Stay true to your values, especially when it's hard to do so.

LEADING THROUGH UNCERTAINTY *BH*

> "Jesus said, 'This sickness will not end in death. No, it is for God's glory so that God's Son may be glorified through it.'"
>
> —John 11:4

Read: John 11:1–16 "The Death of Lazarus"
Jesus learns of Lazarus's illness, but chooses to remain where He is for two more days rather than going immediately to help. His disciples are confused by His actions, but Jesus explains that Lazarus's situation will ultimately reveal God's glory. When Jesus finally decides to return to Judea, the disciples express fear, reminding Him that the region is dangerous. Jesus, however, confidently declares His intention, knowing that His actions will lead to a greater purpose.

As leaders, we often encounter moments of uncertainty or situations where our decisions are not immediately understood by others. Jesus demonstrates that leadership requires faith, patience, and clarity of purpose. Even when others doubt us or fear the unknown, we must remain focused on the bigger picture and the outcomes that align with our mission.

This story also reminds us of the importance of courage. Jesus' decision to return to Judea, despite the risks, shows that effective leadership often requires boldness in the face of danger or criticism. It's not about avoiding challenges, but about trusting in the greater purpose of our work and guiding others through moments of doubt.

Lead your team through moments of uncertainty with faith, courage, and clarity of purpose.

Application: In your leadership today, reflect on moments where you must act despite uncertainty or opposition. Lead with faith and patience, trusting that your actions align with a greater purpose, even when others may not fully understand. Embrace courage, and guide your team through doubt, knowing that bold decisions rooted in clarity will ultimately reveal the bigger picture and impact.

CONNECTING THROUGH EMPATHY *BH*

"Jesus wept."

—John 11:35

Read: John 11:17–37 "Jesus Comforts the Sisters of Lazarus"
Jesus arrives in Bethany after Lazarus has died and is met by Martha and Mary, who are grieving the loss of their brother. Though Jesus knows He will raise Lazarus from the dead, He still takes time to comfort the sisters and share in their sorrow. The shortest verse in the Bible, "Jesus wept," is a powerful reminder of His humanity and empathy.

As leaders, it can be easy to focus solely on solutions or results, especially in challenging circumstances. However, Jesus demonstrates that effective leadership requires compassion and an ability to connect with others on an emotional level. Before performing the miracle of raising Lazarus, Jesus acknowledges the pain and grief of those around Him. This act of empathy strengthens trust and shows that leadership is about more than achieving goals—it's about caring for the people we lead.

Leaders who show genuine compassion foster loyalty and unity within their teams. When team members know their leader values their struggles and emotions, they feel supported and understood. Like Jesus, we must learn to balance decisive action with heartfelt empathy, taking time to connect with others even as we work toward solutions.

> **"People don't care how much you know until they know how much you care."–John Maxwell**

Application: As you lead today, take a moment to show genuine empathy for those you are leading. Acknowledge their struggles and emotions and offer comfort before pushing forward with solutions. By demonstrating compassion, you will build trust and strengthen the unity of your team as you work toward your goals.

LEADERSHIP THAT INSPIRES FAITH BH

> *"Did I not tell you that if you believe, you will see the glory of God?"*
> —John 11:40

Read: John 11:38–44 "Jesus Raises Lazarus from the Dead"
Jesus performs one of His most miraculous signs: raising Lazarus from the dead. Before calling Lazarus out of the tomb, Jesus reminds those present of the power of faith and the glory of God. Though many doubted, Jesus remained focused on demonstrating God's power, giving thanks publicly to the Father to inspire belief in those around Him.

This story highlights the importance of unwavering faith and decisive action in leadership. Jesus shows that leaders must remain confident in their mission even when others doubt. By maintaining His focus on glorifying God and involving others in the process— asking them to roll away the stone and unbind Lazarus—Jesus engages the community and strengthens their faith.

As leaders, we face moments when our decisions challenge the doubts and fears of those around us. Like Jesus, we can lead with confidence and invite others to witness the possibilities that come with trust and belief. When we inspire faith in a greater purpose, we empower our teams to achieve extraordinary outcomes, even in the face of seemingly insurmountable challenges.

Leadership inspires faith by acting decisively, involving others, and staying focused on a purpose greater than ourselves.

<u>Application</u>: Today, lead with unwavering faith in your mission, even when others may doubt. Invite your team to be a part of the process and witness the power of belief in achieving extraordinary outcomes. By staying focused on the greater purpose, you will inspire trust and create a sense of shared accomplishment.

COURAGE IN THE FACE OF OPPOSITION *BH*

> "Then the chief priests and the Pharisees called a meeting of the Sanhedrin. 'What are we accomplishing?' they asked. 'Here is this man performing many signs. If we let Him go on like this, everyone will believe in Him, and then the Romans will come and take away both our temple and our nation.'"
> —John 11:47–48

<u>Read</u>: John 11:45–57 "The Plot to Kill Jesus"
The miraculous raising of Lazarus triggers a wave of belief among many. Yet, it also ignites fear and resistance among the religious leaders. They are more concerned with maintaining their power and position than embracing the truth of Jesus' divine mission. Their fear leads them to plot against Jesus, prioritizing their political security over the salvation He offers.

For leaders, this passage serves as a reminder that doing what is right and impactful often comes with resistance. Jesus' unwavering commitment to His mission, even as opposition grows, exemplifies the courage required to lead in challenging times. Leaders must focus on their purpose, even when others fear change or attempt to undermine progress for personal or organizational gain.

Additionally, it highlights the danger of prioritizing self-interest over greater good. The Pharisees' inability to see beyond their fears blinded them to the truth of who Jesus was. As leaders, we must regularly evaluate our motivations and ensure we are not letting personal fears or ambitions cloud our judgment.

Leadership requires courage to stay committed to the mission, even when faced with resistance or opposition.

Application: Reflect today on your motivations as a leader. Are you prioritizing personal fears or ambitions, or are you focusing on the greater good of your mission? Lead with courage and integrity, even in the face of opposition, and stay committed to the truth that guides your purpose.

A LEGACY OF SACRIFICIAL LEADERSHIP *BH*

"Then Mary took about a pint of pure nard, an expensive perfume; she poured it on Jesus' feet and wiped His feet with her hair. And the house was filled with the fragrance of the perfume."
—John 12:3

Read: John 12:1–10 "Jesus Anointed at Bethany"
This passage captures a powerful act of devotion and sacrifice. Mary's act of anointing Jesus with expensive perfume was not only an expression of deep love, but also a prophetic acknowledgment

of His approaching death. Her action was bold and selfless, drawing criticism from Judas, who was more concerned about financial gain than the significance of the moment.

Mary's act teaches leaders an important lesson about priorities and sacrifice. Leadership often requires costly decisions—investing time, energy, or resources into people and missions that might not offer immediate returns but hold eternal value. Like Mary, leaders must be willing to give sacrificially, even when others do not understand or appreciate the impact of their actions.

Additionally, this moment challenges leaders to remain focused on what matters most. Judas's objection highlights a misaligned perspective; he criticized Mary's generosity while harboring selfish motives. Leaders must guard their hearts against the distractions of greed, pride, or misplaced priorities and instead lead with clarity and purpose.

Leadership requires sacrificial investment in others, focusing on what holds eternal value rather than seeking personal gain or approval.

Application: Take a moment today to evaluate your priorities as a leader. Are you focused on immediate rewards or on making sacrifices for the long-term, eternal value of your work? Lead with selflessness and clarity, staying true to your purpose even when others may not understand or appreciate your actions.

HUMBLE AUTHORITY BH

"They took palm branches and went out to meet Him, shouting, 'Hosanna! Blessed is He who comes in the name of the Lord! Blessed is the King of Israel!'"
–John 12:13

Read: John 12:12–19 "Jesus Comes to Jerusalem as King"

This passage captures Jesus' triumphant entry into Jerusalem, where He is celebrated as King. The crowds welcomed Him with palm branches and praises, but Jesus chose to ride a young donkey, a symbol of humility and peace rather than conquest. This act highlighted the kind of leader He came to be—one who serves rather than dominates.

For leaders, this moment demonstrates the power of leading with humility and purpose. It's easy to be drawn into the recognition and praise of others, but true leadership remains grounded in mission, not applause. Jesus knew that the same crowds who praised Him would soon turn against Him. Still, He stayed focused on His greater purpose of salvation.

Leaders must also understand the balance between authority and humility. Riding into Jerusalem, Jesus embraced His role as King, but did so without arrogance or pretense. This example challenges leaders to walk confidently in their calling while remaining approachable and committed to serving others.

Leadership combines humility and authority, focusing on purpose rather than seeking recognition or approval.

Application: Reflect on how you can lead with both humility and confidence today. Embrace your leadership role with purpose, but remember that true influence comes from serving others rather than seeking praise or recognition. Stay grounded in your mission, regardless of external validation.

DO YOU HAVE TIME TO...? *JA*

"The man who loves his life will lose it, while the man who hates his life in this world will keep it for eternal life."

–John 12:25

Read: John 12:20–36 "Jesus Predicts His Death"

Our key verse, in my opinion, is the greatest lesson from this passage. If we are not willing to deny our own self, we will not inherit eternal life. Even more so, we will not live to the fullest potential that God has set us apart for on this earth. But we've written much about denying self in previous lessons, so I'd like to focus on the scene in this passage.

Jesus reveals a profound truth about purpose and focus. As He arrives in Jerusalem during the Feast of Passover, He knows His mission and the sacrifice that lies ahead. When Andrew and Philip inform Him of Greeks requesting an audience, Jesus' response may seem dismissive. Instead of addressing the request directly, He declares, *"The hour has come for the Son of Man to be glorified"* (John 12:23). John's account doesn't record whether Jesus spoke with the Greeks, but it highlights His unwavering commitment to His purpose.

Jesus' reply emphasizes the urgency and singularity of His mission. At a time when distractions could have pulled Him away, He remains focused on what matters most: glorifying the Father through His sacrifice. This serves as a powerful reminder that leaders must prioritize their time and energy on what aligns with their purpose. While opportunities or requests may seem important, they must be weighed against the mission God has placed before us.

In his book, *Leadership Gold*, John Maxwell shares a lesson he titled, "Don't Manage Your Time—Manage Your Life." In the lesson, he shares the story of a man who filled a jar with marbles, each marble representing one Saturday. He filled enough marbles to observe how much time he still had on earth. He hoped to at least live until he was 75. Every Saturday morning, he would remove one marble. This illustration reminds us of the finite nature of time.[23]

Time is a precious gift from God. Don't waste it because you think you have more or feel entitled to more. Time is not a resource to control, but an opportunity to focus on what truly matters. Live each moment for the purpose and passion God has placed in your life.

Leaders understand that our lives are meant to own our time, not our time own our lives.

<u>Application</u>: Take time today to reflect on your priorities and identify distractions that may pull you away from your God-given mission. Consider how you can better steward the precious gift of time by aligning your actions with your purpose and focusing on what truly matters for His glory.

PATIENCE IN THE LEARNING PROCESS *JA*

"As for the person who hears My words but does not keep them, I do not judge him. For I did not come to judge the world, but to save it."

–John 12:47

<u>Read</u>: John 12:37–50 "The Jews Continue in Their Unbelief"
Despite Jesus' miraculous signs, many Jewish leaders refused to believe in Him, while others who did believe kept their faith hidden out of fear. They prioritized human approval over God's praise, as verse 43 reveals. This reluctance underscores a truth Jesus taught in the Parable of the Sower (Matt 13:1–23): the Word of God, though transformative, can be rejected or diminished when hearts are distracted by worldly concerns.

Leadership often mirrors this challenge. As a leader, your decisions or vision may not always be embraced immediately—or at all—by your team. This isn't necessarily a reflection of poor leadership, but of the complexities of human nature. Your team might lack the perspective you have, need more time to process, or struggle to align with a vision that doesn't yet feel personal to them. Expect resistance and meet it with patience and understanding.

Jesus models this leadership. Even when faced with rejection, He stayed focused on His mission, extending grace and welcoming all who believed. Leaders can emulate this approach by equipping their teams with the knowledge and context needed to understand decisions. When leaders lead with accountability and humility, rather than authority alone, they build trust and foster alignment over time.

> **Leaders take the responsibility to inform their team and graciously walk with them through their understanding.**

Application: Reflect on how you handle resistance to your leadership. This week, practice patience and grace by seeking to understand your team's perspectives and providing the knowledge or context they need to align with your vision. Lead with humility and a focus on fostering trust.

ROLE REVERSAL JA

"You call me 'Teacher' and 'Lord,' and rightly so, for that is what I am. Now that I, your Lord and Teacher, have washed your feet, you also should wash one another's feet."
—John 13:13–14

Read: John 13:1–17 "Jesus Washes His Disciples' Feet"
This scene from John 13 is one of the most iconic illustrations of servant leadership. Jesus, the ultimate leader, does not step away from His position to wash His disciples' feet. Rather, He acknowledges that He is greater than they are in power, position, and status, yet, still demonstrates humility and service to them as His closest team. After He finishes, He states that "no servant is greater than his master" (John 13:16), and instructs His disciples to do likewise (John 13:15). Jesus is not unraveling culture or a social

caste system. Instead, He is showing how those with power, status, wealth, position, and influence should treat people who do not possess the same.

Regardless of the culture you live in, some form of societal hierarchy exists. Social justice warriors seek to level economic inequality to reduce the divide between the rich and the poor. But Jesus never speaks against such a divide. Instead, He teaches and demonstrates how to live and lead, whether you are at the top of society or the bottom, the top of your company or the bottom. Jesus is not seeking to overthrow an earthly government or societal system; He is seeking to revolutionize the government of the heart.

Jesus demonstrated to His disciples that He loved them. Though He was far above them in status, He had their best interests at heart and passionately wanted to serve them to bring them closer to Himself and to each other. I can't imagine the emotional and spiritual bonding that happened in that room the night Jesus was betrayed. And to think, He also washed Judas' feet, knowing Judas would turn on Him that very night. Jesus knew these things and still showed him unmeasured grace and love in the washing of his feet.

Christ-centered leaders are the epitome of servant leaders because they replicate the greatest servant leader of all—Jesus.

<u>Application</u>: This week, follow Jesus' example of servant leadership by performing an act of humility and service for someone in your sphere of influence. Seek no recognition, but focus on showing love and grace, especially toward those who may not expect it or fully appreciate it.

ASSURE YOUR TEAM *JA*

"I tell you the truth, whoever accepts anyone I send accepts Me; and whoever accepts Me accepts the One who sent Me."
—John 13:20

Read: John 13:18–30 "Jesus Predicts His Betrayal"

Jesus finishes washing His disciples' feet and becomes troubled in spirit, knowing what Judas is about to do—even after Jesus poured out so much love to him over the years. He empowers the others by assuring them that anyone who accepts them will also be accepted by Him, and if He accepts them, so will His Father in heaven (John 13:20). For the disciples around the table that evening, what a profound sense of power and acceptance from their leader.

Leaders who assure their teams of their unwavering acceptance foster a deep sense of belonging and empowerment. When leaders affirm that they fully back their team members and their work, they create an atmosphere of trust and support. This reassurance is especially crucial when team members face challenges or represent the leader in high-stakes situations. Knowing their leader stands behind them gives individuals the courage to take ownership of their roles, take risks, and remain confident in their decisions, even in the face of rejection or criticism. Such affirmation signals that the leader values not just the work being done, but the people doing it, reinforcing their importance to the team's mission.

This assurance also cultivates loyalty and unity within the team. When leaders publicly express that they will accept those who accept their team members, it mirrors the same value system they want their team to uphold. It reflects a commitment to fairness and solidarity, inspiring team members to extend the same acceptance and support to one another. By empowering their team in this way, leaders strengthen their collective purpose and model a culture of inclusion and respect that ripples outward to others they encounter. This dynamic not only builds morale but also encourages a shared commitment to the leader's vision and goals.

Leaders who assure their teams that they will accept anyone who accepts them empower their teams to greater influence and productivity.

Application: This week, intentionally affirm each member of your team by recognizing their contributions and expressing your support for their work. Let them know they are valued and trusted to represent the mission, fostering confidence and a sense of belonging.

WHEN THE TEAM CAN'T FOLLOW JA

> "Simon Peter asked Him, 'Lord, where are You going?' Jesus replied, 'Where I am going, you cannot follow now, but you will follow later.'"
>
> —John 13:36

Read: John 13:31–38 "Jesus Predicts Peter's Denial"

Jesus is explaining to Peter and the other disciples the harsh reality that they can no longer physically follow Him, as they have for almost three years. They cannot fathom or comprehend the punishment that Jesus is about to embrace in less than 24 hours. Jesus knows that they love Him, but that they are not ready to endure such hardship in His name.

In the lesson I wrote on Luke 7:1–10, I explained how good leaders understand where their influence is limited and where they need to leverage other leaders' influence. In this passage, we see where the leader must continue without the team. Where Jesus was going, His team was not yet fully prepared to go. Jesus approaches where they are weak and unprepared with grace. He states that Peter will disown Him, and we know through other Scriptures, that Jesus tells all of them that they will scatter on account of Him (Mark 14:27; Matt 26:31). Yet, Jesus encourages Peter that he will follow Jesus later, which was Jesus' foretelling of Peter's death by crucifixion.

Jesus demonstrates a profound leadership principle: the necessity of acting boldly when the team is not yet ready to follow. Despite

Peter's zeal and loyalty, Jesus understands the disciples are not prepared to endure the immense trials that await. Instead of chastising their limitations, Jesus approaches them with grace, foretelling Peter's denial without diminishing his future importance. By affirming that Peter will eventually follow, Jesus sets an example of how leaders can pave the way for their team's eventual growth and success, even when immediate alignment is not possible.

Leadership often demands decisions and actions that the team cannot yet fully grasp or support. There are moments when the leader must venture ahead, making choices that may seem isolating or incomprehensible to the team. However, a wise leader, like Jesus, prepares the way for their team's future participation and development. This includes acknowledging current limitations, providing encouragement for growth, and creating an environment where the team can thrive when they are ready to step into the new challenges. By doing so, leaders not only fulfill the immediate mission, but also cultivate their team's readiness for future endeavors.

Effective leaders act boldly and take responsibility even when their team is not ready to follow but prepare and encourage their team for future growth and readiness to step into greater challenges.

Application: Identify a task or decision that your team may not yet be ready to follow. Act boldly, but also encourage and equip them for future participation by addressing their current needs and fostering growth toward readiness.

TRUST-BASED LEADERSHIP JA

*"Do not let your hearts be troubled.
Trust in God; trust also in Me."*

–John 14:1

Read: John 14:1–4 "Jesus Comforts His Disciples"
Following a despairing conversation in which Jesus tells His disciples they cannot follow Him to where He is going, He reassures them that He is acting with their best interests at heart. He is going to prepare a place for them (John 14:2). He encourages them that, because they know Him, they know the way (John 14:4–6). He assures them they don't need to worry or be troubled but should simply trust Him.

Trust between the leader and the team is a critical component of teamwork. Where there is no trust, the team becomes fragmented. John Maxwell calls trust "the foundation of leadership" in his book *The 21 Irrefutable Laws of Leadership*.[24] Mike Ettore, author of *Trust-Based Leadership* and designer of the "Trust-Based Leadership" concept for training and coaching business executives, underscores this idea. A retired Marine major who served 15 years as a C-level executive in a billion-dollar publicly traded company, Ettore argues that the Marine Corps' maneuver warfare doctrine—which relies heavily on decentralized execution by all members of a unit—"depends first and foremost on a culture of absolute trust among Marines of all ranks."[25]

I recently gave a presentation to a local employee resource group on shaping our environments. I emphasized three absolute must-dos: 1) Connect, 2) Build trust, and 3) Deliver. Before we can expect anyone to trust us, we must establish a connection with them. Once a connection is established, building trust becomes essential for gaining influence. Finally, if we are to shape our environments, we must deliver value to those we've connected with and built trust with; failing to deliver risks losing both trust and connection.

Leaders do not exist to control the team completing the task; they exist to empower the team to complete the task without needing to be controlled. At the heart of this concept is trust.

We can only influence those who trust us, and we will lose their trust if we don't trust them.

Application: Reflect on your connections with your team and identify ways to strengthen trust. Take intentional steps this week to build or deepen trust by engaging authentically, following through on commitments, and demonstrating you value their contributions.

EVEN GREATER THINGS *JA*

"I tell you the truth, anyone who has faith in Me will do what I have been doing. He will do even greater things than these, because I am going to the Father."
–John 14:12

Read: Luke 9:57–62 "The Cost of Following Jesus"
After Jesus reassures His disciples that He is going to prepare a place for them and that He is the way to that place, He then tells them that they will do "even greater things" than He has.

Jesus' promise that His disciples will do "even greater things" (John 14:12) is a profound reminder of the potential God has placed within each of us. Through faith in Him and the power of the Holy Spirit, we are not bound by our limitations but are invited to step into the extraordinary. This doesn't mean we are called to surpass Jesus' significance, but rather that we are empowered to extend His work on an even larger scale, reaching farther and touching lives He commissioned us to transform. Jesus' earthly ministry was geographically confined, but through His Spirit working in us, we can influence the world across generations.

Often, we underestimate what God can accomplish through our willingness to serve. Like the disciples, we may feel unworthy, unprepared, or inadequate to fulfill such a calling. But Jesus assures us that knowing Him is the key. If we remain connected to Him, our efforts, guided by His purpose and power, will have eternal significance. Trust in the gifts God has given you, take bold steps of faith, and allow Him to work through you in ways beyond what you could ever imagine. With God, there are no limits to the impact you can have.

Leaders understand that they must value themselves before valuing others and they believe that they are capable of "even greater things."

Application: Step out boldly this week in an area where you feel unprepared or inadequate, trusting God to work through you. Pray for the Holy Spirit's guidance and take action, believing in the extraordinary potential He has placed within you.

WHERE CONNECTIONS BECOME RELATIONSHIPS JA

"Whoever has My commands and obeys them, he is the one who loves Me. He who loves Me will be loved by My Father, and I too will love him and show Myself to him."
—John 14:21

Read: John 14:15–31 "Jesus Promises the Holy Spirit"
Jesus is closing His last meal with His disciples before He is crucified. He promises to them that He will not leave them alone. He loves them and will always be with them. Jesus is not saying these words only for the disciples who are in front of Him, but for the whole world to know. In verse 22, Judas (not the one who betrayed Him) asks why Jesus doesn't show Himself to the world? Jesus answers that He will come to anyone who loves Him, who obeys His teaching (John 14:23). He will know who truly loves Him by how they live their lives.

Jesus judges us by our behavior, our actions, not our words alone. In the same way, we know who is committed to our teams by their actions. Leaders must be prudent with their time and resources. We must establish a culture of trust so that we can empower our team, but that trust cannot be blind. As teammates show themselves that they are serving the team's needs and not their own, we can trust them more and give them more responsibilities. Like Jesus who will show Himself to those who obey His commands, verifying trust through actions cements connections and builds strong relationships within the team.

I remember when I showed up to my first Force Recon platoon. I wanted to learn from the veterans around me as much as possible, and show them that I was a dependable member of the team. Telling them I was dependable and that they could trust me was not enough for them to do so. I had no deployment experience and had just come from being a security guard at the Presidential Retreat, Camp David. I had to show them that I was dependable, and they could trust me. Although I made plenty of dumb mistakes, I kept a humble attitude and kept learning and showing improvement. By my second platoon, I was promoted to be an assistant team leader.

Trust will lead to strong relationships when it is verified through assessed behavior.

Application: Reflect on how your actions demonstrate your commitment to your team and your values this week. Identify one way you can tangibly build trust—whether by taking initiative, supporting a teammate, or maybe some acts of service that show your commitment to your team.

GROW YOUR CAPACITY TO LEAD *JA*

"I am the vine; you are the branches. If a man remains in Me and I in him, he will bear much fruit; apart from Me you can do nothing."

–John 15:5

Read: John 15:1–17 "The Vine and the Branches"
This passage offers several leadership themes: love, sacrifice, and remaining in Jesus. We cannot truly love unless we remain in the One who is the source of all love, and the greatest form of love is to lay down our lives for our friends (John 15:13).

We often toss around the word "love" as it applies to common affection between people. However, God does not dilute love as we often do. He is love (1 John 4:8). If we are not connected to Him, we cannot truly love because He is the sole source of genuine, real love. If love is the root of leadership, we must remain connected to Jesus to grow into the leaders He has designed us to be.

I firmly believe in the great potential God has placed in each of us. He has stamped His image on us and given us the capacity to influence the advancement of His kingdom. Isn't that a sobering thought? It also alludes to great responsibility. However, it is impossible to achieve the influence He has created us to have if we do not remain in Him.

David Green, the CEO and Founder of Hobby Lobby, explores this concept in his book *Leadership NOT By the Book*. He shares 12 unconventional business principles derived from Scripture, which he applies to running Hobby Lobby. These principles often conflict with traditional corporate strategies for business growth. In the book's epilogue titled, "Leadership by the Book," Green affirms that to be a great leader, one must remain in the will of God through reading His word.[26]

> **Christ-centered leaders understand that their full capacity to influence can only be reached by remaining in Jesus.**

Application: This week, evaluate whether your leadership is rooted in love and connection to Jesus. Take intentional time daily to pray or read Scripture, seeking His guidance and love, so that you can lead others from a place of genuine, God-centered influence.

EXTREME OWNERSHIP *JA*

"If the world hates you, keep in mind that it hated Me first."
—John 15:18

Read: John 15:18—16:4 "The World Hates the Disciples"
Jesus reiterates the statement that He made when washing His disciples' feet: "No servant is greater than his master," and explains that because the world hates Him, it will also hate His disciples. In this intimate time with His disciples, Jesus takes ownership of the hate, hardship, and suffering they will face. He does not leave them to fend for themselves, but takes responsibility for the situations they will undoubtedly encounter and encourages them by promising His presence through the Holy Spirit—the Counselor.

Former U.S. Navy SEALs Jocko Willink and Leif Babin wrote a book titled *Extreme Ownership*. They've since built a leadership consulting business, known as "Echelon Front," around the concepts in the book. The company's motto is: "No matter the problem, leadership is the solution." Their book and consulting approach emphasize that leaders must always take responsibility, drive change, improve situations, and shape their environment for increased productivity and effectiveness. If a leader points to someone, something, or some circumstance as the problem, they remove themselves from affecting a solution. By examining their own actions, influence, decisions, and opportunities, leaders can start working on solutions. Rather than making excuses, leaders must take ownership. Ownership includes holding subordinates accountable for their shortcomings and applying fixes, whether by developing them or, in some cases, removing them. Ownership is not simply saying, "It's my fault," but taking responsibility for the consequences *and* the solutions.[27]

Jesus is the extreme owner. He displays the epitome of extreme ownership by taking responsibility for the hate and suffering His disciples will endure. We don't have to fear what this fallen world throws at us because we have a Savior who stands in the gap between a world of hate and the Great Commission He has entrusted to us: "Go and make disciples" (Matt 28:19).

Exemplary leaders embrace extreme ownership, taking responsibility for challenges and solutions, while empowering their teams to fulfill their missions with courage and purpose.

Application: Reflect on areas in your leadership where you can demonstrate greater ownership. This week, identify one problem within your team or responsibilities, take accountability for its resolution, and lead by example in working toward a solution.

WHEN LEADERSHIP IS A RELAY *JA*

> "But I tell you the truth: It is for your good that I am going away. Unless I go away, the Counselor will not come to you; but if I go, I will send Him to you."
> —John 16:7

Read: John 16:5–16 "The Work of the Holy Spirit"

Jesus explains to His disciples that it is for their good that He goes away (John 16:7). Jesus came to be God incarnate and to save the world from their sins. But His earthly existence was never meant to last. He came, established His church through the Twelve and later through the Apostle Paul, and sacrificed Himself as punishment for the sins of the world. His role was temporal but the Holy Spirit—the Counselor—would come and remain with us forever.

Leadership transitions are inevitable and often necessary for growth, both for the mission and the individuals involved. Jesus' departure was not a loss, but a divine strategy to empower His disciples and the church through the Holy Spirit. Similarly, in leadership roles, the timing of our transition is often guided by the evolving needs of the team and the mission. It's not an indicator of failure but a recognition that leadership is about serving the greater purpose, not clinging to a position. Like Jesus, we must prepare those we lead for the next phase by equipping them, inspiring them, and trusting them to carry on the mission.

As leaders, we are often placeholders for a season, tasked with preparing the ground for the next person to build upon. Just as the Father sent the Son, and the Son sent the Holy Spirit, leadership is a relay, not a solo race. It's important to lead with the awareness that our departure may create space for others to step into their purpose. Whether in professional roles or personal relationships like parenting, success in leadership includes fostering an environment where others can flourish. By embracing this perspective, we model humility, strategic foresight, and a commitment to the overarching mission.

When I first took over as a Marine infantry company commander, I was a first lieutenant while the position called for a seasoned captain. I knew I was a filler until a captain showed up, but I nonetheless had a job to do. After a captain arrived, I was reassigned as the executive officer for the weapons company. Low and behold, the same thing happened again. The current company commander for that company decided to resign earlier than he originally planned, and I was placed in command of the company until a captain showed up three days before we deployed.

Similarly, as parents, we raise our children. We love and lead them from birth. Then adolescence shows up and it seems we lose our influence with them. At that time, I believe good leadership in parenting is surrounding your children with people who love them as you do and who they may listen to and receive influence from in a fresh way.

Leadership is a relay, where equipping others and transitioning with purpose ensures the mission continues and thrives.

Application: Consider your current leadership role and think about how you can intentionally prepare others to step into positions of greater responsibility. Whether in a professional or personal context, look for ways to empower those around you by equipping, inspiring, and trusting them to carry on the mission, even if it means transitioning out of your current role.

VICTORY SECURED JA

"I have told you these things, so that in Me you may have peace. In this world you will have trouble. But take heart! I have overcome the world."
—John 16:33

Read: John 16:17–33 "The Disciples' Grief Will Turn to Joy"
Two passages earlier, Jesus is explaining that the world will hate His disciples, but it's okay because they hated Him first and they only hate His followers because they hate Him. In this passage, Jesus explains clearly that they may have peace despite their troubles because He has overcome the world! What great assurance from their leader: *"this will be hard, but you will win, because I have already claimed victory!"* (Author's paraphrase). Amen!

As a leader, Jesus does not shy away from acknowledging the challenges and opposition His followers will face. He prepares them for reality while also instilling hope and confidence. The assurance that He has already overcome the world serves as a foundation for courage and perseverance, even in the most difficult circumstances. It's a leader's ultimate encouragement—acknowledging the hardships while reinforcing the certainty of victory.

For us today, this message is a call to steadfastness. Life brings trials, opposition, and uncertainty, but as followers of Christ, we can hold fast to the truth that our victory is already secured in Him.

Leaders who emulate this principle inspire their teams to keep pressing forward, reminding them that struggles are temporary, but the mission and the reward are eternal. Jesus' assurance gives us peace in the midst of adversity and the strength to persevere, knowing that the outcome is our secured victory.

> **Great leaders prepare their teams for challenges while inspiring confidence in ultimate victory, offering assurance that their mission will succeed despite the struggles they face.**

Application: When facing adversity or challenges, take a moment today to remind yourself and your team that the victory has already been secured. Encourage others to press forward with confidence, knowing that despite temporary struggles, the mission and ultimate reward are assured in Christ. List three challenges/struggles/adversity that you face in your personal or professional roles that you need to remind yourself that you already have victory over, in Jesus' name.

PRAYING FOR SUCCESS *JA*

> "After Jesus said this, He looked toward heaven and prayed: 'Father, the time has come. Glorify Your Son, that Your Son may glorify You.'"
>
> –John 17:1

Read: John 17:1–5 "Jesus Prays for Himself"

By no means are we to elevate ourselves to the glory of God the Father, or God the Son. However, we do want to learn from Jesus' example here in how He prays for Himself, as we've been seeking to learn from His example throughout this entire journey through the Gospels.

Jesus, a man who is "gentle and humble in heart" (Matt 11:29), is asking God the Father to glorify Him. Why? Aren't we supposed to deny ourselves and put others above ourselves? Of course. Jesus is not glorifying Himself, but asking God to glorify Him. The glory of God the Father upon Him will return to God the Father—"that Your Son may glorify You" (John 17:1).

I believe these words and this picture of Jesus praying to the Father is something we must replicate. We should pray for our own success in the endeavors God has ordained for us. However, we should do so from the humble perspective of bringing glory to the Father through the glory He has brought us. There is no other reason for God to graciously bestow any amount of "success" on us except that it would glorify Him, which leads to our "significance" (see, RLL lesson on Matt 9:27–34). He knows that when our success only glorifies ourselves, it becomes a destructive situation for us. By His grace, He teaches us and molds us to always desire to bring glory to Him.

As leaders, we must cultivate a mindset of stewardship over the opportunities and successes God grants us. When we pray for success, it should come from a heart that desires to reflect God's character and point others toward Him. By keeping our motivations aligned with His glory, we safeguard ourselves from pride and self-centeredness, recognizing that all we have and achieve is by His hand. In this way, we lead with humility and purpose, using our influence to inspire others to glorify God as well.

Christ-centered leaders pray that their success would bring glory to God and not themselves.

Application: Today, when seeking success or progress in your leadership journey, pray with the mindset of bringing glory to God. Ask Him to empower you to reflect His character through your achievements, using your influence to inspire others to glorify Him.

PRAYING FOR OUR TEAM *JA*

"I have given them Your word and the world has hated them, for they are not of the world any more than I am of the world. My prayer is not that You take them out of the world but that You protect them from the evil one."

—John 17:14–15

Read: John 17:6–19 "Jesus Prays for His Disciples"

Jesus prays specifically for His team of twelve disciples—those He broke bread with earlier that night and who had traveled with Him during most of His years of ministry. Why pray for them specifically? Because He has invested in them and empowered them to build His Church long after He is physically removed from them. He will still lead them, but it will be through the Holy Spirit that He sends. Since He will no longer be physically present, He prays that they will have courage and that God the Father will protect them from Satan.

As a leader, do you give your team a task that may cause them to risk their lives, health, reputation, or even livelihood? If so, do you pray for them as they go to execute the task? Sadly, I know I have failed to pray for those I've led and for fellow teammates more often than I've covered them in prayer. During my deployment to Iraq in 2005–2006, I had a regular routine of gathering members of my platoon—and sometimes other units with whom we were going on a mission—to take a few minutes before loading the trucks or helicopters to pray for mission success and safety. Unfortunately, I did not have the same commitment during my next deployment to Afghanistan. I got complacent, lazy, and entitled to God's grace and providence.

On the morning of March 4, 2007, one member of my team was gearing up to go on a routine mounted combat reconnaissance patrol with other teams in our platoon. The rest of us didn't have to get up as early, so we stayed in bed as he was getting his gear ready and others were loading trucks with him. I heard the trucks running outside our hooch. I felt the Spirit nudge me to go and see who wanted to pray, even though I wasn't going on the patrol. I stayed in bed. About five hours later, the patrol returned, having survived an intense firefight as they broke contact out of a complex ambush with the Taliban. One Marine was only minorly wounded. My fellow teammates performed incredibly well in the midst of grave danger. They fought as they had been trained. Unfortunately, the Taliban took control of the narrative and tactically destroyed local American military commanders through information warfare. (The full details of this story are told by my company commander at the time, Fred Galvin, in the book: *A Few Bad Men: The True Story of U.S. Marines Ambushed in Afghanistan and Betrayed in America*)

I share this because I often wonder: what if I had followed the Spirit's leading and prayed with a few guys before that mission? Even if the mission's outcome hadn't changed, how might those I prayed with have been able to see God's hand at work during what became a fight for their lives, their reputations, and for the tremendous leaders who commanded the patrol?

Christ-centered leaders pray for their teams and their teammates in all circumstances.

Application: Today, take time to pray specifically for those you lead or support. Whether they are facing a difficult task or a routine challenge, ask God to guide, protect, and strengthen them. Trust in His providence and be intentional about covering those in your care in prayer, recognizing the power it has, to shape outcomes and build trust within your team.

COVERED IN PRAYER EA

"My prayer is not for them alone. I pray also for those who will believe in Me through their message…"

—John 17:20

Read: John 17:20–26 "Jesus Prays for All Believers"

As we conclude Jesus' High Priestly Prayer, we see Him transition from praying for Himself and His disciples to praying for all future believers. He prays for their unity, that they may share in His glory, and that one day they will reside with Him to witness the glory God has bestowed upon Him.

As leaders, how often do we consider using prayer as a tool in the secular world to navigate tough decisions, challenging conversations, or simply to express gratitude for the positions He has placed us in and the people He has brought into our lives? We often rely on skills and tactics we've developed throughout our careers to address various situations. However, if you're like me, prayer—despite its power and potential impact—is a resource I sometimes overlook or bypass.

Beyond dealing with present challenges, Jesus' prayer in this reading shows us the importance of praying for what is yet to come. I recall learning in a small group years ago that many parents prayed for their children's future spouses. At first, this seemed like a peculiar focus, but over time, I've come to understand how vital God's hand in those future relationships can be. Since then, Christina and I have prayed for the future spouses of each of our children, asking for God's protection over them and that they are led by lives centered on Christ. I now see this as a powerful way to entrust our children—and their future spouses—into God's care, covering them with His faithfulness, righteousness, and security.

In the same way, how can we apply this practice of forward-looking prayer to our secular workplaces? How might we pray today for future events, decisions, or employees, trusting God to guide and prepare the way?

> **Effective leaders recognize the importance of looking beyond present challenges, using prayer to seek guidance for future events, decisions, and the well-being of those they lead.**

Application: Identify one future challenge, decision, or opportunity within your workplace or leadership role. Set aside five minutes each day for the next week to pray specifically for God's guidance and provision in that area. Additionally, include a prayer for the future well-being and growth of your team members, entrusting their journeys to God's care and direction. Track any insights or clarity you gain through this practice.

WORD-LY POWER EA

> "When Jesus said, 'I am He,' they drew
> back and fell to the ground."
>
> —John 18:6

Read: John 18:1–6 "Jesus Arrested"
After Judas betrays Jesus, the soldiers and officers of the high priest seek Him out in the Garden of Gethsemane. Upon finding Jesus, He asks them, "Whom do you seek?" When they respond, "Jesus of Nazareth," He replies, "I am He" (John 18:6). At His words, they are immediately knocked backward to the ground, experiencing the power of God's voice.

This passage is a powerful reminder of the impact our words can have. Just as James warns about the power of the tongue (James 3:5–6), our words carry weight and can profoundly influence those around us—sometimes in ways we don't anticipate.

I recall being a young officer and making a consistent effort to get to know the Marines under my charge. At the time, I viewed these conversations as casual banter, not realizing the gravity they held for the junior Marines. I soon learned that even offhand comments could be taken as directives, prompting immediate action, despite my lack of intent to give a task.

Through experience and reflection, I became more aware of the responsibility I carried with my words. I learned to speak intentionally, ensuring clarity, and to clarify when something was not meant as an order. As we go about our day, let's remember the power our words hold and strive to use them intentionally to inspire and positively influence those around us.

> **Effective leaders understand the power of their words and intentionally use them to inspire, guide, and positively influence those they lead.**

<u>Application</u>: This week, commit to practicing intentional communication by identifying three specific instances where you can use your words to encourage, inspire, or clarify expectations for your team. After each interaction, reflect on the outcomes and ask for feedback to understand how your words were received. Adjust your communication style as needed to ensure your words consistently align with your leadership intentions.

EVEN THE BEST OF INTENTIONS... *EA*

> "Then Simon Peter, who had a sword, drew it and struck the high priest's servant, cutting off his right ear."
> —John 18:10

<u>Read</u>: John 18:8–14 "Peter Cuts Off Malchus' Ear"
As the soldiers and officers of the high priest arrive to arrest Jesus, Peter decides he will not stand for this action. Instead of allowing the soldiers and the high priest to carry out their duties, "Simon Peter, who had a sword, drew it and struck the high priest's servant, cutting off his right ear" (John 18:10). Following this, "Jesus commanded Peter, 'Put your sword away! Shall I not drink the cup the Father has given Me?'" (John 18:11).

Peter's position and response serve as a reminder of two important lessons I have learned during my time as a staff officer.

First, no matter how well-intentioned our actions may be, we may not always be aligned with the goals or intentions of our boss. Communication is critical to ensure that our understanding of our roles and responsibilities matches that of our leadership. To avoid miscommunication, frequent and clear communication up and down the chain of command is essential. In fact, overcommunicating—repeating key points multiple times—might still be necessary to ensure alignment and clarity.

Second, Peter's zeal and passionate defense of Jesus is inspiring. Without resorting to violence, we should ask ourselves how far we are willing to go to support and protect our leaders. One of the Marine Corps' 11 leadership traits is loyalty, a cornerstone of healthy command culture. While disagreements should be addressed respectfully behind closed doors, once decisions are made, we must defend them as if they were our own. Peter's passion and loyalty provide a strong example for us to consider and emulate.

Successful leaders balance loyalty and passion for their mission with clear communication to ensure alignment with their team and superiors.

Application: Reflect on your recent actions or decisions to ensure they align with your leader's goals and intentions. This week, prioritize clear and frequent communication by scheduling at least one check-in with your supervisor to confirm alignment on key tasks or objectives. Additionally, identify one way to demonstrate loyalty and support for your leader's decisions, ensuring that your actions reflect unity and trust within your team.

DISCIPLE JUXTAPOSITION EA

"Simon Peter and another disciple were following Jesus. Because this disciple was known to the high priest, he

> went with Jesus into the high priest's courtyard, but Peter had to wait outside at the door. The other disciple, who was known to the high priest, came back, spoke to the servant girl on duty there and brought Peter in."
>
> −John 18:15−16

Read: John 18:15−18 "Peter's First Denial"
Following Jesus' arrest, He is bound and brought to Annas, the high priest emeritus. Two of His disciples, Peter and an unnamed disciple (widely believed to be John), follow Him. In these few short verses, we see two vastly different responses from the disciples—a contrast that offers a deeper lesson in leadership and behavior under pressure.

Peter, the "rock" upon which Jesus said He would build His church (Matt 16:18), is overcome by fear of being caught. So great is his concern that when asked if he is one of Jesus' disciples, he denies it—marking the first of three denials he will make that night.

In contrast, the unnamed disciple, presumed to be John, remains calm and composed throughout the ordeal. Known to Annas, he follows Jesus into the high priest's courtyard and even arranges for Peter to be admitted by speaking to the servant girl at the door. Despite Peter's fear and denial, John stays connected to the mission and present in the moment.

In comparison, the unnamed disciple exemplifies measured and strategic leadership, maintaining his focus and connection to the mission. Peter, on the other hand, illustrates how fear-based decision-making can compromise integrity and commitment. These two responses serve as a reminder of the importance of self-awareness, courage, and staying steadfast under pressure.

Which disciple's approach will you emulate the next time you face tough decisions under mounting pressure?

Steady leadership requires remaining calm, focused, and mission-oriented under pressure, even when fear threatens to cloud judgment.

Application: Identify a recent or upcoming situation where pressure or fear may influence your decisions. Commit to emulating the calm and mission-oriented approach of the unnamed disciple by preparing a clear plan of action. This week, practice self-awareness by pausing to assess your emotional state in high-pressure moments, and intentionally choose responses that align with your values and mission. Reflect on the outcomes and consider adjustments for future challenges.

THE IMPORTANCE OF TRANSPARENCY IS CLEAR EA

> "'I have spoken openly to the world,' Jesus replied. 'I always taught in synagogues or at the temple, where all the Jews come together. I said nothing in secret.'"
> —John 18:20

Read: John 18:19–24 "The High Priest Questions Jesus"
Following Jesus' arrest and Peter's denial, Jesus is brought before Annas, the high priest emeritus. He is questioned about His disciples and His teachings, and He responds, "I have spoken openly to the world...I always taught in synagogues or at the temple, where all the Jews come together. I said nothing in secret" (John 18:20). Jesus says this to demonstrate that He has not violated any laws or done anything wrong.

Jesus' commitment to speaking openly and publicly throughout His ministry is a valuable reminder of the importance of transparency in leadership. It is crucial to communicate clearly, directly, and truthfully with subordinates. Conversely, if a leader says one thing publicly or to one group, and something completely different behind closed doors or to another group, it fosters distrust and disloyalty among the ranks.

I recall working for a leader who liked to use the phrase "push the narrative," essentially instructing us to tell our Marines what he wanted them to hear instead of what they needed to hear—or even the truth. This approach covered a range of situations, from painting a certain picture for families before deployment, to influencing what outsiders saw in the squadron, to managing day-to-day behavior. Over time, it became apparent that this was not only disingenuous, but often outright dishonest. His behavior bred mistrust among the ranks and led to the kind of unhealthy, behind-closed-doors conversations that Jesus was falsely accused of in this passage.

However, this experience clearly illustrates the importance of transparency. Even if the news is unfavorable, it's critical to address your subordinates swiftly, truthfully, and accurately, remaining genuine to the situation and maintaining your integrity.

Genuine leadership honors transparency and honesty, ensuring that words and actions consistently align, regardless of circumstance.

Application: Today, evaluate a current situation where you need to communicate with your team. Commit to delivering a message that is clear, truthful, and transparent, even if the news is challenging. After the communication, seek feedback from at least two team members to ensure your message was understood and aligned with their expectations. Use this feedback to improve transparency and trust in your leadership.

LIVE OUT YOUR WITNESS EA

"One of the high priest's servants, a relative of the man whose ear Peter had cut off, challenged him, 'Didn't I see you with Him in the garden?' Again Peter denied it, and at that moment a rooster began to crow."

–John 18:26–27

Read: John 18:25–27 "Peter's Second and Third Denials"
After Peter's first denial, now inside the high priest Annas's courtyard, he warms himself by a fire on the cold night. While standing there, he is confronted twice more about being one of Jesus' apostles. Each time, Peter denies knowing Him, attempting to hide his identity. After the third denial, a rooster crows, fulfilling the prophecy Jesus had previously made (John 13:38).

Peter's experience serves as a reminder to consider who we are and how we live out our witness. Do we live in a way that shows we are unashamed of the Gospel and its message? Are we willing to lead by example and make disciples, as commissioned in Matthew 28:19?

Living out our faith in a secular workplace can be challenging and may require a careful approach. Along with an active witness—directly sharing the Gospel—we can maintain a passive witness by demonstrating the fruit of the Spirit as described by Paul in several places, to include Galatians 5:22–23. Without loudly proclaiming our beliefs, we can reflect God's love through our actions and character. In time, these behaviors may open the door to active conversations about the Gospel, allowing us to share Jesus' love and what He has done for us.

Leaders guided by the Spirit can and should demonstrate their faith daily, whether through open proclamation or through a quieter, consistent example of the fruits the Spirit has imbued in them.

Application: Identify one way you can reflect the fruit of the Spirit—such as kindness, patience, or self-control—in your workplace or community this week. Commit to demonstrating this consistently in your interactions. Additionally, pray for an opportunity to engage in an active witness by sharing your faith or values with someone who may benefit from your encouragement or perspective. Track how your actions impact others and how they open doors for deeper conversations.

WHAT IS TRUTH? *EA*

> "...you say that I am a king. In fact, the reason I was born and came into the world is to testify to the truth. Everyone on the side of truth listens to Me."
>
> —John 18:37

Read: John 18:28–40 "Jesus Before Pilate"

When questioned a second time, this time by Pilate in the governor's headquarters, Jesus and Pilate exchange terse words about Jesus' identity and mission. In the course of their conversation, Jesus states, *"...you say that I am a king. In fact, the reason I was born and came into the world is to testify to the truth. Everyone on the side of truth listens to Me"* (John 18:37). Pilate then responds, "What is truth?" (John 18:38).

This interaction reminds us that leaders must operate with moral authority, standing firmly on the truth—even when it's unpopular or leads to unfavorable outcomes. In Jesus' case, declaring the truth about who He is ultimately leads to His death on the cross. Scripture calls Satan the "father of lies," the opposite of truth. By representing the truth that He will soon bear the sins of the world, Jesus disarms Satan's primary weapon: sin.

Are we representing Jesus well as we walk in the Spirit each day? Do we rest in the reality that our sins—past, present, and future—were forgiven the moment we believed? Or do we let Satan's deceptions creep in, even if only slightly, and distort our perception of truth? Even a small deviation can have significant long-term effects. For example, a plane departing New York bound for Los Angeles that's off by just one degree will miss its target by more than 40 miles. A slightly larger variation of eight degrees can land it in San Francisco instead of L.A. This illustrates that maintaining absolute truth is essential, as even minor misrepresentations can lead us far from our intended destination.

Leaders must stand firmly on truth, knowing that even the smallest compromises can lead us off course and undermine our integrity.

Application: Reflect on one area of your leadership or decision-making where you may have been tempted to compromise on truth, even slightly. This week, commit to correcting any missteps by clearly aligning your actions and communications with truth and integrity. Seek feedback from a trusted colleague or mentor to ensure your decisions and leadership remain firmly rooted in truth, and monitor the positive impact this alignment has on your team or mission.

THE STRENGTH TO STAND FIRM *BH*

"Jesus answered, 'You would have no power over Me if it were not given to you from above. Therefore the one who handed Me over to you is guilty of a greater sin.'"

—John 19:11

Read: John 19:1–16 "Jesus Sentenced to be Crucified"
This passage portrays one of the most intense moments of Jesus' journey to the cross. Despite being mocked, beaten, and falsely accused, Jesus remained composed and resolute. He faced Pontius Pilate, who had the authority to release or crucify Him, yet Jesus reminded Pilate that all authority ultimately comes from God. This statement reveals Jesus' unwavering trust in God's plan, even in the face of injustice and suffering.

As leaders, there will be moments when we face opposition, false accusations, or the pressure to compromise. In these moments, it is critical to remain grounded in our principles and trust that God is in control. Jesus did not try to defend Himself or manipulate the situation. Instead, He stood firm in His purpose, knowing that God's plan would prevail.

Leaders are often put in situations where their character is tested. Jesus shows us that true strength is not about controlling outcomes but about trusting in God's sovereignty. When faced with difficult decisions or unjust treatment, we can stand firm, knowing that our authority, like Pilate's, is granted by God. Our role is to lead with integrity, even when it costs us something.

> **True leadership requires the courage to stand firm in the face of opposition, trusting in God's ultimate plan and authority.**

Application: The next time you face opposition, accusations, or pressure to compromise, pause and remember that your authority comes from God. Stand firm in your principles, trusting that God's sovereignty is greater than any immediate circumstance. Reflect on Jesus' example of remaining composed and resolute, and lead with integrity, knowing that the ultimate outcome is in His hands.

SUFFERING DOES NOT ABSOLVE LEADERSHIP *BH*

> "When Jesus saw His mother there, and the disciple whom He loved standing nearby, He said to her, 'Woman, here is your son,' and to the disciple, 'Here is your mother.' From that time on, this disciple took her into his home."
> —John 19:26–27

Read: John 19:17–27 "The Crucifixion of Jesus"
As Jesus hung on the cross, enduring unimaginable pain, He still displayed compassion and concern for others. In His final moments, Jesus entrusted the care of His mother, Mary, to His disciple, John. This act illustrates a profound leadership principle — even in

moments of personal suffering, true leaders remain focused on the needs of others.

Leadership often comes with personal sacrifice. It may involve long hours, difficult decisions, or personal discomfort. But Jesus shows us that leadership is about selflessness and care for those entrusted to us. In the face of hardship, great leaders do not retreat into self-preservation. Instead, they seek to serve and support those under their care.

Jesus' example reminds us that, as leaders, our influence extends beyond tasks and objectives. It touches the lives and well-being of the people around us. Whether leading at the home, the community, or the workplace, we must be willing to sacrifice for those we lead. By prioritizing their well-being, we reflect the heart of a servant leader.

True leadership requires selflessness, even in moments of personal hardship, as we care for the needs of those entrusted to us.

Application: Reflect on the example of Jesus' selflessness, especially in difficult times. Today, consider how you can prioritize the well-being of those you lead, whether at home, work, or in your community. Make a conscious effort to serve others, even when personal sacrifice is required, and lead with a heart of compassion and care, expecting nothing in return.

PERSEVERING TO THE END *BH*

"When He had received the drink, Jesus said, 'It is finished.' With that, He bowed His head and gave up His spirit."
—John 19:30

Read: John 19:28–37 "The Death of Jesus"
In verse 30, we witness the final moments of Jesus' earthly life. His words, "It is finished," signify the completion of His mission. Jesus

had fulfilled every prophecy, every purpose, and every act of obedience required of Him. Even in His final breath, He remained committed to the purpose given to Him by God.

For leaders, this moment serves as a powerful reminder of perseverance and purpose. Effective leadership is not merely about starting strong; it's about finishing well. There are seasons of leadership where exhaustion, discouragement, or doubt may creep in. In these moments, it's tempting to quit or cut corners. But Jesus' example calls us to stay faithful until the mission is complete.

As leaders in our families, workplaces, and communities we must embrace the idea of finishing well. This means honoring commitments, seeing tasks through to completion, and remaining faithful to the purpose God has placed before us. Leadership is not always about instant results; it's about enduring effort. When the work becomes difficult, we can be reminded of Jesus' resolve on the cross, knowing that purposeful leadership leaves a lasting impact.

Great leaders remain faithful to their purpose, persevering until the mission is fully complete.

Application: As you reflect on Jesus' example of finishing well, identify an area in your leadership where you may be tempted to cut corners or give up. Commit to staying faithful and completing the task with perseverance, honoring the purpose and the people entrusted to you, just as Jesus did in His final moments.

BOLD LEADERSHIP IN CRITICAL MOMENTS BH

"Later, Joseph of Arimathea asked Pilate for the body of Jesus. Now Joseph was a disciple of Jesus, but secretly because he feared the Jewish leaders."
—John 19:38

Read: John 19:38-42 "The Burial of Jesus"
Joseph of Arimathea and Nicodemus step forward to care for Jesus' body after His crucifixion. Both men were influential leaders—Joseph a member of the Sanhedrin and Nicodemus a Pharisee—but their previous fear of public association with Jesus had kept them in the shadows. After Jesus' death, however, they boldly stepped into the light, risking their status and reputation to honor Him.

This moment highlights the importance of courage in leadership. True leadership requires bold action, even when it comes with personal risk. Joseph and Nicodemus could have remained silent or distant, but they chose to act with integrity and compassion. Their decision to provide a proper burial for Jesus was a visible act of leadership that demonstrated conviction, courage, and honor.

As leaders, there will be moments when we must make bold decisions that challenge our comfort zones. It might mean standing up for what's right, supporting someone in need, or doing the unseen, difficult tasks that others avoid. Leading with boldness often requires risk—of time, resources, or even reputation—but it's in those moments that our true character is revealed.

Bold leaders act with courage and integrity, even when it comes at personal risk.

Application: Reflect on a situation where you may be hesitant to take bold action due to fear of personal risk. Step forward in courage, trusting that your decision will honor God and reflect the integrity of your leadership, even if it challenges your comfort zone.

LEADING WITH HOPE AND EXPECTATION *BH*

"Finally, the other disciple, who had reached the tomb first, also went inside. He saw and believed."
—John 20:8

Read: John 20:1–9 "The Empty Tomb"

Mary Magdalene discovers the stone rolled away from Jesus' tomb and informs Peter and John. Both disciples run to see it for themselves. Upon entering the empty tomb, John "saw and believed." While they didn't fully understand the significance of Jesus' resurrection at that moment, they knew something extraordinary had happened.

This story reminds leaders of the importance of hope and expectation. Just as Peter and John ran toward the unknown, leaders are often faced with uncertain situations. Instead of retreating, great leaders move forward with expectation, prepared for something new to be revealed. While they may not fully understand every challenge or opportunity at first, they position themselves to see and believe when clarity comes.

As leaders, it's easy to let doubt and fear paralyze our actions. But like Peter and John, we should run toward the unknown, seeking answers with hope and faith. True leadership requires stepping into uncertainty with a heart that expects something good to come from it. When we lead with hope, we inspire others to believe, even when the path ahead isn't clear.

You may have heard the saying, "hope is not a strategy," or, as we say in the military, "hope is not a tactical task." Hope alone is not a plan. However, leaders use hope to lean into a vision that has yet to be realized. Christ-centered leaders go a step further, looking with expectation for a mighty move of God. They then apply excellent leadership to plan the next steps for themselves and their team.

Christ-centered leaders move toward uncertainty with hope and expectation for a mighty move of God, trusting that clarity will come.

Application: As you face uncertainty in your leadership journey, choose to move forward with hope and expectation. Step into the unknown, trusting that God is at work, and take intentional steps to turn that hope into action through planning and perseverance. How will you critically think through your uncertainty this week? Focus your mindset on asking *how* questions and not *can* questions. Critically think, make a plan, and persevere.

RECOGNIZING THE VOICE OF TRUE LEADERSHIP *BH*

> "Jesus said to her, 'Mary.' She turned toward Him and cried out in Aramaic, 'Rabboni! (which means Teacher)."
> —John 20:16

Read: John 20:10–18 "Jesus Appears to Mary Magdalene"
Mary Magdalene stands weeping outside the empty tomb, heartbroken that Jesus' body is gone. Even as Jesus appears to her, she doesn't recognize Him at first. It is only when He calls her by name that her eyes are opened, and she realizes it is her Teacher, alive and present with her.

As leaders, this passage offers a powerful reminder about the value of personal connection and clear communication. Just as Jesus called Mary by name, effective leaders recognize and speak to the individual needs of their team members. People are more likely to follow a leader who sees and acknowledges them personally. When leaders take time to know their people by name, understand their struggles, and call out their potential, they create deeper trust and loyalty.

Additionally, Mary's initial failure to recognize Jesus highlights how easily people can miss important moments when consumed by fear, grief, or distraction. Leaders must create clarity and focus in moments of uncertainty so that their teams do not miss the opportunities right in front of them. Clear, personal communication from a leader can bring clarity and hope in times of doubt.

Great leaders recognize, value, and personally connect with those they lead, inspiring trust and clarity even in uncertain moments.

Application: As a leader, take time to connect with your team on a personal level. Recognize their individual needs, struggles, and strengths. In moments of uncertainty, provide clear communication to help them see the opportunities before them.

LEADING WITH PEACE AND PURPOSE BH

> "Again Jesus said, 'Peace be with you! As the Father has sent Me, I am sending you.'"
> —John 20:21

Read: John 20:19–23 "Jesus Appears to His Disciples"
Jesus appears to His disciples, who are hiding behind locked doors out of fear. His first words to them are, "Peace be with you." This greeting is more than a simple salutation—it's a declaration of calm in the midst of chaos. Jesus follows this with a commissioning, sending them out just as He was sent by the Father.

This moment teaches an essential leadership principle: peace precedes purpose. Leaders must create a sense of peace and calm before they can effectively mobilize their team. Fear and anxiety can paralyze a team, much like the disciples behind locked doors. But when a leader enters the room with calm confidence, it shifts the atmosphere, empowering the team to act with clarity and courage.

Jesus also models the importance of delegation and trust. He sends His disciples to continue His mission, giving them the authority and the power of the Holy Spirit to accomplish it.

Effective leaders do the same. Instead of trying to do everything alone, they empower and trust their team to carry the mission forward. Leadership is not about control—it's about commissioning others to lead with confidence and purpose.

Strong leaders bring peace to fearful situations and empower their teams to take purposeful action.

<u>Application</u>: As a leader, create an atmosphere of peace and calm, especially in times of fear or uncertainty. Then, empower your team by entrusting them to carry out the mission, knowing that their confidence is built on trust and clarity. Position yourself at the point of friction to ensure that your team's actions are purposeful in accomplishing the mission and that you are willing to bear the greatest burdens to mission accomplishment.

STOP DOUBTING *JA*

> "Then He said to Thomas, 'Put your finger here; see My hands. Reach out your hand and put it into My side. Stop doubting and believe.'"
>
> –John 20:27

<u>Read</u>: John 20:24–31 "Jesus Appears to Thomas"
Thomas was not present with the other ten disciples when Jesus first appeared to them following His resurrection. Despite the testimonies of all the others, Thomas remained hardheaded and skeptical about Jesus raising Himself from the dead. A week later, Jesus confronted Thomas of his doubts and stood in front of him as his resurrected Lord. Thomas then believed and declared Jesus as his Lord and his God (John 20:28).

We can pick on Thomas and chastise him for not believing when he heard that Jesus had risen, but we should first be honest with ourselves of our own doubting spirit. The year 2024 filled me with doubts in several areas of my life. No matter how much God answered prayers for me, I still let Satan's lies enter in and cast doubts in my heart.

I once took part in a Bible study series by Rick Warren with my church some years ago and I remember Rick stating that when we rationalize, what we really are doing is providing ourselves with "rationale lies." I thought to myself, 'that's spot on!' When we rationalize, we only see things based on our own understanding within our natural boundaries. No matter how God has revealed Himself to us or how many times, we so easily refer back to what we understand. That's exactly where Satan wants to keep us and exactly from where Christ wants to free us.

As leaders, we bear the responsibility of initiating freedom from doubt, both for ourselves and for those we lead. Clear communication of vision, coupled with grace and understanding, builds trust and dispels uncertainty within the team. By fostering an environment of collaboration and mutual reliance, we empower our teammates to overcome individual doubts. The shared resolve of the team strengthens its forward momentum, driving everyone closer to the shared vision.

Leaders dispel doubt by fostering trust, clarity, and collaboration, empowering their teams to overcome uncertainty and achieve their vision.

Application: Reflect on areas of doubt in your leadership and confront them with the truth of God's faithfulness. Create an environment where open communication and grace can help dispel uncertainties in your team, fostering a collective belief in the mission and vision.

LEADERS PROVIDE *JA*

"He said, 'Throw your net on the right side of the boat and you will find some.' When they did, they were unable to haul the net in because of the large number of fish."
—John 21:6

Read: John 21:1–14 "Jesus and the Miraculous Catch of Fish"
When Jesus first called some of His disciples, they were fishing. It was their trade. After Jesus' death and resurrection, the disciples who were fishermen returned to the trade they knew. Though they were trained and empowered to build Jesus' Church, they returned to what they did best. They lacked the confidence to do His work. It would be out of their comfort zone and likely a large risk to themselves, their livelihood, and that of their families.

Jesus meets them in Galilee and gives them instructions the same way He did when He first called them to follow Him and become "fishers of men" (Luke 5:1–11). After not catching any fish all night, He instructs them to cast their net. Once again, like the day they first met Jesus, their catch was too large to haul into the boat, so they towed it to shore.

When uncertainty mounts in our lives, Jesus wants us to turn to Him. If we are never in a situation to need Him, then why would we ever turn to Him. The one thing that we know about uncertainty is that it is certain. The question is: How will we handle it? The disciples left the ministry and returned to what they knew. Their uncertainty grew as what they were good at was not producing for them. But Jesus showed up and met their uncertainty with His provision.

I have countless stories of facing uncertainty in the military. It's a fact of war and our training prepared us for it. Many times, I've faced situations well out of my control and had to operate in the midst of the uncertainty. But I'd like to share with you the uncertainty I faced during my transition out of the military. I had accepted a job, and after a year in the job, I decided that it was not the right fit for me. I knew I wanted to get into the leadership development space, but wasn't sure what that looked like. My last day was on a Friday and by Tuesday of that week, I had one job offer and two other individuals interested in working with me in the leadership development space. Now, as I write this, neither of those opportunities are what I am currently doing but all of them have created connections and growth in my life. I share this to say that what Jesus was speaking to me at that time was, 'I am your provision. I will always meet your needs.'

As leaders, we must seek God—Jehovah Jirah, our Provider—for our provisions. We then must serve as providers for our teams. Leaders inspire the change they wish to see. They lead the transformation that is going to take the team and organization to the next level. They take ownership and responsibility in providing the support their team needs to accomplish the mission.

Effective leaders meet their team members where they are, provide support, inspire them to fulfill their calling with confidence, and drive their success.

<u>Application</u>: Reflect on the uncertainties you're facing right now. Turn to God as your provider and trust that He will meet your needs. As a leader, take ownership of your team's needs, offering them the support and vision they need to move forward with confidence and purpose.

LEADERSHIP DEVELOPMENT JA

"I tell you the truth, when you were younger you dressed yourself and went where you wanted; but when you are old you will stretch out your hands, and someone else will dress you and lead you where you do not want to go."

−John 21:18

Read: John 21:15–25 "Jesus Reinstates Peter"
Following our key verse, John writes in verse 19, that Jesus said this to Peter to indicate the death by which he would glorify God. Jesus empowers Peter to be the "rock" on which He builds His Church. Peter spends the rest of his life establishing Jesus' Church before the Romans execute him by crucifying him upside down, according to traditional accounts.

Leaders are not self-made men or women. They are not naturally born to lead while others are born to follow. Leaders are developed. We are all capable of developing into leaders and as Red Letter Leadership attests, Jesus commands us all to lead (Matt 28:19). For leaders to be developed, they must humble themselves to learning and developing and have someone willing to develop them.

Though Acts 1:8 accounts Jesus' last spoken words to His disciples before ascending to heaven, this last passage of John displays Jesus directly commissioning Peter to lead His Church. As Jesus had demonstrated through His words and example, Peter's leadership will require his sacrifice, his service, and a whole lot of love to accomplish his mission to establish the Church.

Jesus' investment in Peter underscores the importance of having a guide who sees potential, provides instruction, and calls out greatness even in the midst of imperfection. For those seeking to lead, the path demands selflessness, a commitment to learning, and the courage to take on a mission larger than oneself.

Great leaders develop leaders, not subordinates.

Application: Consider the leaders who have shaped you along the way. Embrace the opportunity to both learn from and invest in others, recognizing the importance of selflessness and sacrifice in developing leadership. As you continue your journey, seek to call out the greatness in those around you, fostering their growth and empowering them to lead with purpose.

EPILOGUE

BE HIS WITNESS THROUGH YOUR LEADERSHIP *JA*

"But you will receive power when the Holy Spirit comes on you; and you will be My witnesses in Jerusalem, and in all Judea and Samaria, and to the ends of the earth."
—Acts 1:8

Read: Acts 1:1–11 "Jesus Taken Up into Heaven"

As we wrap up our journey through the four Gospel accounts of Jesus, consider a few ways in which Jesus exemplified leadership as a recap of our study.

1. He humbled Himself to the task of leading and to His own development as a leader.
2. He walked and spoke with integrity and grew His credibility as an influencer.
3. He asked specific individuals to partner with Him in His ministry and they became His closest Twelve teammates.
4. He cast vision for His team.
5. He directed their plans but did not micromanage them.
6. He invested 1:1 personal time with them.
7. Those who responded most favorably to His influence, He invested even more (Peter, James, and John).
8. He established a culture of trust and of decentralized execution of the mission.
9. He empowered His team to carry out His will and exponentially multiply His impact.
10. He understood His environment and addressed opposition.
11. He personally connected with those He and His team sought to serve.
12. He remained focused on the purpose for which He came.
13. He spoke clearly and communicated His intent.

14. He invested in communication with those who were willing to listen rather than those seeking to criticize.
15. He restored His team's unity when individual actions within the team fractured it.
16. When the leaders He developed were capable of continuing His vision and mission without His direct involvement, He departed while assuring them of His supervision and support.

This is not an exhaustive list of the lessons in leadership Jesus showed but merely a few highlights.

Following Jesus' commission in Matthew 28:19, for His disciples to "go and make disciples," He instructs them in Acts 1 where to go. He first tells them to go to their local community (Jerusalem). He then tells them to go and make disciples in their own region and country (Judea). He also calls them to make disciples of their social enemies (Samaria). Lastly, He tells them to go to the ends of the earth. There is no place we go where we should not be focused on carrying out the commission He's given us as leaders.

Though we will become great leaders when we submit ourselves to Christ Jesus and commit to our own leadership development through His example, that is not the only purpose to learning how Jesus led. We learn how Jesus led and do likewise so that we can continue the work of His original team of twelve. We lead how Jesus led so that we will make disciples of Jesus, not of us. We lead to develop other leaders.

Christ-centered leaders lead to advance God's kingdom, not their own.

Application: Reflect on the leadership principles Jesus exemplified and identify one to emulate in your daily life this week. Whether it's investing in someone 1:1, casting vision for your team, or fostering a culture of trust, take intentional steps to lead like Jesus and inspire others to continue His mission. Let your leadership be a testimony that points others to Him.

ACKNOWLEDGEMENTS

The contents of this book were originally to add value to those on the Red Letter Leadership email list. As part of Red Letter Leadership's desire to develop Christ-centered leaders, we simply chose to draw lessons from the Gospel accounts of Jesus and send them out every morning to our email list. Our email list is full of people who received the writings, gave us great feedback, and encouraged us by sharing how the lessons spoke to them at the time they needed to hear it. We want to thank those who received the initial emails that are now compiled into this book for their encouragement, support, feedback, and for sharing the lessons with others such as people at their church, their workplace, their family, and even sports teams they coached. We believe that these lessons have impacted lives well before the publishing of this book and that is why we moved to offer these lessons now in print.

* * * * *

I thank my wife most of all. She has stood by me and has been the rock for my family through six overseas deployments (four of which with four or more children at home) and many more months away for training. As I transitioned out of the military, she continued to work hard as our homemaker and my helper while also returning to her profession as a speech pathologist which allowed me to spend time on projects such as this book. If this book added any value to you, it would never have happened without the consistent behind the scenes work of my wonderful and most beautiful bride, Sarah.

I would also like to thank my children. We first adopted four children from the Pennsylvania Foster Care System before adopting two more from Ethiopia a few years later. Then God blessed us with a biological daughter following my wife's obedience to donate a portion of her liver to an 11-month-old boy. Our children have seen a lot and suffered a lot before they came to be in our family. Then, as inexperienced parents who love Jesus, we adopt them. In addition to being inexperienced, my job in the military required me to leave often and for months at a time. My children are resilient, and although I have not been the best father to them, the one that they deserve, they have been a tremendous blessing to me. I have experienced the love of God through them as my children. I pray that they will always keep Jesus close to them as their closest friend. They have sacrificed so much, and I am so grateful.

To my children, Sammy, Benji, Joseph, Crystal, Brea, Amanda, and Natalie, thank you for allowing me to be your dad, for loving me when I was home and when I wasn't, for forgiving me when I failed you, and for filling our home with memories and the character that has become our family.

Glory be to God for His goodness and to His Son Jesus, who made a way for us to experience the fullness of God through His death, resurrection, and sending us His Spirit.

—Jordan

* * * * *

First and foremost, I want to thank my wife — my anchor, my confidant, and my unwavering supporter for the past 21 years. Through the highs and lows of Army life, she has remained steady and faithful, enduring the demands of multiple combat deployments, constant relocations, and the unpredictability of a 24-year military career. We've moved 16 times, started over in new places again and again, and yet she has faced each transition with grace, strength, and a quiet resilience that has held our family together. This book would not exist without her belief in me and the sacrifices she has made so I could pursue my calling.

Second, I want to thank my three amazing daughters, who have shown strength beyond their years as military children.

They have endured the challenge of moving every one to three years — changing schools, leaving behind friends, and starting over in new communities. Through it all, they have handled each transition with grace, courage, and a style all their own. Their resilience, adaptability, and kindness inspire me daily. I am so incredibly proud to be their dad.

In closing, I want to thank all the mentors in my life, past and present, who have made such a huge impact on me. So many people invested their time, energy, and wisdom into me — often when I didn't deserve it — and I carry their influence with deep gratitude. I would be remiss if I didn't also thank my Lord and Savior, King Jesus. His grace has sustained me, His truth has guided me, and His presence has been my constant, both in seasons of peace and in times of war. To Him be the glory.

—Ben

* * * * *

I am profoundly grateful to those who have held up my arms, as Aaron and Hur did for Moses, allowing this work to come to life, not by my strength alone, but by the grace of God through the faithfulness of others. To my beloved wife, Christina, thank you for walking beside me in faith, prayer, and purpose. Our journey together has shaped the rhythm of my leadership and refined my heart for this calling. To my children—Ayden, Sydney, Levy, Madyson, and Kaytlyn—you are the most humbling and honest picture of leadership God has ever given me. Loving and leading you has been both the greatest challenge and highest honor of my life.

To Spencer Waters, my brother in Christ who helped guide me back into the light when I needed it most—thank you for your quiet strength and unwavering presence. To Pastor Garrett Ericson, your encouragement and passion for the Gospel breathed life into this project. You've sharpened me like iron sharpens iron. A heartfelt thank you to Jordan and Ben, who walked alongside me in writing this book. Your insights, creativity, and steady hands helped shape each lesson into something worthy of the message we felt called to share. Lastly, I am deeply indebted to every unnamed leader whose wisdom and sacrifice have helped me see further by standing on the shoulders of giants—thank you for showing me what it means to lead with grace, truth, and courage.

—Eric

INDEX

A

Abilities (also "ability"): 15, 19, 39, 41, 92, 96, 116, 122–124, 155, 167, 180, 182, 205, 240, 249, 256–257, 260, 275, 287, 289, 293, 296, 303, 307–308, 312, 321, 325, 329, 359–361, 365–366, 375, 402–403, 407, 415, 432–433, 437, 442

Accountability: 8, 27, 35, 44, 76, 106, 112–113, 137, 201, 230–231, 240, 303, 338, 340, 349–350, 378–379, 405, 450, 461

Accountable: 7, 44, 60, 100, 106, 122, 187, 202, 217, 231, 240, 285–286, 324, 378, 460

Action (also as in "taking action" and "your/our actions"): 5, 7, 10, 12, 25–26, 31–32, 39, 46–48, 51, 57–58, 64–65, 69, 76, 80, 82, 105–106, 118–119, 125–127, 135–136, 138–139, 143, 146–147, 155–157, 161–162, 165–166, 169, 175–178, 183, 186–187, 189, 195–197, 201–202, 212, 222, 226, 228–229, 232–233, 243, 254, 259, 263, 268–274, 277–278, 280, 286, 292, 298, 304–305, 307, 317, 319–320, 324–325, 343, 346, 350, 357, 366–367, 370–371, 382- 384, 386, 388, 397, 404–405, 407, 411, 417, 421–422, 425–427, 429, 439–443, 446, 449, 454, 457–458, 460, 469–471, 473–475, 477, 481–483, 485, 494

Adapt: 19, 56, 278, 359

Adding Value: 53, 87–88, 122–123, 162, 329, 376

Adversity (see also "opposition"): 12, 38, 39, 233, 236, 243, 356, 375, 377, 378, 383, 440, 464

Advice: 5, 110, 219, 223, 235, 318

Approachable: 76–77, 100, 110, 194, 204, 359, 447

Alignment: 12, 40, 64, 152, 320, 372, 388, 405, 431, 450, 454, 471, 477

Assurance: 57, 78, 131, 165, 452, 463–464

Authority: 11, 15, 18, 30, 41–43, 45–48, 53, 64, 66, 74, 76, 88, 97, 101–102, 108–114, 118, 136, 138, 141, 155–156, 159, 167–168, 178–181, 189, 197–200, 203, 208, 213–214, 217, 243, 253–254, 268–269, 274–275, 289–290, 303, 312–313, 325, 338, 367, 369, 372, 387, 406–407, 415–416, 440, 446–447, 450, 476–478, 484

Awareness: 26, 51, 230, 234, 289, 336, 431, 437–438, 462, 472–473

B

Behavior: 19–20, 80, 106, 123, 172, 186, 188, 202, 221–222, 256, 263, 269, 328, 369–370, 383, 401, 416–417, 425, 436, 457–458, 472, 474–475

Betrayal: 27, 130–131, 133, 226–227, 232, 240, 378, 382–383, 452

Boldness: 58, 212, 389, 405, 441, 481

Boundaries: 181, 298, 310, 411, 486

Burden: 16, 29, 34, 43, 60–61, 81, 102, 116, 118, 218, 325, 381, 391, 419, 485

C

Calling: 11, 28, 44–45, 48, 66, 69, 72, 75, 86, 104, 147, 154, 161, 233, 272–273, 331, 361, 392, 396, 398, 401, 430, 447, 456, 488

Calm: 45, 51, 78, 176–177, 231–232, 299–300, 385, 419, 472–473, 484, 485

Capabilities: 186, 230

Challenge(s) (see also "obstacles"): 7, 9–11, 36, 39, 53, 58, 66, 68, 86, 95, 97, 99, 102, 132, 134, 138, 142–143, 163, 169, 172, 188, 196, 229–230, 233, 235, 243, 266, 270, 274–275, 284, 288, 299, 305, 309, 314, 319, 322, 330, 357, 359–360, 362, 374–375, 378, 381, 383, 390–391, 420, 425, 434–435, 439, 441, 444, 449, 452, 455, 461, 463–464, 468–469, 482

Character (see also "integrity"): 23, 29, 37–39, 65, 70, 132, 166, 191–192, 218, 236, 287–289, 323–324, 348, 356, 384, 403, 416, 421–422, 429, 465, 475, 478, 481

Clarity: 108–109, 177, 226, 228–229, 243, 251, 270, 275, 292, 309, 361, 366, 398, 406, 437, 441–442, 446, 470–471, 482–486

Collaborate (also "collaborating" and "collaboration"): 5, 36, 64, 101, 168, 200, 286, 310–311, 316, 347–348, 358, 486

Comfort (also "uncomfortable"): 13–14, 23, 37–39, 41, 47, 56–57, 66–67, 72–73, 85, 86–87, 103, 117, 127, 132, 134, 142–143, 152–153, 176, 195, 206, 260, 272, 281, 332, 334, 362, 376, 384, 405, 419, 432, 443, 455, 479

Comfort zone: 10–11, 34, 47, 56, 58, 92, 133, 143, 152–153, 180, 267, 409, 414, 481, 487

Commitment: 8, 27, 49–50, 68, 74, 86, 91, 97, 125, 131, 133, 153, 170, 194, 203, 227, 233, 270, 272–273, 277, 287–288, 298, 320, 322, 330, 334, 338, 341–342, 355, 362, 388, 421, 433, 440, 445, 448, 452, 462, 466, 472–473, 480, 489

Communication (see also "speaking" and "responding"): 44, 64–65, 80, 122, 124, 131, 193–194, 198, 207, 228, 275, 316, 319, 343, 363, 409, 417, 439, 471, 473, 483, 493–494

Commitment: 8, 27, 49–50, 68, 74, 86, 91, 97, 125, 131, 133, 153, 170, 194, 203, 227, 233, 270, 272–273, 277, 287–288, 298, 320, 322, 330, 334, 338, 341–342, 355, 362, 388, 421, 433, 440, 445, 448, 452, 462, 466, 472–473, 480, 489

Compassion: 4, 14, 35, 41, 66, 77, 82, 113, 118, 159, 166, 184–185, 190–191, 221, 271, 273–275, 290–291, 302, 307, 345–346, 363–364, 382, 404, 406–408, 442–443, 478–479, 481

Confidence: 12, 49, 88, 131, 164, 176–177, 179–180, 186, 210, 228, 231, 234, 242–243, 267, 269, 274–275, 288, 291–292, 322, 338, 392, 402–403, 415, 424, 432, 439, 440, 444, 447, 453, 463–464, 484–485, 487–488

Conflict (as a noun and verb, and "conflict resolution"): 64, 67, 85, 93–94, 100, 108–109, 113, 119, 122, 232, 236, 330, 350, 382–383, 387, 440, 459

Confrontation (also "confront" See also "adversity" and "opposition"): 26, 76, 106, 111, 123, 134–135, 146, 169, 177, 186, 194, 210, 233, 262, 270, 299, 301, 323, 349, 368–369, 420, 427, 475, 485

Connecting (with others and with God): 13, 19, 189, 194, 211, 231, 270, 285, 319, 343–344, 358, 382, 386, 409, 421, 429, 434, 442–443, 455–457, 459, 472, 483–484, 488, 493

Consistency: 5, 12, 30, 37, 51, 83, 131, 175, 226, 262, 280, 287, 307, 351, 384, 410, 438–440, 469, 474–475

Control: 14–15, 23, 28, 34, 42–43, 62, 76, 85–86, 118, 136, 146, 156, 174, 215–216, 262, 279, 281, 304, 325, 327–328, 338, 361, 382, 387, 405, 448, 455, 467, 475, 478, 485, 487
Conviction: 103, 133–135, 182–183, 216, 236, 269, 285, 367, 383–385, 388, 439–440, 481
Courage: 4, 21, 24–25, 28, 49, 76, 78–79, 95, 106, 131, 133–134, 140, 165, 194, 233–234, 236, 242, 292, 302–303, 388, 430–431, 441–442, 444–445, 452, 461, 463, 466, 472, 478, 481, 484, 489
Culture: 4, 17–18, 68, 79, 94, 103, 106, 141, 153–154, 200, 216, 236, 239, 242, 248–249, 252–253, 267, 281, 290, 310–311, 312, 328–329, 339, 342, 346, 354, 358–359, 385, 388, 405, 408–409, 416, 450–452, 455, 458, 471, 494

D

Decision: 6–8, 10, 32, 44, 48, 53, 57, 86, 88, 90, 129, 132, 143, 163, 165, 199, 218, 236, 243, 259, 275, 279, 282, 285, 304, 320, 324–325, 338, 347, 349, 350, 357, 360, 362, 370–371, 379–380, 385, 388, 392, 405, 416, 421, 430, 434, 436, 439, 440–442, 444, 446, 449–450, 452, 454, 460, 468–469, 471–473, 477–479, 481
Dedication: 67, 272, 312
Delegation: 167–168, 432, 484
Deliver: 42, 58, 84–85, 89, 117, 258, 300, 303–304, 326, 335, 343, 361, 420, 423, 426, 455, 474
Determination: 273, 299, 300, 342, 356, 364
Development: 10–11, 99, 111, 158, 174–175, 180, 223–224, 256, 270, 280, 285, 287, 324, 335, 347, 380, 391, 454, 488
Devotion: 32, 80, 170, 205, 227, 342, 372, 376, 445

Direction (also "redirection"): 4, 11, 64, 89, 101, 110, 131, 140, 174, 205, 250, 259, 272, 276, 318, 322, 325, 351, 356, 403, 439, 469
Discernment: 7, 8, 24, 83, 215, 293, 392, 406
Discipleship: 57, 86, 271
Discipline: 4, 7, 10, 12, 15, 23, 25, 37–38, 44, 57, 83, 110, 116, 225–226, 286–287, 356, 370, 375, 380
Dishonesty: 135, 288
Distraction: 16, 44, 170–172, 317–318, 338, 342, 381, 446, 448–449
Dominance: 15, 203, 254

E

Empower: 16, 17, 49, 54, 62, 64–65, 81, 88, 92, 100, 154, 165, 167, 175, 193, 216, 221, 223, 228, 243, 268, 302, 305, 319, 328, 338, 354–355, 365, 381, 400, 403–404, 408–409, 415–416, 432, 444, 452, 455–456, 458, 461, 463, 465–466, 484–487, 489
Encouragement: 14, 50, 57, 124, 276, 285, 291, 308, 325, 341, 353, 365, 397, 402–403, 412, 435, 454, 463, 475
Endurance: 120, 134, 340
Environment: 4, 12, 17, 20, 58, 64, 69, 74, 81, 100, 103, 114, 124–125, 139, 160–161, 175–176, 188, 191–193, 196, 212, 222, 224–225, 231–232, 236, 240, 242, 250, 272, 303, 317, 319, 326, 339, 341–342, 345, 346, 348, 350, 358, 365, 383, 388, 391, 405, 416, 424, 426, 454–455, 460
Equip (also "equipped"): 3, 10, 12, 26, 101–102, 121–122, 229, 280, 305, 319, 336, 342, 381, 392, 399, 410, 414, 417, 450, 454, 462, 463
Evaluation: 165, 348
Example (as in "set(s) an example" or "setting an example"): 8, 80, 112, 194, 269, 284, 330, 454
Execute (as in "executing a task" or "decentralized execution"): 54, 179, 228, 259, 265, 328, 455, 466

F

Failure: 51, 75, 78, 112, 131, 136, 178, 192, 216, 229, 236, 239, 255, 288, 368, 375, 378, 414, 419, 431–432, 462, 483

Faith: 3, 4, 10, 23, 28, 30, 33–34, 41–42, 44–46, 48, 50–51, 55–57, 68, 80–82, 84, 88–92, 94, 96, 99, 106–107, 113, 115–116, 120–123, 126, 131, 143–144, 146, 159, 161, 172, 174, 179–180, 185, 188, 193, 198, 204–205, 209, 213–214, 222, 227, 237, 239, 242–243, 252, 255, 258–259, 262, 266, 272, 274, 289–290, 298–303, 305, 319, 330–331, 349–350, 352, 353, 357–360, 363, 371, 377–378, 380–381, 403–404, 410–414, 419, 425–426, 435, 437, 440–444, 449, 456–457, 468, 475, 480, 482, 486

Faithful: 23, 30, 55, 68, 82, 96, 120–123, 126, 146, 237, 262, 350, 371, 413, 435, 440, 468, 480, 486

Family: 4, 6, 7, 12, 21, 23, 25, 29, 30, 36–37, 40–41, 45, 48, 55, 67–68, 74–75, 82, 96–97, 103, 105, 114–115, 122, 132, 140, 147, 168–171, 173, 177–178, 180, 220, 227, 250, 253, 255, 261, 283, 298, 300, 305, 308, 342, 344–347, 349, 351, 366, 401, 421, 424–425, 434

Fear: 6, 18, 34, 36, 43–45, 55, 57, 78–79, 88, 120, 130, 134, 152, 163, 182–183, 210–212, 228, 232, 234, 236, 259, 267, 299–300, 327, 337–338, 377–378, 383–384, 418–420, 430–431, 441, 444–445, 449, 460, 472–473, 480–485

Feedback: 183, 194, 224–225, 315, 358, 436–437, 439, 470, 474, 477

Focus (also "focusing"): 22, 34, 36, 47, 51–53, 55, 57, 61–63, 70, 75, 77, 79, 82, 88, 91, 93, 98, 107–111, 113, 115, 117, 121, 123, 127, 165–166, 168–171, 190, 199, 219, 221, 227, 231, 240, 270–271, 276–278, 282, 286, 292, 296–297, 311–314, 320, 324, 326–327, 331, 337–343, 346–348, 350–351, 357–358, 365, 372, 378, 387, 400, 404, 407, 410, 413–414, 416, 418–421, 423, 426, 429, 432, 435, 441–451, 468, 472, 479, 483

Follow: 3, 8–12, 14, 23–24, 26, 39–40, 44–45, 48–49, 52, 54, 60, 62, 67–68, 71, 73, 79, 83, 86, 94–95, 98–99, 101, 108, 114, 118–120, 126–128, 130–133, 136–137, 141–142, 145, 147, 152–153, 158–160, 163–166, 169, 172, 178, 190, 195, 197, 200, 205–207, 216–217, 219, 222, 224, 227–229, 231–232, 236–237, 242–243, 250, 260, 263–266, 269, 271–272, 275–276, 278, 280, 283–284, 288–289, 293, 299, 305–308, 311–313, 319, 324, 329, 330, 333, 336–337, 339, 341–342, 350, 360–361, 363, 372, 375, 377, 382–383, 385–387, 401–403, 417, 420–424, 426–427, 430–431, 433, 438–441, 451, 453–456, 463, 467, 470–473, 483–485, 487, 489, 494

Follower: 11, 14, 39, 48–49, 52, 95, 101, 114, 119, 120, 132, 160, 163, 166, 172, 190, 195, 197, 200, 206, 222, 228–229, 232, 242–243, 263, 280, 299, 307, 333, 336–337, 350, 360, 372, 382–383, 420–421, 424, 427, 431, 438, 463

Followership: 166, 336, 337

Forgive (also "forgiven"): 9, 24, 25, 35, 47, 60, 94–95, 130–131, 135, 212–213, 240, 256, 262, 274–275, 293–294, 304, 346, 358, 368, 417, 427–428, 476

Foundation: 3, 12, 17, 39–40, 51, 58, 71, 84, 110, 114, 116, 126, 153, 219, 222, 236–237, 266, 287, 292, 332, 358, 407, 421, 431, 433, 455, 463

G

Give (as in "give to" and "giving"): 30–31, 33, 58, 67, 73, 86, 98, 113,

121, 127–128, 201, 205, 208, 217, 221, 223, 307–308, 346, 360, 364, 372, 376, 401, 415, 427–428, 443, 484
Goal (also "goals"): 7–8, 11, 17, 42, 59, 62, 64, 167–168, 171, 217, 219–221, 227, 248, 273, 277, 310, 320–321, 337, 355–356, 361, 369, 407, 410, 414, 420, 435, 442–443, 452, 471
Grace: 24, 28–29, 35, 56–59, 64, 66–67, 70, 80–81, 92, 94, 100, 110, 112–113, 131, 138, 143–144, 169, 178, 211, 221, 240, 254–255, 284, 286, 294, 332, 346, 354, 368, 370, 382–383, 386, 396, 397, 400, 412–413, 417, 427–428, 431, 434, 450–451, 453–454, 465–466, 486
Gracious: 3, 158, 160, 255, 415, 450, 465
Gratitude: 60, 162, 353, 354, 435, 468
Greatness: 9, 17, 91–92, 102, 104, 207–209, 282, 310, 354–355, 375, 489
Growth (as in personal and team growth): 8, 11, 17, 37–38, 44, 49, 57, 63, 65, 67, 70–71, 75, 85, 110–111, 113, 117, 169, 173–175, 180–181, 188, 204, 206–207, 216, 224–225, 255, 267, 280, 286–288, 296, 306, 315–316, 324, 333, 335–336, 339, 345–346, 348–349, 353–355, 358–359, 361–362, 364, 375, 380, 402–403, 408, 410–411, 432–433, 438, 454, 459, 461, 469, 488–489
Guard: 56, 82–83, 112, 140–141, 143–144, 146, 181, 187, 322–323, 379, 384, 446, 458
Guidance: 51, 54, 60, 63, 79, 83, 88, 172, 174, 204, 212, 228–229, 235, 251, 259, 263, 271–272, 276, 319, 325, 339, 353, 356, 358–359, 365, 374, 392, 397, 412, 432, 438, 457, 459, 468–469
Guide: 3–4, 11, 32–33, 37, 44, 61, 65, 83, 93–95, 110, 122, 146, 154–155, 165, 177–178, 184, 189, 221, 233, 238, 252, 273, 288, 319–320, 325, 350, 380, 406–407, 411, 420, 429, 433, 439, 442, 445, 456, 462, 467–468, 470, 475, 489

H

Holiness: 24–25, 37–38, 62, 86, 106, 154, 282, 322
Holy: 4, 11, 24, 71, 79, 83, 91, 147, 156, 162, 183, 203, 221, 224, 240, 248, 252, 262–265, 272, 278–279, 282, 324–325, 392, 421–422, 456–457, 460–462, 466, 484
Honesty: 27, 474
Hope: 11, 14, 22, 36, 57, 113, 118, 131, 135, 165, 179, 188, 229, 233, 285, 291, 301, 337, 352–353, 377, 382, 412, 424, 448, 463, 481–483
Humility: 4, 8–9, 12, 19, 22–23, 27, 30–32, 35, 55, 60, 76, 80–81, 91, 93–95, 100, 103–105, 109–110, 112–114, 117, 137, 140, 153–154, 157, 164–167, 183, 188, 194, 201, 211, 216, 222, 234, 253, 254, 260, 287–288, 293, 296–297, 304, 306, 310, 336, 339, 350, 357–359, 370, 374–376, 379, 380, 382–383, 386, 399–400, 404–408, 416, 425, 431, 436–437, 447, 450–451, 462

I

Impact: 41, 52, 65, 82, 97, 125–126, 133, 141, 157, 168, 172, 175, 178, 180, 201, 222, 225, 272–273, 296, 305, 313, 322, 353, 364, 366, 370, 380, 386, 400, 402, 404–405, 407, 411, 413, 421, 426–427, 432–433, 435, 442, 445–446, 457, 468–469, 475, 477, 480
Influence: 5, 15, 17, 19, 41, 47, 63–65, 69, 80, 83, 92, 96–97, 103, 118–120, 124–125, 136, 143, 146, 155, 157–160, 165, 171, 178, 181, 183, 187, 191, 197, 200–201, 204, 222, 225, 228, 252–254, 260–261, 269, 288, 290–291, 297–298, 301, 303, 307,

309, 311–312, 322–324, 328, 335–336, 345, 352–355, 364, 374, 378, 382, 401, 403, 405, 411, 421–422, 429, 439, 447, 451–453, 455, 456, 459–460, 462, 465, 469–470, 473, 479
Initiative: 227, 313, 327, 458
Inspiration: 338
Inspire: 22, 31, 64–65, 70, 100, 118–119, 124–125, 155, 165–166, 169, 175, 177, 179, 186, 189, 196, 228, 269, 291, 310, 329, 353, 363–364, 382, 385–386, 388, 390, 401–404, 409–411, 443–444, 464–465, 470, 482, 488
Instruction: 6, 34, 54–55, 57, 94, 147, 158–159, 228, 303, 424, 487, 489
Integrity: 4, 11–12, 23, 27, 37, 55, 65, 76, 101, 106, 112–114, 119, 121, 130–131, 133–134, 136–137, 146, 165, 187, 201, 214–215, 222, 235–238, 242, 262–263, 269, 288, 292, 317, 322,–324, 330–331, 349–350, 359–360, 383–384, 387–388, 397–399, 402, 404–405, 407, 431, 440–441, 445, 472, 474, 477–478, 481
Intentional: 23, 44, 54, 59, 63, 108, 166, 173, 217, 225, 234, 257, 265, 287, 313, 316, 323, 336, 341, 344–345, 355–356, 376, 396–397, 403, 407–409, 412, 436, 453, 456, 459, 463, 468, 470, 482, 494
Intentionality: 12, 44, 409
Involvement: 54, 147, 314, 494

J

Joy: 21–23, 37, 72–74, 103, 133, 143, 171, 214, 262, 281, 291, 463
Judgment: 7, 35, 59, 66–67, 70, 103, 188, 212, 276, 281, 314, 350, 415–417, 427–428, 445, 472

K

Kind (also, "kindness"): 14, 23, 146, 166, 200, 262, 397, 475

L

Learning: 48, 54, 162, 164, 221, 254, 313, 336, 346–347, 376, 391, 406–407, 424, 436, 449, 458, 468, 489
Listen: 56, 58, 63, 79, 87–88, 93, 111, 117–118, 143, 146, 171–172, 183, 190, 197, 225, 235, 238, 243, 272, 285, 287, 294–297, 307, 342, 351, 363–364, 382, 409, 415, 423–426, 438, 462, 476, 494
Love: 8, 13, 23, 28–30, 35–36, 38, 56, 61–62, 66, 70, 84, 87, 96–100, 105, 112, 115–116, 118–121, 125, 129–133, 140–141, 144, 146–147, 153, 171, 189–190, 197–198, 200, 203–204, 208, 211, 213, 215, 220–221, 224, 227, 240–242, 248, 254, 258, 260–262, 264–265, 281–284, 286, 293, 295, 298, 302, 326, 329, 333–334, 342, 346, 348–350, 366–368, 370, 372, 374, 382, 386, 397, 406–407, 410, 412, 434, 445, 447, 451–453, 457, 459, 462, 475, 478, 489

M

Management: 85, 167, 206, 232, 271, 424
Marriage: 27, 95–96, 114–115, 202–203, 219, 342, 373
Mature (also "maturity"): 63, 204, 391, 432
Mentor: 158, 167, 204, 211, 217, 223–224, 231, 234–235, 276–277, 303, 307, 314, 337–338, 340–341, 354, 365, 410, 477
Mentoring: 211, 314, 341, 410
Mentorship: 234–235, 365
Mercy: 17, 23, 59, 61, 70, 94–95, 110, 144, 177, 209, 283–284, 294, 350, 357, 363
Model: 12, 27, 41, 64, 98, 131, 133, 158, 165, 228, 266, 270, 319, 326, 338, 369, 380, 386, 425, 427–428, 450, 452, 462, 484
Motivation: 136, 229, 273, 338, 367, 371, 407, 445, 465

O

Obedience: 31, 33, 48, 74, 79, 96, 109, 152–153, 212, 250, 335, 347, 396
Objective: 48–49, 54, 107, 170, 182, 184–185, 207, 310, 321, 357, 471, 479
Obstacle: 88, 319, 387–388, 414, 418
Opposition: 5, 59, 63, 67–68, 71, 120, 122, 133, 138–140, 146, 168, 211–212, 230, 236–237, 242, 266, 292, 311, 317, 320–321, 357, 369–370, 378, 382–384, 390, 417–418, 422, 433, 440, 442, 444–445, 463, 477–478
Organization: 7, 10, 21, 25, 54–55, 91, 106, 112, 153, 164–165, 167–168, 195, 197–198, 222, 236, 242, 267, 277–278, 297, 308, 310–311, 313, 315–316, 322–323, 347, 351–352, 401, 410, 424, 427, 439, 445, 488
Ownership: 69, 86, 112, 220, 239, 267, 452, 460–461, 488

P

Patience: 23, 131, 262, 269, 274–275, 392, 406–407, 413, 441–442, 449–450, 475
Peace: 15, 18–19, 23, 45–46, 67, 94, 104–105, 201, 210, 226, 262, 300–302, 330, 338, 382–383, 447, 463–464, 484–485
Performance: 29, 198, 224, 263, 272, 288, 400, 425–426
Perseverance: 172, 181, 186, 188, 207, 356, 463, 480, 483
Perspective: 33, 46, 59–60, 85, 108, 135, 140–141, 169, 193, 195, 224–225, 248, 254, 261, 292, 295, 303–304, 327, 334, 339, 351, 359, 373–374, 403, 406–407, 410, 418, 420, 424, 436, 446, 449–450, 462, 465, 475
Planning: 53–54, 216, 259, 321, 346, 483
Prayer: 16, 31–32, 34, 36, 50, 76, 83, 105–107, 125, 146, 154, 158, 213, 230, 253, 270, 283, 308–309, 318–319, 326, 355–357, 368, 380–381, 404, 466–469, 486
Preparation (also "be prepared," "prepare to," "prepare for," "leaders prepare," and "must prepare"): 10, 14, 50, 121, 135, 139, 141, 159–160, 163, 188, 195, 198, 206, 228, 266, 306, 325, 331, 333–334, 377, 462, 464
Presence (also "be present"): 16, 29, 73, 85, 122, 222, 227, 229, 232, 240, 277, 299–300, 311, 317–318, 325, 337, 383, 420, 460
Priorities: 15, 27, 96, 115, 125, 129, 147, 187, 227, 349, 410, 421, 439, 446, 449
Prioritize: 16, 38, 48, 55, 57, 63, 67, 72, 86, 97, 125, 161, 168, 184, 199–200, 215, 224, 227, 271, 276, 298, 306, 324, 326, 340, 342, 349, 365, 371, 380–381, 420, 425–426, 440–441, 448–449, 479
Proficiency: 4, 12, 216, 287
Purpose: 3–4, 9–11, 16, 24, 30, 32–34, 44, 52, 55, 57, 59, 62–64, 66–67, 72, 76, 85, 92, 106–108, 111–112, 115–116, 126, 128, 131, 133, 135, 144, 147, 152, 155, 161, 167, 170, 181, 188, 195, 207, 218–221, 232–234, 243, 250, 257, 270–271, 273–274, 276–278, 292, 298, 319–321, 326, 338, 360, 362, 366–367, 371–373, 375, 377–378, 387–388, 391, 398–399, 401, 405, 408, 410, 412–413, 420–424, 430, 435, 441–442, 444–449, 452, 456, 461–462, 465, 478, 480, 484–485, 488–489, 494

R

Reaction: 17, 46, 51, 78, 177, 232, 234, 274, 299, 302, 347, 360
Readiness: 9, 122, 273, 454
Recognize: 5, 12–13, 17, 22, 24, 35–36, 38, 42, 56–57, 70, 75, 83, 108, 123–124, 141, 162–163, 166, 168–170, 178, 183–184, 200, 202, 235,

253–256, 257, 269, 276, 289–290, 293–294, 310, 315, 322, 325, 328, 330, 352–353, 358, 363–364, 367, 375, 381, 390–391, 401–404, 408, 431–432, 437–439, 468, 483, 484
Redeem: 3, 17, 50, 62, 64, 258
Redeeming: 258
Redemption: 3, 52, 70, 133, 265, 364, 368
Reflection: 10–12, 23, 35, 94, 116, 182–183, 225, 270, 308–309, 330, 358, 449, 469
Relationship: 9, 26–27, 35–36, 44, 53, 55, 94–95, 97–98, 114–115, 140, 165, 189, 218, 226, 240, 298, 316, 324, 340–341, 343, 345, 348, 427–429, 431, 457–458, 462, 468
Repentance: 60, 109, 262, 276, 293, 333
Reputation: 12, 17, 28–29, 109, 138–139, 157, 165–166, 180, 187, 269, 289, 364, 466–467, 481
Resilience: 10, 21, 28, 68, 103, 131, 165, 188, 207, 229, 232, 287, 319, 375–376, 378, 381, 439
Resolve: 4, 50, 93–94, 109, 131, 134, 177, 228, 233–234, 269, 273, 292, 362, 381, 480, 486
Resource: 11, 30–33, 39, 41, 47, 50, 56, 90, 92, 99–102, 111, 123, 128, 132, 142, 155, 204, 217–218, 256, 276, 326, 329, 362, 366, 370–371, 392, 396, 404, 414, 446, 458, 481
Respect: 65, 96, 106, 113, 157, 191, 204, 215, 221, 253, 256, 260, 263, 310, 334, 343, 358–359, 405–406, 408,–409, 452, 471
Responding: 28, 36, 51, 161, 169, 231, 275, 364, 369, 382–383
Responsibility: 13, 37, 39–40, 57, 60, 64–65, 81, 92, 101–102, 112, 115, 120–121, 123, 136, 155–156, 184, 195–196, 199, 204, 216, 242, 249, 313, 323, 371, 380, 388, 405, 440, 450, 454, 459–461, 463, 469, 486, 488

Rest: 25, 43, 47, 52, 57, 60, 64, 94–95, 112, 114–116, 131, 135–136, 140, 157, 165–167, 184–186, 192, 200–201, 217, 239–240, 242–243, 252, 263, 270–271, 278–279, 287–288, 305, 346, 363, 378–379, 381, 405, 413, 416, 421–422, 427–428, 466, 476, 489
Risk: 6–7, 17, 56, 65, 91, 122, 182, 219, 239, 292, 328, 332, 340, 359, 388, 414, 441, 452, 455, 466, 481, 487

S

Sacrifice: 13, 15, 24, 29, 38–39, 59, 62, 72–73, 76, 94, 99, 101, 103, 112, 132–133, 137, 140, 152–153, 159, 190, 198–199, 204, 208, 223, 233, 237, 240, 242, 260, 264–265, 272–273, 355, 360–362, 368, 376, 380, 386, 396, 427, 433–434, 445–446, 448, 459, 461, 479, 489
Salvation: 116, 163, 170, 256, 262, 283, 343, 362, 378, 386, 434, 444, 447
Selflessness: 100, 264, 386, 408, 479, 489
Servant: 21, 30–31, 41–42, 62, 94, 102–103, 111, 120–123, 125, 140, 165, 199, 208, 231, 251, 260, 270, 289, 326, 345–346, 362, 370, 379–380, 403, 433, 450–451, 460, 470, 472, 474, 479
Service: 13, 52, 59, 61, 82, 90, 94, 103, 128, 131, 137, 157, 180–181, 199, 219, 227, 242, 265, 270–271, 300, 310, 317, 328–329, 344, 347, 379, 404, 412, 450–451, 458, 489
Speaking: 3, 19, 87, 97, 101, 105, 139, 178, 181, 210, 216, 224, 269, 325, 397, 406, 408, 423–424, 428, 430–431, 472–473, 488
Standard: 3, 12, 23–26, 29, 60, 74, 95, 98, 105–106, 112–113, 119, 202–203, 231, 237, 240, 269, 283, 286, 319, 347–350, 368, 384, 398
Stewardship: 32, 86, 111, 123, 366, 371–372, 465

Strategy: 140, 461, 482
Strength: 3, 5, 9–10, 14–15, 18–19, 28, 39–40, 49, 58, 60, 64–65, 76, 78, 81, 83, 85, 94–95, 100–101, 104, 116, 121, 124, 155, 162, 166, 172, 179, 182, 186, 188, 193, 212, 217, 219–220, 230–231, 233, 253, 256–257, 272, 275–276, 280, 292–294, 302, 305, 307, 311, 319–322, 327–328, 331, 344, 365, 381, 387–388, 397, 399–400, 402–403, 408, 413, 417, 427, 429, 438–439, 442–443, 452, 456, 464, 467, 477–478, 484, 486
Structure: 183, 203, 378–379
Submission: 18, 31, 96, 98, 100, 153, 237, 355, 415–416
Support: 5, 36, 40–41, 47, 49, 55, 68, 70, 91–92, 101–102, 115, 122, 140, 166, 168–169, 171, 191, 200, 204, 219, 224, 230–231, 243, 256, 276, 291, 305, 310, 316–317, 322, 329, 339, 346, 349, 353–354, 358, 363, 365, 378–379, 383, 400, 408, 414, 427, 433, 440–441, 443, 452, 454, 458, 467, 471, 479, 481, 488, 494
Surrender: 15, 18, 30, 33, 40, 85–86, 116, 140, 271–272, 305, 325, 331

T

Teamwork: 93–94, 141, 167, 290, 306, 328, 400, 455
Testify: 87, 90, 139, 248, 255, 399, 416, 440, 476
Testimony: 75, 93, 96, 138, 159, 178, 255, 298, 303, 389–390, 407, 411–412, 428–429, 440, 494
Transformation: 9, 26, 37–38, 364, 386, 404, 411, 488
Trust: 10, 12, 27, 31–34, 36, 40, 43, 45–46, 55, 57, 65, 70, 76–77, 79, 83, 90–91, 99, 112–113, 118, 123–126, 131, 135, 146, 152, 164–165, 174, 177, 180–181, 188, 191, 193, 197, 227–229, 231, 235, 250–252, 258–259, 269, 272, 282, 292, 295, 297, 299–300, 302, 315, 325, 328, 331, 338, 343–344, 356–359, 362–363, 371, 382, 390–392, 397, 399–400, 403, 408–409, 414–416, 420–422, 431–432, 435, 437–439, 441–444, 450, 452–458, 462–463, 467–468, 471, 473–474, 477–478, 481–486, 488, 494
Truth: 4, 10, 15, 30, 35, 58, 61, 65, 68–69, 71–72, 74, 76, 83–84, 88, 98, 101–102, 104–105, 107–111, 113, 116–120, 124, 126–127, 130–131, 133, 138–141, 143–144, 146–147, 169, 173, 200, 203–204, 215, 217, 224, 234, 248, 251, 255, 257–258, 266, 292, 294–296, 307, 320, 325, 330–333, 335, 350–352, 354, 362, 367, 369–370, 372–374, 376, 378–379, 382, 384–385, 389–390, 392, 396–397, 406–407, 410, 416–417, 423–425, 430–433, 437, 444–445, 448–449, 451, 456, 461, 463, 473–474, 476–477, 486, 488

U

Unity: 3, 25, 64–65, 74, 93, 95, 135–136, 240, 251, 284, 310, 320–321, 408, 428, 442–443, 452, 468, 471, 494

V

Value: 4, 7–8, 55, 57–58, 64, 76, 91, 106, 114, 144, 178, 183, 222, 226–227, 233, 236–238, 262, 266, 274, 287, 298, 300, 310, 317, 319, 344–345, 348–350, 359, 372, 375, 384, 388, 401, 405, 408, 439–442, 452, 458, 473
Vision: 9, 11, 64, 131, 167, 179–180, 190, 195–198, 228–229, 233, 243, 250–251, 254, 271, 278, 290, 298, 302–303, 320–322, 331, 374, 409–410, 424, 437, 439–440, 449–450, 452, 482, 486, 488, 494

W

Weakness: 9, 15, 18–19, 28, 81, 162, 191, 229, 235, 293, 302, 384, 438

Willing: 6, 11, 19, 21, 35–36, 40–43, 56, 58, 63, 72–73, 78, 92, 99, 101, 114, 119, 128, 132–134, 140, 153, 180–181, 198, 204–205, 228, 230, 239–240, 267–268, 272–274, 276, 285, 306, 315, 330–331, 345, 355, 358–364, 372, 374, 386–387, 396, 406, 409, 411–412, 437–438, 446, 448, 456, 471, 475, 479, 485, 489, 494

Wisdom: 4, 6, 35, 49, 75–76, 81, 85, 108, 122, 158, 173, 178, 235, 293, 295–297, 304, 319–321, 325, 369–370, 372–374, 379, 397, 406, 424–425

Worry: 33–34, 210, 214, 223–224, 258, 324, 327, 338, 377, 400, 455

NOTES

THE BOOK OF MATTHEW

1. Matt Chandler, "*The Beatitudes,*" RightNow Media, 2022, Bible study series, Session 3, 2:35 https://app.rightnowmedia.org/en/player/video/744026?session=745006&position=37.
2. Martin Luther, the great 16th Century Reformer, is attributed to stating "I have so much to do today that I'm going to need to spend three hours in prayer in order to be able to get it all done." The most authoritative source to attribute this statement to Luther is from the *Cyclopedia of Religious Anecdotes* published in 1923 and compiled by James Gilchrist Lawson.
J. Gilchrist Lawson, *Cyclopedia of Religious Anecdotes* (Fleming H. Revell Company, 1923), 303.
3. The Voice of the Martyrs (VOM) is an organization founded by Pastor Richard Wurmbrand and his wife, Sabina, after being imprisoned for their Christian witness in Communist Romania. VOM "serves persecuted Christians in the world's most difficult and dangerous places to follow Christ." Read more about the organization and stories from the persecuted at https://www.persecution.com/.
4. Although John C. Maxwell book specifically cites the Golden Rule, in speaking and teaching on this book, he has referend his paraphrase of the Golden Rule, "treat others how they want to be treated," as the "Platinum Rule."
John C. Maxwell, *Every Communicates, Few Connect* (United States: HarperCollins Leadership, 2010), 241–242.
5. This quote is attributed to Nick Saban in memes, across social media posts, and blog websites. However, there is uncertainty if the quote originated with Nick Saban or if he was quoting someone else when he said it.
6. John C. Maxwell, *The 15 Invaluable Laws of Growth* (New York, NY: Hachette Book Group, Inc., 2012), 1.
7. John C. Maxwell, *The 15 Invaluable Laws of Growth* (New York, NY: Hachette Book Group, Inc., 2012), 121.
8. Roger Fisher, William Ury, and Bruce Patton, *Getting to Yes: Negotiating Agreement Without Giving In* (New York, NY: Penguin Group, 2011), 19.
9. Lee Strobel, *The Case of Christ* (Grand Rapids, MI: Zondervan, 1998).

THE BOOK OF MARK

10. This statement comes from Bible.com's Introductory commentary on the Book of Mark and is used in this lesson to stress that Jesus brought a form of leadership that was radical to the culture and understanding of power at the time. "YouVersion," A Digital Ministry of Life Church, https://www.bible.com/bible/111/MRK.INTRO1.NIV.
11. John C. Maxwell, *Leadership Gold* (United States: HarperCollins Leadership, 2008), 1.
12. Marcus Lutrell, *Lone Survivor: The Eyewitness Account of Operation Redwing and the Lost Heroes of SEAL Team 10* (United States: Little, Brown and Company, 2007).
13. The quote was heard by John C. Maxwell. In the first edition of his book, *Developing the Leader Within You*, he wrote, "you can love people without leading them, but you cannot lead people without loving them."
John C. Maxwell, *Developing the Leader Within You* (Nashville, TN: Thomas Nelson, Inc., 1995), 8.

THE BOOK OF LUKE

14. John C. Maxwell, *Leadership Gold* (United States: HarperCollins Leadership, 2008), 66.
15. "First who, then what" is a concept that Jim Collins promotes in his book *Good to Great*. It's the idea that you find the right people and then build the vision and organization with those people.
Jim Collins, *Good to Great* (Random House Business Books, 2001).
16. The Voice of the Martyrs, "Loving His Enemies," *The Voice of the Martyrs*, Vol. 58, No. 6, June 2024, 4–7.
17. John C. Maxwell, *Leadership Gold* (United States: HarperCollins Leadership, 2008), 49.
18. John C. Maxwell and Chris Hodges, *Jesus, the High Road Leader* (Maxwell Leadership, 2024), 14.
19. John C. Maxwell, *Developing the Leader Within You* (Nashville, TN: Thomas Nelson, Inc., 1995), 10.

20. This quote from Maxwell was heard spoken by Maxwell at the International Maxwell Conference in August 2024 in Orlando, FL. It is likely found in one of his many books on personal growth.
21. John C. Maxwell, *The 21 Irrefutable Laws of Leadership, 25th Anniversary Edition* (United States: HarperCollins Leadership, 2022), 13.
22. John C. Maxwell, *High Road Leadership* (Maxwell Leadership, 2024), 31 and 99.

THE BOOK OF JOHN

23. John C. Maxwell, *Leadership Gold* (United States: HarperCollins Leadership, 2008), 114.
24. John C. Maxwell, *The 21 Irrefutable Laws of Leadership, 25th Anniversary Edition* (United States: HarperCollins Leadership, 2022), 67.
25. Mike Ettore, *Trust-Based Leadership* (Fidelis Leadership Group, LLC, 2019), 195.
26. David Green with Bill High, *Leadership NOT by the Book* (Grand Rapids, MI: Baker Books, 2022).
27. Jocko Willink and Leif Babin, *Extreme Ownership* (St Martin's Press, 2015). Echelon Front's homepage: https://echelonfront.com/.

ABOUT THE AUTHORS

JORDAN AMES

Jordan is a leadership consultant and coach and founder of Red Letter Leadership. He is a retired Marine Raider with 21 years of active service. He is a Maxwell Leadership Certified Coach and holds Master's and Bachelor's degrees in History. Jordan and his wife, Sarah, are the proud parents of seven, six of whom he and Sarah adopted. He served as a Presidential Security Guard, a Force Recon Marine, a Marine Special Operator, an Infantry Officer, and completed his service as a Special Operations Officer. He is passionate about his own personal development as a leader and helping others grow their leadership capacity to advance God's kingdom purposes.

BEN HUNTER

Ben is a seasoned leader with over 24 years of military experience, having served in various Special Operations, Airborne Infantry, Stryker, and Mechanized Infantry units. Ben creates winning teams and fosters effective communication to ensure clarity and alignment within diverse groups. He is a General Downing Scholar and Carlucci Fellow with a Master's degree in Public Policy from Duke University. Ben is the proud father of three and has been married to his wife, Lori for 21 years.

ERIC ALBRIGHT

Eric is a retired Marine Corps officer and aviator with over 20 years of military leadership experience, including over 250 combat missions in the cockpit of an AV-8B Harrier Jet. He has led aviation departments, driven organizational change, shaped future leaders as chief instructor for the Marine Corps' Expeditionary Warfare School, and has led the team in direct support of the Presidential Airlift Mission. Eric is currently a business owner, consultant, church leader, and host of the podcast, "Make the Choice: A Podcast for Men". He holds a Master's in Leadership studies, dual Bachelor's degrees, and shares five children with his wife, Christina.

Though we are *in* this world, we must not be *of* this world

Leadership is all about influence—and your influence grows when it's grounded in integrity and driven by purpose. At **Red Letter Leadership**, we help leaders expand their impact and influence by following the words and example of Jesus Christ. Whether you're leading a business, a ministry, or your family team, our **leadership coaching** is designed to deepen your walk with Christ while sharpening your leadership skills so that you are empowered, energized, and equipped to impact your world for the kingdom of God.

Let's keep growing together.

Visit www.redletterleadership.com or scan the QR code below to allow us to be a part of your leadership development journey.

Red Letter Leadership Website

Lead with integrity.

Live with purpose.

Influence the world for Christ through your leadership

www.ingramcontent.com/pod-product-compliance
Lightning Source LLC
Chambersburg PA
CBHW050131240426
43673CB00043B/1636